WordPerfect® for LINUX® Bible

D1519104

WordPerfect® for LINUX® Bible

Stephen E. Harris
with Erwin Zijleman

IDG Books Worldwide, Inc.
An International Data Group Company

Foster City, CA ✦ Chicago, IL ✦ Indianapolis, IN ✦ New York, NY

WordPerfect® for LINUX® Bible

Published by

IDG Books Worldwide, Inc.

An International Data Group Company
919 E. Hillsdale Blvd., Suite 400
Foster City, CA 94404

www.idgbooks.com (IDG Books Worldwide Web site)

The image of the Linux penguin Tux was created by Larry Ewing (lewing@isc.tamu.edu), using the Gimp graphics program (http://www.gimp.org/). The image was subsequently modified for use by IDG Books Worldwide on this book's cover by Tuomas Kuosmanen (tigert@gimp.org). Tuomas also used the Gimp program for his work with Tux.

Screen shots of Corel Corporation Web pages are copyright © 1999 Corel Corporation and Corel Corporation Limited, reprinted by permission.

ISBN: 0-7645-3374-6

Printed in the United States of America

10 9 8 7 6 5 4 3 2 1

1B/RU/QX/ZZ/FC

Distributed in the United States by
IDG Books Worldwide, Inc.

Distributed by CDG Books Canada Inc. for Canada; by Transworld Publishers Limited in the United Kingdom; by IDG Norge Books for Norway; by IDG Sweden Books for Sweden; by IDG Books Australia Publishing Corporation Pty. Ltd. for Australia and New Zealand; by TransQuest Publishers Pte Ltd. for Singapore, Malaysia, Thailand, Indonesia, and Hong Kong; by Gotop Information Inc. for Taiwan; by ICG Muse, Inc. for Japan; by Norma Comunicaciones S.A. for Colombia; by Intersoft for South Africa; by Eyrolles for France; by International Thomson Publishing for Germany, Austria and Switzerland; by Distribuidora Cuspide for Argentina; by Livraria Cultura for Brazil; by Ediciones ZETA S.C.R. Ltda. for Peru; by WS Computer Publishing Corporation, Inc., for the Philippines; by Contemporanea de Ediciones for Venezuela; by Express Computer Distributors for the Caribbean and West Indies; by Micronesia Media Distributor, Inc. for Micronesia; by Grupo Editorial Norma S.A. for Guatemala; by Chips Computadoras S.A. de C.V. for Mexico; by Editorial Norma de Panama S.A. for Panama; by American Bookshops for Finland. Authorized Sales Agent: Anthony Rudkin Associates for the Middle East and North Africa.

For general information on IDG Books Worldwide's books in the U.S., please call our Consumer Customer Service department at 800-762-2974. For reseller information, including discounts and premium sales, please call our Reseller Customer Service department at 800-434-3422.

For information on where to purchase IDG Books Worldwide's books outside the U.S., please contact our International Sales department at 317-596-5530 or fax 317-596-5692.

For consumer information on foreign language translations, please contact our Customer Service department at 800-434-3422, fax 317-596-5692, or e-mail rights@idgbooks.com.

For information on licensing foreign or domestic rights, please phone +1-650-655-3109.

For sales inquiries and special prices for bulk quantities, please contact our Sales department at 650-655-3200 or write to the address above.

For information on using IDG Books Worldwide's books in the classroom or for ordering examination copies, please contact our Educational Sales department at 800-434-2086 or fax 317-596-5499.

For press review copies, author interviews, or other publicity information, please contact our Public Relations department at 650-655-3000 or fax 650-655-3299.

For authorization to photocopy items for corporate, personal, or educational use, please contact Copyright Clearance Center, 222 Rosewood Drive, Danvers, MA 01923, or fax 978-750-4470.

Library of Congress Cataloging-in-Publication Data

Harris, Stephen E.
    WordPerfect for Linux Bible/
Stephen E. Harris.
        p. cm.
    Includes index.
    ISBN 0-7645-3374-6 (alk. paper)
    1. WordPerfect (Computer file). 2. Word processing
I. Zijleman, Erwin. II. Title
Z52.5.W65H336   1999
652.5'5369–dc21   99-15719
                                        CIP

ABOUT IDG BOOKS WORLDWIDE

Welcome to the world of IDG Books Worldwide.

IDG Books Worldwide, Inc., is a subsidiary of International Data Group, the world's largest publisher of computer-related information and the leading global provider of information services on information technology. IDG was founded more than 30 years ago by Patrick J. McGovern and now employs more than 9,000 people worldwide. IDG publishes more than 290 computer publications in over 75 countries. More than 90 million people read one or more IDG publications each month.

Launched in 1990, IDG Books Worldwide is today the #1 publisher of best-selling computer books in the United States. We are proud to have received eight awards from the Computer Press Association in recognition of editorial excellence and three from Computer Currents' First Annual Readers' Choice Awards. Our best-selling *...For Dummies*® series has more than 50 million copies in print with translations in 31 languages. IDG Books Worldwide, through a joint venture with IDG's Hi-Tech Beijing, became the first U.S. publisher to publish a computer book in the People's Republic of China. In record time, IDG Books Worldwide has become the first choice for millions of readers around the world who want to learn how to better manage their businesses.

Our mission is simple: Every one of our books is designed to bring extra value and skill-building instructions to the reader. Our books are written by experts who understand and care about our readers. The knowledge base of our editorial staff comes from years of experience in publishing, education, and journalism — experience we use to produce books to carry us into the new millennium. In short, we care about books, so we attract the best people. We devote special attention to details such as audience, interior design, use of icons, and illustrations. And because we use an efficient process of authoring, editing, and desktop publishing our books electronically, we can spend more time ensuring superior content and less time on the technicalities of making books.

You can count on our commitment to deliver high-quality books at competitive prices on topics you want to read about. At IDG Books Worldwide, we continue in the IDG tradition of delivering quality for more than 30 years. You'll find no better book on a subject than one from IDG Books Worldwide.

John Kilcullen
Chairman and CEO
IDG Books Worldwide, Inc.

Steven Berkowitz
President and Publisher
IDG Books Worldwide, Inc.

Eighth Annual
Computer Press
Awards ≥1992

Ninth Annual
Computer Press
Awards ≥1993

Tenth Annual
Computer Press
Awards ≥1994

Eleventh Annual
Computer Press
Awards ≥1995

IDG is the world's leading IT media, research and exposition company. Founded in 1964, IDG had 1997 revenues of $2.05 billion and has more than 9,000 employees worldwide. IDG offers the widest range of media options that reach IT buyers in 75 countries representing 95% of worldwide IT spending. IDG's diverse product and services portfolio spans six key areas including print publishing, online publishing, expositions and conferences, market research, education and training, and global marketing services. More than 90 million people read one or more of IDG's 290 magazines and newspapers, including IDG's leading global brands — Computerworld, PC World, Network World, Macworld and the Channel World family of publications. IDG Books Worldwide is one of the fastest-growing computer book publishers in the world, with more than 700 titles in 36 languages. The "...For Dummies®" series alone has more than 50 million copies in print. IDG offers online users the largest network of technology-specific Web sites around the world through IDG.net (http://www.idg.net), which comprises more than 225 targeted Web sites in 55 countries worldwide. International Data Corporation (IDC) is the world's largest provider of information technology data, analysis and consulting, with research centers in over 41 countries and more than 400 research analysts worldwide. IDG World Expo is a leading producer of more than 168 globally branded conferences and expositions in 35 countries including E3 (Electronic Entertainment Expo), Macworld Expo, ComNet, Windows World Expo, ICE (Internet Commerce Expo), Agenda, DEMO, and Spotlight. IDG's training subsidiary, ExecuTrain, is the world's largest computer training company, with more than 230 locations worldwide and 785 training courses. IDG Marketing Services helps industry-leading IT companies build international brand recognition by developing global integrated marketing programs via IDG's print, online and exposition products worldwide. Further information about the company can be found at www.idg.com.   1/24/99

Credits

Acquisitions Editor
Andy Cummings

Development Editor
Melanie Feinberg

Technical Editors
Jason Grenier
W. Wayne Liauh
Philip Rackus

Copy Editors
Eric Hahn
Corey Cohen
Marti Paul

Production
IDG Books Worldwide Production

Proofreading and Indexing
York Production Services

About the Authors

Stephen E. Harris is the founder and president of QwkScreen, a software development and consulting firm dedicated to making the computer screen a friendlier place. Author of the best-selling titles *WordPerfect 7 Bible* and *WordPerfect Suite 8 Bible*, Steve is a proud member of the Corel Beta Squad. He lives in the woods of western Massachusetts with his wife Githa, three cats (Tiger, Becky, and Chester), bears, deer, turkeys, and other assorted wildlife. You can find Steve, plus more WordPerfect solutions and links, at http://www.qwkscreen.com.

Erwin Zijleman began his career as a development sociologist, specializing in urban sociology and education in third-world countries, particularly Southeast Asia. He now works as a software scientist, specializing in PC office applications. Erwin has served as a beta tester for Microsoft, Borland, and WP Corporation products. Currently, Erwin tests almost exclusively for Corel. He lives near Amsterdam, in the historic center of Leiden, with his cat (Bagu).

This book is dedicated to everyone in the open source community, who are working wonders through a collective labor of love.

Foreword

When we posted the free version of Corel WordPerfect 8 for Linux on CNET last December, we expected a flurry of downloads.

What we got was an avalanche—82,925 download attempts by Linux enthusiasts in the first 12 hours. As we spread WordPerfect 8 for Linux to popular mirror sites around the Web, users rushed to get their hands on this full-powered word processor, which handles documents seamlessly between applications and across platforms. WordPerfect 8 for Linux was not just an instant hit—it became one of the biggest software releases of the year, with over 900,000 download attempts to date.

This success is a tremendous validation of our Linux strategy. We have proven that the Linux community wants access to commercial, mainstream applications such as WordPerfect, and we intend to deliver them.

Just as we're excited about bringing WordPerfect 8 to Linux, we are also delighted that Steve Harris, with expert assistance from Erwin Zijleman, is porting his best-selling WordPerfect guidance to the Linux venue. Full of expert tips and examples, *WordPerfect for Linux Bible* provides 100 percent of what you need to master WordPerfect for Linux.

In celebration of both the software and book release, Corel Corporation has arranged with IDG Books Worldwide to package the full Personal Edition of WordPerfect 8 for Linux with *WordPerfect for Linux Bible*—you won't find a bigger bargain!

Corel WordPerfect 8 for Linux—Personal Edition is an ideal office solution that delivers the same amazing array of features as the Windows version. Click and type with the Shadow Cursor. QuickFind with a single click. Check spelling and grammar on the fly. Automate with macros. Format tables in a flash. Create hyperlinks automatically. Corel WordPerfect 8 for Linux—Personal Edition unleashes your full productivity potential at home, at school, and in the office.

Whether you're new to WordPerfect or a seasoned veteran coming over to Linux, *WordPerfect for Linux Bible* is an easy-to-use, accessible guide to the program's powerful features. Steve and Erwin show you how to get up and running quickly in WordPerfect for Linux, and then reveal their secrets to everything from creating memos, letters, and reports to formatting, handling, and printing documents. They give you clear, step-by-step instructions and plenty of illustrations in this hands-on tutorial reference.

Welcome to WordPerfect 8 for Linux—Personal Edition, and welcome to *WordPerfect for Linux Bible*—I highly recommend them both!

Mike Cowpland, president and CEO
Corel Corporation

Preface

Things move fast in the software business! There has been a tremendous upsurge in interest in using Linux for desktop applications. With the sudden success of WordPerfect 8 for Linux, including its "Killer App" award at the LinuxWorld conference, we figured that the world was ready for its first book on a mainstream Linux application.

We only had to take the instructions from our *WordPerfect for Windows Bible*, replace the Windows screen shots with Linux ones, and send it off. Right? Well, that's what we thought, but it wasn't that easy. We had various desktop possibilities to consider, new installation procedures, and enough variations throughout the book to make the "translation" to Linux an exciting, and sometimes hair-raising, experience.

But here it is! You're holding the first book devoted to a user application for the Linux desktop. Plus, this book's CD contains the program itself — the Personal Edition of WordPerfect 8 for Linux. This is an exciting business!

Here's What You Get

This book comes with

+ Complete instructions on installing and using WordPerfect 8 for Linux

+ The ready-to-install Personal Edition of WordPerfect 8 for Linux on CD

+ The KDE 1.1 desktop environment, which we consider to be the best platform for running WordPerfect 8 for Linux

Of course, you purchased this book for its clear, brief descriptions and step-by-step instructions for using WordPerfect for Linux. We also hope that you're pleased with our exclusive in-line tips that pack more goodness into every page. In place of tedious introductions and summaries, bulleted summaries begin, and concise lists of cross-references conclude, each chapter.

If writing computer books isn't an art, we'd like to think it's akin to a craft or a science. Our aim is to deliver a huge amount of information in an easy-to-use, accessible format. We hope you're pleased.

What's in This Book?

Here's some of what you will find in this book:

Part I, "Getting Started," shows you how to install and configure WordPerfect for Linux, then get up and running, typing and editing from day one. You learn how to copy and move information, proofread on the fly, use keyboard shortcuts, and manage your screen. You become an instant expert with Format-As-You-Go, Make It Fit, and other great time-saving features, and learn where to turn for further help.

Part II, "Basic Training," shows you how to undo mistakes and safeguard your work. You learn how to manage your files and use the Corel Versions archiving utility. You also get creative with fonts and clip art, master printing techniques, and create Web pages.

Part III, "Writing with WordPerfect," shows you the tricks to speed up your work with WordPerfect's powerful correction and proofreading tools. You see how to edit, review, and format documents, as well as work with columns and tables.

Part IV, "Working with Large Documents," shows you how to organize with bullets and outlines, insert document references, and master WordPerfect's superb large document handling facilities.

Part V, "Honing Your Skills," explains how to work quickly with ExpressDoc templates, projects, and styles, perform spreadsheet calculations, sort information, and create professional-looking publications by applying graphic lines, borders, and fills. You also discover how to format equations and create effective charts and graphs.

Part VI, "Customizing and Automating," shows you how to fine-tune WordPerfect to the way you work. You learn how to create custom toolbars and keyboards, mass-produce with labels and merge, and automate repetitive tasks by recording and playing macros.

The appendixes provide a quick reference to WordPerfect's diverse settings, lists of the best links for WordPerfect for Linux, Corel information and help, the latest on Linux, and other interesting information. Last but not least, you get a description of what's on your *WordPerfect for Linux Bible* CD.

Conventions Used in This Book

This book uses a few conventions to distinguish various elements of the instructions and display:

✦ Key1+Key2 (as in Ctrl+V) means that you press and hold the first key, press the second key, and then release both keys.

+ Menu ➪ Command1 ➪ Command2 indicates a menu to choose, then the command and subcommands to select. So Tools ➪ QuickCorrect ➪ SmartQuotes is just a short way of saying: "Open the Tools menu and choose QuickCorrect, then choose SmartQuotes from the submenu that appears."

+ Text that you type appears in **bold**.

+ New terms appear in *italic*.

A mouse or other pointing device is a necessity for most Windows programs. These standard mouse actions are used throughout the book:

Action	What You Do
Point	Move the mouse to place the pointer on a screen item.
Click	Press and release the left mouse button once.
Double-click	Quickly press and release the left mouse button twice.
Right-click	Press and release the right mouse button. A shortcut menu (QuickMenu) of context-sensitive choices appears.
Drag	Point to what you want to drag, press and hold the left mouse button, move the mouse, then release the button. You can also drag across text to select it.

A "click" becomes a "tap" if you are using a pen device; "left" becomes "right," and vice versa, if you're using the left-handed mouse setup. (Some mice have a way to single-click where others double-click.)

Icons Used in This Book

The *WordPerfect for Linux Bible* features special text sidebars indicated by various icons:

 Marks a shortcut or neat idea. (*Tip:* And this is an in-line tip!)

 Provides extra information, such as what to do in special situations.

 Warns you when you can lose data, mess up your document, or damage your setup if you aren't careful. This icon may also tell you what to do if you encounter problems.

For the Latest Updates . . .

Change is constant in this business. For the latest on updates, fixes, and upgrades, check out my Web site at www.qwkscreen.com, where you'll find lots of tips and some bonus material. (You can also get to my Web site through the IDG Books Worldwide Web site at www.idgbooks.com.) I also maintain links to discussion groups, sources of fonts and clip art, and many other resources.

Any comments, suggestions, criticisms, corrections, or requests? Please send them to me at steveh@qwkscreen.com. Thanks. I hope this book is helpful!

Acknowledgments

While any shortcomings are my own, this massive work is necessarily a team product involving publishers, editors, designers, proofreaders, indexers, and typesetters, as well as promotion and sales people. Publishing is an exciting business, but it's also stressful and competitive. Thankfully, the dedicated pros with whom I deal at IDG Books Worldwide temper the demands of deadlines with nurturing and care for writers. Because it's impossible to name each person in this process, please allow me to extend my heartfelt thanks to everyone in this hardworking group.

I want to single out Melanie Feinberg for her wonderful editing job on the less-polished sections of the book.

Special thanks to Andy Cummings for listening to our ideas, then joining in with purposeful enthusiasm. You really get things rolling!

To W. Wayne Liauh, many thanks for making time in your busy schedule to apply your technical expertise to a number of our chapters. Thanks also to Phil C. Rackus and Jason Grenier at Corel for doing their share—and at a moment's notice, no less.

This project owes much of its success to the generous and constant support from many dedicated folks at Corel. Thanks to Mike Cowpland for help in getting this project rolling, and to Nicholas Blommesteijn and Stephen Hillier in Linux product development. Special thanks to Chip Maxwell for chasing down WordPerfect for Linux CDs and everything else.

To my co-author, Erwin Zijleman, I can't begin to express my gratitude. Aside from the fact that it would have been impossible to do this book without you, it wouldn't have been half the fun!

As always, I must thank my attorney/agent Joel L. Hecker, Esq., for his wise counsel and support. Finally, a very special acknowledgment to my wife Githa, who had the pleasure of reading drafts of new chapters and enduring my crazy schedule. Yes, we finished in time for our vacation!

Steve Harris

Contents at a Glance

Contents

Part III: Writing with WordPerfect 219

Chapter 12: Writer's Lib 221

Chapter 13: Editing Techniques 237

Part V: Honing Your Skills   411

Chapter 20: Working Quickly with ExpressDoc Templates and Styles 413

Chapter 21: Doing Calculations in WordPerfect 429

Part VI: Customizing and Automating   543

Chapter 26: Fine-Tuning WordPerfect 545

Chapter 27: Customizing Toolbars, Menus, and Keyboards 571

Chapter 28: Mass Producing with Labels and Merge 579

Getting Started

◆　◆　◆　◆

◆　◆　◆　◆

Getting Up and Running

Welcome to WordPerfect 8 for Linux! When Corel posted a free download version of WordPerfect 8 for Linux, it became an instant hit in the Linux community. This book brings you the complete retail version on CD, and tells you all you need to know to get the most out of WordPerfect for Linux.

If you just bought this book and CD package, you're probably eager to get started. Rest assured that WordPerfect 8 for Linux is easy to install — you'll be up and running before you know it.

Before you install WordPerfect 8 for Linux, either from this CD or from a separate package, examine this chapter to see what Linux, and WordPerfect for Linux in particular, are all about.

What Is Linux?

Just what is Linux and where does it come from? Linux is the brainchild of Linus Torvalds, who decided to write a compact version of the powerful UNIX operating system while he was a student at the University of Helsinki in Finland.

Instead of trying to sell Linux, Torvalds gave it away. He had the foresight to make Linux into a pioneering open source operating system that anyone could modify. Thousands of programmers from all over the world joined Linus in his crusade to create a sophisticated, complex, powerful, and *free* operating system.

The latest Linux kernel, as well as many supporting programs, can always be downloaded free of charge. In most cases, it is more convenient to buy a Linux *distribution* (a complete package with installation) from a third party, but if you have the time to download everything you need, feel free to do so!

Linux is powerful and free, but what does it have to offer me? Here are some Linux benefits:

◆ ◆ ◆ ◆

In This Chapter

Install WordPerfect
for Linux

Customize your
WordPerfect
installation

Start WordPerfect 8
for Linux

Use the WordPerfect
interface

Perform
administrative tasks
in WordPerfect

Customize your
desktop for easy
access to
WordPerfect

◆ ◆ ◆ ◆

✦ You get a true, stable, multitasking environment that can run several programs at once.

✦ Linux comes with the X-Window graphics subsystem (Xfree86 in most packages) that supports a graphical user interface such as KDE or GNOME.

✦ You'll find hundreds of software applications (the list grows longer by the day), most of which can be downloaded free of charge.

✦ You get built-in support for networking and Internet access.

✦ You get an operating system that runs like greased lightning — even on your old 486!

Linux improvements are being made even as you read this page. If you encounter a problem, you can expect to find a fix within days.

Most software developers are working on Linux versions of their popular applications. Corel Corporation, for example, is working on bringing WordPerfect Office 2000 to Linux, as well as its award-winning CorelDRAW! package.

What Is WordPerfect 8 for Linux?

On December 17, 1998, Corel released a free download version of WordPerfect 8 to the Linux community. The program was an instant hit; hundreds of thousands grabbed a copy of the world's most powerful word processor.

Commercial versions of WordPerfect 8 for Linux are now available, including the version on this book's CD, as described in Table 1-1.

Table 1-1	
Available Versions of WordPerfect 8 for Linux	
Version	*Features*
Free download	A fully functional word processor that offers unlimited personal (non-commercial) use for registered users.
Personal retail edition	Like the free download, a fully functional word processor that offers unlimited use, plus telephone support and a number of extra features like drawing and charting tools, an equation editor, ExpressDocs, a font installation utility, and a large number of fonts and graphics.
WordPerfect 8 for Linux Bible edition	Everything in the personal retail edition (except telephone support), plus the KDE desktop environment.

Features in All Versions of WordPerfect 8 for Linux

All versions of WordPerfect 8 for Linux, including the free download, contain the following features:

✦ File compatibility across the DOS, Windows, UNIX, and Macintosh platforms, including Word 97 for Windows.

✦ WP File Manager to search and open files, create directories, change file modes, and more—without having to remember Linux commands.

✦ Shadow Cursor to point, click, and begin typing anywhere on the page.

✦ Instant spelling and proofreading suggestions.

✦ Corel Versions, to keep track of document revisions for workgroup collaboration.

All versions of WordPerfect 8 for Linux can also perform the following tasks:

✦ Move, rotate, and size graphics. Wrap and contour text around an image. Draw objects directly on top of text, group graphics, and add color gradient fills or patterns.

✦ Size table rows, and join and split cells with a single click.

✦ Publish to HTML, complete with hyperlinks and bookmarks. Convert Web files directly into WordPerfect format.

✦ Create Internet links automatically from text beginning with `www`, `ftp`, `http`, `mailto`, and more.

✦ Drag guidelines to change margins and columns directly on your page.

Additional Features in the Retail and *WordPerfect Bible* Editions

All versions, other than the free download, also include:

✦ Advanced drawing and charting applications with online help

✦ Nearly 150 fonts plus a font installer utility

✦ Adobe Acrobat reader

✦ 5000 clip art images

✦ 200 photos

✦ Over 180 textures

✦ Netscape Navigator Web browser

✦ Over 90 ExpressDoc templates

✦ Print queue manager

✦ Font installation utility

✦ Custom database creation utility

That's quite a package, especially when you consider that all of these features are included on your *WordPerfect for Linux Bible* CD!

Installing Linux

Before you can install WordPerfect for Linux, you have to install Linux on your system. If you're downloading and installing Linux on your own, it can be a complicated process, so refer to one of the numerous books dedicated to installing and using Linux. If you're using a Linux package distribution (such as Red Hat Linux, S.u.S.E. Linux, Debian Linux, Slackware Linux, or Caldera Open Linux), use the installation guide and setup program from your package.

 Tip   If you need more help, check out these IDG Books Worldwide books on the Linux operating system: *Linux for Dummies*, *Red Hat Linux Secrets*, and *Linux Configuration & Installation*.

Installing an X-Window Desktop Environment

All Linux distributions come with an *X-Window graphics subsystem* (also known as *X*) and an *X-Window manager*. The graphics subsystem handles all the graphics displayed on your screen and interacts with your mouse, graphics adapter, and display. Most Linux distributions use the XFree86 graphics subsystem, but commercial alternatives like MetroX and AcceleratedX are often used as well.

The X-Window manager runs on top of the graphics subsystem and determines the look and feel of the graphical user interface. The default X-Window manager for the RedHat distribution (fvwm95) comes with a taskbar similar to that in Windows 95/98/NT. You can always switch to other X-Window managers or install a new X-Window manager.

Some X-Window managers, such as the widely adopted KDE, add their own desktop icons, menu bars, and taskbars. Because KDE comes with many applications in addition to the X-Window manager, it is called an *X desktop environment*. KDE includes a powerful file manager, a complete help system, a text editor, an image viewer, screensavers, games, and many other tools and applications. Other X desktop environments include GNOME and CDE.

The authors of this book used Version 1.1 of the KDE X desktop environment, as seen in certain screen shots. You'll find KDE for Red Hat 5.1/5.2 on this book's CD, along with installation instructions. (See Appendix C for details.)

Installing WordPerfect 8 for Linux

Once you have Linux up and running, it's time to install WordPerfect 8 for Linux. To install WordPerfect 8 either from the retail package or your Bible CD:

1. Boot Linux.

2. Type **startx** to start the X-Window system, from which you can run WordPerfect's graphical setup program.

3. Open a terminal window and mount your *WordPerfect for Linux Bible* CD-ROM by typing the command **mount /dev/cdrom /mnt/cdrom**. The CD mount directory "/mnt/cdrom" may differ on your system.

4. Go to the /mnt/cdrom directory (or the directory you specified) by typing **cd /mnt/cdrom** in the terminal window, then type **./install.wp** to start the WordPerfect setup program and display the license information (see Figure 1-1).

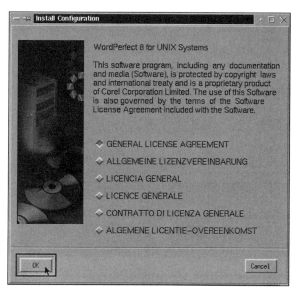

Figure 1-1: Starting the WordPerfect 8 for Linux setup

5. Click OK and specify where you want to install the software (see Figure 1-2). Most Linux programs are installed under /usr/local, so /usr/local/wp8 is the default location.

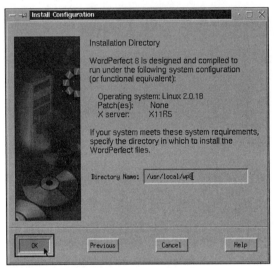

Figure 1-2: Specifying the WordPerfect installation directory

6. Click OK, then select the installation you want (see Figure 1-3):

- *Minimum,* to install the programs and data to run WP and print documents

- *Medium,* to include grammar checking and the thesaurus

- *Full,* to include system administration help, online help, macros, macro help, WP Draw and sample graphics, sample WP documents, learning files, third-party font installation, and sound capabilities.

We recommend the full installation: we can't pass up the macro, graphics, font, and template features.

If you have installed a previous version of WordPerfect for Linux, you can specify its directory as a pattern directory, which keeps your current printer and other settings.

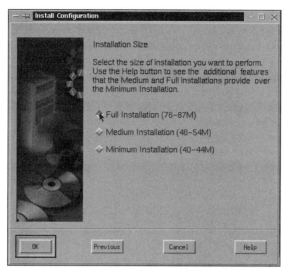

Figure 1-3: Selecting the installation type

7. Click OK and enter your registration number (see Figure 1-4). (The
registration number for the software on this book's CD is located in a text file
("Registration Key") on the CD itself.) The registration number is on the
registration card if you bought a package.

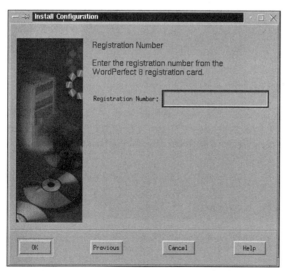

Figure 1-4: Entering your registration number

8. Click OK. WordPerfect now asks if you want to update the magic numbers file. We recommend clicking Yes, because this action adds the WordPerfect document to the defined file types under Linux.

9. Click OK, then select language modules to install (see Figure 1-5). This sequence enables you to use the writing tools for the supported languages, and even run a fully localized version of WordPerfect 8 for Linux by specifying a startup option (see Chapter 26, "Fine-Tuning WordPerfect"). You'll also be asked to pick the default language.

Figure 1-5: Installing language modules

10. Click OK, highlight each printer you want to use with WordPerfect for Linux, then click Select (see Figure 1-6). (Hold Ctrl to select multiple printers.)

11. Assign your printers to a valid destination, normally "lp" (see Figure 1-7). (More information on printer destinations can be found in the documentation with your Linux distribution.)

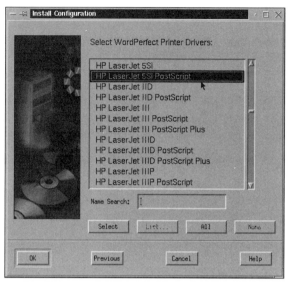

Figure 1-6: Selecting printers to use with WordPerfect

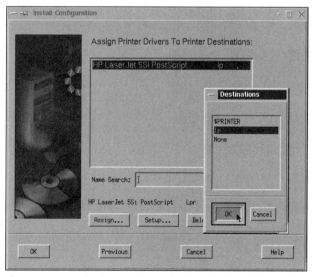

Figure 1-7: Assigning a printer destination

12. Click OK. You'll now be asked if you want to install the CDE desktop icon, the online manual, and the Netscape Navigator browser (see Figure 1-8). Make sure that you install the desktop icon (for use later in this chapter).

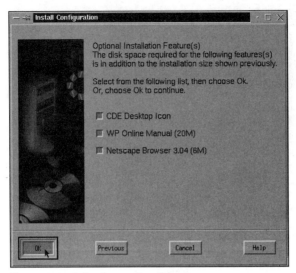

Figure 1-8: Selecting optional features

13. The install review list will be displayed (see Figure 1-9). To change an item, highlight it in the listing and click OK.

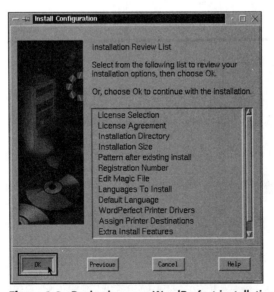

Figure 1-9: Reviewing your WordPerfect installation

14. Click OK to begin installing the WordPerfect files (see Figure 1-10).

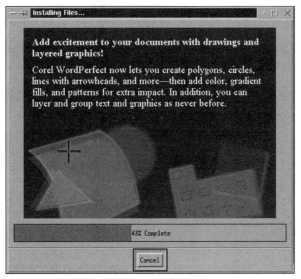

Figure 1-10: Installing the WordPerfect files on your system

15. After all the files have been copied, additional late-breaking product information may be displayed. Browsing this information is valuable in most cases.

Now you're ready to run WordPerfect 8 for Linux!

Starting WordPerfect for Linux

To start WordPerfect for Linux:

1. Open a terminal window and use the "cd" command (in most cases, cd /usr/local/wp8) to go to your WordPerfect directory (see Figure 1-11).

2. Go to the directory wpbin.

3. Type **./xwp** to start WordPerfect.

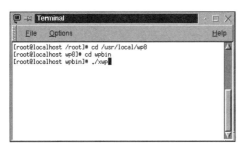

Figure 1-11: Starting WordPerfect from a terminal window

Using the WordPerfect 8 for Linux Interface

If you've ever used a Windows version of WordPerfect, WordPerfect 8 for Linux will look familiar. No matter which X-Window manager you use, you always see a WordPerfect document window and a WordPerfect program window when you start WordPerfect (as shown in Figure 1-12). When you open a second document, a second document window opens, and so forth.

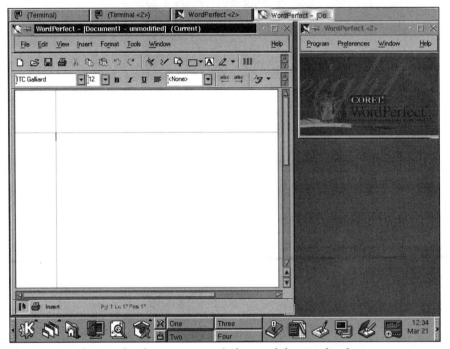

Figure 1-12: The WordPerfect Program Window and the WordPerfect document window

Use the WordPerfect program window to manage the document windows and adjust general WordPerfect settings (see Chapter 26, "Fine-Tuning WordPerfect"). Working with multiple windows requires some practice in the beginning. For example, if you have an open dialog box in one document window, you won't be able to work in another document window until the dialog is closed. This situation occurs only one instance of the WordPerfect program is running, even though you have multiple document windows.

Features of the WordPerfect for Linux interface are similar to those in the Windows version, and most operations are identical. The document formats are identical—

no conversion is required to send documents between the two versions. The main differences between the two versions follow:

✦ In Linux, the WordPerfect program window is separate from your document windows.

✦ File paths under Linux do not have drive letters and the backslash (\) is used instead of the forward slash (/). A typical document name (including the path) will be `/usr/local/wpdocuments/Chapter11.wpd` in Linux, compared to `C:\MyDocuments\Chapter11.wpd` in Windows.

You get a hands-on feel for the interface in Chapter 2, "Writing a Letter," then learn tons of screen tricks in Chapter 3, "Mastering the WordPerfect Interface."

Using Virtual Desktops

Opening separate windows for all your documents may be a bit confusing in the beginning, but it comes with the benefit of *virtual desktops* that your X-Window manager provides. Suppose you have three WordPerfect document windows you want to display full-screen. Just move each document window to a separate desktop! You can even display the WordPerfect program window on all the desktops (see Chapter 3, "Mastering the WordPerfect Interface").

Most X-Window managers offer at least four virtual desktops. The KDE X-Window manager has eight. Under KDE, use Ctrl+F1 to Ctrl+F8 to switch to the desktop you want to use. You can also use Ctrl+Tab to switch to the next available desktop.

Note

A virtual desktop is not the same as a *virtual screen*. The virtual screen offers extra screen space. For example, if you run Linux with 800 · 600 pixels, you can set up a virtual screen of 1,024 · 768 pixels. When you position the mouse cursor at the border of the screen, the display scrolls to show the rest of your screen. The X-Window system can give you both virtual desktops and virtual screens, but virtual desktops are normally the better option for WordPerfect.

Specifying WordPerfect Startup Options

In some cases, you'll find it useful or even necessary to start WordPerfect with one or more of the startup options described in Chapter 26, "Fine-Tuning WordPerfect." Two startup options deserve special attention:

✦ The -adm (administrator) option that enables you to install fonts (see Chapter 8, "Fonts Fantastic") and change certain system settings (see Chapter 26, "Fine-Tuning WordPerfect").

✦ The -lang option that enables you to run a localized (non-English) version of WordPerfect (only if you have installed the language modules).

For example, to launch WordPerfect as an administrator, type **./xwp -adm** in the command line, as shown in Figure 1-11. To use the Dutch version of WordPerfect, type **./xwp -lang nl**. To launch WordPerfect as an administrator and use the Dutch version of WordPerfect, type **./xwp -adm -lang nl**.

The easiest way to use startup options is to include them in your WordPerfect desktop icon or menu item, as described in a following section.

Setting Up Easy Ways to Launch WordPerfect

Hmmm . . . is there an easier way to start WordPerfect for Linux? Fortunately, there are several ways! You can:

✦ Create a WordPerfect alias to simplify the launch command

✦ Add a clickable icon to your desktop

✦ Add WordPerfect items to your desktop's program menu

Creating a WordPerfect Alias

To define a simplified alias for launching WordPerfect:

1. Using a text editor, open the file bash_profile in your home-directory $HOME. This directory will be /root if you logged in as root, but to make sure you go to the right directory, type **cd $HOME** to get there.

2. Add the following line (adjust the path if you installed WordPerfect in another directory):

```
alias wp='/usr/local/wp8/wpbin/xwp'
```

This line enables you to start WordPerfect for Linux by just typing **wp** in a terminal window.

Tip
Use the editor that comes with your X-Window manager (for instance, xedit when you use fvwm95, or kedit when you use KDE) to edit the bash-profile file. If the editor can't find the file, you probably have to enable an option to allow editing of .dot (hidden) files.

Adding a WordPerfect Icon to Your Desktop

Adding a desktop icon to your desktop is an even easier way to launch WordPerfect (see Figure 1-13).

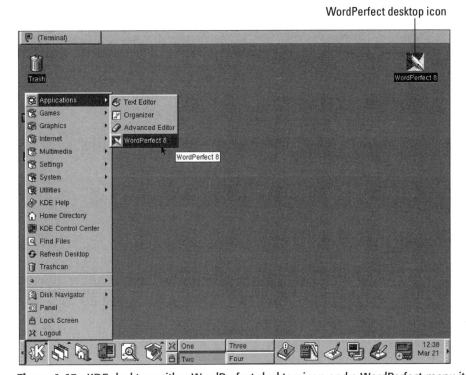

Figure 1-13: KDE desktop with a WordPerfect desktop icon and a WordPerfect menu item

Check the documentation for your X-Window manager to see how to install a desktop icon. If you installed the KDE X desktop environment on this book's CD, adding a desktop icon is easy:

   1. Right-click the KDE desktop and click New ➪ Application (see Figure 1-14).

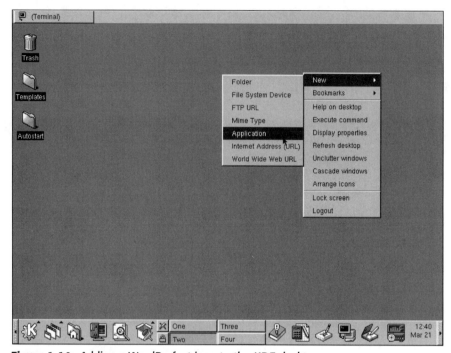

Figure 1-14: Adding a WordPerfect icon to the KDE desktop

2. Add the path to the WordPerfect executable (for instance, /usr/local/
wp8/wpbin/xwp) to the Execute box (see Figure 1-15).

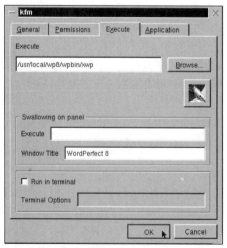

Figure 1-15: Specifying execute information
for your WordPerfect desktop icon

3. Select an icon for WordPerfect and click OK. The WordPerfect icon will be added to your desktop.

Tip

WordPerfect comes with an icon for the CDE desktop environment. Most other desktop environments will be able to use this icon as well, so make sure you installed it (see the preceding "Installing WordPerfect 8 for Linux" section).

To use the CDE desktop icon that comes with WordPerfect, use your desktop's file manager to copy the icons located in /usr/local/wp8/wplib/dt/appconfig/icons/c to /opt/kde/share/icons, and give the icons the extension .xpm.

Adding WordPerfect to Your Program Menu

Still another way to launch WordPerfect is by adding a selection to your desktop's program menu (refer to Figure 1-13). To add WordPerfect to your KDE program menu:

1. Click K ➪ Utilities ➪ Menu Editor.

2. Right-click the category to which you want to add WordPerfect and click New (see Figure 1-16).

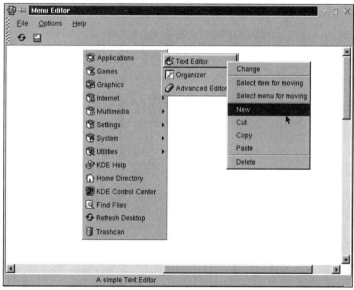

Figure 1-16: Adding a WordPerfect item to Applications category of the KDE program menu

3. Add the program information to the Execute box (see Figure 1-17), as described in Step 2 in the preceding "Adding a WordPerfect Icon to Your Desktop" section.

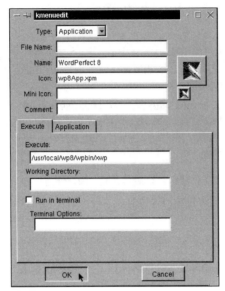

Figure 1-17: Adding program execution
information for the menu item

4. Select an icon for WordPerfect, as described in Step 3 of the preceding
"Adding a WordPerfect Icon to Your Desktop" section, then click OK to add
WordPerfect to the menu.

Tip

Create separate menu items for launching WordPerfect with special startup
options, such as the administrator function or a different language.

Customizing WordPerfect for Linux

The WordPerfect for Linux setup program installs a default WordPerfect
configuration on your system. This configuration can be customized completely to
your wishes. You'll probably want to install extra fonts (see Chapter 8, "Managing
Fonts"), customize your printer settings (see Chapter 10, "Printing Documents,
Booklets, and Envelopes"), fine-tune the WordPerfect environment (see Chapter 26,
"Fine-Tuning WordPerfect"), and customize toolbars, menus, and keyboards (see
Chapter 27, "Customizing Toolbars, Menus, and Keyboards").

For information on customizing your X-Window environment, refer to your
X-Window manager's online help and documentation.

Well, now it's time to use WordPerfect 8 for Linux! So why not turn to Chapter 2 and
write a letter?

For More Information. . .

On	See
WordPerfect startup options	Chapter 26
Configuring a printer	Chapter 10
Installing additional fonts	Chapter 8
Fine-tuning WordPerfect	Chapter 26
Customizing toolbars and keyboards	Chapter 27
Mastering the WordPerfect interface	Chapter 3
Getting started	Chapter 2

✦   ✦   ✦

Writing a Letter

The best way to get to know WordPerfect 8 for Linux is to start using it! The WordPerfect text techniques in this chapter enable you to get off to a flying start with WordPerfect 8 for Linux. Let's experience the ease of writing a letter in WordPerfect.

A Quick Tour of WordPerfect's Screen

So, without further ado, start WordPerfect and take a look at the writing screen:

1. Boot Linux.
2. Type **startx** to start your X-Window manager.

 Tip

To start the X-Window manager automatically after booting Linux, edit the file /etc/inittab and change the default runlevel to runlevel 5 (X11). Check your Linux user's guide or ask your system administrator for more information on editing the inittab file. (If you use WordPerfect to modify the system default files, make sure to save them as ASCII files.)

3. Open a terminal window and go to the directory containing the WordPerfect for Linux executable. For instance, type **cd /usr/local/wp8/wpbin**.
4. Type **./xwp** to start WordPerfect for Linux.

 Tip

You can create an alias, add WordPerfect to the Linux menu, or create a shortcut on the desktop to make it easier to start WordPerfect (see Chapter 1, "Getting Up and Running").

This sequence brings you to the WordPerfect document window. Unless you've changed WordPerfect's default settings, your screen should look like Figure 2-1.

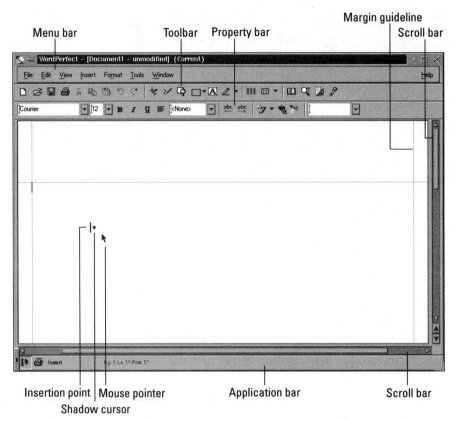

Figure 2-1: WordPerfect's document window

Chapter 3 explores the screen particulars. For now, the best way to learn WordPerfect is to jump right in and start typing. Mind you, it's not like learning to drive a car. You're not about to careen off the monitor into the depths of your computer's hard disk.

Writing a Letter

Now the fun begins. Yes, thanks to WordPerfect's features, typing can actually be fun (especially compared to a manual typewriter or basic text editor).

On the blank document screen, create your letter:

1. Type **Dear George**, then press Enter to end the line.

2. Press Enter again to skip a line, then type **WordPerfact 8 for Linux is a delite . . .** (including the misspellings) and the remainder of the paragraph as shown in Figure 2-2.

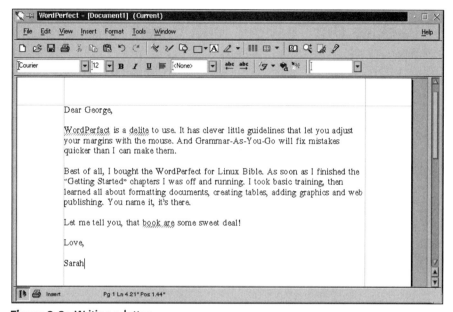

Figure 2-2: Writing a letter

3. Press Enter two more times, then type two paragraphs of praise for the *WordPerfect for Linux Bible* (just kidding), followed by a closing.

As you type, note how text automatically wraps to the next line. Press Enter only when you want to end a paragraph or force the beginning of a new line. Notice, too, that your misspelled words are underlined with hatched red lines. (Questionable grammar may be underlined in blue, as you'll see shortly.)

Correcting Mistakes

The advantages of a word processor quickly become apparent when correcting mistakes.

Fixing Typos

To erase the character you just typed (the one to the left of the insertion point), press Backspace. Pressing the Delete key erases the character to the right of the insertion point.

If you followed directions, you typed "WordPerfact" instead of "WordPerfect" in the second line of the letter. Click the mouse or use the arrow keys to position the insertion point in front of the *a*. Press Delete, then type **e**. Note how the red crosshatching disappears, indicating that the spelling is now correct.

Backing Out Changes with Undo

Use Undo when you want to reverse your last *editing action*. An editing action can be the words you just typed or the characters you deleted. Almost anything that changes the format of your document counts, such as when you change the line spacing, put a phrase in italics, set tabs, center a line, or move a margin guideline. Undo sends you back to where you were before. (Scrolling or saving your document cannot be undone, because no editing has taken place.)

To reverse editing actions by using Undo:

1. Click the Undo button on the toolbar, click Edit ➪ Undo, or press Ctrl+Z.

2. Repeat Undo to backtrack your editing session, one action at a time, for as many Undos found in your document.

WordPerfect allows up to 300 levels of Undo (see Chapter 6, "Working without Worries").

Redoing Undo

To reverse your Undos with Redo, click the Redo button on the toolbar. (You can also click Edit ➪ Redo.) When there are no more Redos, the Redo arrow on the toolbar appears dim.

Proofreading-As-You-Go

WordPerfect comes with a powerful set of instant proofreading tools, including Grammar-As-You-Go and automatic typo correction. You can turn any automatic feature on and off from the Tools menu. (All the features, except Grammar-As-You-Go, are initially turned on.)

Spell-As-You-Go

When you typed "WordPerfact", you probably noticed that its red underlining appeared immediately. The underlining is produced by Spell-As-You-Go, a great WordPerfect feature that highlights possible mistakes as you type them. You can right-click a marked word (such as "delite"), then click one of the suggested replacements. When there are more than six suggestions, you can point to More and pick from the remainder of the list (see Figure 2-3).

Prompt-As-You-Go

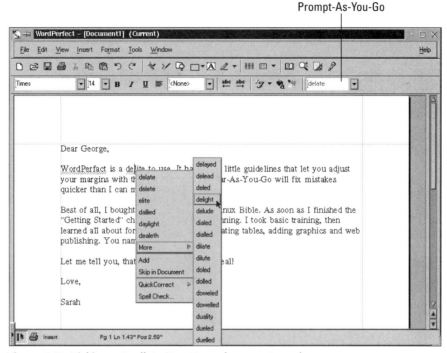

Figure 2-3: Picking a Spell-As-You-Go replacement word

The Spell-As-You-Go QuickMenu, which appears when you right-click on a misspelled word, gives you four other choices:

✦ *Add* places the word in the user word list, so the word won't be flagged as an error again. Your "skip words" can include the names of friends and places, or technical terms not in WordPerfect's word list.

✦ *Skip in Document* has the same effect as Add, but only for this document.

✦ *QuickCorrect* puts the word, with its replacement, in your user word list, to correct future errors instantly (see "QuickCorrect" later in this section).

✦ *Spell Check* takes you to the Spell Checker, where more options are available.

If you want to turn off Spell-As-You-Go, click Tools ⇨ Proofread ⇨ Off.

For details on the Spell Checker and word lists, see Chapter 12, "Writer's Lib."

Prompt-As-You-Go and the Instant Thesaurus

You can also correct the word or phrase at the insertion point by selecting from the Prompt-As-You-Go replacements on the property bar. Possible spelling corrections appear in red. Blue text is used for possible grammar fixes. When there's no problem, and the word appears in black, Prompt-As-You-Go turns into an Instant Thesaurus. Simply click a replacement synonym from the list (see Figure 2-4).

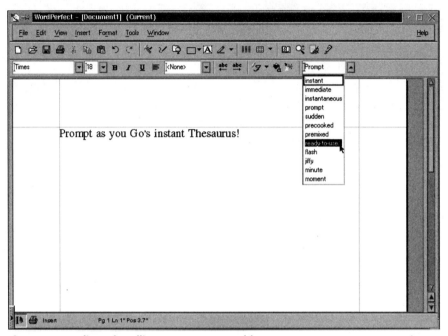

Figure 2-4: In lieu of spelling or grammar problems, Prompt-As-You-Go turns into an Instant Thesaurus

Prompt-As-You-Go checks your grammar and spelling, even when Grammar-As-You-Go and Spell-As-You-Go are off. To turn off Prompt-As-You-Go, click Tools ➪ Proofread ➪ Prompt-As-You-Go, and uncheck Prompt-As-You-Go. (Turning off this feature may speed up your display.)

Automatic Typo Correction

WordPerfect can correct your misspelled or mistyped word automatically, so long as there is only one close replacement. For example, if you type "informtion", leaving out the *a*, the program can ascertain what you meant. Likewise, when you transpose two characters, as with "transpsoe", the program can usually correct your mistake.

This automatic correction is on by default, so it may take you by surprise. To turn it off, click Tools ➪ QuickCorrect, and disable "Correct other mis-typed words, when possible."

QuickCorrect

QuickCorrect is the original form of instant correction. There's no guesswork, because the word you type, with its replacement, must be in your user word list.

Try typing **adn**, **alot**, or **july**, and, of course, **potatoe**, to see your mistakes corrected instantly. Note that the correction does not appear until you type a space (or press Enter), indicating that you have completed the word.

If nothing happens when you type these words, make sure that QuickCorrect is turned on. To do so, click Tools ➪ QuickCorrect, then click "Replace words as you type." Remove the check to turn off QuickCorrect.

QuickCorrect comes with a starting list of replacement words. The beauty of the feature is that you can add your personal mistakes to the list, together with the correct spelling, so next time these mistakes are instantly corrected. QuickCorrect is also great for shorthand abbreviations, and it can liberate you from the Shift and apostrophe (') keys. See Chapter 12, "Writer's Lib," for details.

Grammar-As-You-Go

Grammar-As-You-Go is another great proofreading tool. To turn it on, click Tools ➪ Proofread ➪ Grammar-As-You-Go. (Spell-As-You-Go will be on as well.)

Now when you type "That book are some sweet deal!", "book are" should be underlined in blue. A right-click shows that there is a problem with subject-verb agreement. You can select either "books are" or "book is" to correct the situation. (You can also select replacements from the Prompt-As-You-Go list on the property bar.) No grammar checker is perfect, however, so treat the flags as possible errors. Don't feel that you have to get rid of every underline!

More Instant Correction Options

Click Tools ➪ QuickCorrect to take a look at the instant correction options under the various sections:

✦ *QuickCorrect* (shown in Figure 2-5) enables you to add misspellings or abbreviations, along with their replacements, to the QuickCorrect list manually.

✦ *QuickLinks* instantly transforms phrases you specify into hypertext links that you can click to jump to an Internet address. For example, type **@Corel** to create an instant link to Corel's home page at http://www.corel.com. (This example is predefined in your installation.)

✦ *Format-As-You-Go* provides automatic sentence corrections, instant bullets, and other conveniences. For example, the start of a sentence in WordPerfect is normally capitalized automatically.

✦ *SmartQuotes* turns straight quotation marks into printer's curly quotes.

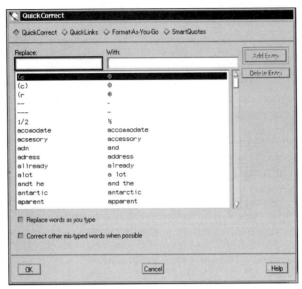

Figure 2-5: QuickCorrect replacement list

For more on Format-As-You-Go and SmartQuotes, see Chapter 4, "Becoming an Instant WordPerfect Expert." Chapter 12, "Writer's Lib," features in-depth coverage of QuickCorrect.

Getting Around the Screen

By now, you've probably noticed the two basic ways to move around the screen:

✦ By using the arrow (directional) keys

✦ By using the mouse

Most keyboards have four arrow keys — often grouped in an inverted "T" — for moving up, down, left, and right. The arrow keys on the numeric keypad (if you have one) can also be used, provided the Num Lock light is off. As you press the arrow keys, the insertion point (the blinking vertical bar, also known as the cursor) moves around the screen.

Using the Shadow Cursor to Click and Type

Now, move the mouse and notice the shadow cursor that enables you to click anywhere in the screen and start typing (as shown in Figure 2-6). Try moving the mouse and clicking to get the hang of the shadow cursor. When the shadow cursor is set to appear in text, it disappears after you stop moving the mouse.

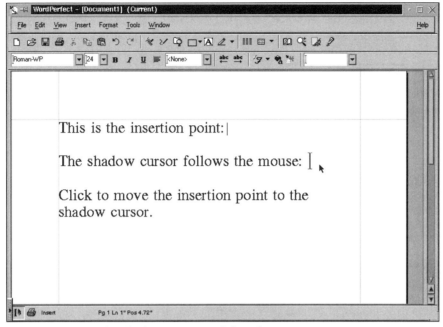

Figure 2-6: Using the shadow cursor to click and type

Tip   Normally the shadow cursor appears only in your document's white space, not in the text. You can have it snap to margins, tabs, an indent, or spaces. You can also change its color and shape.

The shadow cursor can do lots of clever operations, as you'll see in Chapter 3, "Mastering the WordPerfect Interface," but it takes a while to get comfortable with this feature. For now, you may want to turn it off by clicking the Shadow Cursor button on the application bar at the bottom of your screen.

Caution   If you click the left mouse button when the pointer is in the left margin, WordPerfect selects (highlights) the nearest sentence. If this happens, remove the highlight by clicking anywhere between the margins.

Inserting Text versus Typeover

As you type, you're normally in *insert* mode—words spread out and wrap around to the next line as you type. To see how this works as you edit your letter, go back to the first line of the letter and place the insertion point immediately after "WordPerfect". Press the spacebar, then type the words "for Linux". Notice that, as you type, the text after the insertion point is pushed to the right and down. That's what word processing is all about.

At times, though, you may want to correct your document or add to it by typing over the existing text. Suppose, going back to the letter in Figure 2-2, you'd rather "change" the margins than "adjust" them. Go back and position the insertion point in front of the *a* in "adjust." Now, press the Insert key several times and observe how the Insert status on the application bar at the bottom of your screen toggles between Insert and Typeover. (You can also click the Insert/Typeover button on the application bar to switch modes.) Leave it at Typeover for the moment and type **change** over "adjust". Notice how the text doesn't move in typeover mode. Toggle back to Insert mode.

Inserting the Date and Time

So far, you've been so busy typing and editing your letter that you haven't put in the date. Click where you want the date to appear, then press Ctrl+D (Insert ⇨ Date/Time ⇨ Insert), as shown in Figure 2-7.

If you check "Keep the inserted date current," the same date appears, but there's a difference. A *date code* is inserted that refreshes the date each time you open or print your document. This is a handy way to ensure that your letter reflects the current date if you plan to send it later. However, if you want a record of when the letter was sent, leave this option unchecked. Otherwise, the date will change every time you look at the letter.

Figure 2-7: Inserting the date

If you dislike the available date or time formats, click New Format to design a custom format. Just pick the format you want from the available date and time codes (see Figure 2-8). Click Insert Date Code or Insert Time Code to place each code in the "Edit date format" box. Add any punctuation, spaces, or text, then click OK to apply your custom format to any date you insert afterwards. (To change the date format for all your documents, edit the Document Style, as explained in Chapter 15, "Formatting Your Document.")

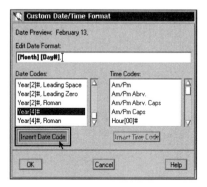

Figure 2-8: Creating a custom date/time format

Selecting Text

One of the most powerful and flexible features of WordPerfect is its capability to perform operations on selected (blocked) text and graphics. You can move, copy, or delete highlighted information, or change the format of your text. You can even save your block as a file on its own. You have almost as many ways to select information as you have things to do with the information. Try these two basic selection techniques:

✦ *Using the mouse.* Drag the mouse across the information you want to select, as shown in Figure 2-9, then release the mouse button. (If you start dragging near a margin guideline, make sure the pointer is still an arrow or I-bar, or you'll drag the guideline instead.) As you drag across words, selection switches from character-by-character to word-by-word if WordPerfect's "Select whole words instead of characters" option is checked. To turn this option on or off, switch to the WordPerfect program window and click Preferences ➪ Environment.

✦ *Using the keyboard.* Place the insertion point where you want to start your selection, then press F8. (Press F12 if you're using the DOS-compatible keyboard.) Use the arrow keys to select text one character or line at a time. Press the spacebar to extend the selection word-by-word, or press any character to extend to the next occurrence of that character.

Tip

For many operations on a single word (such as making it bold or italic), simply place the insertion point anywhere in the word, then press Ctrl+B or Ctrl+I. You don't need to select the word.

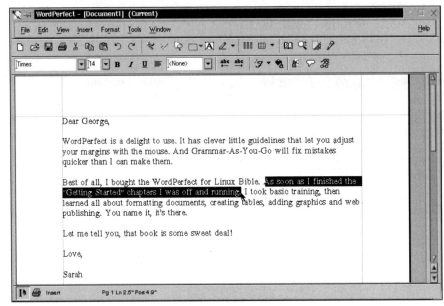

Figure 2-9: Select text by dragging the mouse

To remove a selection:

✦ Click anywhere in the document (except for the left margin)
✦ Press F8 (F12 for the DOS-compatible keyboard)

Moving and Copying Text

Now that you know how to select text, you can move text around to rearrange your ideas, or copy text to avoid typing it again. Essentially, there are two ways to move and copy:

✦ By cutting or copying the selected information (text or graphics) to the Clipboard, then pasting it to the new location
✦ By dragging the information with the mouse and dropping it into place

Moving and Copying via the Clipboard

The *X clipboard* is a holding area (or buffer) to which you can cut, copy, or append information, then paste it to another location in the current file, in another file, or even in another file in another application.

To move or copy via the Clipboard:

1. Select the information.

2. Place the selection in the Clipboard in either of two ways:

   • To move the information, click the Move button on the toolbar. (You can also press Ctrl+X or click Edit ➪ Cut.) The selection will disappear from its place in the document and be transferred to the Clipboard.

   • To copy the information, click the Copy button on the toolbar. (You can also press Ctrl+C or click Edit ➪ Copy.) The selection will remain in its place in the document, and a copy of the selection will be placed in the Clipboard.

3. Move the insertion point to where you want to put the information.

4. Click the Paste button on the toolbar. (You can also press Ctrl+V or click Edit ➪ Paste.)

When information is in the Clipboard, the Paste button on the toolbar is highlighted, and you can paste it in as many places as you want. Your selection stays in the Clipboard until it's replaced by your next cut or copy operation, or until you exit your X-Window manager.

Using Paste Simple

Normally, the pasting part of the move or copy process pastes your text at the new location with its original font size, style, color, and other attributes. For example, if you paste the word "**bold**" in between the words "*large italic*", the result looks like the following: *large* **bold** *italic*.

Press Ctrl+Shift+V to paste simple a copy of the text, so that it looks the same as the text at the insertion point, like this: *large bold italic*.

When you use Paste Simple on a blank line, the text takes on the default font size, style, and color.

Unlike Cut, Copy, and Paste, Paste Simple does not appear on either the default menu bar or the toolbar (Paste Special on the Edit menu is a different feature). To add Paste Simple to the toolbar, turn to the customizing instructions in Chapter 27, "Customizing Toolbars, Menus, and Keyboards."

Appending to Information in the Clipboard

Instead of replacing the Clipboard's contents each time you copy, you can append to it, then paste both the old and the new:

1. Select some text, then click Edit ➪ Append. (Select the necessary blank space or line to separate your clipboard items.)

2. Move the insertion point to where you want to copy the Clipboard's contents.

3. Click the Paste button. (You can also press Ctrl+V or click Edit ⇨ Paste.)

This time, your last two selections are copied. You can append to the Clipboard as many times as you want. The entire contents of the Clipboard are always pasted. There's no history by which you can go back and select only the Clipboard information from two "appends" ago.

Using the Mouse to Drag and Drop

For nearby moving or copying, try using the mouse to drag and drop:

1. Drag to make your selection, then release the left mouse button.

2. Put the mouse pointer on the selected text, then drag it to the new location.

To move the information, release the mouse button. To copy the information while leaving the original intact, hold down the Ctrl key while you release the mouse button. The mouse pointer looks slightly different when you press Ctrl, as shown in Figure 2-10.

If you drag while holding down the right mouse button in Step 2, a QuickMenu appears at the new location that lets you choose between move and copy. It even offers you move simple and copy simple features, both of which work like paste simple.

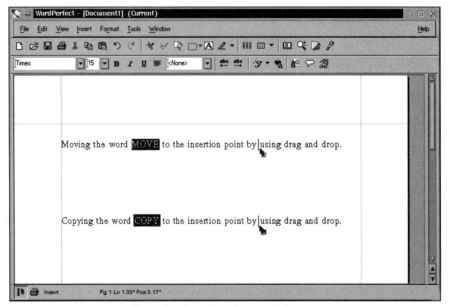

Figure 2-10: Moving and copying by using drag and drop

Making a Bold Impression

Writing is about expression. While the words themselves have primacy, the manner in which they are displayed visually can add (or detract) from their impact. With a word processor (and its associated printer), you no longer have to use the crude underlining method required with a typewriter to emphasize a point or identify a title. To use bold and italic instead:

1. Click the Bold button or the Italic button on the property bar. (You can also press Ctrl+B or Ctrl+I.)

2. Type your text, then repeat Step 1 to turn off the effect.

To make text you already typed bold or italic, first select the text, or place the insertion point anywhere on a single word.

Note how the Bold or Italic button is recessed when its attribute is active at the insertion point. You can click the recessed button to remove bold or italic.

WordPerfect includes a host of other features to embellish your text. The full range of text effects (including font, size, color, and other attributes) is described in Chapter 8, "Fonts Fantastic."

Changing Line Spacing

The ability to adjust line spacing (the amount of white space between each line of text) is another great word processing convenience. To change your line spacing:

1. Place the insertion point anywhere in the paragraph where you want the change to begin, or select the paragraphs you want to change.

2. Click Format ➪ Line ➪ Spacing.

3. Type the line spacing you want (see Figure 2-11). You can also click the little arrows, or press the up and down arrows on your keyboard.

Figure 2-11: Changing line spacing

Tip   If you work with line spacing often, you can add the line spacing button to the text property bar (see Chapter 27, "Customizing Toolbars, Menus, and Keyboards").

Saving and Naming Your Document

Your letter is finished and corrected, so now save it as a file on your hard disk. (In most cases, save your document before it's finished, in case of a power outage or other unforeseen event.)

The title bar at the top of your screen should read "WordPerfect - [Document1]." This title means that you are in the first document window (you can have up to nine documents open concurrently), and that you have yet to save your letter and give it a name.

To save and name a new document:

1. Click the Save button on the toolbar. (You can also click File ➪ Save, or press Ctrl+S.)

2. Type a name for your document in the "Filename" box (see Figure 2-12), then click Save.

Tip   You can give your documents descriptive names of any length, with spaces between words. Keep them reasonably short for display purposes, and don't use any of the following characters: * + = [ ] : ; . " < > ? / \ |. WordPerfect for Linux does not append a default extension to the name you type.

For information on placing your files into particular directories, see Chapter 7, "Managing Your Files."

Printing Your Document

Now that your letter is saved to disk, it's ready to print:

1. Click the Print button on the toolbar. (You can also click File ➪ Print, or press F5.)

2. Click OK (see Figure 2-13).

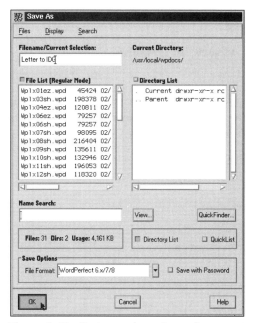

Figure 2-12: Saving and naming a document

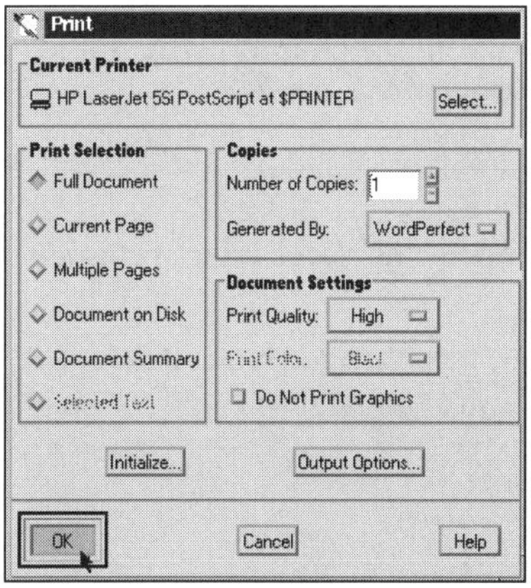

Figure 2-13: Printing your document

Various printing options are covered in Chapter 10, "Printing Documents, Booklets, and Envelopes." Setting up a printer under Linux is covered in Chapter 1, "Getting Up and Running."

Closing Your Document

Now that your letter is finished, you can close the document window:

1. Click File ⇨ Close.

2. If you have changed your document since it was last saved, the "Save changes to . . . ?" prompt appears (refer to Figure 2-14). To save the latest changes, click Yes. To discard the latest changes, click No. To continue editing your document, click Cancel.

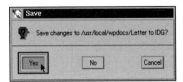

Figure 2-14: You're prompted to save the latest changes when closing the document window

Exiting WordPerfect

You've covered a lot of word processing territory in this chapter! Why not leave the program and take a break before examining the screen details?

To exit WordPerfect:

1. Click the WordPerfect taskbar button to open the WordPerfect program window.

2. Click Program ⇨ Exit. If an open document has changed since it was last saved, answer the "Save changes to . . . ?" prompt as described previously.

For More Information . . .

On	See
WordPerfect for Linux basics	Chapter 1
Mastering the WordPerfect interface	Chapter 3
Using Undo and Redo	Chapter 6
Using the Spell Checker and word lists	Chapter 12
Checking your grammar	Chapter 12
Using QuickCorrect	Chapter 12
Using QuickLinks, Format-As-You-Go, and SmartQuotes	Chapter 4
Using the shadow cursor	Chapter 3
Customizing toolbars	Chapter 27
Working with fonts	Chapter 8
Organizing files in directories	Chapter 7
Printing and information	Chapter 10

✦   ✦   ✦

Mastering the WordPerfect Interface

As you learned in the preceding chapters, WordPerfect makes it easy to get up and running as well as type and edit text. Now it's time to get acquainted with a number of friendly screen features (and tricks) that make working in WordPerfect for Linux a pleasurable experience.

Getting Around the Screen

Start WordPerfect for Linux to display the WordPerfect document window shown in Figure 3-1. From here, you can take an in-depth look at WordPerfect's screen features.

Switching Windows with Your Linux Taskbar

Linux is a *multitasking environment*, which means that it allows several programs to be active at a time, sharing your computer's resources according to each program's needs. Therefore, most X-Window managers provide a taskbar, similar to the KDE taskbar shown in Figure 3-1, with buttons to click to switch among your active programs, including the WordPerfect program. Each WordPerfect document window also has a taskbar button, so you can click the taskbar buttons to switch between your open documents.

You can point to a document button on the taskbar to see the name of the document it contains. The program button simply says "WordPerfect."

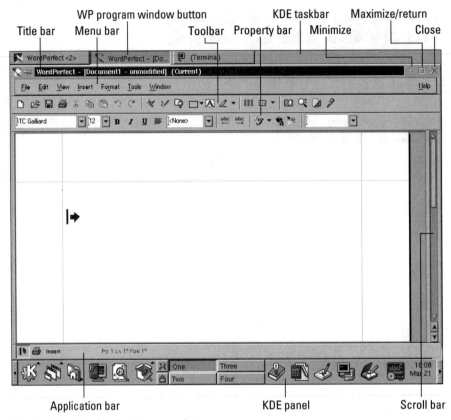

Figure 3-1: WordPerfect's screen features

In most cases, you can right-click taskbar buttons to display context-sensitive selections, such as closing a program.

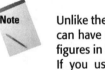

Note   Unlike the Microsoft Windows graphical user interface, the Linux X-Window system can have different faces, depending on which X-Window manager you use. Some figures in this book show the KDE X-Window manager, provided on the book's CD. If you use another X-Window manager, certain screen features vary, but the WordPerfect program window and document windows look the same. (For more information on X-Window managers and KDE, see Chapter 1, "Getting Up and Running.")

KDE also has a panel on the bottom of the screen. This panel can be used to start applications and switch to other virtual desktops (see Chapter 1, "Getting Up and Running").

What Are Those Little Buttons?

Several little buttons display in the upper corners of the WordPerfect document window. Table 3-1 explains the purpose of each button. If you're using an X-Window manager other than KDE, the appearance of your buttons is likely to differ.

Table 3-1
Little Buttons at the Top of Your Screen

Upper-Left Buttons

Click This Button	*To*
The Document Control button	Display a menu of window choices, such as closing the window, minimizing the window to a taskbar icon, changing the size of the window, or moving the window to another virtual desktop (see Chapter 1, "Getting Up and Running"). The Sticky menu option also has its own button.
The Sticky button	This button, a picture of a tack, can be quite useful when you are using more than one virtual desktop. When you click the Sticky button, the document window (or the WordPerfect program window) displays on all your virtual desktops.

Upper-Right Buttons

Click This Button	*To*
The Minimize button	Shrink (minimize) your document to a button on the taskbar.
The Maximize button	Enlarge (maximize) the document to fill the entire screen.
The Return button	Return a maximized window to its previous size.
The Close button	Close the document window.

Resizing a Document Window

When a document window is not displayed full-screen, you can drag the borders to shrink or stretch it. To increase or decrease both the width and height, drag one of the corners (see Figure 3-2).

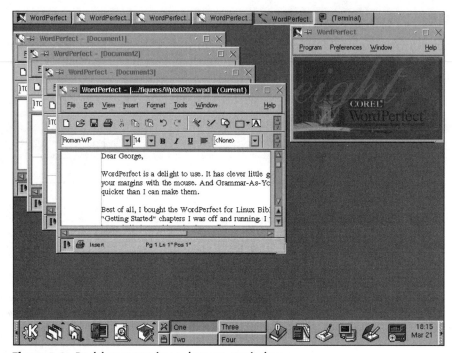

Figure 3-2: Resizing or moving a document window

Using Title Bar

The *title bar* of a document window displays the name of the program, along with the name of the document on which you're working. You can drag the title bar to move the window to another location. (Double-click the title bar to maximize and return the document window display alternately.)

Using the Menu Bar

Nearly every program command and feature can be accessed by clicking items on the *menu bar*. Selections are arranged logically under categories. Many menu selections lead to submenus (Edit ➪ Select) or dialogs (Edit ➪ Find and Replace). These selections are indicated by right-pointing triangles for submenus or ellipses (. . .) for dialogs.

To navigate menus and select items with the mouse:

1. Click the menu bar.

2. Point to the menu bar to move from menu to menu.

3. Click to select an item.

To navigate menus and select items with the keyboard:

1. Select a menu by pressing the Alt key plus the underlined letter (or press the Alt key alone to go to the left of the menu bar).

2. Scroll the menus by using the arrow keys.

3. Press Enter to select the highlighted item.

To exit a menu without making a selection, click on the document, or press Esc until you return to your document.

Using Toolbars

Toolbars provide quick mouse access to frequently used features. You can even put the icon for another program (such as a calculator) on a toolbar to launch it right from your screen (see Chapter 27, "Customizing Toolbars, Menus, and Keyboards").

A little downward-pointing triangle on a button's right (as for the Highlight and Tables buttons) indicates a list or palette from which to make your selection.

You can select various custom toolbars for particular tasks (such as Format, Graphics, or Outline Tools) or create a custom toolbar of your own. Click View ⇨ Toolbars or right-click anywhere on a toolbar to add or remove toolbars.

Note   In WordPerfect for Linux, you can't move a toolbar to another location, as with WordPerfect for Windows.

Using the Property Bar

The *property bar* is a chameleon-like toolbar that presents a different set of features depending on the current task (such as drawing, tables, or outlining). Select some text and note how the property bar changes, while the toolbar items remain the same.

As with other toolbars, you can customize the buttons of a property bar. (See Chapter 26, "Fine-Tuning WordPerfect," for more information.)

Using Scroll Bars

The *scroll bars* along the right side and bottom of the screen enable you to move quickly through long documents. Because you normally scroll WordPerfect documents up and down (not from left to right), you may want to remove the horizontal scroll bar to free some screen space (switch to the WordPerfect program window, click Preferences ➪ Display, and uncheck Horizontal). The scroll bars shown in Figure 3-3 have the following features:

✦ *Scroll arrows*. Click the up or down arrow to scroll line by line or row by row. Hold a button down to scroll continuously.

✦ *Scroll boxes*. As you move through your document, the scroll boxes move along the scroll bars, indicating your relative position. (The length of the scroll box indicates the proportion of the document on display.) Drag a scroll box to scroll quickly to another location.

✦ *Page up* and *page down buttons*. To scroll one page at a time, click the page up or page down button. (Click a blank spot above or below the scroll box to scroll one screen at a time.)

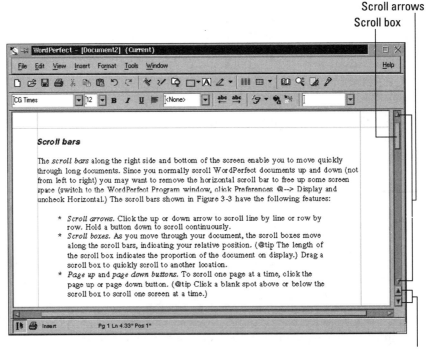

Figure 3-3: Scroll bars and page up and down buttons

Tip   You must click the screen to move the insertion point and make your scrolling stick. Otherwise, you jump back to your original screen location when you press a key.

Using the Application Bar

Located at the bottom of your screen, the *application bar* shows you valuable information (like the cursor position and the page number). The *application bar* enables you to display or hide screen features (like the shadow cursor) and insert information in your document (like the date). You can customize application bar selections and display (see Chapter 26, "Fine-Tuning WordPerfect").

Displaying QuickTips

Rest the pointer on a menu, toolbar, property bar, or application bar selection for a second or two to trigger a descriptive *QuickTip* (see Figure 3-4).

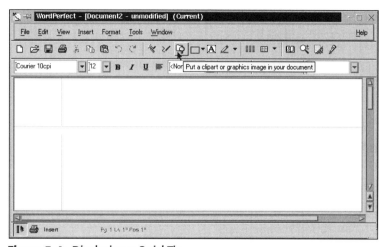

Figure 3-4: Displaying a QuickTip

Using Dialogs and QuickMenus

Today, working with applications involves a continuous series of selections. Dialogs and QuickMenus present two handy ways to communicate your wishes.

Dialogs

Dialogs, or dialog boxes, present choices in a variety of ways. You can drag a dialog around the screen by the title bar, or press Esc to dismiss the dialog without making a choice.

The dialogs shown in Figures 3-5, 3-6, and 3-7 illustrate the dialog characteristics and features described in Table 3-2.

Dimmed options
Radio button

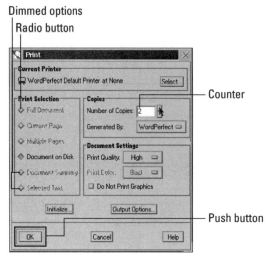

Counter

Push button

Figure 3-5: Features illustrated by
the Print dialog

List box

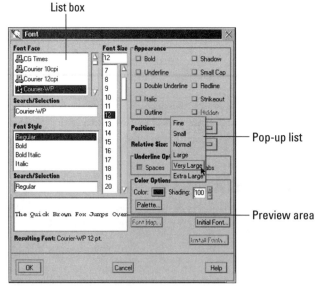

Pop-up list

Preview area

Figure 3-6: Features illustrated by
the Font dialog

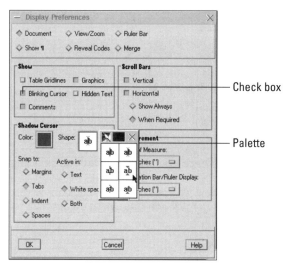

— Check box

— Palette

Figure 3-7: Features illustrated by the Display Preferences dialog

Table 3-2
Common Dialog Items

Item	How to Use It
Sections	Click the sections to display the group of options you want.
Pop-up list	Click the arrow to display the list of options, then click the option you want.
Counter	Type a number or click the arrows to change the value (also known as a spin box).
Push button	Click to perform an immediate action. These buttons — also called command buttons — can chain to lower-level dialog boxes.
Radio buttons	Click the option you want. You can only select one.
Check boxes	Click to check the options you want. You can select more than one.
List box	Click the arrows to scroll the list, then click your selection.
Palette	Click to trigger a visual display of colors or tools from which to choose.
Preview area	View the effect of your selections before they're applied.
Text box	(Not shown, but the Name box in the Save File dialog is an example.) Type your entry or selection.
Dimmed options	Options that are not available at that moment. For instance, in the Print dialog, the Selected text item is dimmed (not available) because no text is currently selected.

You can use the following keystrokes in a dialog:

✦ Tab to go to the next part

✦ Shift+Tab to go to the previous part

✦ Arrow keys to switch among buttons or scroll a list

✦ Enter to activate the highlighted button

QuickMenus

As you work, the program keeps track of where you are and what you're doing. The *QuickMenu*, like the property bar, goes a step further by anticipating what you want to do next. To see how this works, type a few words, then right-click anywhere in the typing area to display the normal text QuickMenu (shown in Figure 3-8).

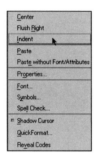

Figure 3-8: Normal text QuickMenu

Point and click to select a QuickMenu item. To dismiss the QuickMenu, press Esc or click the left mouse button anywhere outside the menu.

Tip

QuickMenus in WordPerfect for Linux are a bit tricky, because you have to click much more quickly than in the Windows version. If you can't get the QuickMenu to stay on the screen, press and hold down the right mouse button instead of just clicking it.

Now, select some text and right-click your selection. This time, the formatting selections are replaced by Cut, Copy, and Block Protect — actions you are likely to do with selected text (see Figure 3-9). Right-click in the left margin for a QuickMenu to do such tasks as select a sentence or adjust your margins.

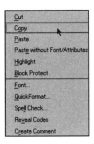

Figure 3-9: Selected text QuickMenu

Cascading and Tiling Windows

If you have several WordPerfect document windows open, you can click the Window menu in the current document to:

✦ *Cascade* the windows as shown in Figure 3-2. The active window has a highlighted menu bar. Click anywhere on an inactive window to bring it to the foreground. You can then maximize the window.

✦ *Tile* your windows as shown in Figure 3-10. (Four windows display in a matrix.) This option is especially useful for comparing two documents. You can tile documents top to bottom or side by side.

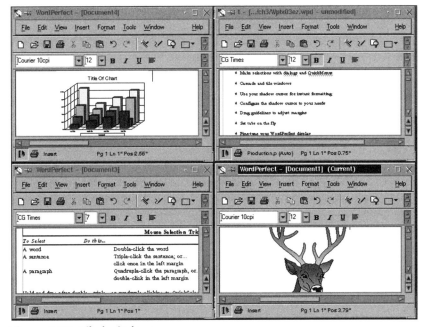

Figure 3-10: Tiled windows

Taking Visual Shortcuts

WordPerfect presents a lively, even playful, working environment. In addition to such features as toolbars and QuickMenus, WordPerfect has several visual tools designed specifically for a text environment.

Performing Shadow Cursor Tricks

WordPerfect's shadow cursor has emerged as a full-fledged formatting tool. The shadow cursor is also something of a paradox: an intuitive, time-saving feature that can be more annoying than helpful initially. Before you decide that it's driving you nuts, try these tricks:

1. Open a blank document, then move the mouse around. See how the shadow cursor follows the pointer, indicating where the insertion point will land when you click.

2. Move the shadow cursor to the center of a line, so that arrows point in both directions, then click and type. Your text is centered automatically.

3. Point at the left margin, click and type; then point at the right margin and do the same. See how your text is first left-justified, then right-justified.

If these tasks feel natural, consider that without the shadow cursor, nothing would be happening! Your blank document is exactly that to your mouse, so you must start from the top-left corner of the page.

Formatting reports, letters, flyers, and cards is simple, but it's also disconcerting—with a casual click, you can insert a bunch of formatting codes inadvertently. You can get rid of them immediately with Undo (Ctrl+Z), but the feature still takes some practice.

Turning the shadow cursor on and off

The preceding exercise leads to the next feature — ways to turn the shadow cursor on and off:

✦ Click the Shadow Cursor button on the application bar at the bottom of your screen.

✦ Click View ➪ Shadow Cursor.

✦ Right-click in your document and click Shadow Cursor.

Inserting graphics with the shadow cursor

Turn on your shadow cursor and try this trick:

1. Click and drag anywhere in a white space (as shown in Figure 3-11).

2. Release the mouse, click Image From File, select an image, then click Insert.

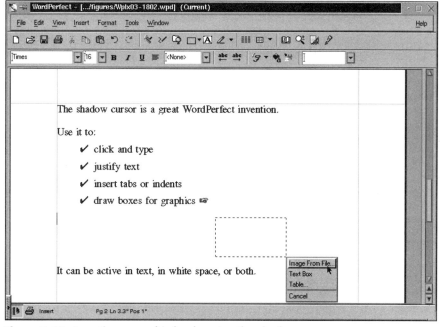

Figure 3-11: Inserting a graphic by dragging the shadow cursor

You could also have selected a text box (see Chapter 9, "Working with Graphics") or a table-in-a-box (see Chapter 16, "Formatting with Columns and Tables").

Configuring your shadow cursor

While you're likely to be content with most features (such as toolbars) as they come out of the box, you should know about the options for the shadow cursor. To configure your shadow cursor:

1. Switch to the WordPerfect program window, then click Preferences ➪ Display.

2. Select any of these shadow cursor settings:

- Click the Color palette to change the color of your shadow cursor.

- Click the Shape palette to pick a different shape when you're pointing to text (see Figure 3-12).

- Pick whether you want the shadow cursor to snap to (and insert formatting codes for) margins, tabs, indents, or spaces.

- You can have the shadow cursor appear when your pointer is in text (active in text), in white space, or both.

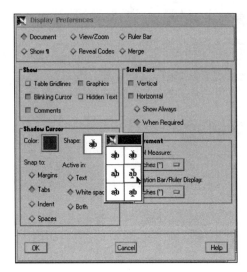

Figure 3-12: Configuring your shadow cursor

Recommended shadow cursor settings

If you don't want to experiment, try these shadow cursor settings: a shape for text of two little triangles, snap to margins (text justification without inadvertent tabs and spaces), and active in both. And don't forget how easy it is to turn the shadow cursor on or off by clicking its button on the application bar.

Displaying the Ruler

WordPerfect's ruler, shown in Figure 3-13, is handy for viewing and adjusting margins, tabs, and columns. Click View ➪ Ruler to display or remove the ruler. See Chapter 15, "Formatting Your Document," for tips on its use.

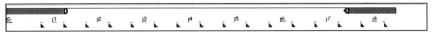

Figure 3-13: WordPerfect's ruler

Dragging Guidelines

One of the most clever features of the WordPerfect screen is the dotted *guidelines* that you can drag to adjust your side, top, and bottom margins. Other guidelines enable you to adjust page headers and footers, or column margins and spacing. Even tables sport guidelines around cells without lines.

Just drag the guideline to the new position to change your margin settings (see Figure 3-14). Normally, the line snaps to an interval on an invisible grid, as explained under display preferences in Chapter 26, "Fine-Tuning WordPerfect." (If you mess up your margins, press Ctrl+Z to restore them.)

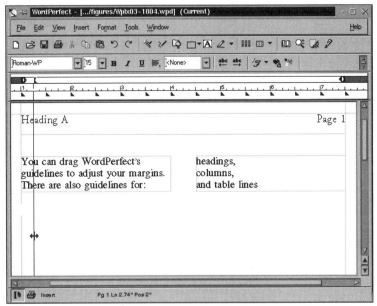

Figure 3-14: Adjusting a margin by dragging its guideline

Tip   Because WordPerfect for Linux does not display the new margin settings as you drag, display the ruler before you drag the margin guidelines.

To select which guidelines you want to see, click View ⇨ Guidelines, and then check the ones you want.

Setting Tabs on the Fly

You can also use the ruler and tab icons to change your tab settings on the fly:

1. Click View ⇨ Ruler, then drag one of the tab marker triangles on the ruler to change your tab settings. Click View ⇨ Ruler to hide the ruler.

Note that wherever tabs are set, a *tab icon* displays in the left margin. When you work in Draft view (explained in the following "Choosing How Your Document Appears" section), you must switch to Page view temporarily to see the icons.

2. Click the tab icon to display the ruler bar.

3. Drag the markers to remove or adjust the settings (see Figure 3-15).

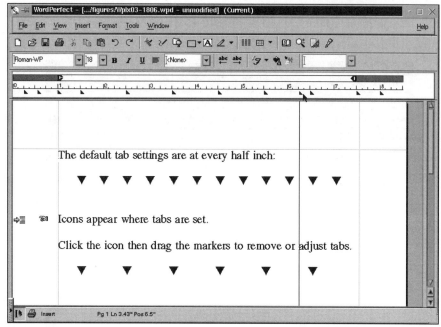

Figure 3-15: Setting tabs on the fly

4. Click your document when you're finished. The ruler bar disappears and your new settings take effect from that point forward.

For complete information on using and setting tabs, turn to Chapter 15, "Formatting Your Document."

Setting Up Your Linux Screen

Most X-Window managers enable you to customize your display. Here's a useful trick: autohide your taskbar and panel to provide more room for displaying your documents. You can then point to where your documents are hiding and trigger them whenever necessary.

If you use KDE, here's how to customize the panel and taskbar:

1. Click K ⇨ Panel ⇨ Configure to set the location and style for the KDE panel, and to position or hide the KDE taskbar (as shown in Figure 3-16). (Don't select the Hidden taskbar setting unless you want to remove it permanently from view.)

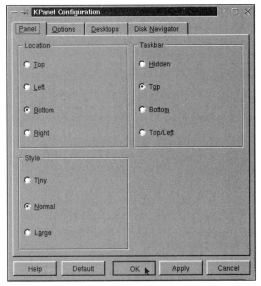

Figure 3-16: Customizing the KDE panel and taskbar

2. Click the Options tab to autohide the panel or taskbar (see Figure 3-17). You can also set the delay before the panel or taskbar disappears. (Hide the KDE panel by clicking the triangle on either end of the panel instead.)

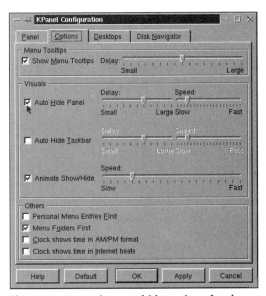

Figure 3-17: Setting autohide options for the KDE panel and taskbar

Another way to display more information on the screen is to switch to a higher screen resolution (refer to your Linux manual for screen setup instructions). Instead of trying to fit more information on the screen, consider using virtual desktops (see Chapter 1, "Getting Up and Running").

Fine-Tuning Your Document Window Display

Early DOS versions of WordPerfect showed the typewriter's influence on the word processor. The screen was analogous to a plain sheet of paper, and many features could be accessed by using shortcut keys.

Many WordPerfect users (including fans of the earlier DOS versions) don't realize that the graphical user interface versions of WordPerfect give you almost total control over which screen features appear and how documents display. Aside from the title bar and the menu bar, all screen gadgets are optional.

Selecting Screen Features to Display

The View menu gives you control over which screen features display (other than the scroll bars.)

To select the toolbars to display or hide (including the property bar and application bar), click View ➪ Toolbars, and check the bars you want (see Figure 3-18).

Figure 3-18: Selecting the toolbars to display

To change your scroll bar display, switch to the WordPerfect program window and click Preferences ➪ Display. Then check or uncheck the vertical and horizontal scroll bars.

Choosing How Your Document Appears

The View menu gives you three document display modes from which to choose:

✦ *Draft* lets you see the substance of what you're typing without the distraction of top and bottom margins, page headers, footers, or footnotes. Pages are separated by thin horizontal lines, so you don't "jump" from page to page.

✦ *Page* shows your document as it will look when printed — complete with margins, headers, footers, and footnotes. Information that doesn't print (such as a document comment) is represented by an icon.

✦ *Web Page* converts your document to a Web page automatically and puts you in the HTML editor (see Chapter 11, "Web Writing and Publishing"). Watch out, though — HTML's formatting is not as sophisticated as native WordPerfect, so you can lose WordPerfect formatting when you switch back and forth.

Zooming Your Display

Zoom lets you shrink or expand your display of text and graphics anywhere from 25 to 400 percent. (Zoom doesn't affect how your document prints.)

To zoom your document, click View ⇨ Zoom or click the Zoom button on the toolbar. Select a set zoom factor or specify any percentage (Other on the toolbar list) from 25 to 400 (see Figure 3-19).

Figure 3-19: Specifying a zoom percentage

Zoom also offers these display options:

✦ *Margin width* displays your text in the full width of the window, with minimal white space outside of the margins. Characters usually display larger, but you'll see fewer lines at one time.

✦ *Page width* displays the full left and right margins (the text usually appears smaller).

✦ *Full page* displays your entire page at once (minus top and bottom margins in Draft view). This view is handy for print preview and page layout, but not for editing.

Selecting Other View Options

The View menu has five other options:

✦ *Graphics*, when turned off (unchecked), displays images as blank rectangles. This option speeds your display and doesn't affect how the graphics print.

✦ *Table Gridlines*, when checked, displays table lines as dimmed, dotted lines, and no graphic fills appear. This option speeds your display and doesn't affect printing.

✦ *Hidden Text* turns the display of hidden text on (so it can be seen and printed) or off. (Hidden text and comments are explained in Chapter 13, "Editing Techniques.")

✦ *Show¶*, when checked, displays various nonprinting symbols onscreen for every space, hard return, tab, indent, flush right, soft hyphen, advance, or center page.

✦ *Reveal Codes* displays your document's formatting codes. (See the following "Revealing the Hidden Formatting Codes" section.)

Discovering the Keys to Success

If you're looking for tricks and shortcuts, don't forget the keyboard. For example, to erase from the insertion point to the end of the line, simply press Ctrl+Delete. When it comes to speed, there is no contest between the keyboard and the mouse. Compare the following: clicking the page down box on the scroll bar and then clicking the screen to move the insertion point; or just pressing Alt+PgDn on the keyboard.

Keyboard Features

The typewriter keyboard was an excellent device for entering text. Shown in the now-standard "enhanced" version in Figure 3-20, the computer keyboard includes powerful and versatile features, as described in Table 3-3.

Figure 3-20: Enhanced Keyboard

Table 3-3 Keyboard Features	
Feature	**Description**
Numeric keypad	Found on most full-sized keyboards, it's handy for performing calculations and entering numbers (when Num Lock is on).
Function keys	The pre-mouse standard for performing specific program operations. The best-known function key is F1, for help.
Shift	Enables all keys, including the function keys, to perform two operations.
Ctrl and Alt	Enable the other keys to do multiple functions, just like the Shift key. When used in combination with Shift, Ctrl and Alt provide more possibilities than you can probably remember. Alt+characters open menus. Ctrl turns character keys into easy-to-remember function keys, such as Ctrl+B for bold type or Ctrl+Shift+B to insert a bullet.
Arrow keys	Enable you to move around the screen quickly. Like most other keys, they repeat when you hold them down.
Special-purpose keys	Insert, Delete, Home, End, PgUp, and PgDn are special-purpose keys. These keys can be handy, especially when used in conjunction with other keys (such as Ctrl, Alt, and the arrow keys).
Esc	A quick way out of dialog boxes, menus, and other places.

Changing Keyboards

Various WordPerfect functions can be assigned to particular keys or key combinations. A set of key assignments constitutes a keyboard definition.

WordPerfect for Linux comes with a special Equation Editor keyboard, plus a number of standard keyboards:

✦ _XWP8_ keyboard, the default keyboard for WP for Linux.

✦ _WPWin8_ keyboard, also known as the CUA (Common User Access) keyboard, uses standard Windows key assignments.

✦ _WP60DOS_ keyboard enables those who cut their teeth on a DOS version of WordPerfect to feel right at home. F12 selects text, instead of F8. Print is Shift+F7. F7 closes a document.

✦ _XWP51_ , _XWP60_, and _XWP70_ keyboards, older WordPerfect for UNIX keyboards.

To change keyboards:

1. Switch to the WordPerfect program window and click Preferences ➪ Keyboard.

2. Highlight the keyboard you want to use and click Select (see Figure 3-21).

Figure 3-21: Changing keyboards

If you're used to the Windows keyboard, you'll be comfortable with the Linux keyboard — all the basic keys are identical. In Chapter 27, "Customizing Toolbars, Menus, and Keyboards," you learn how to customize a keyboard definition to your liking.

Note   Note that certain keystrokes on your WordPerfect keyboard are likely to be pre-empted by your X-Window manager. In KDE, these keystrokes include:

Ctrl+F1 through Ctrl+F8 take you to virtual desktops 1–8

Ctrl+Tab takes you to the next virtual desktop

Alt+Tab switches to the next application

Alt+F1 through Alt+F3 perform various Linux functions

Alt+Ctrl+Fx and Alt+Ctrl+Shift+Fx (where Fx is any function key) result in a new login. Don't use them.

Using Navigational Keystrokes

You have seen how to go to another location by using the scroll bars. You will find, however, that the arrow keys and other keyboard shortcuts shown in Table 3-4 are usually the quickest way to get around a document. Keyboard shortcuts also move the insertion point as they change your location. The default XWP8 keyboard and the WP60DOS keyboard are shown in the following tables. The Windows keyboard is not shown, because most of the common keystrokes are implemented in the same way as in the XWP8 keyboard.

Table 3-4 Navigational Keystrokes		
To Move the Insertion Point	*Linux or Windows Keystroke*	*WP60DOS Keystroke*
One character left/right	the left arrow/the right arrow	the left arrow/the right arrow
One word left/right	Ctrl+the left arrow/the right arrow	Ctrl+the left arrow/the right arrow
One line up/down	the up arrow/the down arrow	the up arrow/the down arrow
One paragraph up/down	Ctrl+the up arrow/the down arrow	Ctrl+the up arrow/the down arrow
To the end of the line	End	End
To the beginning of	Home	Home, Home, the left the line arrow
To the beginning of the line (before codes)	Home, Home	Home, Home, Home, the left arrow
Up one screen	PgUp	Home, the up arrow
Down one screen	PgDn	Home, the down arrow
Up one page	Alt+PgUp	PgUp
Down one page	Alt+PgDn	PgDn
To the beginning of the document	Ctrl+Home	Home, Home, the up arrow
To the beginning of the document (before codes)	Ctrl+Home, Ctrl+Home	Home, Home, Home, the up arrow
To the end of the document	Ctrl+End	Home, Home, the down arrow
For heavy-duty moving within your document, click Edit ⇨ Go To (or press Ctrl+G) to display the Go To dialog box shown in Figure 3-22.		

Figure 3-22: Using Go To

Using Other Keystrokes

Other keyboard shortcuts to WordPerfect features include the insertion keystrokes, the deletion keystrokes, and the control-alpha shortcut keys.

Insertion Keystrokes

The following keystrokes insert various formatting codes in your text.

To Insert	Linux or Windows Keystrokes	WP60DOS Keystrokes
Hard Page or Column Break	Ctrl+Enter	Ctrl+Enter
Hard Space	Ctrl+spacebar	Ctrl+spacebar
Hard Hyphen	Ctrl+-	Ctrl+-
Soft Hyphen	Ctrl+Shift+-	Ctrl+Shift+-

Deletion Keystrokes

The following is a list of deletion keystrokes you can use.

To Delete	Linux or Windows Keystrokes	WP60DOS Keystrokes
Selected text	Delete	Delete
Current character	Delete	Delete
Character to the left	Backspace	Backspace

To Delete	Linux or Windows Keystrokes	WP60DOS Keystrokes
Word	Ctrl+Backspace	Ctrl+Backspace
Rest of the line	Ctrl+Delete	
Rest of the page	Ctrl+Shift+Delete	

Control-Alpha Shortcut Keys

Most of the control-alpha shortcuts in Table 3-5 and Table 3-6 are easy to remember (such as Ctrl+B for bold and Ctrl+I for italics). The control-alpha combinations from V to Z are worth memorizing. Ctrl+Z can undo all the combinations in this section!

Table 3-5 Control-Alpha Shortcut Keys		
Ctrl+Function	**Linux or Windows Keyboard Character**	**WP60DOS Keyboard Character**
Select All	A	
Turn on/off bold	B	B
Copy selection to the Clipboard	C	C
Insert date text	D	
Justify center	E	
Find QuickMark	Q	F
Find and replace text	F	
Go to	G	
Paragraph Format		G
Turn on/off italic	I	I
Justify full	J	
Toggle case of selected text	K	
Justify left	L	L
Create new document	N	
Resume normal font		N
Insert page number	P	P
Set QuickMark		Q

Continued

Table 3-5 *(continued)*

Ctrl+Function	Linux or Windows Keyboard Character	WP60DOS Keyboard Character
Justify right	R	
Save	S	
Outline body text	H	
Turn on/off underline	U	U
Paste Clipboard contents	V	V
Insert WordPerfect characters	W	
Display Document information		W
Cut selection to Clipboard	X	X
Undo	Z	Z

Table 3-6
Ctrl+Shift Alpha Shortcut Keys

Ctrl+Shift+Function	Linux or Windows Keyboard Character	WP60DOS Keyboard Character
Expand Abbreviations	A	
Insert bullet	B	
Insert date code	D	
Set QuickMark	Q	
Redo	R	
Save All	S	
Paste Clipboard contents without formatting	V	
Undelete	Z	
Table of Contents Define		Z

Tip   None of the WordPerfect keystrokes is chiseled in stone, especially the control-alpha key combinations. If you're using a DOS-compatible keyboard, for example, you may want to change Ctrl+S from insert sound clip to save. (See Chapter 27, "Customizing Toolbars, Menus, and Keyboards.")

Revealing the Hidden Formatting Codes

No discussion of WordPerfect's interface should fail to mention the hidden formatting codes that govern appearances. Your ability to work with the codes behind the scenes can make all the difference between the program controlling you, and you controlling the program. The formatting codes manage every aspect of document display and print — page margins, font type and size, using bold and italics, and inserting graphics and centering text.

You can reveal (or hide) the formatting codes in either of the following ways:

✦ Right-click the text area and click Reveal Codes.

✦ Click View ➪ Reveal Codes.

When you view the formatting codes, as shown in Figure 3-23, your screen is split into text and code windows. You can drag the box on the divider line to enlarge or shrink the Reveal Codes window.

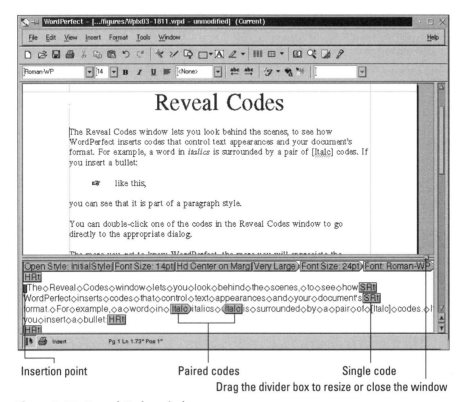

Figure 3-23: Reveal Codes window

Notice that spaces in Reveal Codes are represented as diamond-shaped bullets, and formatting codes appear as sculptured boxes. The small red rectangle in the bottom part of the screen corresponds to the normal insertion point in the text window above.

The two types of formatting codes in the Reveal Codes window follow:

✦ *Single* (or open) codes that appear as square icons, such as HRt for hard return.

✦ *Paired codes* that point toward each other. When you put a word in italics, for example, it has an italic code on either side to turn the feature on and off. Deleting either one of the codes deletes the pair.

Note   Each new document begins with an Initial Document Style code (which cannot be deleted) based on the Default Document Style (see Chapter 15, "Formatting Your Document").

Reveal Codes has the following handy editing features:

✦ A QuickTip description appears when you point to a code icon.

✦ You can delete a code by dragging it up or down out of the Reveal Codes window and dropping it. As usual, you can undo such a deletion with Ctrl+Z.

✦ An associated dialog box appears when you double-click a code. You can then change your font from Times to Courier, for example, or your spacing from double to single. (This technique only works with single codes — not paired on/off codes.)

The appearance of the Reveal Codes window can also be customized. See Chapter 26, "Fine-Tuning WordPerfect," for more information.

The more you use Reveal Codes, the more you appreciate how it helps you to understand and control your document's format. If you don't want to look at the codes, fine. But if your document is behaving strangely — for example, you delete a paragraph and your screen suddenly fills with large, bold type — an accidental or leftover formatting code probably is the culprit. Place the insertion point where the problem starts, open the Reveal Codes window, and delete or modify the offending code.

For More Information . . .

On	See
Starting WordPerfect quick and easy	Chapter 1
Basic typing and editing	Chapter 2
Using the ruler bar and setting tabs	Chapter 15
HTML editing	Chapter 11
Using hidden text and comments	Chapter 13
Setting the default Initial Document Style	Chapter 15
Customizing your Reveal Codes display	Chapter 26
Customizing WordPerfect's display	Chapter 26
Using Reveal Codes	Chapter 4
Customizing toolbars, menus, and keyboards	Chapter 27

✦   ✦   ✦

Becoming an Instant WordPerfect Expert

Now that you've learned the basics, you probably think, "This is great so far, but I guess it'll take another year to learn the sophisticated stuff, like fine-tuning font sizes and line spacing, drop caps, heading styles, and fancy tables." No way! You're going to try out these features right now. Plus, this chapter points the way to other easy-to-use (yet powerful) WordPerfect features discussed in following chapters.

QuickFinding with a Single Click

If you're looking for the previous or next occurrence of the current word or selection, searching doesn't get quicker than this: click the QuickFind Previous button or the QuickFind Next button on the property bar.

The QuickFind buttons match on whole words only. For example, if you select the "quick" in "quicker" and click a button, you'll match only on the word "quick"—not "QuickFinder," Chapter 13, "Editing Techniques," discusses the finding tricks.

Using Format-As-You-Go

Chapter 2 discussed how WordPerfect fixes your spelling, typos, and grammar on the fly. Now click Tools ➪ QuickCorrect ➪ Format-As-You-Go, and take a look at the instant sentence corrections and formatting (see Figure 4-1).

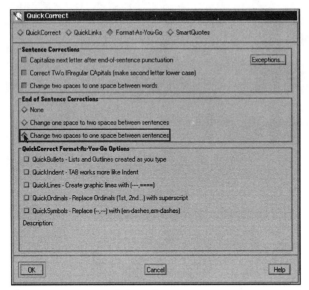

Figure 4-1: Format-As-You-Go

Instant Sentence Corrections

The sentence correction options make typing much easier:

✦ *Capitalize next letter after end-of-sentence punctuation* means that you don't
  have to bother with the Shift key when you start most sentences. (You still
  have to use Shift after headings without punctuation.)

✦ *Correct TWo IRregular CApitals (make second letter lowercase)* gets rid of this
  annoying typo. (Use QuickCorrect entries for exceptions. For "UMass,"
  replace "umass" with "UMass" and you won't even have to type the initial
  caps!)

✦ *Change two spaces to one space between words* is great in these days of
  proportional fonts, when it's difficult to discern the spacing between words.

You'll probably want to select an end-of-sentence correction, either to turn one
space between sentences to two, or two to one. (When using a proportional font,
one space is the standard punctuation for books, newsletters, and most other
publications.)

There Must Be Exceptions . . .

Most sentences end with a period; so do most abbreviations. If you click the
Exceptions button, you'll see a list of words that don't signal the end of a sentence
(such as "corp." or "inc."), as shown in Figure 4-2. Of course, if your sentence ends
with an exception, it's back to the Shift key.

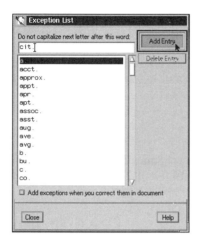

Figure 4-2: There must be exceptions.

As you can see from the list in Figure 4-2, all single letters with a period are ignored (as with "a.m.", "i.e.", or "P.O."). You can add other abbreviations to the list manually, such as op. cit. (two entries).

To add exception words automatically, check Add exceptions when you correct them in document. Then, when you Backspace over the capitalized letter and correct it (before ending the word), the preceding abbreviation is added to the list.

Other Format-As-You-Go Choices

Other options for Format-As-You-Go include the following:

✦ *QuickBullets* begins a bulleted list when you type **o, *, O, ^, >, +,** or **-** as the first character on a line, followed by a tab or indent. You can also type a number (for a numbered list), **i** or **I** (for Roman numerals), or a letter (for an alphabetical list), followed by **.,**), or **-,** and then a tab or indent. To end the list, press Enter ➪ Backspace.

✦ *QuickIndent* creates a hanging indent paragraph (one that begins with an indent, followed by a back tab) when you press Tab at the beginning of any paragraph line except the first. If the first line already starts with a tab, you end up with a regular indented paragraph instead. You can also press Tab anywhere in the first line to indent the remainder of the paragraph from that tab stop.

✦ *QuickLines* converts four or more hyphens (-) at the start of a line into a horizontal line. (Type four or more hyphens, then press Enter.) Four or more equal signs (=) insert a double line.

✦ *QuickOrdinals* changes the "st", "nd", or "rd" of ordinal numbers to superscript (1st, 2nd, 3rd).

✦ *QuickSymbols* changes -- (two hyphens) to an en dash (to indicate a range of numbers) or --- (three hyphens) to an em dash (to indicate a break in a sentence).

SmartQuotes

The SmartQuotes options (Tools ➪ QuickCorrect ➪ SmartQuotes) let you substitute the curly printer's quotes in place of the straight-up-and-down variety. You even get different styles from which to choose (see Figure 4-3).

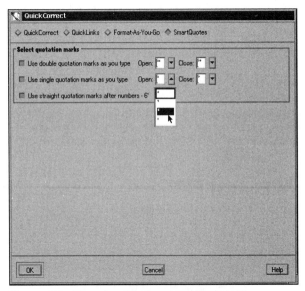

Figure 4-3: Changing the SmartQuote character

Be sure that "Use straight quotation marks after numbers" is checked when you use SmartQuotes. With this feature checked, the abbreviations for inches and feet will remain straight, as they should be.

Making It Fit

Have you tried writing a one-page résumé, but even though you've taken out every extra-redundant superfluous word, some text still manages to squiggle over to the next page? You need Make It Fit!

Are you a student about to turn in an 11-page paper, and your professor set a page limit of 10? You need Make It Fit!

Are you a desktop publisher creating a six-page flyer, but your text and graphics take up only five and one-half? You need Make It Fit! Read on to discover this wonderful feature.

Sizing a Document to Fit a Specified Number of Pages

To size your entire document to fit a specified number of pages:

1. Click Format ➪ Make It Fit, and specify the number of pages you want (see Figure 4-4).

2. Check the items that you are willing to allow WordPerfect to adjust, and click Make It Fit.

Figure 4-4: Using Make It Fit

WordPerfect then makes several passes of your document to determine the best combination of adjustments to make, and voilà! It fits! If you don't like the results, press Ctrl+Z to undo.

If you make further changes to your document, you can run Make It Fit again.

Tip   Use Make It Fit even when the current and desired number of pages are the same. If your flier is five and one-half pages, you're already on the sixth page, so Make It Fit expands it to a full six.

The Make It Fit feature shrinks or expands your document up to 50 percent. Unlike most other formatting features, it places these codes in your Document Style (see Chapter 15, "Formatting Your Document"), rather than in the text.

Dressing Up Your Work with Drop Caps

Suffering from drop cap envy? WordPerfect has the cure! No experience is required to start off your flier, newsletter, article, or chapter with this traditional flourish. In addition to drop caps, raised caps and many other font effects can be used (Figure 4-5).

T he default Drop Cap is three lines tall, positioned in the text.

M ove surrounding text down with a raised cap.

You can drop the first word, or several characters.

arious fonts add a dramatic flourish.

R everse your drop cap with 1% font shading and 100% fill.

E xperiment with margin positions and borders for new effects.

Figure 4-5: Drop cap sampler

Even though the drop cap displays as a fancy graphic, the spell checker and other writing tools treat it as regular text. To create your own drop cap:

1. Place the insertion point in an existing paragraph, or where you want to begin a new paragraph.

2. Click Format ⇨ Paragraph ⇨ Drop Cap. The first character of your paragraph, or the first character you type, is given the default drop cap treatment.

3. Place the insertion point before the drop cap, and click the Drop Cap Style button to pick another style (as shown in Figure 4-6). Then customize your drop cap by using any of the options in Steps 4-8.

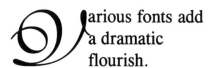

Tip   Pick the "XA" style in the lower-right corner to turn off a drop cap, or press Ctrl+Z to undo any changes you make.

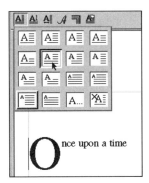

Figure 4-6: Picking a drop cap style

4. Click the Drop Cap Size button to select a height from two to nine lines. You can even select Other from the list to specify the precise in-between height.

5. Click the Drop Cap Position button to select In Text (the default) or In Margin (the drop cap will be 100 percent in the margin). Click Other to specify exactly how much you want to move the surrounding text down, or how far you want to move the drop cap into the margin (see Figure 4-7).

Figure 4-7: Specifying a precise drop cap position

6. Click the Drop Cap Font button to specify a special font face, style, appearance, color, or shading for your drop cap. (Try both a plain and decorative font to see the difference.)

7. Click the Drop Cap Border button to specify any kind of border or fill. (See Chapter 23, "Adding Graphic Lines, Borders, and Fills," for complete details.)

8. Click the Drop Cap Options button to include any number of characters or the whole first word in the drop cap (Figure 4-8). You can also check any of the following:

   • *Wrap text around drop cap* (the default) keeps paragraph text from printing over the drop cap.

   • *Allow for descender* wraps paragraph text around parts of drop characters that extend below the baseline on which the characters sit.

   • *Allow for diacritic* moves drop characters with diacritical marks down slightly.

Figure 4-8: Specifying drop cap options

Creating Custom Styles Quickly

Suppose that you just created some nice formats for paragraphs and headings you would like to use in future documents. For example, you may publish a regular sales brochure or newsletter that you want to give a consistent, professional appearance. By using *QuickStyles*, you can save the format, fonts, and other attributes as styles to use over and over again.

To create a custom style with QuickStyle:

1. Format the text of an existing paragraph (for a heading, body text, and so forth) the way you want all paragraphs of that type to look.

2. Click the paragraph, then click the Select Style list on the property bar and click QuickStyle (Format ➪ Styles ➪ QuickStyle).

3. Give the style a name and description (see Figure 4-9).

Figure 4-9: Creating a custom style by using QuickStyle

4. Click the "Paragraph" style type, then click OK. The style you just created now appears with your other document styles listing (see Figure 4-10).

5. If you want to use the style in other documents as well, click Options ➪ Copy ➪ "Personal Library" ➪ OK.

Figure 4-10: Your style now appears with your other document styles

By saving your custom paragraph style to the personal library, or to a shared library if you are on a network, you can use the style in new documents you create. (For more information on styles, see Chapter 20, "Working Quickly with ExpressDocs Templates and Styles.")

QuickFormatting Your Headings

QuickFormat is even quicker than QuickStyles — you don't even have to give your style a name. QuickFormat is great for applying the same style to all the headings in a document. To use QuickFormat:

1. Click in your formatted heading or paragraph and click the QuickFormat button. (You can also click Format ⇨ QuickFormat, or right-click your document and click QuickFormat.)

2. Decide to transfer Fonts and Attributes (such as the font size and color), Paragraph Styles (formatting applied paragraph-by-paragraph), or Both. Choose Fonts and Attributes to apply only the current font and attributes to other text, character-by-character, without saving them to a style (Figure 4-11).

Figure 4-11: Selecting the formatting features to transfer

3. Your pointer turns into a paint roller with which you can click the other headings to transfer the style, or a paint brush if you're applying only the character attributes (see Figure 4-12).

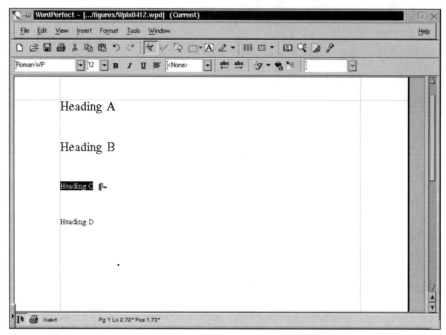

Figure 4-12: Applying the QuickFormat style to other headings

4. When you're finished applying the style, click the QuickFormat button to turn it off.

Creating Fancy Tables in No Time

With WordPerfect, you can create tables in no time. Simply click where you want the table to appear, click the Tables button, then drag to create the desired table size. Or double-click the Tables button and specify the number of columns and rows.

First try creating a 6 · 7 table, as shown in Figure 4-13. Then you'll learn how to format the table.

Figure 4-13: Creating a table

SpeedFormatting a Table

Formatting a table is easy with WordPerfect's SpeedFormat feature. The following steps show you how to use SpeedFormat to apply a professional-looking style (as in Figure 4-14) to your entire table.

Cyclops Software Sales					
	1st Quarter	2nd Quarter	3rd Quarter	4th Quarter	Total
1997					
1998					
1999					
2000					
2001					

Figure 4-14: SpeedFormat provides professional-looking table styles you can apply instantly

Try the following with the 6 · 7 table you just created:

1. Type **Cyclops Software Sales** in the upper-left cell, then type **1997**, **1998**, **1st Quarter**, and **Total** in the cells shown in Figure 4-15.

2. Point to the top of the "1997" cell, then drag to select all of the year cells, as shown in Figure 4-15.

3. Click the Table QuickFill button to QuickFill the dates for the remaining years.

4. Drag to select the "1st Quarter" cell and the three cells to its right. Click the Table QuickFill button.

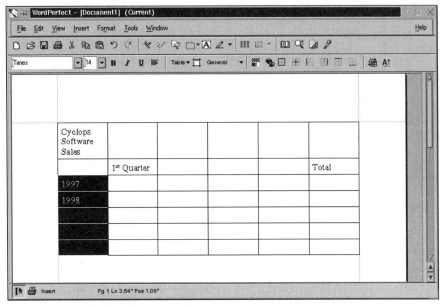

Figure 4-15: Selecting the year cells

5. All the text should now be filled. Now right-click the table anywhere and click SpeedFormat. Highlight the Header Fill Double style or any other style you like, and click Apply (see Figure 4-16).

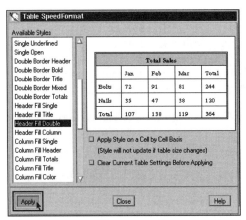

Figure 4-16: Applying a SpeedFormat style to your table

In Praise of the QuickMark

Bookmarks are great for keeping your place when you're reading a book. WordPerfect has invented the electronic equivalent to bookmarks — the QuickMark.

To set the QuickMark, just press Ctrl+Shift+Q. To move the insertion point to the QuickMark, press Ctrl+Q. (The DOS keystrokes are Ctrl+Q and Ctrl+F, respectively.)

You're allowed one QuickMark per document. Each time you set it, it moves to the new location, just like moving a paper bookmark. (You can see the QuickMark in Reveal Codes.)

Click Tools ⇨ Bookmark for options to set a QuickMark at the current location every time you save a document, and to return to the QuickMark the next time you open it.

There's also a Save Workspace setting to insert QuickMarks in your open documents automatically when you exit, then reopen your documents and return to where you left off when you restart WordPerfect (see Chapter 26, "Fine-Tuning WordPerfect"). Regular bookmarks are described in Chapter 13, "Editing Techniques."

Using Boilerplate

Format-As-You-Go, Make It Fit, drop caps, Table SpeedFormat, QuickStyles, QuickFormat, and the QuickMark — these are but a few of the handy, powerful features WordPerfect provides. You'll find many more goodies in the chapters to come.

Wait . . . before you go, here's one powerful tool that's so easy you don't even have to click a button! You'll never find this tool in those glossy full-page ads. In fact, it isn't a WordPerfect feature at all, just a basic technique you can employ with any word processor: *boilerplate*. Boilerplate is simply a preformatted document (such as a letterhead, resume, or cover sheet) that you can use over and over again. It's not a style, or a quick-anything, but a reusable copy of your previous work.

Just open the document you want to use as a boilerplate, add the new text, and save the file under a different name. With those simple steps, you'll have a proven format and perhaps much of the text as well.

For More Information . . .

On	See
Tricks with Find and Replace	Chapter 13
Fixing spelling, typos, and grammar on the fly	Chapter 2
Changing the Initial Document Style	Chapter 15
Applying borders and fills	Chapter 23
Using ExpressDocs and styles	Chapter 20
Creating and formatting tables	Chapter 16
Saving your workspace	Chapter 26
Using bookmarks	Chapter 13

✦　　✦　　✦

Getting Help

No matter how intuitive and powerful your software, it's only as good as the support it provides. With fierce price competition in the software industry, the days of toll-free, unlimited telephone support are over. However, you can find more readily available, easy-to-use support for WordPerfect than ever before, including the PerfectExpert, independent journals, and a vibrant user community. Whether you're a beginner looking to format a letterhead, or an expert user researching the technical minutiae, answers to your questions are close at hand.

Getting Help in WordPerfect

In most cases, the quickest way to an answer is by way of the extensive online help facilities:

+ Help topics on all aspects of WordPerfect for Linux

+ Context-sensitive PerfectExpert help with the task at hand

+ Troubleshooting help

Note
For general help on Linux, use the `man` command to display manual pages. For example, if you want to know how to change file permissions with the `chmod` command, type `man chmod` in a terminal window to display all the information you need. Most X-Window managers offer additional help information as well, and there's also extensive Linux information available on the Internet (see Appendix B, "WordPerfect and Linux Web Links").

Exploring the Help Topics

Most online help is found under the Help Topics dialog. Press F1 or click Help ⇨ Contents, then select the type of help you need:

✦ *Search (Index)* is usually the quickest and surest way to find a help topic. Type the first few letters of the topic (as in Figure 5-1), then double-click the entry you want and click Go To.

Figure 5-1: Looking up a help topic in the index

✦ *How Do I* organizes help into sections of related tasks (see Figure 5-2). Double-click an item to display further information in a new window (see Figure 5-3).

Figure 5-2: Selecting a topic from "How Do I"

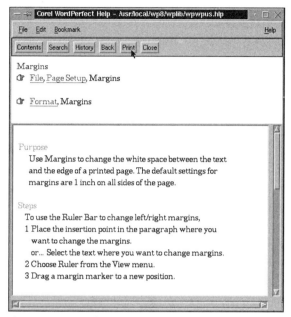

Figure 5-3: Displaying "How Do I" information

✦ *Glossary* is the place to look for short descriptions of terms used in and around the program.

✦ *Menu Commands* describes the options available in the WordPerfect menus systematically. Go here when you want to know more about a certain command.

✦ *Corel WordPerfect Bars* provides more information on the WordPerfect tool-bars, the property bar, and the application bar (see Chapter 3, "Mastering the WordPerfect Interface").

Help with Using Help

When a help topic is displayed, you can click the hyperlinks for further help on specific tasks or related concepts (see Figure 5-4).

The buttons on top of the help window perform other useful operations, including:

✦ *History* displays a list of recently opened help topics.

✦ *Back* returns to the previous topic.

✦ *Print* gets a hard copy.

Click Bookmark ⇨ Define to define a bookmark. This setting will make it easy to come back to the topic in the future.

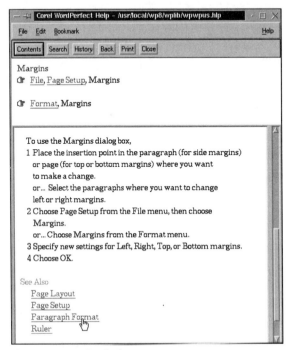

Figure 5-4: Using help

Getting PerfectExpert Help As You Work

For advice and assistance as you go about your tasks, click the PerfectExpert button (or click Help ⇨ PerfectExpert).

Clicking PerfectExpert displays the context-sensitive PerfectExpert help panel, with helpful tips, relevant help selections, and buttons to call up features to complete your work (see Figure 5-5). Panel selections change depending on whether you're editing text, inserting bullets, creating a table, or so forth. PerfectExpert help follows in whatever direction you want to go.

Drag the panel to the most convenient location. Click the PerfectExpert button again to close the panel, or click the close button in the upper-right corner.

Getting Other Context-Sensitive Help

You can get context-sensitive help in three additional ways:

✦ Hold the mouse pointer over a screen selection to display its QuickTip.

✦ For general information on a dialog or highlighted menu selection, press F1, or click the dialog Help button.

✦ Press Shift+F1, then click an item or press keystrokes.

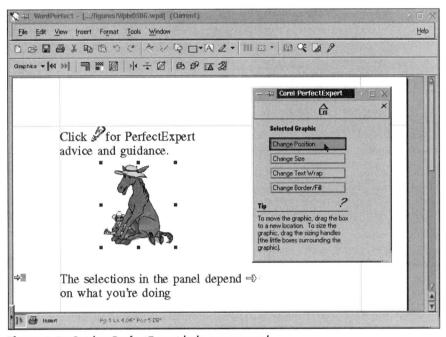

Figure 5-5: Getting PerfectExpert help as you work

Getting Internet and Other Help

Outside of WordPerfect, there are several directions in which you can turn for help.

Getting Internet Support

If you're hooked up to the Internet, you'll find comprehensive, up-to-date support at Corel's Web site:

1. Click Help ➪ Online Help.

2. Select the topic in which you are interested:

- *WWW WP Manual:* a Web-based manual for WordPerfect.

- *WWW WP Knowledge Base:* the database used by technical support.

- *WWW WP Support:* the WordPerfect for Linux support page (see Figure 5-6).

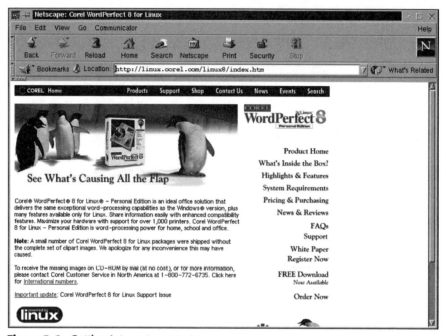

Figure 5-6: Getting Internet support

Getting Other Outside Help

Other help outside of the program includes:

✦ *Various Corel support services.* Click Help ➪ Search for Help On and search for "Corel support services" for details.

✦ *Corel support newsgroups.* Recently, a WordPerfect for Linux newsgroup was added to the Corel support newsgroups. Connect to the news server `cnews.corel.ca` to access the Corel support newsgroups.

✦ *The QwkScreen Web site* at `http://www.qwkscreen.com`, where you'll find tips, tricks, and links to other resources and newsgroups.

✦ Lots of valuable information on Linux and WordPerfect for Linux can be found on the World Wide Web. The list of links in Appendix B, "WordPerfect and Linux Links," is a good start.

For More Information . . .

On	See
Mastering the WordPerfect interface	Chapter 3
Linux and WordPerfect Web links	Appendix B

✦   ✦   ✦

Basic Training

✦ ✦ ✦ ✦

In This Part

✦ ✦ ✦ ✦

Working without Worries

WordPerfect 8 for Linux's automated features enable beginning and advanced users to accomplish complex tasks quickly. However, as anyone experienced with computers knows, you can lose work even faster than you create it. That's why this chapter shows you how to work safely as well as quickly.

Safeguarding Your Work

None of WordPerfect's sophisticated, time-saving tools will do you any good if your work is lost because of an editing mistake or a hard disk crash. You can't recover what you don't save. This simple logic often escapes many computer users, even though saves and backups are easy to perform.

WordPerfect provides automatic backup and undo features that you can configure to your needs. It also features Corel Versions, a full-fledged archiving utility for tracking and safeguarding multiple file revisions.

You should make safety a regular part of your working habits. For example, a final save before a drastic editing action can be done with the click of a button or the press of a key. As for daily backups, they should be as regular a habit as bathing or brushing your teeth.

You can lose all or part of your work in several ways. Fortunately, you also have several ways to protect your work. Table 6-1 shows what can go wrong, the safeguards you can take, and how to recover when an accident occurs.

Table 6-1
Safeguarding Your Work

What Can Go Wrong	Safeguards	How to Recover
A recent deletion or editing change was a mistake.	Automatic.	Use Undo to reverse your editing actions (1 to 300, see "Using Undo as your first line of defense," later in this chapter).
Your work gets messed up, so you want to go back to where it was five minutes ago.	Automatic timed backups, plus regular saves that you make.	Close your screen file without changes, then reopen the file or saving backup.
Your WordPerfect application freezes, and you must restart WordPerfect.	Timed backups.	Rename or open the timed backup file when you restart WordPerfect.
You change your mind about the changes you just saved and want to go back to the save before that.	Turn on the original document backup feature in WordPerfect or Presentations.	Replace the current document with the .BK! copy.
Today's edits made a mess of your file, so you want to start over.	Daily backups to disk or tape.	Restore yesterday's copy.
You need a file from several days or weeks ago that you have since deleted or changed.	Keep backups going back several days, weeks, or months.	Restore the appropriate backup copy.
Your computer and backups are lost because of fire, flood, or theft.	Archive a copy of your full backup off-site on a regular schedule.	Restore to another computer from your archived copy.

QuickSaving Your Work

Think of the save feature as QuickSave: simply click the Save button on the toolbar, or press Ctrl-S on the keyboard (Ctrl+F12 for the WP DOS keyboard).

If you get into the habit of QuickSaving your document every few paragraphs, you won't have to worry about losing your work in most situations. The only drawback is that your options for restoring recent changes are reduced, because you're constantly replacing your backups.

Making Timed Backups

For everyday hazards, timed document backup is a critical line of defense. At the interval you specify, WordPerfect automatically makes a backup copy of every window that has changed since the last save.

Timed backups are deleted automatically when you exit the program normally, but if a power failure occurs, or you get kicked out of the program for some reason, the backups are preserved. You can recover your documents from the timed backups when you restart WordPerfect, so you'll never lose more than a few minutes of work.

To make timed backups:

1. Switch to the WordPerfect program window and click Preferences ⇨ Files.

2. Check "Timed Document Backup every x minutes," and specify the number of minutes.

WordPerfect's automatic backups are named `wp_bkX.Y.Z`. X is a sequential backup number, Y is the code number of the process that crashed, and Z is the name of the user who was editing the document.

For example, if you logged in as `root` and had four documents open when the WordPerfect process 353 crashed, the resulting backups would be named `wp_bk1.353_root`, `wp_bk2.353_root`, `wp_bk3.353_root`, and `wp_bk4.353_root`.

To learn how to access a timed backup, see "Restoring from a Timed Document Backup" later in this chapter. For more on setting WordPerfect's backups, see Chapter 26, "Fine-Tuning WordPerfect."

Making Original Document Backups

WordPerfect also has an *original document backup* safeguard that (if you turn it on) makes a copy of your original disk document each time you save your screen changes to disk. The backup goes into the same directory as the original file, using the same name and a .BK! extension.

If original document backup provides another level of protection, why is it off by default? Well, it offers no additional crash protection, and the backups clutter your directories. (They aren't deleted when you exit the application, as are your timed backups.) The feature is only useful when you save a document, then decide you want to revert to the previous version instead.

Backing Up Your Data

Don't expect WordPerfect to take care of all your disaster-prevention and recovery needs. It can deal with things that go on within its programs and restore most of your work when the lights go out, but it can't do anything if your hard disk goes "belly-up" because of a computer virus or mechanical failure. What if your machine is stolen? Unlikely, perhaps, but why chance losing weeks, months, even years of work and records?

Forget about losing your hard disk. What happens if you discover two days later that you deleted the wrong file? Suppose you rewrite a section of your term paper or report and decide after a couple days that the old version was better. There's only one way to protect your work in these situations. You must back up your data!

If you have copies of your work, you're fine. If you don't, you're helpless. If nothing else, at the end of the day, go to the directory where you keep your important documents and copy them onto floppies. See Chapter 7, "Managing Your Files," for details on copying files.

Note   If your work is on a network drive, your files are probably backed up and archived on a regular schedule. See your network administrator for details.

If you have many files to back up, use a tape drive, Recordable-CD, or other removable storage device. You can then use a file manager, or even better, a third-party backup program to:

✦ Copy numerous files from different directories in one operation.

✦ Store your backups in a highly compressed format.

✦ Automatically run your backups at the time you designate.

✦ Save your file settings and other options (such as to back up only the files you changed since the last backup).

What to back up

Back up anything you don't want to lose. In most cases, it doesn't make sense to back up your operating system or applications, because you probably have CDs or disks for them anyway. Focus on your data. Other backup candidates are the WordPerfect system files that can be found in the directory /root/.wprc. This directory contains your WordPerfect settings, your styles, and your additions to the writing tools word lists. If you back up these files, you won't have to redo all your custom settings manually if you ever need to reinstall WordPerfect.

When to back up

You never know when an accident will occur, or how far back in time you'll want to go. Think about keeping backups by the month, by the week for the last four weeks, and by the day for the current week. With ten sets of backups, you can keep records for the whole quarter:

Backup Group	Backup Set Names
Daily	Monday, Tuesday, Wednesday, Thursday
Weekly	First Week, Second Week, Third Week
Monthly	First Month, Second Month, Third Month

To provide a comprehensive three-month backup:

1. Perform a full backup every Friday evening.

2. Perform an incremental backup (of additions or changes since Friday) on Monday, Tuesday, Wednesday, and Thursday.

3. On the last Friday of every month, perform an additional full backup.

If you're making tape or CD backups, you probably can save tapes or CDs by appending multiple backups on a single tape or CD — especially the incremental daily backups.

As another precaution against fire, flood, theft, or some other unforeseen disaster, you can make an additional backup copy every Friday to archive at a separate location.

Recovering Your Work

Suppose that you lost (or messed up) a file. Because you took the proper precautions, you're not going to break into a cold sweat. The first thing to do is nothing; don't even close the document! Take a minute to size up what happened, then select the appropriate recovery procedures from the following sections.

Using Undo As Your First Line of Defense

If something goes wrong with your document, think of Undo as your first line of defense. The Undo history maintained with your file enables you to reverse your most recent editing changes (such as deletions, insertions, new font sizes, moving graphics, or copying text).

In WordPerfect you can click Edit ⇨ Undo/Redo History to undo or put back any number of selected actions at once (see Figure 6-1).

Figure 6-1: Using WordPerfect's Undo/Redo history

You can also click Options in the Undo/Redo History dialog to specify how many Undos to retain (1 to 300), and whether they should be saved with your document (see Figure 6-2). Saving your Undos with the document enables you to retrace your steps later, but it does make your files bigger and may enable someone else to see what you've changed.

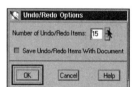

Figure 6-2: Specifying WordPerfect's Undo/Redo options

WordPerfect also has an Undelete feature (assigned to Ctrl+Shift+Z) that enables you to restore, at the insertion point, any of the last three deletions.

Going Back to Your Disk Document

As an alternative to undoing step-by-step when your screen document gets messed up, you can discard your screen changes, then restore the file from your last save to disk:

1. Click File ⇨ Close.

2. When asked to save changes to your document, click No to clear the screen without saving your changes to disk.

3. Open your document normally.

Restoring from a Timed Document Backup

If both your screen and disk documents are messed up in WordPerfect, you may be able to make a reasonably graceful recovery from the automatic timed document backup. To restore from a timed document backup:

1. Close the screen document.

2. Go into backup directory specified in the WordPerfect Program window under Preferences ➪ Files and look for wp_bkX.Y.Z, where *X* is the number of the document window you were using and *Z* is your user ID (*Y* is the number of the WordPerfect process that crashed).

3. Open the document in WordPerfect and make sure it's all right.

4. Click File ➪ Save As.

5. Locate and highlight the original document, then click Save.

6. Answer Yes to the "Replace this name?" prompt.

If the last timed backup was after the problem with the document, then this procedure will be of little benefit. However, it's worth a try.

Recovering from a Crash

If an application kicks you out of the system, or your computer crashes and you must reboot, you can recover your work from the timed backup files. To recover from a crash:

1. Restart the application.

2. As you reenter the program, you are asked if you want to use a timed backup (see Figure 6-3).

Figure 6-3: Recovering from a timed backup file upon reentering WordPerfect

3. Click File Manager to browse the timed backups and click Open to retrieve your backup (the backup files are named wp_bkX.Y.Z, where *X* is the number of the document window you were using), then continue with Step 4. You can also click Rename to preserve your backup in case you need to restore it later. Click Delete only if you're sure that you won't need the backup.

4. If the backup you opened is more recent and complete than the original on disk, you can click File ▷ Save As to save the backup document to the original filename.

Note

If you open or rename your backup files upon reentering WordPerfect, you can click File ▷ Document ▷ Add Compare Markings to compare the backup to the file on disk (see Chapter 13, "Editing Techniques"), then decide which one to use.

Going Back to the Save Before Last

If original document backup is turned on, you can undo both the current and last sets of changes by restoring the save before last:

1. Click File ▷ Close to exit the screen document. (Answer "No" to any "Save Changes?" prompts.)

2. Click File ▷ Open, then go to the document's directory (*not* the backup directory), and open the associated .BK! file.

3. After making sure that this file is the proper version, click File ▷ Save As, click the document you are replacing, then click Save.

Restoring from a Periodic Backup

To recover from a daily, weekly, or monthly backup, perform either of the following tasks:

✦ If you backed up files by using the Open File dialog box, use the same procedure to copy the file(s) back from the backup disk to the directory.

✦ If you used a backup program, follow the program's restore procedures.

Repairing a Damaged Document

Sometimes a WordPerfect document will become damaged such that you can't open it, or it crashes WordPerfect when you edit or save it. When this happens, try running one of the utilities available to repair damaged documents. Most of these utilities run under Windows. Under Linux, you can try to start WordPerfect with the -recover startup option. This option will regenerate documents that are not functioning properly. For more information on startup options, see Chapter 26, "Fine-Tuning WordPerfect."

One of the most powerful utilities is WP8REST.EXE. This utility was originally designed to fix problems with password-protected files, but it turned out to be a great tool for repairing various other document problems, such as corrupted files.

This utility will work with documents created in WordPerfect 6.x and newer. The utility can be downloaded from Corel's FTP site at `ftp://ftp.corel.com/pub/WordPerfect/wpwin/8/wp8rest.exe`. After starting the program, the name of the corrupted file must be entered. The utility will repair the document and save the repaired file with the wps1 extension.

Tracking Changes with Corel Versions

Corel Versions acts like a super Undo by storing multiple updates to your files in one backup, as they evolve toward their final form. Its facilities for annotating revisions and identifying authors are especially useful when a team is working on the same documents.

You can track revisions to any type of file, including graphics. You can specify the number of revisions to keep, store them in a highly compressed form, and compare versions side by side.

Saving Versions of a File

To start an archive of the current file onscreen:

1. Click File ➪ Version Control ➪ Save Current.

2. Specify any of the following (see Figure 6-4):

- *Make first version permanent:* to keep the original from being replaced when the maximum number of temporary versions is reached.

- *Save version to a single location:* to store the versions in the default Versions directory. When you remove the check, versions are saved in the same directory as the original file.

- *Max number of Tem versions:* to specify the number of temporary versions to keep before being replaced by newer versions.

Figure 6-4: Starting a version archive

To save subsequent versions of the file:

1. Click File ➪ Version Control ➪ Save Current.

2. Check Permanent to make this a permanent copy that doesn't count toward the number of temporary copies (see Figure 6-5).

3. Add any descriptive comments, such as "Technical review incorporated," or "Includes Meera's comments."

Tip   To type multiline comments, keep typing without pressing Enter. Otherwise, you'll submit the version with what you've typed so far.

Figure 6-5: Adding a version to your archive

Retrieving a Previous Version of a File

To retrieve a previous version of a file:

1. Click File ➪ Version Control ➪ Retrieve Current.

2. Select the version you want and click Retrieve (Figure 6-6).

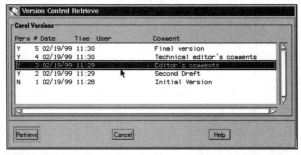

Figure 6-6: Retrieving a previous version of a file

3. Choose whether you want to replace your screen document with the retrieved version. If you choose No, a new file is created. (The versions are stored in one combined archive file. If you want to work with a particular version, you have to open it and save it as a new file.)

Setting Archive Defaults

To set archive defaults, including where the versions are stored and the number of versions:

1. Click File ➪ Version Control ➪ Preferences.

2. Specify the default archive location and the default number of temporary versions (see Figure 6-7).

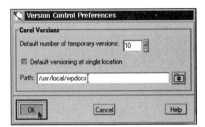

Figure 6-7: Setting archive defaults

Backing Up Your Archives

By backing up your Versions file, you get a backup of the file's entire version history automatically. If you store your archives in the default Versions directory, simply back up the directory to make a copy of the history for all your archives at once.

Copying, Moving, or Deleting an Archive

Each file's archive is stored in a special .CV file, which you can't edit directly in WordPerfect. The archive file's name includes the full name and path of the original file, with dollar signs ($) to indicate the slashes (/). For example, versions of the file `research proposal.wpd` in the directory /usr/local/wpdocs will be stored in the archive `$usr$local$wpdocs$research proposal.cv`.

Corel Versions can find a file's archive as long as the archive is in either the file's directory or the default Versions directory. You can, therefore, move an archive freely between the two directories. For example, if your workgroup shares a common default Versions directory, you can move an archive to the shared directory so that others can use it, then move it back after everyone is finished.

Use the File Manager to copy, move, or delete archives:

1. Click File ➪ Open.

2. Select the appropriate file.

3. Click Files ➪ Corel Versions ➪ File ➪ Copy to copy an archive (see Figure 6-8), click Files ➪ Corel Versions ➪ File ➪ Move to move an archive, and click Files ➪ Corel Versions ➪ File ➪ Delete to delete an archive.

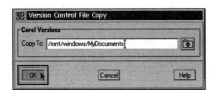

Figure 6-8: Copying, moving or deleting an archive

No Recycle Bin Diving

Make sure you use the tools WordPerfect offers to save your work. Unlike Microsoft Windows, Linux does not have a Recycle Bin. When you delete a file, there's no way to get it back.

For More Information . . .

On	See
Setting WordPerfect's backup intervals	Chapter 26
Managing files	Chapter 7
Comparing documents	Chapter 13
Recovering files on a network drive	Your network administrator
Using an external backup program	The program's manual or help

✦   ✦   ✦

Managing Your Files

With computers, all your documents are always within easy reach . . . if you can find them. With the help of the WordPerfect file-management tools, you can organize your work so that you'll never misplace a letter or report. If you do happen to lose a document, you can locate it in short order.

The WordPerfect file-management facilities offer a number of improvements to those facilities delivered with Linux. Using WordPerfect's Open dialog box as your file-management control center, you can organize your stuff without ever leaving the program. As you play with WordPerfect's file-management features for a while, you'll discover many functions (such as find, view, open, save, name, move, copy, rename, delete, and print). You can even perform QuickFinder searches to find the paper your dog ate.

Note This chapter refers to the Open dialog box for convenience, but all WordPerfect file-management dialog boxes (such as Save As) work in the same way.

Organizing Your Files

The first step in managing your files is to organize. The programs, documents, graphics, and other files on each drive are stored in *directories* (equivalent to *folders* in Windows). Directories can also contain *subdirectories:* files can be organized in a logical hierarchy (or tree), much as you organize the drawers, sections, and folders of a filing cabinet (see Figure 7-1). Note in the illustration how the user's documents are organized into separate "school," "work," and "letters" directories. The "letters" directory, in turn, has separate subdirectories for "business" and "personal."

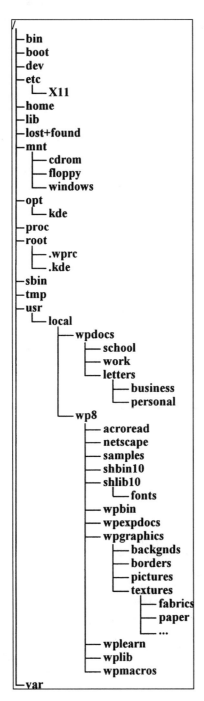

Figure 7-1: Partial illustration of one user's directory tree

The tree helps you to see the path to your document's directory. In the title bar of your WordPerfect document window, you see the likes of /usr/local/wpdocs /personal/loveletter.wpd, where /usr/local/wpdocs/personal is the path to your directory and loveletter.wpd is the particular file. The path plus the filename gives a file its unique identity. That's how you can have two files with the same name in different directories.

Note

Windows users should note the absence of drive letters under Linux, such as "A:" and "C:". Under Linux, your hard drive space is divided into any number of *partitions*, which are referred to the same way as any other directories.

The root directory under Linux appears as "/" at the top of your directory tree. Temporary storage, including floppy and CD drives, can be "mounted" for Linux access. You can also mount your DOS or Windows drives on your system to access them directly from WordPerfect 8 for Linux. See your Linux guide for detailed mounting instructions.

Navigating Directories

To get started, click File ⇨ Open, then browse through the directory list to see how your directories are organized (see Figure 7-2). Use the scroll bar to navigate the open directory. You can also click the Name Search section, then type the first letter of the filename. To jump to a subdirectory, double-click its name in the right window. Click ".." to move up a directory.

Double-click a directory to open it. The name and path of the selected directory are shown in the Current Selection at the upper-left.

Opening Files

To work on an existing file, you can either open the file in the current document window, or go to the WordPerfect program manager to open a file in another window. You can also go the program manager to open a new, blank document window, then save your work to a new file.

Opening a File in the Current Document Window

To open a file in the current document window, click the Open button (File ⇨ Open), then select the file and click Open. The current document will close, and you will be prompted, if necessary, to save any changes.

Selected file   Selected directory

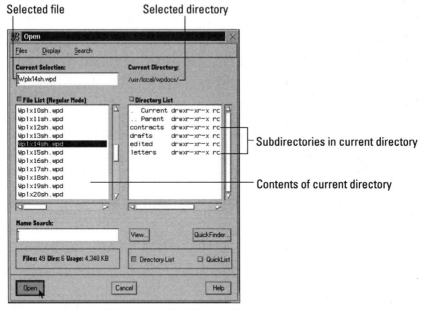

Figure 7-2: Open dialog box, with directory list on right

Opening or Creating a File in a New Document Window

To open or create a file in a new document window:

1. Switch to the WordPerfect program window. (Double-click the document window title bar to shrink the document window, if necessary.)

2. Click the Program menu, then do one of the following:

   • Select from the last ten documents on which you worked at the bottom of the Program menu (see Figure 7-3).

   • Click Open Window, then locate and select a document.

   • Click New Window to open a blank document window. You can then start typing, or click File ➪ Open to open an existing document in the new window.

You can have up to 100 windows open at a time, depending on your computer's memory.

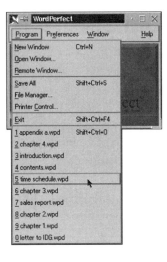

Figure 7-3: Opening one of the last ten documents on which you worked

Previewing Files Before You Open Them

When you're not sure which file you want, use the file-management viewer to take peek at various files before you open a document window. Otherwise, you have to open and close each file until you find the one you want.

To preview a file as shown in Figure 7-4, select the file, then click the View button. You can then click other files in the list to view their contents in the viewer.

Figure 7-4: Previewing a file

Converting Text from Other Formats

WordPerfect 8 for Linux shares a common file format with WordPerfect 6, 7, and 8 for Windows, as well as WordPerfect 9. You can exchange documents freely between Linux and Windows versions of WordPerfect.

Older WordPerfect documents (including those created in WordPerfect 5.x) are converted automatically when opened into WordPerfect for Linux. WordPerfect also provides conversion filters that enable you to work with many common and not-so-common document formats, including ASCII, ANSI, Ami Pro, Applix Words, and Microsoft Word 6.0/7.0 and 97.

When you open or insert a document created in another word processor, the converter displays its best guess as to the document's format, but enables you to make the final choice (see Figure 7-5).

Figure 7-5: Converting text from another format when opening it in WordPerfect

In the conversion process that follows, a few formatting and other features may get lost or changed along the way. Depending on the nature of the conversion, you may find it necessary to delete codes and perform other edits to format the document the way you want it to appear in WordPerfect. (The Reveal Codes window is especially suited to this task.)

When you save a converted document that you edited, you can choose to save it back to its original format rather than save it as a WordPerfect document (see Figure 7-6). Be careful when you save files meant to be used in their original format, such as ASCII system files.

As a general rule, the less formatting involved, the better text converts. Try to avoid such complexities as tables, columns, headers, footers, page numbering, bullets, styles, graphics, sound clips, and hypertext. Often Rich Text Format (RTF) can be used as an intermediary between two word processing programs. RTF uses text codes to preserve basic type and formatting elements. Unformatted ASCII and ANSI files offer the lowest common denominator for text transfers.

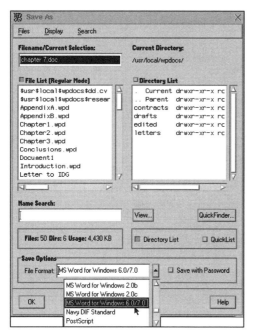

Figure 7-6: Saving converted text after it has been edited in WordPerfect

Customizing Your File-Management Display

Your file-management dialog boxes have various display options that you can customize to the way you work. For example, you can choose to display descriptive names for your documents or sort them by date in reverse order.

To customize your file-management display:

1. Click @open (File ⇨ Open).
2. Click the Display menu to make the temporary menu selections described in Table 7-1.
3. Click Change File Manager Setup to specify any of the List and General options in Table 7-1.

Table 7-1
File-Management Display Options

Option	Enables You to
Menu Selections	
Show File View	Preview files before you open them.
Show WP descriptive Names	Display the descriptive name and type from the document summary, along with the file name and size. (See "Adding Descriptive Summaries to Documents" later in this chapter.)
Show Dot Files	Display Linux configuration files starting with ".". (Normally leave off so you won't alter Linux system files.)
Change File Manager Setup	Access the File Manager Setup dialog box (see Figure 7-7) to specify List and General options.
List Options	
List	Select the file, directory, or QuickList you want to customize.
Change Entry Options	Select items to display in standard and descriptive listings, such as the file name, descriptive name, last update, and owner.
Sort By	Select the list item to sort on.
Sort Order order	Change the way files are sorted to ascending or descending
Truncate Filenames	Specify the maximum filename length that will appear in the dialog box, to leave room for other items in the listing.
General Options	
Directory List/QuickList Startup-Mode	Select whether to display the Directory List, QuickList, or both by default.
File List Startup Mode	Select whether to default to the regular filename display or to display including the descriptive names from document summaries.
Prompt for Password...	Select whether or not a password is required to view the descriptive names for locked (protected) files, and whether they are included in search results. (For more about passwords, see the section "Password-Protecting Your Files" in a following section of this chapter.)
Ask for Confirmation on File Deletions	Have a chance to change your mind when deleting files.

Option	Enables You to
Show Sort Information with List Labels	Display the item on which a list is sorted, such as the Filename or Last Update.
Number of Spaces between List Columns	Set how widely list items are separated.
Change Default File Format	Change the format in which your documents are saved normally.

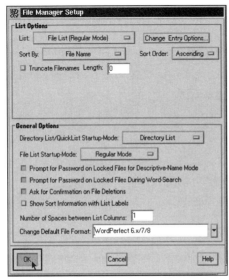

Figure 7-7: File Manager setup options (options vary with the list selected)

Changes you make will be reflected in any dialog box that displays files, not just the Open dialog box. (And yes, you can also adjust file preferences in any file dialog box — not just Open.)

You can also adjust the size of any file dialog box: just drag a side or corner of the box.

Tip Widening the display puts more details on view.

Going Straight to Your Favorite Files

Most likely, 90 percent of your work is stored in five or six directories. So, why search all over the place for what you need? WordPerfect's QuickList feature provides an ingenious solution.

Using a QuickList

By adding entries to the QuickList, you can go straight to the directories and documents you use regularly. Click QuickList in the Open dialog box to display your QuickList (see Figure 7-8). Directories are preceded by [D]; files are preceded by [F]. QuickList also displays descriptions that you added to your files. (For more information, see "Adding Descriptive Summaries to Documents" in a following section.) Double-click an entry to open the actual directory or document.

Figure 7-8: Displaying the QuickList

Building Your Own QuickList

When you first display your QuickList, you'll see that WordPerfect has already created entries for such things as your document and macro directories. But you can add any directories or files you want. To add your favorite directories and files to the QuickList:

1. Right-click the QuickList, click Edit QuickList, then click Add.

2. Type the name and path of the directory or file (see Figure 7-9).

Figure 7-9: Adding an item to the QuickList

3. Type a meaningful description of the directory or file for your QuickList display.

Editing or Deleting a QuickList Item

To edit or delete a QuickList item, right-click the QuickList, click Edit QuickList, then select the item and click Edit or Delete.

Note   To avoid QuickList clutter, only keep items you use regularly.

Updating the QuickList Automatically

When you click Preferences ⇨ Files, you'll notice an Update QuickList with Changes selection in the bottom right. When this option is selected, your standard QuickList entries for templates, graphics, macros, and so forth are updated automatically if you change the directory.

Performing File-Management Tasks in WordPerfect

You can perform all file-management tasks — such as moving a file from one directory to another — from within any WordPerfect file dialog box (like Open or Save).

However, to operate on more than one selected file or directory an a time, you must use the File Manager accessed by clicking Program ⇨ File Manager in the WordPerfect program window. You will not be able to select multiple files or directories from any of the file dialog boxes accessed via a document window.

The following sections give basic instructions for performing file-management tasks in WordPerfect. For all of these tasks, the first step is to open a file dialog box like Open or Save (use the File Manager for any of the operations involving multiple files). Then follow the steps for the specific operation.

Selecting files

Click individual files in any file dialog box to select them. To select a consecutive group of files in the File Manager, click the first file, then hold the Shift key and click the last file.

To select two or more nonconsecutive files in the File Manager, hold the Ctrl key as you click each file.

Click a blank spot in the listing to deselect all the files, or hold Ctrl and click files to deselect them one at a time.

Copying a File or Directory to Another Directory

WordPerfect provides an easy-to-follow way to copy a selected file or directory (with its contents) to another directory.

To copy a file or directory to another directory:

1. Select the file or directory to be copied.

2. Click Files ⇨ Copy.

3. Type the name of the target directory and click OK.

Use the program window's File Manager to copy multiple files or directories at once.

Moving a File or Directory

To move a selected file or directory:

1. Click Files ⇨ Move/Rename.

2. Type the name of the target directory and click OK.

Use the program window's File Manager to move multiple files or directories at once.

Renaming a File or Directory

To rename a selected file or directory:

1. Click Files ⇨ Move/Rename.

2. Type the new name, then click OK.

Deleting a File or Directory

To delete a selected file or directory, click Files ➪ Delete, or press Delete.

Use the program window's File Manager to delete multiple files or directories at once.

Changing File Permission Modes

Every file and directory has three levels of permission for read, write, and execute modes that are assigned to three sets of users: User (the creator of the file), the Group to which the creator belongs, and Other (anyone outside the Group). By default, a file's permissions are set to X. However, you may want to change these permissions. For example, you may want to permit others to read your files, but not edit (write) them.

You must be the user or have Root privileges in Linux to be able to change modes.

To change the mode of selected files or directories:

1. Click Files ➪ Change Mode.

2. Check or uncheck the permission mode you want to change (see Figure 7-10).

Figure 7-10: Changing file permission modes

For more on using file and directory permissions, refer to the documentation from your Linux distribution.

Printing Files

To print selected files directly from a file dialog box, click Files ➪ Print File(s).

The Print dialog box opens as usual.

Creating or Deleting a Directory

Creating a new directory is useful particularly when saving a file; if, for example, you're creating the first file for a new project and want to save it in a project folder. Instead of saving the file in a different directory and creating the new one later, you can do it all in one fell swoop.

To create a directory:

1. Go to the directory where you want to create a new directory.
2. Click Files ➪ Create Directory.
3. Type a name for the directory, then click OK.

To delete a directory and its contents, click the directory and press the Delete key.

Password-Protecting Your Files

Password-protect is one feature that's easy to miss. Perhaps that's how it should be—then you won't password-protect a document and forget your password.

Sometimes, however, you may need to prevent others from searching, viewing, altering, or printing a document. Be warned, however: password-protected files can still be moved, copied, or deleted without using the password.

You can select enhanced password protection to provide greater security and case-sensitive passwords. If your document has a password of "TigeR," for example, it cannot be opened with "tiger" or "Tiger".

The password-protect feature is found only in the Save As dialog box. To password-protect a file:

1. Click File ➪ Save As.
2. If you're saving a new file or want to rename your file, type the filename and path.
3. Check "Save with Password," then click Save.
4. Select either Enhanced or Original password protection (see Figure 7-11).
5. Type your password, then click OK.

Asterisks appear as you type, in order to safeguard the password from prying eyes.

6. Retype the password to confirm, then click OK again.

Figure 7-11: Password-protecting a file

From this point forward, anyone trying to preview, open, or print your document is prompted for your password. So remember it!

To remove password protection from a file, open the file, click File ➪ Save As, and remove the "Save with Password" check.

Adding Descriptive Summaries to Documents

You can attach descriptive summaries to your documents to categorize, annotate, and locate your work, thereby helping you find the files you want more quickly. The summaries appear in file dialog boxes, and you can also search on them.

Although summaries are not printed normally, this feature is available. You can also save summaries to a separate document.

To attach a descriptive summary to your current document, click File ➪ Properties ➪ Document Summary and fill in the fields (see Figure 7-12). (You can also right-click your document and click Properties.)

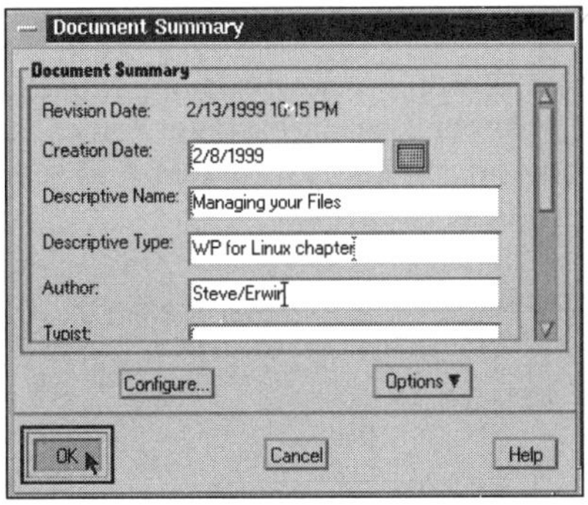

Figure 7-12: Creating a document summary

Ten fields are included in WordPerfect's default document summary configuration. If you don't see what you need, you can customize your summaries with more than 50 fields, from Abstract to Version Number. Here's what you do:

1. Click File ⇨ Properties ⇨ Document Summary ⇨ Configure, and select or deselect any of the available fields.

2. Drag with the middle mouse button (both buttons on a two-button mouse) to rearrange the fields in the box (see Figure 7-13).

3. To use the new configuration for your new documents, click Use as Default.

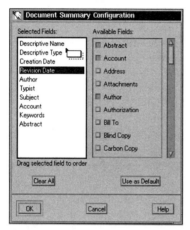

Figure 7-13: Customizing document summaries

Searching for Files

If you don't know the location of your file, call on QuickFinder for help. QuickFinder is a powerful search tool that can, for example, track down every letter that mentions a particular person or company.

You can search for files by file pattern (such as Chapter*.*), words or phrases, summary fields (such as a descriptive name or typist), or date range. You can also create an index of all the words in a collection of documents for super-fast searches (see "Building Fast Search Indexes" in a following section.)

You can also run QuickFinder from the Search Results list to make a second or third pass using refined search criteria.

Doing a QuickFinder Search

To do a QuickFinder file search on a file's name, contents, or other properties:

1. Click File ➪ Open, then click QuickFinder.

2. To search for a filename, type a partial or complete name in the File Pattern box (see Figure 7-14). (You can also include the * or ? characters for wildcard searches, as described in the next section.)

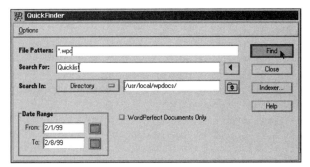

Figure 7-14: Searching for filenames or contents

3. To search for a term in a document's contents, type a word or phrase for which to search in the Search For box.

Tip

You can search for multiple words or phrases. For example, to look for either *open* or *file*, type the words without quotation marks. To look for a phrase, use quotation marks, as with "open file".

4. From the Search In pop-up list, choose whether you want to search the directory, subtree (the current directory plus its subdirectories), or QuickFinder index. Then select a directory or index from the accompanying list.

5. Specify a From date, a To date, or both if you want to limit your search to files revised within a date range. (Click the mini-calendars at the right of the date boxes to select dates quickly.)

6. Choose to search for WordPerfect documents only or all file types.

7. Click Find to start your search. The results will be displayed in a Search Results listing (see Figure 7-15).

8. Select the file for which you were looking in the list, or click Close to return to your original directory.

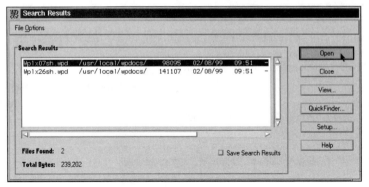

Figure 7-15: QuickFinder search results

Tip   If you're not sure which file in the search results list is the one you want, click View to preview the file.

Searches match on partial filenames, but only on whole words in file contents. For example, a search on "list" matches on "Booklist.wpd," as well as on any document containing the word "list." However, the word "enlisted" in a document's contents will not match.

Tip   If you get a long list of matching files, click QuickFinder in the Search Results dialog box to search within the list.

Searching with Wildcards

Use the "*" (zero or more characters) or "?" (one character) wildcard in the File Pattern box if you're not sure of the exact name or contents. For example, "Te*.wpd" matches on all WordPerfect documents starting with "Te." A search on "wild*d" finds all files containing "wildcard" or "wildcatted."

Searching for a Word String or Pattern

If you click the drop-down list to the right of the Search For box in the QuickFinder dialog box, you can specify combinations of words or phrases for which to search within a document or portion of a document (see Figure 7-16). When describing the Search For contents, you can use any of the text search operators shown in Table 7-2.

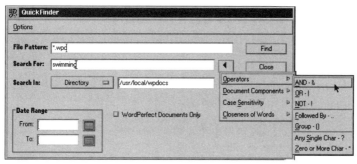

Figure 7-16: Specifying a Search For word string or word pattern

Table 7-2 Text Search Operators		
Search Operator	*Sample Query*	*Selects*
(none)	swimming	Files that contain "swimming"
(none)	swimming beach	Files that contain "swimming" and "beach"
& or "and"	swimming & beach	Files that contain "swimming" and "beach"
quotes	"beach ball"	Files containing the phrase "beach ball"
| or "or"	swimming | "beach ball"	Files that contain "swimming" or the phrase "beach ball"
!	! swimming	Files that don't contain "swimming"
..	beach .. umbrella	Files that contain "beach" and an "umbrella" sometime after the first "beach"
( )	! (beach and umbrella)	Files that don't contain both "beach" and "umbrella"
/page	/page watermelon cantaloupe	Files with "watermelon" and "cantaloupe" on the same page
/paragraph	/paragraph watermelon cantaloupe	Files with "watermelon" and "cantaloupe" in the same paragraph
/sentence	/sentence watermelon cantaloupe	Files with "watermelon" and "cantaloupe" in the same sentence
/line	/line watermelon cantaloupe	Files with "watermelon" and "cantaloupe" in the same line
/subject	/subject recipe	Files with "recipe" in the Subject field of their file description
/descriptive_name	/descriptive_name lasagne	Files with "lasagne" in the Descriptive Name field of their file description

Doing Advanced Searches on File Content

In addition to searching on a word string or pattern, as described in the preceding section, you can use other advanced options when searching the contents of files:

1. Click File ⇨ Open, then click QuickFinder.

2. Specify your search text in the Search For box.

3. Click the drop-down list to the right of the Search For box to specify any of the following (see Figure 7-17):

   - *Operators:* to select any of the operators described in Table 7-2 above.

   - *Document components:* to limit the search to certain document components, such as the first page or a selected summary field.

   - *Case sensitivity:* to select whether to match on the case of your search text.

   - *Closeness of words:* to limit the search for strings to words in a document, on a page, in a paragraph, in a sentence, on a line, or even within a chosen number of words.

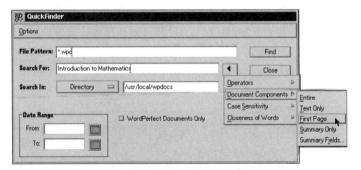

Figure 7-17: Doing advanced searches on file content

4. Click Find to find the files that meet the criteria you entered. Remember, if your results list is too large, you can click the QuickFinder button and enter more criteria to narrow the search.

Building Fast Search Indexes

Normal searches by content can be painfully slow, but you can create highly compressed Fast Search indexes of every word in every file for the directories you specify. Instead of reading a collection of files from top to bottom, which can take a fair amount of time, QuickFinder searches your index automatically in a second or two!

Note

Indexes cost you some hard disk space. The size of an index depends on several factors, but figure about 1/50th the size of the original files. If you are indexing 100MB of files, for example, the index may take 2MB of hard disk space.

Creating a Fast Search Index

You can index any combination of files or directories. To create a Fast Search index:

1. Click File ➪ Open, then click QuickFinder ➪ Indexer.

2. Click Create and give the index a name.

3. Specify each directories or files to Index, then click Add to include them in the list (Figure 7-18). (Click Include Subtree to index subdirectories as well.)

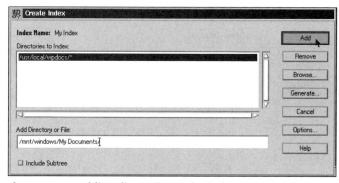

Figure 7-18: Adding directories to the index

4. Click Options to override any of the general indexing settings. (See "Setting QuickFinder indexing options" below.)

5. Click Generate to build the index.

Setting QuickFinder Indexing Options

Click Options while building an index to specify the Fast Search indexing options described in Table 7-3. (See Figure 7-19 to check out the Options dialog box.)

General options can be set from the main Indexer dialog box by clicking Indexer Options ➪ Preferences.

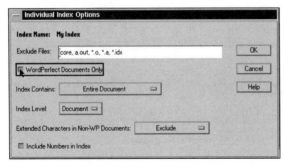

Figure 7-19: Setting Fast Search indexing options

Table 7-3
Fast Search Indexing Options

Option	Enables You to
Exclude Files	Exclude file types you can't open in WordPerfect, or those you don't use.
WP Documents Only	Restrict the index to WordPerfect documents only (indexing may be much faster).
Index Contains	Build an index containing complete documents, text only, or summaries only.
Index Level	Index words down to the page, paragraph, or sentence to enable searching on closeness of words. (The lower the level, the bigger the index.)
Extended Characters	Tell the indexer how to handle non-letter or number characters, such as the Euro symbol, in non-WP documents. Leave at Exclude unless you must search on them. Otherwise, interpret them as ANSI for Windows documents or ASCII for DOS documents.
Include Numbers in Index	Index numbers as well as words. Excluding numbers may speed your searches a bit.

Editing or Updating a Fast Search Index

Of course, when you create new files or change existing ones, they won't be part of an existing index. And you may also decide that you want to change index options at some point. You don't need to re-run the index completely in these cases:

you can just edit (to change the options) or update (to add new or modified files). To edit or update a Fast Search index:

1. Click File ➪ Open, then click QuickFinder ➪ Indexer.

2. Select the index to edit or update, then click any of the following options:

    • *Edit:* to change the index properties.

    • *Generate:* to update or rebuild the index. You can index modified and new files only or index all the files.

Normally, it's much faster to update an index than to rebuild it. However, searches tend to slow down with a heavily updated index. When that happens, rebuild the index.

For More Information . . .

On	See
Searching Internet locations	Chapter 14
Specifying text search criteria	Chapter 20

✦   ✦   ✦

Fonts Fantastic

C H A P T E R

8

For all its fancy charts and graphics, WordPerfect still uses writing as its fundamental means of communication. While the keyboard may be more impersonal than the pen, easy-to-use font technology gives you new ways to enhance your flyers, invitations, newsletters, and other desktop publications.

Welcome to the Font Family

The terms *typeface* and *font* are used interchangeably to refer to a group of letters, numbers, and other characters that share a distinctive design. A set of related fonts is often called a *font family*. For example, WordPerfect's Futura Medium font family has members for medium (plain text), medium italic, bold, and bold italic.

Tip   Stick to one or two font families in a document — perhaps one for text and one for headings. Too many fonts make your work look cluttered and unprofessional.

Related families can compose an *extended font family*. Using the Futura example, you find related families of light, book, heavy, black, light condensed, medium condensed, and bold condensed fonts — all based on the same basic typeface, but with varying degrees of "boldness," more and less space for each letter, and so forth. Other extended font families can include thin, roman (upright), engraved, oblique (italic), demibold, extra bold, and ultra bold fonts.

Characters stand upon an invisible *baseline*, and the size of the type is measured in *points* (of which there are 72 to the inch) for a single-spaced line (see Figure 8-1). The spacing between the lines of type, known as *leading* (pronounced *ledding*), was literally fixed by strips of lead in the days of metal type.

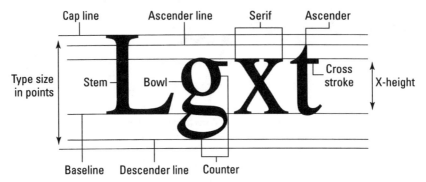

Figure 8-1: Elements of fonts

Another font characteristic is its *x-height*, or the height of a font's lowercase letters, exclusive of their *ascenders* and *descenders*. Two fonts can the same point measurement, yet have a different x-height:

Book Antiqua Arial

Other elements are the *bowl* (curved or semicircular line of a letter such as *a, b,* or *d*), *stem* (main stroke of a letter like *L*), and the *cross stroke* in an *f* or *t*. You should also examine the *counters*, or spaces enclosed in various letters like *a, b, d, e,* and *g*.

Classifying Fonts

Fonts can be classified in many ways—this chapter makes no attempt to cover all font classifications. Instead, the purpose here is to provide a working knowledge of how different types of fonts can be used to enhance your message.

Fixed and Proportional Fonts

Fixed or *monospaced* fonts are similar to typewriter text. Every character has the same width. A "W" takes up the same amount of space as an "I." (Fixed fonts are handy when you must align numbers or other characters in columns of text.)

Proportional fonts allocate spacing according to each letter's shape and size. For example, the narrow characters of the fixed Courier font are fleshed out with exaggerated serifs and cross-strokes:

`Courier with fixed spacing.`
CG Times with proportional spacing.

Scalable and Nonscalable Fonts

A *scalable* font can be enlarged or reduced to almost any point size, depending on the capabilities of your printer. For example, Times New Roman can be scaled to 14.6 points. With *nonscalable* fonts, you must select one of the predetermined sizes that come with the font.

All laser, inkjet, and dot-matrix printers support both scalable and nonscalable fonts. Typewriters and the older daisy-wheel printers support only nonscalable fonts.

Built-in and Downloadable Fonts

You can also distinguish between fonts that are *built in* or *internal* to your printer, and *downloadable* or *soft* fonts stored in your computer. Printer fonts have distinctive icons in your font lists (see Figure 8-2).

Figure 8-2: You can identify printer fonts by their icons

Soft fonts are also called *graphical* fonts. WordPerfect 8 for Linux comes with nearly 200 Type 1 PostScript graphical fonts. These high-quality fonts are often preferred by professional typesetters.

Soft fonts take longer to print than built-in fonts. However, with today's sophisticated printers and faster machines, the difference in speed is usually negligible, unless you're doing commercial, high-volume printing.

Distinguishing Font Styles

The font classifications in the preceding section discussed technical characteristics instead of style. Although it's good to have this technical background, you usually work with scalable fonts and focus on matters of style.

Serif and Sans Serif Fonts

A basic stylistic distinction is made between fonts with *serifs* to finish off the tops and bottoms of letters, and those that are *sans serif* (without serifs). Either style works well in larger sizes, as for headlines:

Headlines can be Serif

...or Sans-serif

In smaller sizes, serifs improve the readability of type by leading your eyes through the text. That's why almost every book, newspaper, or magazine you read is composed in serif fonts.

Other Style Distinctions

Beyond serif and sans serif, type styles can be classified in a myriad of ways. In *Collier's Rules for Desktop Design and Typography*, David Collier identifies seven useful categories, as shown in Table 8-1.

Table 8-1 Collier's Seven Classes of Type		
Class	**Description**	**Examples**
Old Style	Resembles handwriting, with inclined curves and contrasting thickness in strokes	Classical Garamond, Goudy Old Style

Class	Description	Examples
Transitional	Less analogous to handwriting	Transitional 521, Schoolbook, Baskerville
Modern	Marked by an abrupt contrast between thick and thin strokes, and thin horizontal serifs	Bodoni, Normande
Geometric	Geometric shapes, with little stroke contrast and circular bowls	Futura, Avant Garde
Humanist	After Roman inscriptions, with contrasting stroke thickness or slightly fluted stems	Humanist 521, Gill Sans, Optima
`Slab Serif`	Heavy square serifs, with or without brackets	Geometric Slabserif, Lotus Line Dr., Courier New
Digital	New fonts that appear computer-generated rather than drawn by hand	Orbit, Amelia

WordPerfect 8 for Linux does not include all of the examples in Table 8-1.

You can also classify fonts according to usage. Here, fonts often are divided into six categories:

✦ *Text fonts* are easy to read and work well in a wide range of sizes. Roman-WP, Courier-WP, and Goudy Old Style are good examples of text fonts.

✦ *Display fonts* create good, solid headlines. Display fonts don't work for normal text. Amelia Regular, Futura Black, Bodoni-WP, and Swiss 721 Black Extended are good examples of display fonts.

✦ *Decorative fonts* can add a flourish or set a festive mood for announcements and invitations. Bank Gothic, Bernhard Modern, Enviro D, Caslon Open Face, and Engravers' Gothic are examples of decorative fonts.

✦ *Old world fonts*, such as Caslon Open Face, Charlesworth, Engravers' Old English, Zapf Chancery, and Letter 686 give your document a sense of the past.

✦ *Fun fonts* for informal use include Goldmine Normal, Hobo-WP, Informal 011, ITC Benguiat, Kids Normal, and Pipeline Normal.

✦ *Specialty fonts* include the WordPerfect fonts for iconic and typographic symbols that you can use to add bullets, check boxes, and other special touches to your documents.

Recognizing Font Subtleties

As you work with fonts, you'll find that subtle differences in design convey substantial differences in impression. The *HP LaserJet Journal* points out, for example, that its Albertus, Antique Olive, and Univers fonts appear similar, yet have distinct "personalities" (see Figure 8-3).

Ideas, Ltd.

The Albertus headline is showy and distinctive – good for an ad agency's letterhead.

Hilda's Housecleaning

The Antique Olive headline has a casual look – good for friendly neighborhood services.

Death Valley Savings & Loan

The Univers headline is serious and trustworthy – good for a bank.

Figure 8-3: Similar fonts that convey different impressions

Note   Because font names can be trademarked—though font styles cannot—you may run into similar fonts with different names. Examples are Architect/BluePrint, Futura/ Modern Industrial/Torino, Swiss/Arial/Helvetica, and Univers/Zurich.

Installing Fonts in WordPerfect

With the proliferation of inexpensive, high-quality fonts, your creative possibilities are endless. The retail and WordPerfect Bible editions of WordPerfect for Linux come with more than 100 Type 1 fonts, but you can install many more. Your printer may come with useful fonts as well.

Tip   In Linux, you can't use the TrueType fonts used by many Windows and Macintosh programs, but you may find Type 1 fonts in unexpected places. For example, even an old version of CorelDRAW for Windows comes with hundreds of Type 1 fonts.

Every font used in WordPerfect must be installed in WordPerfect for Linux. The initial WordPerfect installation installs only basic text fonts plus the special

WordPerfect characters and symbols (see the following "Using Special Characters and Symbols" section). To access all the WordPerfect fonts that come with your CD, use the following installation procedures. Follow the same procedures to install Type 1 fonts you may have elsewhere on your hard drive or another CD.

To install (and remove) fonts for use in WordPerfect:

1. Mount the CD if you're installing the WordPerfect fonts or fonts from another CD. (Mounting instructions are located in Chapter 1, "Getting Up and Running.")

2. Start WordPerfect with the Administrator startup option (-admin), as described in Chapter 1.

3. Click Format ⇨ Font, then click the Install Fonts button.

4. Select the font type to install (see Figure 8-4):

   • *Type 1* to install Type 1 PostScript fonts, such as those on your WordPerfect for Linux Bible CD.

   • *HP LaserJet* to install bitmapped HP LaserJet fonts. These fonts come in many styles, but always have a fixed size.

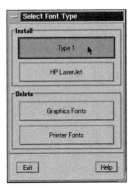

Figure 8-4: Installing fonts in WordPerfect

5. Change the Font Directory and the .pfb Directory to the directory with the fonts you're installing (on the *WordPerfect for Linux Bible* CD, this directory is normally /mnt/cdrom/fonts.)

6. Select the fonts you want to install from the Available Fonts list, then click Install (see Figure 8-5). (If you don't see any fonts, make sure you specified the correct fonts directory.)

7. When prompted, click Yes to copy the fonts to the fonts directory so WordPerfect can find the copied fonts (see Figure 8-6).

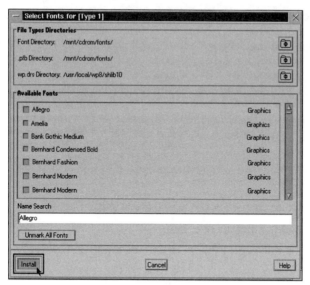

Figure 8-5: Selecting the fonts to install

Figure 8-6: Copying fonts to the fonts directory

8. When prompted, exit the font installer and restart WordPerfect.

Once your fonts are installed, you can display and print the Linux Fonts.wpd reference list on your *WordPerfect for Linux Bible* CD. This document displays examples of 184 fonts you can install.

To remove fonts from WordPerfect, click Format ⇨ Fonts ⇨ Install Fonts, then select the font type to remove (refer to Figure 8-4) and select the fonts you want to remove.

Note   You can also run the Font Installer outside of WordPerfect, though it only installs fonts for use in WordPerfect. The program, named xwpfi, is found in the subdirectory shbin10.

Changing Font Appearances

Font possibilities don't end when you select a font. WordPerfect provides various ways you can emphasize text or change its appearance (see Figure 8-7). You can also emphasize text by varying its size (see Figure 8-8) or using capitals (see Figure 8-9).

Put words in bold to make them **stand out** from the rest of the pack.

Add more subtle *emphasis* with italics. Use italics for titles of books and journals cited in reports.

Avoid underlining, it's a <u>messy holdover</u> from the typewriter days.

Don't overuse bold and italics, *or they will quickly lose their effectiveness*.

For extra emphasis, see how to reverse text in Chapter 8.

Standard Roman fonts can be altered by the program to produce italic or bold type, but for the most accurate results install the carefully crafted variations as specific fonts. For example, the Geometric Slabserif 703 group from Bitstream has individual fonts for:

Light
Light Italic
Medium
Medium Italic
Medium Condensed
Bold
Bold Italic
Bold Condensed
Extra Bold
Extra Bold Italic
Extra Bold Condensed.

Figure 8-7: Varying font appearances

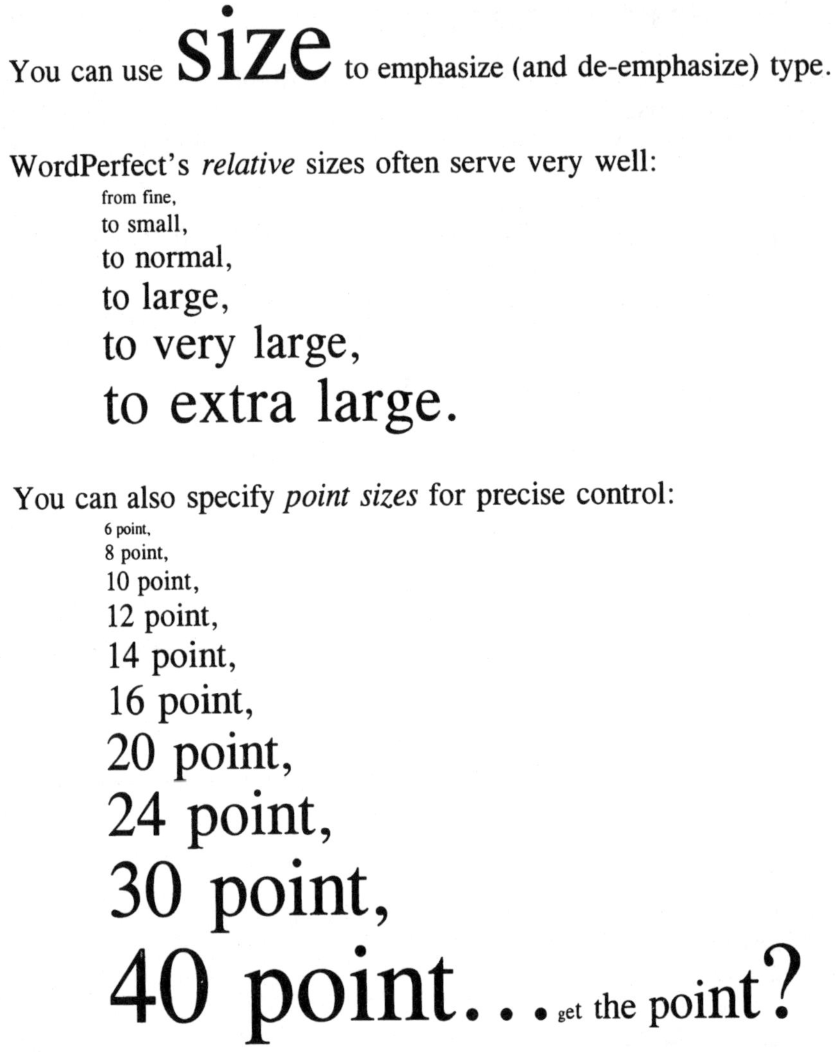

You can use size to emphasize (and de-emphasize) type.

WordPerfect's *relative* sizes often serve very well:

from fine,

to small,

to normal,

to large,

to very large,

to extra large.

You can also specify *point sizes* for precise control:

6 point,

8 point,

10 point,

12 point,

14 point,

16 point,

20 point,

24 point,

30 point,

40 point... get the point?

Figure 8-8: Varying font size

SOMETIMES it is a nice touch to open a chapter.
Use SMALL CAPS to avoid OVERPOWERING the line.

All caps in headlines can be...

BOXY AND HARD TO READ

Mixed upper and lower-case is...

More Natural to the Reader's Eye

Whatever you do...

Avoid Screamers!

(exclaimation points) in headlines.

Figure 8-9: Varying capitalization

WordPerfect has other appearance attributes you can use to create special effects:

You can use double-underlines for totals in calculations:

$$13$$
$$\underline{x\ 4}$$
$$=52$$

QuickChanging Fonts from the Property Bar

The quickest way to change the font face or size is from the drop-down lists on the property bar. Just click and scroll a listing, then click your selection. Click the Font Color button on the property bar to select another color from the palette.

The QuickFonts button on the property bar provides quick access to any of your last ten font-attribute combinations (see Figure 8-10). Selections display in their actual size, color, and appearance.

Click Font to bring up the Font dialog

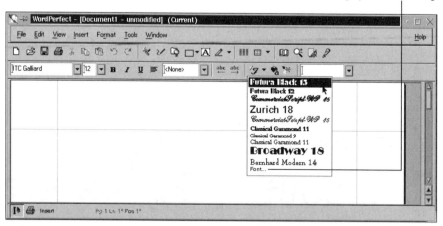

Figure 8-10: Selecting a QuickFont from the property bar

Select the text (or place the insertion point on the word you want to change) before making a property bar selection. Put the insertion point in a space to change the font from the insertion point forward.

Using the Font Dialog Box

The Font dialog box is your font command center (see Figure 8-11). You can access this dialog box in several ways:

✦ Click Format ➪ Font.

✦ Right-click in your text, then click Font.

✦ Click the QuickFonts button, then click Font.

✦ Press F9 (Ctrl+F8 on a DOS-compatible keyboard).

✦ Double-click a font code in WordPerfect's Reveal Codes.

Your chosen font options are applied to your selected text. If you did not select any text, your changes apply from the insertion point forward. If the insertion point is in a word, the changes apply to the single word.

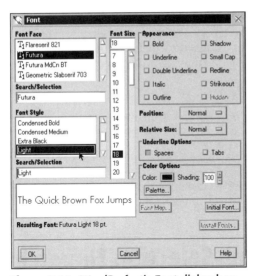

Figure 8-11: WordPerfect's Font dialog box

Selecting a font face, size, and style

When you open the Font dialog box, the font characteristics at the insertion point are displayed in the window at the bottom. You can select the font face and size, and specify a font style available with that face. You can type a custom font size, such as 12.6, for scalable fonts.

Changing the color or shading of your text

If your printer supports color, click the Color button, and then pick a color from the palette, using the arrow keys or the mouse. You can also vary the shading from 1 to 100 percent. (You can also pick a font color from the property bar.)

Changing the font position

Click the Position list to create smaller superscript or subscript characters:

$$E = mc^2$$

$$H_2O$$

Changing the relative font size

Click the "Relative size" list to select from six relative sizes ranging from fine to extra large, computed as percentages of your normal document font. (To customize relative size percentages, see Chapter 26, "Fine-Tuning WordPerfect.")

Selecting the font appearance

You can check (and preview) one or more of the Appearance attributes to apply to your text.

Selecting underline options

When underlining text in WordPerfect, you can specify whether you want to underline Tabs and Spaces as well. Your selection stays in effect until you change it.

Understanding the Font-Selection Hierarchy

When working with fonts in WordPerfect, you need to understand the font-selection hierarchy, from low to high, used to determine the current font:

✦ The printer initial font

✦ The document initial font

✦ The last font used in your document

When you open a new document, you start with the *printer initial (default) font* for the currently selected printer. This font has the lowest priority.

The *document initial (default) font* is the same as the printer initial font, unless you change it for the current document (instructions for this operation are provided below). Finally, the last font selection you make while working in your document (inserting a font code) overrides both the printer initial font and the document initial font.

To change your initial document font:

1. Click Format ⇨ Font.
2. Click Initial Font and select the font to be used as the initial document font.

Using Special Characters and Symbols

WordPerfect installs special Type 1 fonts that provide a large number of special characters and symbols from which to choose.

Some special characters are used for the familiar bullets, em dashes, decimal-align characters, and dot leaders. You can insert many others (such as Greek letters and trademarks) into regular text or use them for other purposes (such as custom bullets or attention-getters). Figure 8-12 displays some uses of special characters.

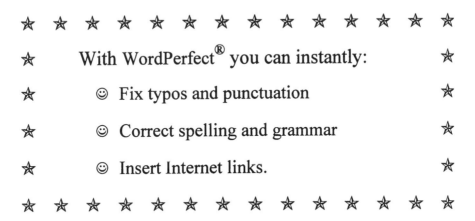

Figure 8-12: A few of the thousands of characters and symbols available

The WordPerfect characters are grouped in 14 sets, numbered from 1 through 14 (set 0 is the ASCII characters and symbols on your keyboard). Figure 8-13 lists the sets with examples.

WordPerfect's Character Sets

Set	Type	# Chars	Examples
0	ASCII	126	A a B b C c @ # $ ^ & * ([
1	Multinational	241	Á á Â â Ä ä À à Å å Æ æ
2	Phonetic	144	ɑ ɒ ɓ ʙ ɔ ç ɕ ʹ ʺ ː ˑ ˇ
3	Box Drawing	87	▌ ▀ – │ ┐ ┤ ┴ ┼ = ╟ ╓
4	Typographic	101	● • ¶ ¿ £ ½ ® ℞ ff ▶
5	Iconic	254	♡ ♂ ♀ ♫ 🖂 ✎ ✔ ✪ ☻
6	Math/Scientific	237	± ≥ ∝ ∑ ∞ → ↓ ▶ ∏
7	Math/Sc. Ext.	228	⌈ ∏ ‖ { ⊔ ⌀ ⌐
8	Greek	218	Α α Β β Β ϐ Γ γ
9	Hebrew	122	ח ז ו ה ד ג ב א
10	Cyrillic	249	А а Б б В в Г г
11	Japanese	62	ヲ オ キ ツ テ ホ ヒ ン
12	Cur. Font Symbols		(reserved)
13	Arabic	195	٢ ٤ ج خ ز ش ط ع ل ئ ﻹ
14	Arabic Script	219	٣ ٢ چ ج ٿ ٿ ٹ ژ خ گ

Figure 8-13: Sampling of WordPerfect characters

Inserting Special Characters and Symbols

To insert a special character or symbol:

1. Place the insertion point where you want the character to appear, then press Ctrl+W or click Insert ⇨ Symbol. (You can also click the Symbols button on the property bar.)

2. Click the "Character Set" pop-up list and click the character set you want (see Figure 8-14).

3. Click the character you want, then click Insert.

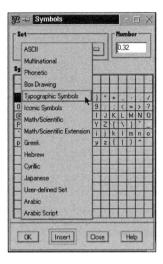

Figure 8-14: Selecting a character set

Special Character Tips and Tricks

Use the following tricks when inserting special characters or symbols:

✦ Double-click a character to insert it.

✦ Keep the dialog box open and click the screen where you want to insert the next character.

✦ Type a character's two-digit pair of numbers in the Number box. For example, type **4,12** to insert the Japanese yen symbol (¥) — the 12th character in the fourth set.

Tip

Create QuickCorrect abbreviations for special characters you use regularly (see Chapter 12, "Writer's Lib") — then just type the abbreviation. You can also assign characters to particular keystrokes (see Chapter 27, "Customizing Toolbars, Menus, and Keyboards").

For More Information . . .

On	See
Creating QuickCorrect abbreviations	Chapter 12
Assigning characters to keystrokes	Chapter 27
Working with graphics boxes	Chapter 9
Using cut, copy, and paste	Chapter 2
Adding borders to graphics	Chapter 23

✦   ✦   ✦

Working with Graphics

Working with graphics is a dream in WordPerfect. You get thousands of clip art images (plus photos and textures) that you can use to liven up your newsletters, fliers, reports, cards, or any other kind of document. WordPerfect has the unprecedented ability to handle practically every graphic format around, giving you the freedom to assemble and use graphics from a myriad of sources.

Distinguishing Types of Graphics

Graphics in desktop publishing fall roughly into three categories:

- ✦ *Vector* graphics, created by drawing, charting, and CAD programs. They form pictures out of mathematical lines and curves, and don't lose their sharpness as you change their size or shape.

- ✦ *Bitmap* (*raster*) images, composed of thousands of *pixels* (tiny squares), created by scanners and paint programs. The resolution (sharpness) of a bitmap depends on the size of its pixels, often expressed in dots per inch (dpi). The smaller the pixels the higher the resolution, but the bigger the file size.

- ✦ *Metafile* graphics are a hybrid of bitmap and vector components.

Bitmaps are good for fine art and photographs with subtle shadings and vivid detail, though they often have ragged edges ("raggies") when enlarged. Vectors are best for line art and drawings (such as clip art). Their file size is usually much smaller than comparable bitmaps, which can gobble up disk space by the megabyte.

WordPerfect lets you import graphics in any of the formats in Table 9-1.

Table 9-1
Importable Graphic Formats in WordPerfect for Linux

Graphic Format	Filename Extension	Graphics Type
Bitmap	.BMP, .DIB	Bitmap
CALS Compressed	.CAL	Bitmap
CompuServe GIF	.GIF	Bitmap
Computer Graphics Metafile	.CGM, CMF	Vector
Corel PHOTO-PAINT	.CPT	Bitmap
CorelDRAW	.CDR, .CDT, .PAT, .CMX	Bitmap
Encapsulated PostScript	.EPS	Vector
Enhanced Windows Metafile	.EMF	Metafile
H-P Plotter (HPGL)	.HPG, .HP, .PLT	Vector
JPEG	.JPG, .JPE	Bitmap
Kodak Photo CD	.PCD	Bitmap
Macintosh PICT	.PCT	Metafile
OS/2 Bitmap	.BMP	Bitmap
PC Paintbrush	.PCX	Bitmap
Portable Network Graphic	.PNG, .GIF	Bitmap
Sun Raster files	.RAS	Bitmap
Tagged Image Format File	.TIF	Bitmap
TruevisionTarga	.TGA	Bitmap
Windows Metafile	.WMF	Metafile
WordPerfect Graphic	.WPG	Metafile
X11 Bitmap Standard		Bitmap
X Window Image Dump	.XWD	Bitmap

Caution Graphics handling in the initial release of WordPerfect 8 for Linux can vary, depending on your graphics adapter and X-Window server. For example, a graphic in a particular format may import without an error message, but not display, on a machine running AcceleratedX, but display properly on a system running Xfree86. (In some cases, you can just resize the box to see the image.)

If you have a problem handling a particular graphics format on your system, use the appropriate service pack from Corel. Look on the Web site at `http://www.corel.com/support/ftpsite/index.htm`.

In addition, you can preview any of these image types in any file management dialog box (such as Open or Save).

Understanding the Graphics Box

When you add a chart, clip art, picture, or other graphic object to a document, the graphic object placed into a container, or frame, known in WordPerfect as a *graphics box*. You can think of the graphics box as a super picture frame that enables you to:

✦ Move the graphic around

✦ Stretch or shrink the contents

✦ Group or layer multiple graphics

✦ Set off the graphic with borders and fills

✦ Control the flow of text around the graphic

✦ Add descriptive captions

When a Graphics Box Isn't a Graphics Box

You'll see how to perform graphics box operations in short order. First, however, you must understand when a graphics box isn't a "graphics" box:

✦ When it contains text

✦ When it contains a table

You put text or a table in a graphics box so that you can drag it around, add borders, and do all the other things you can do with a graphics box. The only thing you cannot do is enlarge or shrink the table or text — just the box. (An equation-in-a-box is different, because this object is text is treated as a graphical object.)

What's a Graphics Box Style?

Click Insert ➪ Graphics ➪ Custom Box, and take a look at the graphics box styles from which you can choose (see Figure 9-1). These styles are prepackaged combinations of graphics box attributes (anchor, border, fill, caption, and so on), suited to various types of graphics and text. For example, when you compare the standard text box to the Sticky Note box, you'll see that the standard box is wide, sets off the text with a thin border, and is positioned to the side of your text. The Sticky Note is narrow and borderless, has a yellow fill, and sits on top of your document text.

Figure 9-1: Graphics box styles

Rather than examine each style in detail, the following sections show how you can change the attributes of any box to fit your needs.

Adding Graphics

You can add graphics to your work in several ways:

✦ Create your own art in a drawing or painting program.

✦ Insert watermarks (see Chapter 15, "Formatting Your Document") and tables-in-a-box (see Chapter 16, "Formatting with Columns and Tables").

✦ Create equations (see Chapter 24, "Creating Equations") and charts (see Chapter 25, "Charting Data").

✦ Insert clip art.

✦ Create text boxes.

✦ Insert other graphic objects, such as an image that you captured from the Internet (see Chapter 11, "Writing and Publishing for the Web").

This chapter covers creating your own art, importing clip art and other types of graphics, and creating text boxes, but the basic steps can be applied to any graphics process.

Inserting Clip Art or Any Other Graphic

WordPerfect comes with 5,000 clip art images. To insert a clip art image in WordPerfect:

1. Click the Clip Art button (Insert ➪ Graphics ➪ From File).

2. Browse through the clip art. Click View to display a preview of the selected image (see Figure 9-2).

Figure 9-2: Previewing clip art before you insert

3. Double-click the filename of the image you want to insert, or select the file and click Insert.

The selected graphic appears in your document inside a graphics box.

4. Drag the graphic box to the desired location, then click outside the box to deselect it.

Drawing Graphics Boxes with the Shadow Cursor

WordPerfect's shadow cursor makes it a cinch to insert graphics. To draw a graphics box with the shadow cursor:

1. Click the Shadow Cursor button on the application bar, if necessary, to turn on the shadow cursor.

2. Drag anywhere in your document's white space (except in a line of text) to draw a box.

3. Release the mouse, then select the type of box you want from the menu that appears (Figure 9-3).

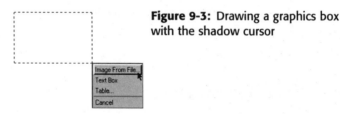

Figure 9-3: Drawing a graphics box with the shadow cursor

Follow the procedures described elsewhere, depending on the type of graphics box:

- For Image from File, see the previous section, "Inserting Clip Art or Any Other Graphic."

- For Text Box, see "Creating a Floating Text Box" in the following section.

- For Table, see "Creating a Table-In-A-Box" in Chapter 16, "Formatting with Columns and Tables."

Creating a Floating Text Box

By enclosing text in a graphics box, you can *float* (position) the text anywhere on the page, independent from the rest of your document text. This feature is useful for creating a *pull quote* of an excerpted line or phrase, in a larger or display typeface, to draw the reader's attention to an article or story. You can also apply other graphics box treatments to your text box, such as a shadow, border, or fill.

To create a floating text box:

1. Click Insert ⇨ Text Box.

2. Type your text, using your favorite fonts or formatting (see Figure 9-4). (Click the shadow cursor to center or right-align your text.)

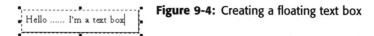

Figure 9-4: Creating a floating text box

Creating an In-Line Text Box

An in-line text box enables you to apply special treatment to selected text, just as with a floating text box, but the box stays put within the line of text:

1. Type your line of text.

2. Select the words you want to put in a box, then click the Text Box button (Insert ⇨ Text Box).

Creating a Sticky Note

You can use the Sticky Note box, which sits on top of your document, to write notes to yourself. To create a Sticky Note:

1. Click Insert ➪ Graphics ➪ Custom Box.

2. Select the Sticky Note Text box, then click OK.

3. Type and format your sticky note text, then click outside of the box when you're done.

Creating Reversed Text

When text is in a box, you can *reverse* it (make the text white in a colored background instead of dark on a white background). To do this:

1. Click the edge of the box to select it.

2. Click the Graphic Fill button and select a solid fill of the color you want.

3. Click in the text box, select the text, then click the Font Color button to preview and select white or another contrasting color for your text.

Selecting Graphics and Text Boxes

Many graphics box operations (including moving and deleting) begin by selecting the box. Click anywhere in a standard graphics box to select it and display the sizing handles (see Figure 9-5).

Figure 9-5: Sizing handles appear around selected boxes

When you click in a text box (including a Sticky Note or button), a border of dashes appears around the box to indicate that you're in text edit mode (refer to Figure 9-4). You can move or size a text box in edit mode, but sometimes you'll need to select the box alone (to delete it, for example) by pointing to the border and clicking (see Figure 9-6). (You can also right-click a text box and click Select Box.)

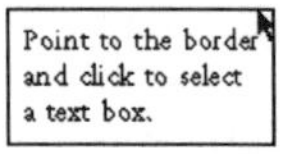

Point to the border and click to select a text box.

Figure 9-6: Point to the border and click to select a text box

If you're editing the text within the box and want to select the box instead, first click outside the box, and then click the border.

Displaying and Hiding Graphics

When you're editing text on a slower machine, you can click View ➪ Graphics to hide your graphics and speed scrolling. The graphics will still print.

Mastering Graphics Box Techniques

You can right-click a graphics box to edit it, or select the box and select items from the property bar. When you have multiple graphics in a document, you can click the Previous button or the Next button on the property bar to go from graphic to graphic.

Try this WordPerfect exercise to get the hang of the basic graphics box techniques:

1. Open a blank new document, click Insert ➪ Graphics ➪ From File, insert a clip art item, then:

   • Click outside the graphics box to deselect it. (Click the box to select it again.)

   • Click anywhere within the box to drag it to another location. (Hold Ctrl to make a copy.)

   • Drag a corner handle to size the image proportionally (see Figure 9-7).

Figure 9-7: Drag a corner handle to size an image proportionally

   • Drag a side handle to stretch or squeeze the image (Figure 9-8).

Figure 9-8: Drag a side handle to stretch or squeeze the image

- • Press Delete to remove the box.

2. Click Insert ➪ Text Box, then do the following:

- • Click the middle of the box with the shadow cursor to center the line.

- • Type and format some text, just as you would in a document. (You can even use Reveal Codes in a text box.)

- • Click outside the box to deselect it, then point to the border and click to select just the box.

- • Position the pointer anywhere along the border, and then drag the box (see Figure 9-9).

- • Drag a handle to stretch or shrink the amount of text that displays. Note how the size of the text doesn't change.

Figure 9-9: Click the border to drag a text box

One more thing: When you double-click a graphic image, you'll open WP Draw, the drawing component that comes with WordPerfect. You can edit the image in WP Draw.

Layering Graphics Boxes

WordPerfect's *drawing layer* lets you arrange a stack of overlapping graphics boxes. The drawing layer also enables Sticky Notes (which lie on top of your text) and watermarks (which go behind it).

Practice layering different kinds of graphics boxes in the following exercise:

1. Type some text.

2. Click Insert ➪ Graphics ➪ Custom Box.

3. Select the Sticky Note Text box, put some text in it, and then click outside the note.

4. Create another Sticky Note Text box.

5. Click the Graphics Wrap button ⇨ Behind Text to put the second note behind the text (Figure 9-10).

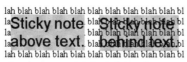

Figure 9-10: Sticky Notes above and behind text

6. Insert three graphics from the clip art collection, and place them in a stack by dragging them on top of each other.

7. Select a graphic, and then click the Graphics Up and Graphics Down buttons to move it up and down in the stack (see Figure 9-11). Click Graphics ⇨ To Front and Graphics ⇨ To Back to move it to the top or bottom of the stack.

8. Click the Previous button or the Next button to select different graphics in the stack.

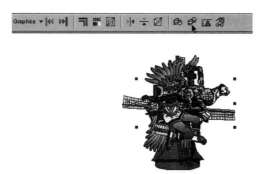

Figure 9-11: Moving graphics up and down the stack

For more on layering graphics, see "Creating Your Own Art" later in this chapter.

Grouping Graphics Boxes

In WordPerfect, you can group graphics boxes, then drag them around as one. This feature is especially handy for superimposing text on graphics.

The following exercise teaches you how to group graphics boxes.

1. Click the Clip Art button (Insert ⇨ Graphics ⇨ From File) and insert an image of a coyote and a speech balloon, as shown in Figure 9-12.

2. With the speech balloon selected, click the Graphics Flip Vertical button to flip it from left to right, and then drag it over to the coyote and click outside of the box to deselect it.

3. Click Insert ⇨ Text Box, and type what the coyote is saying.

4. Drag the handles to shrink the box around your text, and then drag the box to position it over the speech balloon. (You'll also want to remove the border, as described in a following section.)

5. While holding Shift, click the coyote, click the text box, and then click the balloon. Notice how handles appear around the group as you click (see Figure 9-12).

Figure 9-12: Hold Shift as you click each graphic to select a group

6. Click Graphics ⇨ Group to lock the graphics together.

You can now drag the graphics around and position them in relation to text as a group. Editing changes (such as to the border or fill) apply to every individual graphic, not the rectangle around the group.

To separate the boxes in a group, right-click one of the graphics and click Separate.

Editing the Appearance of a Graphics Box

You can change the appearance of a graphics box in your document by changing its style, border, or fill.

Changing the Style of a Graphics Box

To change the style of a graphics box (such as from Image to Figure), select the box and click Graphics ⇨ Style, or right-click the box and click Style.

Changing the Border or Fill of a Graphics Box

To change the border or fill of a graphics box, select the box and click the Graphics Flip Vertical or the Graphics Fill button, and then select a border or fill from the palette (see Figure 9-13).

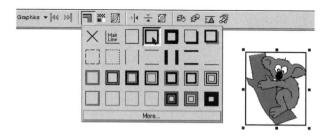

Figure 9-13: Changing the border of a graphics box

To access the full range of border and fill customization options, click More on either the Border or Fill palette, or right-click the graphic and click Border/Fill (see Figure 9-14).

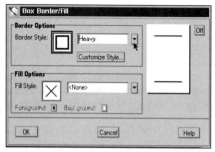

Figure 9-14: Accessing all the border and fill options

See Chapter 23, "Adding Graphic Lines, Borders, and Fills," for more on customizing borders and fills.

Changing the Size, Position, and Spacing of a Graphics Box

Once you add a graphics box to a WordPerfect document, you'll probably want to change its size or position. You may also want to change its inside or outside spacing.

Specifying a Precise Graphics Box Size

While the mouse is the quickest tool for resizing a graphics box, you can also give it a precise size:

1. Select the graphic and click Graphics ➪ Size.
2. Specify one of the following width and height options (Figure 9-15):
   - *Set:* to specify a particular width or height.
   - *Full:* to fill the width of the column, cell, or page, or the height of the page.
   - *Maintain proportions:* to adjust the width or height to the contents of the box automatically.

Figure 9-15: Specifying a precise graphics box size

Changing the Anchor Type and Position

Every graphics box in WordPerfect has one of the following *anchors* to position it in relation to text:

✦ *Page* (Image, Sticky Note, Table, Watermark): lets you attach the graphics box to the entire page (watermark), or to a particular location on the page, so it doesn't shift as you add or delete text.

✦ *Paragraph* (Figure, Text): keeps the graphics box attached to a particular paragraph as you edit text, even when the paragraph shifts to another page.

✦ *Character* (Button, Inline Text): treats your graphics box as a single character that shifts along the line as you edit your text.

To change a graphic's anchor type and position:

1. Select the graphic and click Graphics ⇨ Position.

2. Select an anchor from the "Box placement" list (see Figure 9-16).

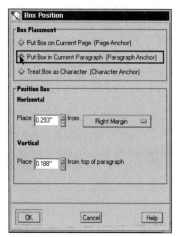

Figure 9-16: Changing the anchor type

3. Specify the positioning options for the type of anchor you selected.

Note To use a graphic of your scanned signature in e-mail or a fax, set the anchor to character or paragraph to keep it attached to the closing phrase.

Adjusting the Inside or Outside Spacing of a Graphics Box

To adjust the space between the contents and border of a graphics box in WordPerfect, or the space between the border and the text surrounding the box:

1. Select the box, and then click Graphics ⇨ Border/Fill ⇨ Customize Style.

2. Click the Inside and Outside space palettes to specify the spacing you want (see Figure 9-17).

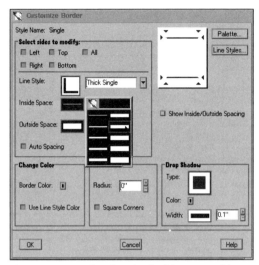

Figure 9-17: Adjusting the inside or outside space of a graphics box

Creating and Editing Captions

You can add captions to your WordPerfect images with either identifying text, or automatic numbering (such as Figure 1, Figure 2, and so forth) used for document references. You can employ several positioning, appearance, and numbering style options in customizing captions.

Adding a Caption to a Graphics Box

To add a caption to a graphics box:

1. Click the box and click the Graphics Caption button.

2. Type the caption text you want (see Figure 9-18). (Use the property bar selections to change the font face, color, and other attributes.)

Figure 9-18: Default caption for a second coyote

Figure 2

Editing a Caption

To edit a caption, select the graphic and click the Graphics Caption button.

Deleting a Caption

To delete a caption, right-click the graphic and then click Caption ➪ Reset. Reset not only deletes the caption, but also returns the caption style (if it has been altered) to the default for that type of graphics box.

Changing the Position of a Caption

The default caption position for most graphics box styles is outside of the border, at the bottom left. To change the caption's position, right-click the graphic, click Caption, then specify a different position, either inside or outside of the border (see Figure 9-19).

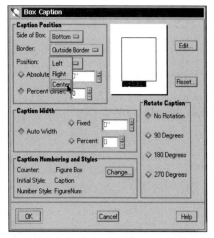

Figure 9-19: Changing the position of a caption

Rotating a Caption

You can rotate a caption in 90-degree increments, as shown in Figure 9-20. This feature is handy when you want to print a caption along the side of a graphics box, rather than across the top or bottom.

Figure 9-20: Caption rotated 90 degrees

To rotate a caption, right-click the graphic, click Caption, and select a rotation of 90, 180, or 270 counterclockwise degrees.

Adjusting the Caption Width

You can adjust the width of a caption to the layout of your graphics and text. This feature is useful if you are printing a caption on the side of a graphic (see Figure 9-21), or if you are rotating a caption printed at the top or bottom.

To adjust the width of a caption, right-click the graphic, click Caption, and specify either a fixed width or a percentage of the box's width.

Figure 9-21: The same caption at two different widths

Controlling the Flow of Text Around a Graphic

The impact of a graphic comes primarily in its relation to the textual elements. In preceding sections, you learned how to layer graphics above and behind text. In many cases, however, you'll want your text to flow around a graphic. Figure 9-22 illustrates a few of the possibilities.

To change the flow of text around a graphic:

1. Select the graphic and click the Wrap Text button (or right-click the graphic and click Wrap).

2. Select the wrap you want (see Figure 9-23):

   • *Neither side:* to have the graphics box stand alone.

   • *Square:* to align text with the sides of the box.

   • *Contour:* to wrap text around the image within the box, when there's no border. (Text also contours to a border with rounded corners.)

   • *Behind Text/In Front of Text:* to place the graphic behind or in front of the text.

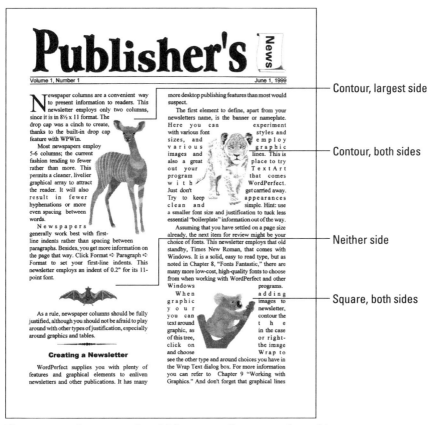

Contour, largest side

Contour, both sides

Neither side

Square, both sides

Figure 9-22: Some ways in which text can flow around graphics

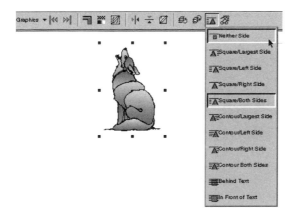

Figure 9-23: Changing the flow of text around a graphic

With a square or contour wrap, you also specify the side around which it wraps. The "Largest Side" option causes the text to flow around the side of the box where there is the most white space.

Creating a Custom Graphics Box Style

You can create a custom graphics box style for all your documents, with the particular border, fill, anchor, content, spacing, caption, wrap and other options you want:

1. Click Format ➪ Graphics Styles ➪ Box ➪ Create.

2. Give your style a name, and specify the options you want (see Figure 9-24).

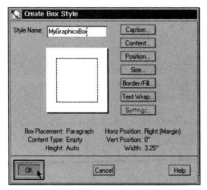

Figure 9-24: Creating a Custom Graphics Box Style

To insert your custom graphics box, click Insert ➪ Graphics ➪ Custom Box and select your style from the list.

Changing the Properties of a Graphic Image

In addition to moving or sizing a graphics box, you can change the properties of the image within it. Use the image tools to crop, rotate, scale, or flip an image, or adjust such attributes as its brightness, contrast, color, and fill:

1. Select the graphic and click the Graphic Image Tools button to display the Image Tools palette, as shown in Figure 9-25.

2. Use any of the tools shown in Table 9-2 to change the properties of your image.

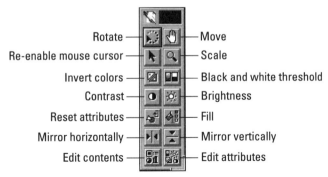

Rotate — Move
Re-enable mouse cursor — Scale
Invert colors — Black and white threshold
Contrast — Brightness
Reset attributes — Fill
Mirror horizontally — Mirror vertically
Edit contents — Edit attributes

Figure 9-25: Image Tools palette

Table 9-2
Image Tools

Image Tool	Lets You
Rotate	Rotate the image around a selected point (see Figure 9-26)
Re-enable mouse cursor	Re-enable the mouse cursor to move the image
Invert Colors	Switch the colors of the image to their complements
Contrast	Adjust the contrast of the image
Reset Attributes	Reset the image display to its original state
Mirror horizontally	Flip the image left to right
Edit Contents	Edit the image in WP Draw
Move	Move the image within the box
Scale	Zoom the entire image in or out, or zoom (crop) a selected part of the image; you can also reset an image to its original size
BW threshold	Display a color image in black and white, and select a dividing line (threshold) between black and white (see Figure 9-27)
Brightness	Adjust the brightness of the image
Fill	Select normal fill, no fill (transparent image with background showing through), or white fill (the image displays in outline with white fill)
Mirror vertically	Flip the image top to bottom
Edit Attributes	Access all the image-editing tools from one dialog box and specify precise numeric settings (see Figure 9-28); you can also specify the image print parameters

To reposition the Image Tools palette, drag its title bar. Click your document to dismiss the palette.

Figure 9-26: Rotating an image

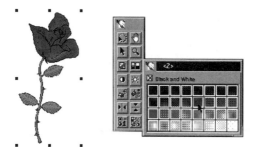

Figure 9-27: Selecting a threshold when converting a color image to black and white

Figure 9-28: Setting all the image attributes at once

Creating Your Own Art with WP Draw

While WordPerfect comes with an extensive collection of clip art and backgrounds, a hand-drawn object may be just the touch you need for your slide, drawing, menu, or brochure. WP Draw enables you to draw and edit a variety of shapes, including lines, arrows, circles, and rectangles. Here are some hands-on tips for editing shapes and applying fills, shadows, and other special effects.

Types of Graphic Objects

WordPerfect comes with a variety of graphic objects that you don't have to draw by hand:

- ✦ Horizontal and vertical graphic lines
- ✦ Clip art
- ✦ Charts
- ✦ Borders and fills

The preceding section "Inserting Clip Art or Any Other Graphic" describes the insertion of clip art. For more information on creating charts, see Chapter 25, "Charting Data." For more information on borders, fills, and lines, see Chapter 23, "Adding Graphic Lines, Borders, and Fills."

Drawing Basic Shapes

You can draw several types of shapes directly on a WordPerfect document. Click Insert ⇨ Shape to draw any of the objects shown in Figure 9-29.

When drawing a polyline or polygon, click wherever you want to add a joint, then double-click to complete the shape.

Tip   Hold Shift while drawing a line or polyline to draw at exact horizontal, vertical, or diagonal angles. Hold Shift when drawing a rectangle to draw a square.

Every shape is in a graphics box that you can reshape and customize. You can change the attributes of a selected shape from the property bar, such as adding ends to a line to turn it into an arrow, or drag points to change the shape or direction (Figure 9-30).

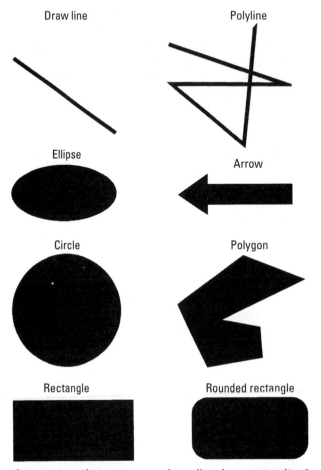

Figure 9-29: Shapes you can draw directly on a WordPerfect document

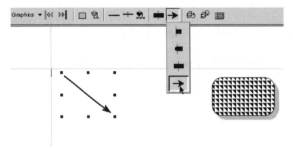

Figure 9-30: Use the property bar to change the attributes of a selected shape

Using the WP Draw tools

To create more complex shapes and combine shapes and other graphics in a single drawing, use the WP Draw tools. Click Insert ➪ Graphics ➪ Draw Picture to use the tools directly in a document (see Figure 9-31). Or, double-click a graphic to open the draw program.

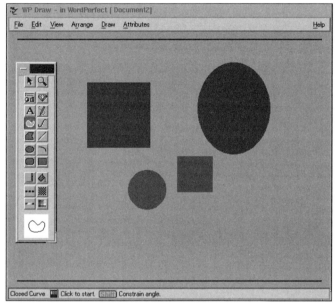

Figure 9-31: Drawing a complex shape in WordPerfect with the WP Draw drawing tools

Using the Rulers, Grid, and Snap To

The rulers and grid help you draw and position objects exactly. You can have the objects you create "snap to" grid intervals, even when they're not displayed. (The ruler and grid do not print.)

Click View ➪ Ruler to toggle the display of the ruler, View ➪ Grid to toggle the grid display, and View ➪ Snap to Grid to toggle Snap To Grid.

To customize grid and Snap To features, click View ➪ Grid/Snap Options, then specify:

✦ The horizontal and vertical Snap To spacing between dots (see Figure 9-32).

✦ The interval between dotted grid lines.

✦ The *snap zone*, or how close an object can get to an alignment guide before it snaps to the guide.

Figure 9-32: Specifying grid and Snap To options

Click File ➪ Preferences ➪ Display to set the default settings for the ruler and the grid.

Drawing More Complex Shapes

In addition to the basic shapes, you can also attempt the more advanced shapes illustrated in Table 9-3.

| | Table 9-3 | |
| | **Advanced Shapes** | |
Shape	*How to Draw It*	*Constraint When Holding Shift*
Elliptical arc	(1) Drag to create the line, then release the mouse button (2) Move the pointer to size the arc, then click	Creates a circular arc
Curve	(1) Click wherever you want to change the direction of the curve (2) Double-click to end	Places points at horizontal, vertical, and 45-degree angles
Closed curve	Same as curve	Places points at horizontal, vertical, and 45-degree angles
Freehand shape	Drag the mouse in any direction, then release when finished	No difference when holding down Shift

All the objects can be found in the Draw menu. For instance, Click Draw ⇨ Curve to draw a curve. You can also use the WP Draw palette (see Figure 9-33). Click File ⇨ Exit to return to your WordPerfect document and insert your drawing.

Figure 9-33: Using the WP Draw palette to insert shapes in your drawing

Selecting Objects

You must select objects before you can edit them. To select objects in the drawing window, click the Drawing Select button, then click the object. Hold Ctrl or Shift to select multiple objects.

To select all the objects at once, click Edit ⇨ Select ⇨ All. You can also click a blank area and click Select All. (Press Ctrl and click to deselect objects one at a time.)

Moving, Copying, and Sizing Objects

Objects in the drawing window are in graphics boxes that you can move, copy, or size like any other, using any of the techniques described previously in this chapter.

Editing Objects

You can edit the attributes of selected objects (such as the border, fill, shadow, color, or line style) by selecting an object and choosing the appropriate options from the Attributes menu.

Using Edit Points to Reshape an Object

Certain irregular drawn objects shapes have *edit points* on their lines, which you can drag to alter the shape of the object. To use edit points to reshape an object:

1. Right-click the object and click Edit Points.

2. Drag any of the points to reshape the object.

3. If the object is a curve, closed curve, or freehand line, you can also click a point and drag a control handle on the direction line (see Figure 9-34).

Figure 9-34: Click a point and drag a control handle to reshape a curved object

Right-click points for additional options, depending on the type of object.

Using Undo and Redo

When moving or editing objects, you can click Edit ⇨ Undo or Edit ⇨ Redo to undo or restore your latest editing action.

Arranging the Order of Overlapping Objects

When you have two or more overlapping objects, you can arrange their order in the stack (see Figure 9-35). Right-click an object, then click one of the following:

✦ *Front* to move the object to the foreground

✦ *Back* to move the object to the background

You can also click Arrange ⇨ Front and Arrange ⇨ Back.

Grouping Objects

Once you've arranged your objects the way you want, you can group them into a single object, so they can all be moved or worked on together:

1. Click the graphics while holding Shift, or click Edit ⇨ Select ⇨ All to select all the objects.

2. Click Arrange ⇨ Group.

The grouped objects can now be moved, sized, and edited as one. To separate the group back into individual objects, select and click Arrange ⇨ Ungroup.

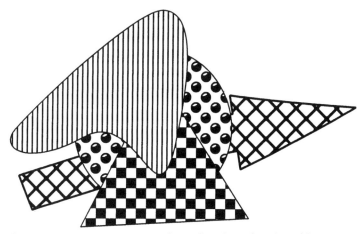

Figure 9-35: You can arrange the order of overlapping objects

Rotating, Skewing, and Flipping Objects

You can right-click an object to rotate or skew (slant) the object (see Figure 9-36). Click Arrange ➪ Flip Left/Right, or Arrange ➪ Flip Top/Bottom to flip objects. (You can group objects, then rotate, skew, or flip them as one.)

Figure 9-36: Skewing an object

Creating Text Objects in the Drawing Window

You can create a text box or line of text in the drawing window, much as you create a text box or line of text in WordPerfect. Text created this way becomes a graphic object to which various effects (such as the rotating and skewing described previously) can be applied.

To create a text box or line in the drawing window:

1. Click the Draw Text button from the WP Draw Palette or click Draw ➪ Text and drag the width of the box you want. This sequence will open the WP Draw text editor (see Figure 9-37).

2. Click Format ➪ Font to select the font face, style, and size you want.

3. Type your text.

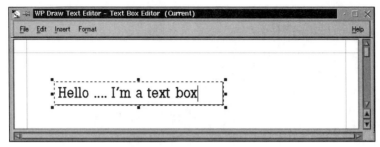

Figure 9-37: The WP Draw Text Editor

4. Click File ➪ Close when you're finished.

A text box expands downward as you type (drag a side handle to widen or narrow it). Text on a line cuts off beyond the right end.

Applying effects to text objects

You can apply effects to text objects, such as size, skew, and rotate (see Figure 9-38), just like any other object.

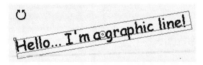

Figure 9-38: Rotating a text object

To turn your text into graphics with fills and outlines, select the text, then click Attribute ➪ Fill.

For More Information . . .

On	See
Inserting watermarks	Chapter 15
Creating equations	Chapter 24
Charting data	Chapter 25
Capturing Web graphics	Chapter 11
Adding graphic borders and fills	Chapter 23
Generating caption lists	Chapter 18

✦   ✦   ✦

Printing Documents, Booklets, and Envelopes

◆ ◆ ◆ ◆

In This Chapter

Use all the print selection tricks

Print multiple pages and copies

Do two-sided printing

Add a binding offset

Create custom print settings

Publish booklets

Print envelopes

Select a printer

Control the progress of your print jobs

Print to a file

◆ ◆ ◆ ◆

While WordPerfect does wonders for your input, it also enables easy production and transmission of quality output. The program's printing facilities do everything from finding the mailing address for an envelope to creating booklets ready to be stapled down the middle. You can customize almost every aspect of printing.

Printing All or Part of a Document

To print all or part of a WordPerfect document:

1. Click the Print button on the toolbar, or click File ➪ Print. (You can also press F5; Shift+F7 on a DOS keyboard.)

2. Specify what you want to print:

   - *Full document* or *Current page* to print the entire document, or the page at the insertion point (see Figure 10-1).

   - *Multiple Pages* to print particular pages, secondary pages, chapters, or volumes (see the following section, "Printing Multiple Pages").

   - *Document on Disk* to print a document without opening the document first.

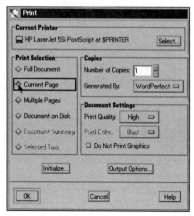

Figure 10-1: Printing the current page

> • *Document Summary* to print only the document summary. (Click Output Options and check "Print Document Summary" to print both the document and its summary.)
>
> • *Selected text* prints text you selected.

Selected text prints in the same page position as it appears onscreen. To start printing at the top of the page, enter a hard page break (Ctrl+Enter) just before your selected passage. Press Ctrl+Z to remove the break after your passage prints.

> **3.** Specify the number of copies, print quality, color, and other options discussed in the sections to follow.
>
> **4.** Click OK.

To print your entire document with the current settings in one step, click File ➪ Print Document.

Printing Multiple Pages

Click File ➪ Print, then select Multiple Pages and click OK to print particular pages, secondary pages, chapters, or volumes (see Figure 10-2).

The volumes you specify take precedence over other settings, followed by chapters, secondary pages, and pages. For example, if you type **3** in the Chapter(s) box, only pages from Chapter 3 will print, even if pages from other chapters are specified.

If your document has multiple sections (that is, you have reset the page numbers along the way), you can designate the section, followed by a colon (:), in the Page(s) box. For example, if you specify **3:2-5**, pages 2-5 in the third section will print.

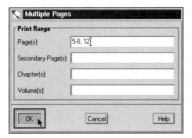

Figure 10-2: Printing multiple pages

To print only odd or even pages, see the following "Two-Sided Printing" section.

For more on numbering pages, see Chapter 14, "Controlling Text and Numbering Pages."

Printing a Document on Disk

You don't have to open a document in order to print it. To print a document on disk:

1. Click File ➪ Print, check "Document on disk," click OK and specify the file you want to print.

2. Specify the pages, copies, and other options, just as you do for a screen document.

Tip

You can also print documents from the Open dialog box (see Chapter 7, "Managing Your Files").

Printing Multiple Copies

To print multiple copies of your document:

1. Click File ➪ Print, specify what you want to print, then specify the number of copies you want (see Figure 10-3).

2. Choose whether to let WordPerfect or the printer generate the copies. Letting the printer generate copies results in faster output, but copies are *grouped* by page instead of *collated* (all the pages of the first copy are printed, then all the pages of the second, and so forth).

Caution

The number of copies (like other print settings) stays the same for the remainder of the current session, unless you change the setting.

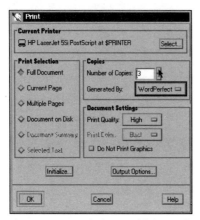

Figure 10-3: Printing multiple copies

Specifying the Print Quality, Graphics, and Color

To print a document in a hurry (or to save on ink or toner), you can print your text and graphics at a lower print quality. You can also choose not to print graphics — perhaps to proofread text without the distraction of graphics. If your printer supports color, you can print either in color or black and white.

To specify the print quality, graphics, and color:

1. Click File ➪ Print.

2. Specify what you want to print, then select any of the following:

   • Specify High, Medium, or Draft in the Print Quality list (see Figure 10-4). Print quality choices vary from printer to printer.

   • To print your document without graphics, check "Do Not Print Graphics."

   • If you have a color printer, you can choose either Black (black and white) or Full Color in the Print Color list.

Two-Sided Printing

Few desktop printers support double-sided printing (duplexing), but you can usually print pages on one side, then turn them over and print on the other. Because there are always at least as many odd pages as even ones, consider printing the even pages first. With this strategy, you never have a page left in the paper tray after printing the reverse side.

The following method works on many printers:

1. Click File ➪ Print, specify what you want to print, then click Output Options and check "Print in reverse order."

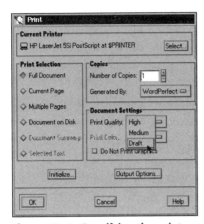

Figure 10-4: Specifying the print quality, graphics, and color

2. In the Output Options dialog box, click Print Odd/Even Pages and select Even (see Figure 10-5). Then click OK to close the Output Options dialog box and OK to print.

Figure 10-5: Two-sided printing

3. When the even pages are printed, turn the pages the opposite way and reload them.

You may have to experiment a bit to get the proper page orientation for your printer.

4. Repeat Steps 1 and 2, but now uncheck "Print in reverse order" and print the odd pages.

Various printers handle pages differently, so experiment on a small scale to find the two-sided printing method that works for you.

Caution   Your printer manual may warn you that paper jams can result if you try to print on both sides of the page with your printer. Better-quality, long-grain paper is less likely to jam. Also, let the paper from a laser printer cool before turning it over, so the ink powder cures and doesn't smudge your roller.

Adding a Binding Offset

When you create a document to be printed and bound, you can add an offset to keep text from disappearing into the bound margin. The offset shifts text away from the bound edge.

To apply a binding offset:

1. Click File ➪ Page Setup ➪ Two-Sided Printing.

2. Select the edge from which text will be shifted (see Figure 10-6).

Figure 10-6: Adding a binding offset

3. Specify the distance that you want to shift the text.

4. If your printer supports duplex printing, select one of the duplexing options.

5. Click OK.

Printing Booklets

Booklet printing is a simple and ingenious way to print small phone directories, instructions, menus, and other pamphlets.

The secret of booklet printing is that you first subdivide each physical page of your document into two logical pages. (If you subdivide the page into more than two logical pages, you get an error message when you try to print them as a booklet.) When you print your document as a booklet, your printed pages come out in proper sequence, ready to staple and fold as a booklet. The page can be divided either horizontally or vertically.

To print your document as a booklet:

1. Place the insertion point at the beginning of the file, then click File ➪ Page Setup ➪ Page Size.

2. To change to a landscape (horizontal) page layout, select a landscape paper definition.

Tip The landscape letter-size paper makes a handy booklet when folded in half length-wise. In its normal (portrait) orientation, letter-size paper makes an attractive menu or brochure.

3. To subdivide your pages, click File ➪ Page Setup ➪ Subdivide Page, then specify 2 columns and 1 row (see Figure 10-7).

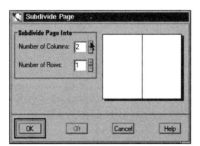

Figure 10-7: Subdividing landscape pages to create a booklet

4. You may want to click File ➪ Page Setup ➪ Margins to specify smaller margins, in proportion with your smaller pages. (A smaller font can be helpful too.)

5. It helps to set up page numbering (Format ➪ Page ➪ Page Numbering ➪ Numbering) to arrange your pages after they're printed.

6. Make any editing or formatting changes to your document. (If you want to get fancy, create a title page.) Use Make It Fit (see Chapter 4, "Becoming an Instant WordPerfect Expert") to adjust to the number of pages you want. To preview how your pages will print, click the Zoom button on the toolbar to switch to Full Page zoom (see Figure 10-8).

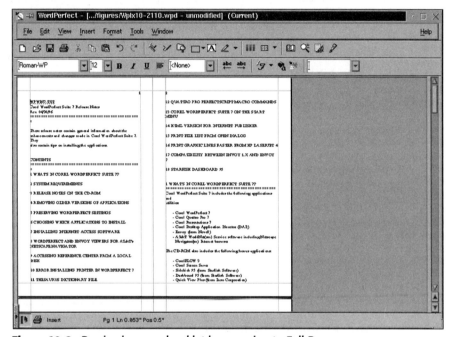

Figure 10-8: Previewing your booklet by zooming to Full Page

7. Now print your booklet. Click File ➪ Print ➪ Output Options, check "Booklet Printing," then click OK to close the Output Options dialog box and OK to print the booklet. Four booklet pages print on each physical page (two on each side). A 14-page booklet, for example, prints on four pages.

8. Follow the prompts to reinsert your pages into the printer, one page at a time, removing any printer pauses.

9. Assemble the pages in the proper order, then fold them. Your booklet is finished!

Printing Envelopes

When you print an envelope, WordPerfect picks up the mailing address from your letter automatically (if the address is in a standard position followed by hard returns). You can also specify precise address positions, and create a bar code out of the ZIP code automatically (see the following "Specifying Address Positions and Bar Code Options" section). To print an envelope:

1. Select the mailing address if it is not in a standard position.

2. Click Format ⇨ Envelope. The last return address you used is displayed (see Figure 10-9). The mailing address also appears if WordPerfect found it or you selected it.

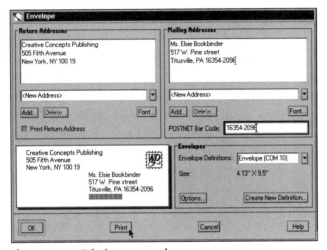

Figure 10-9: Printing an envelope

3. Use the current return address or select an address from the drop-down list. You can also type the return address.

4. If you want to change the font for the return address, click Font. (Be sure that "Print return address" is checked if you want the return address to print.)

5. Specify the mailing address, select another, or change its font, just as you did for the return address in Steps 3 and 4.

Tip   Add a new mailing address to the drop-down list to avoid typing it again.

6. Select an envelope from the "Envelope definitions" drop-down list, then click Print.

To print envelopes with mailing lists and form letters, see Chapter 28, "Mass-Producing with Labels and Merge."

Specifying Address Positions and Bar Code Options

To specify precise positions for the return or mailing address on the envelope, or to choose whether and where to print a USPS bar code automatically, click Options from the Envelope dialog box (see Figure 10-10).

You can adjust the horizontal and vertical positions for both the return and mailing addresses. The adjustments you make apply to all envelopes you print by using that envelope definition.

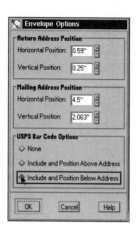

Figure 10-10: Changing address positions and bar code options

Including a USPS POSTNET bar code with the mailing address can speed mail sorting and delivery. The code is a computer-readable interpretation of the ZIP code (5 or 9 digits) or the 12-digit Delivery Point Bar Code (DPBC). You can position the code above or below the address, or withhold the code altogether.

Creating a New Envelope Definition

If your envelope isn't among the listed definitions, you can create a new definition for it:

1. Click Format ➪ Envelope ➪ Create New Definition.

2. Give your envelope a name (see Figure 10-11).

3. Select an envelope size or specify a custom width and height.

4. Specify the paper location, printing adjustments, and font orientation, as described in "Creating a Custom Page Definition," in Chapter 15, "Formatting Your Document."

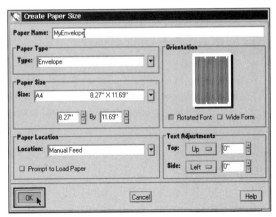

Figure 10-11: Creating a new envelope definition

Deleting an Envelope Definition

You can't delete an envelope definition with the normal creation route. An envelope definition is just another page definition, however. To delete an envelope definition, click File ⇨ Page Setup ⇨ Page Size, select the envelope definition you want to delete, then click Delete.

Preparing to Print

Various technologies for printing to paper are still the mainstay of desktop publishing. You can save paper and toner or ink (and spare some trees) by ensuring that your work is in polished form before you print. Check spelling and grammar, then Zoom to a full-page view to see that it has a pleasing format.

Also, be sure that the printer you want is displayed on the application bar and ready to go. If you need to change your current printer selection:

1. Click File ⇨ Print ⇨ Select.

2. Select the printer you want to use (see Figure 10-12).

The selected printer will be the standard printer until you select another printer.

Controlling the Progress of Your Print Jobs

Suppose you launch the printing of a 72-page report, only to say "Uh-oh, I didn't mean to do that." What do you do? You can cancel your print job, but your software will probably process your print job too quickly to avoid printing. You may have to head straight for the printer.

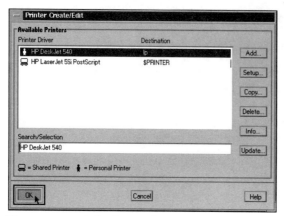

Figure 10-12: Selecting a printer

Catching Up with Your Print Job

When you print your document, the *printer driver* first puts the information into a format that your printer understands and stores it in a temporary file. While the temporary print file is being created, the "Preparing document for printing" message appears.

If the print job is large, or if your job is queued behind others, you may be able to catch it by switching to the WordPerfect program window and clicking Program ⇨ Printer Control. If the job is still active, it appears in the queue list. To stop the process, select the print job and click Cancel (see Figure 10-13). To pause a print job, click Hold.

Stopping a Job That Is Printing

Chances are, however, that the job is already feeding into your printer's memory and pages are spewing out of your printer. Your printer may have a reset button to clear its memory. However, if the job is more than a couple of pages long, more pages will be sent from your computer to the printer.

So what is the quickest and surest way to bring printing to a halt? Lift the paper out of your printer's input bin or pull out the paper tray. (Don't try to stop a page already feeding through the printer.) You can then cancel what remains of the job in the queue and reset your printer, or turn it off and back on after a few seconds to clear its memory. These tips are general suggestions; consult your printer manual for the best way to stop your printer.

Figure 10-13: Canceling a print job

Adding a Printer

WordPerfect 8 for Linux uses its own printer drivers. Normally, these drivers are added during the installation process for WordPerfect (see Chapter 1, "Getting Up and Running"). However, if you change your printer or install a new one, you must add the printer to your list of available printers in WordPerfect:

1. Click File ⇨ Print ⇨ Select.

2. Click Printer Create/Edit ⇨ Add.

3. Click Printer Driver Files (*.prs) if you already have a driver for your printer, or click Additional Printer Drivers (*.all) if you have the ALL file on your hard drive and need to create a printer driver (see Figure 10-14).

 Tip   If no printers appear in the Printers list, you may need to specify the directory in which your PRS or ALL files are stored. Normally, the ALL files will be stored in the shlib10 directory (such as .usr/local/wp8/shlib10) and PRS files will be stored in the directory /root/.wprc (the directory that contains all your personal settings).

4. Select the printer(s) you want to add, then click OK.

5. If you are creating a new printer driver, the Create Printer dialog box will appear (see Figure 10-15). You can specify a different Printer Filename, then click OK, or simply click OK to confirm the filename.

Figure 10-14: Adding a printer

Figure 10-15: Making a printer available in WordPerfect

Printing to a File

In some cases, you may want to print a document to a file. If your document already is a file, why would you want to print it to another file? Here's the situation. The printer you want to use is not connected to your system or network, or your document won't be printed by the application you're using.

Say that you want to send the newsletter you created to a service bureau to print on their color PostScript printer. Set up and select the PostScript printer (you just need the printer driver, not the printer itself), print to a file on your hard drive or removable storage, then send the file (physically or electronically) to the service bureau.

To print to a file:

1. Click File ➪ Print ➪ Select, then select the destination printer from the list.

2. Click Printer Create/Edit, then click Setup.

3. Click Destination, then select Disk.

4. Type a filename and print the document (see Figure 10-16).

To resume printing to your printer rather than to a file, select the printer and reset the destination to its original setting.

The file to which you print is no longer a WordPerfect document. Instead, the file is in a printer format that can be fed to the printer on the receiving end.

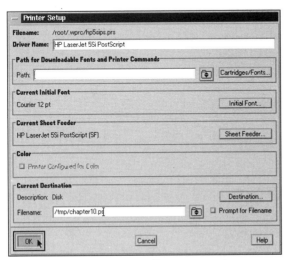

Figure 10-16: Printing to a file

For More Information . . .

On	*See*
Setting up printers	Linux manual
Publishing to HTML	Chapter 11
Customizing WordPerfect pages	Chapter 15
Numbering pages	Chapter 14
Printing from the Open dialog box	Chapter 7
Using Make It Fit	Chapter 4
Creating mailing lists and form letters	Chapter 28
Creating a custom page definition	Chapter 15

✦   ✦   ✦

Writing and Publishing for the Web

Web writing is here to stay. If you need to publish to the Web, WordPerfect has unsurpassed facilities for creating Web documents. This chapter explores the software's Web options.

Understanding Web Terms

Before you plunge into Web writing, take a quick look at Table 11-1, which has some of the Web terms you encounter along the way.

Table 11-1	
Essential Web Terms	
Term	**Description**
Client	Program on a network (such as Netscape Navigator) that makes requests to the server program on another computer (such as a Web server).
Flame	Incendiary newsgroup posting that provides more heat than light. Self-extinguishing when ignored.
Home page	First page that you come to when you launch your browser or visit a Web site.
HTML	Codes or "tags" for text, titles, formatting, backgrounds, graphics, links, and other Web page features.

Continued

Table 11-1 *(continued)*

Term	Description
Hypertext	A special type of database system in which text, pictures, and other objects can be linked creatively, so that information can be accessed through a variety of non-sequential paths.
Internet	A global "network of networks" connecting millions of computers and hundreds of millions of users who exchange data, mail, news and opinions. The operators of each independent host computer decide which Internet services to use and which local services to provide to the global Internet. The terms "Web" and "Internet" are often used interchangeably, though there are technical distinctions between the two.
Intranet	In-house network in which members of an organization publish information and interact with each other much as they do on the global Internet. While intranet users can get out to the Internet, access from the Internet to the intranet is usually restricted by a security firewall to prevent unauthorized access.
Internet Service Provider (ISP)	Commercial vendor or organization that hosts Web sites and provides dial-up access to the Internet. They also serve large companies by providing a direct connection from the company's networks to the Internet.
Newsgroup	Online discussion group or forum, in which you can view and post messages.
Online service	Commercial vendor (such as America Online) that provides individuals with both Internet access and other online services, such as user "chat" rooms, accessible only by subscribers.
Portal	Web site, such as Yahoo, which serves as a "door" to diverse services and information. A portal provides links to many other Web pages, many of which are commercial sponsors.
Search engine	Program that searches for Web documents or newsgroup postings containing specified keywords or text.
Spam	Junk e-mail or newsgroup postings. Whatever you do, don't respond to it! If you ask to be "removed" from a mailing list, you'll just confirm that your address is valid and that you read their messages.
Surfing	Going out into the Internet in search of information, using a browser or search engine.
Thread	Related messages in a newsgroup.
URL	Uniform Resource Locator (or Web address). The Internet equivalent of a pathname to contact a site or locate a file.
Web browsing	Exploring the Web with browser software (such as Netscape Navigator or Microsoft Internet Explorer).

Term	Description
Web	The World Wide Web. The Web is a collection of documents (called "pages") located on computers all over the world. You view a Web page by typing its URL or clicking a hypertext link on a page.
Web, or Internet, publisher	Tools for creating HTML documents.
Web editor	Editing screen of your Internet publisher.
Web link	A hyperlink attached to highlighted words or an image that contains the URL (address) of a Web document. Click the links to jump from page to page on the Internet.
Web pages	Scrollable hypertext documents with HTML formatting codes that you see on the Web.
Web site	A collection of related Web pages. Corel's Web site, for example, has many pages attached to it.
Web server	Computer where Web sites are stored. One service provider (such as a university) can support many sites on their Web server, but you can set up a Web site on a personal computer as well (see Chapter 17).
Webcasting	Web broadcasting. Delivers the latest information (or junk news and commercials) to your desktop automatically.

What's a Web Document?

A Web document is written in HTML, and can be viewed in Netscape Navigator (the browser that comes with most Linux distributions), other browsers across the Internet, or within your company's intranetwork (or intranet).

So What, Exactly, Is HTML?

HTML, or HyperText Markup Language, is a collection of styles, indicated by tags, to enhance the appearance of plain (ASCII) text documents when viewed in a Web browser. For example, to display the previous heading, "So What, Exactly, Is HTML?" on the Web, you write something like the following in HTML:

```
<H2><STRONG><FONT FACE="Arial">So What, Exactly, Is
HTML?</FONT></STRONG></H2>
```

Notice how the text is surrounded by the following three pairs of on/off tags to "mark up" its format and appearance:

✦ <H2> and </H2> to apply the Heading 2 style

✦ <STRONG> and </STRONG> to put it in boldface

✦ <FONT FACE="Arial"> and </FONT> to change the font

Wait a second . . . doesn't this look familiar? Change the paragraph codes to hard returns, "strong" to "bold," "H2" to "very large," and you'll see that HTML tags are essentially the same as the WordPerfect markups in Reveal Codes.

If you're getting the idea that WordPerfect is also a markup language, you have the right idea. And, just as you don't have to type or see the codes in WordPerfect, you don't have to type HTML tags in WordPerfect's Web writing facilities.

Why Reinvent the Wheel?

So, why not use WordPerfect in the first place, instead of bothering with HTML? The reason: A uniform, basic format was required for the viewing of scientific documents on the Internet that displayed roughly the same way on any machine, using any output device, from monitors to Braille readers. The resulting specification of tags described a basic document, employing just a few fonts and styles, that could link to other documents on the Web.

What HTML Doesn't Do

Because HTML documents are designed to scroll on the screen and jump to other pages via links, they don't have page numbers, margins, headers, footers, or watermarks. Likewise, the documents don't contain fill, footnotes, or vertical lines.

HTML is (and was meant to be) much less sophisticated than WordPerfect, precisely because its purpose was to transmit ideas, not to publish complex formats. That's also why you get the "You may lose some formatting permanently!" warning when switching from Page view to Web Page view in WordPerfect.

Because HTML documents are plain text files, you cannot embed graphics, sound, and other multimedia elements in them, as with a WordPerfect document. These objects must be stored separately and referenced by HTML tags.

Multimedia Additions to HTML

Well, that was the idea . . . before the Web's explosive growth and commercialization started pushing HTML to incorporate textured backgrounds, tables, flashing text, sound clips, and other multimedia frills and thrills.

When you visit some Web sites, you see rotating 3-D graphics, video, and other advanced features. These are not HTML code, but behind-the-scenes programs (or applets) created in Java, Shockwave, and other languages that can be transferred over the Internet. (The HTML code simply defines how applets are activated.) You may have to download and install (often free) plug-ins (or extensions) to Netscape Navigator to experience various animation, audio, and video thrills.

Tip For the latest information on the evolving HTML standards, visit the home page of the World Wide Web Consortium at `http://www.w3.org`. QwkScreen's Web site, `http://www.qwkscreen.com`, contains links to this and other Web publishing sources.

How Do You Create Web Pages?

WordPerfect comes with two Web-publishing options:

✦ WordPerfect provides a Web Page view, which lets you compose and edit HTML documents directly.

✦ You can publish a copy of your WordPerfect document to HTML.

Creating Web Documents in WordPerfect

To create a Web (HTML) document:

1. Open an existing document you want to publish to HTML, or open a new blank document.

2. Click the Web Page View button (View ➪ Web Page) to switch to the Web editing (Internet Publisher) environment. (You can also click File ➪ Internet Publisher ➪ Format as Web Document.)

3. Unless the document is blank, you receive a warning message that you can lose any formatting that isn't HTML-compatible. Check the option at the bottom if you don't want to see the warning the next time you choose Web View (see Figure 11-1). (You may want to save your document under a different name before switching to Web View.)

4. Upon entering the Web editor (see Figure 11-2), create and format text, tables, hyperlinks, graphics, and so forth, much as you would in a normal document.

5. Click the View in Web Browser button (View ➪ View in Web Browser) to see how the page will look in your browser.

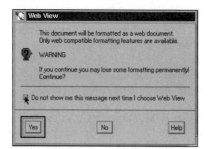

Figure 11-1: Disabling the Web View warning

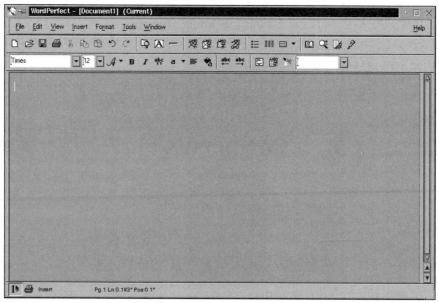

Figure 11-2: Web editing (Internet Publisher) environment, with slate-colored background and custom tools

6. Click the Publish to HTML button (File ⇨ Internet Publisher ⇨ Publish to HTML), then specify the filename and location to which you're publishing (see Figure 11-3).

WordPerfect saves a copy of the Web document in HTML format with a .HTM extension. Any graphics, sound clips, or Java applets are stored in a subdirectory with the document's name and a .HTG extension.

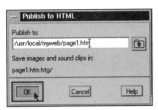

Figure 11-3: Specifying the HTML filename

Tip   You can also publish to HTML by clicking File ➪ Send to ➪ HTML.

Specifying Names for Web Documents

Give careful consideration to how you name your Web documents. In particular, find out from your Web administrator what naming conventions you should follow. If you're putting up a new site, your home page (the page where folks land when they pay a visit) may require a specific name (such as `index.html` or `welcome.html`).

Note that Web pages can have either of two extensions: .HTM or .HTML. You may have to use the full .HTML extension if your page is going up on a UNIX (or Linux) server, particularly for your home page. Again, check with your Web administrator.

Specifying Locations for Documents and Graphics

While browsing the Web, you've probably come across plenty of "Location Not Found" messages and little icons indicating missing graphics. You don't want that to happen with your Web pages. In WordPerfect for Linux, you don't have worry about file locations for graphics, sound clips, Java applets, and so forth. WordPerfect links and stores all objects automatically in a directory that has the same name as the document, but adds a .HTG file extension.

Working in the Web Editor

When you work in the Web editor, you'll notice that your menus and dialog boxes are restricted to the HTML possibilities, not the full set of WordPerfect features. The Format menu, for example, has just a few choices, compared to the vast array of features available when you create a normal WordPerfect document. You'll also discover a few features that aren't normally available (such as creating a Web form or Java applet).

Click Format ⇨ Font for an example of what's different in HTML (see Figure 11-4). You'll notice that there are fewer options. All the available options have their HTML equivalents.

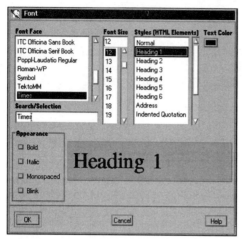

Figure 11-4: You'll find different options when changing the font properties

You'll be happy to see that Spell-As-You-Go and other proofreading tools are still available. Text is text, no matter where you put it.

Giving Your Web Page a Title

To title your Web document — the title is the text that displays in the title bar of the Web browser — click the Web Properties button on the toolbar, then click Custom Title and type the title you want. If you don't specify a title, the first occurrence of the highest-level heading in your document appears instead.

Applying Web Styles

When formatting HTML text for titles, headings, bulleted lists, and so forth, you have only 12 paragraph styles from which to choose. These styles fall into two categories:

✦ Styles that change text size, appearance, or format

✦ Styles for creating outlines and lists

Click the Web Style button on the toolbar (Format ⇨ Font) to apply the various styles (see Figure 11-5), described in Table 11-2.

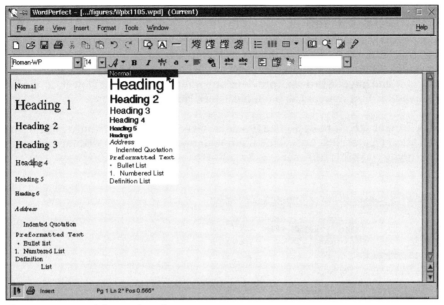

Figure 11-5: Applying Web styles

Table 11-2	
Web Document Styles	
Style	***Description***
Heading 1	Largest heading
Heading 2–6	Headings of decreasing importance, marked for the Table of Contents
Address	Italic text
Indented Quotation	Adjusts the margins for indented quotes (has a special outline type)
Preformatted Text	Monospaced font
Bullet List	Creates a bulleted list (contains paragraph numbers and an outline code set to Bullets)
Numbered List	Creates a numbered list (contains paragraph numbers and an outline code set to Numbers)
Definition List	Creates a list of definitions (contains an outline code set to Definitions)

Changing Fonts

Because HTML documents need to display on every computer and monitor, there's generally little you can do with fonts in HTML. Even font colors don't show up in all browsers. As for the typeface, it's best to stick to basics. A fancy headline font may look just fine in your browser preview, but when most people view it on the Web, the headline font appears as plain old Times New Roman.

Click Format ➪ Font to apply the typeface, size, color, and attributes you want to Web text (Figure 11-6). Just remember, your special font may display as a standard font in your visitor's browser.

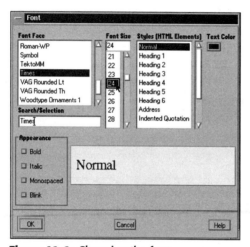

Figure 11-6: Changing the font

Creating a Home Page

Now for some fun. In the following sections, you create the home page shown in Figure 11-7.

Note that the Table of Contents in Figure 11-7 has underlined hyperlinks to other sections. Start by creating the sections, then create the Table of Contents at the top.

Beginning from a blank screen, first create a "Web Styles" section:

1. In the Web view, type **Web Styles**, then click the Web Styles button on the toolbar and apply the Heading 2 style to the text.

2. Click the Web Horizontal Line button (Insert ➪ Horizontal Line) to underline your heading.

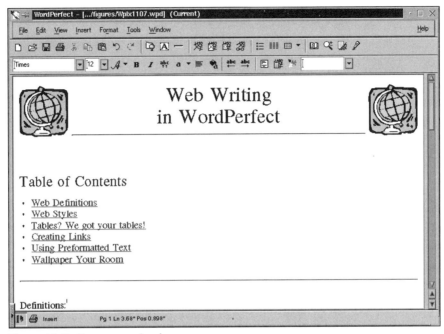

Figure 11-7: Your upcoming home page

3. Type the text underneath the heading, as in Figure 11-5, and apply the various Web styles to create a gallery of samples.

Tip To change the length, thickness, or justification of a horizontal line, right-click the line and click Edit Horizontal Line.

Previewing Your Creations

The Web editor provides a good representation of how your page will appear in a browser, but it's still a WordPerfect document, not an HTML document.

To see how your creation really looks, click the View in Web Browser button on the toolbar (View ➪ View in Web Browser). This sequence creates a temporary HTML copy of the document and launches your default browser (typically Netscape Navigator) for display. (To see your actual HTML code in the browser, click View ➪ Page Source.)

When you're finished admiring your work, exit Navigator and return to the Web editor. Better yet, leave Navigator up and switch back to WordPerfect.

Tip If WordPerfect does not start your browser, check the browser settings. Click File ➪ Internet Publisher ➪ Browser Preferences to adjust the current settings.

Using Justification and Line Breaks

Are you ready to create the fancy stuff at the top of the home page? Go to the beginning of your document. Press Enter a few times if you need to make some room at the top.

1. Click the Justification button on the property bar and center the title line.

2. Type **Web Writing**, then click Insert ➪ Line Break. The line break takes you to the next line without ending the paragraph, so the two lines of your title don't get separated.

3. Type **in WordPerfect** and press Enter.

4. Click the Justification button and then click Left.

5. Select the title and apply the Heading 1 style.

Adding Graphics

You add graphics to Web documents much as you do in WordPerfect (see Chapter 9, "Working with Graphics"). There are fewer options in HTML documents, of course. You can anchor to the character or paragraph, but not the page. You can position left, right, or center within the paragraph. To add graphics to your page as shown in Figure 11-7:

1. Click the Insert ClipArt button (Insert ➪ Graphics ➪ From File), then select the image you want to add to your Web page.

2. Right-click the graphic, click Position, then choose between a paragraph anchor and a character anchor. In this case, select the paragraph anchor.

3. Drag the graphic to the upper-left corner, then drag a corner handle to adjust it to a reasonable size.

4. Use copy and paste to add a copy of the image to the upper-right corner.

5. Click the end of your title and insert a horizontal line.

When you preview or publish your Web pages, you get a "Conversion In Progress" message for each graphic that WordPerfect converts to either the GIF (default) or JPEG format for viewing on the Web.

Adding Symbols

For the most part, don't use Ctrl+W symbols in your Web documents. Other than the trademark and copyright symbols, accented characters, various length dashes, and SmartQuotes, symbols aren't supported by HTML.

Creating Bulleted Lists

Next, create the bulleted list for your table of contents:

1. Select the Heading 3 style, then type **Table of Contents** and press Enter.

2. Click the Web Bullets button on the toolbar (Insert ➪ Bullets & Numbering), click OK, type **Web Definitions**, press Enter, type **Web Styles,** and press Enter again.

3. Add more bulleted entries for the Table of Contents, as shown in Figure 11-7. (Include one for "Wallpaper Your Room," which will be the topic that your secondary Web page will link to.)

4. Press Enter ➪ Backspace to end the list.

If you click Insert ➪ Bullets & Numbering, you see that there are only three bulleted list options in the Web editor:

✦ *Bulleted*, as shown in Figure 11-8. (The actual appearance of bullets is determined by the browser.)

✦ *Numbered*, to create a list of items with standard Arabic numbers.

✦ *Definition*, employing the hanging indent paragraph style, to present an unnumbered list of items with explanations on the right.

Figure 11-8: Bullets and numbering selections in the Web editor

Because the lists in the Web editor are outline styles, you can press Tab or Shift+Tab to change the levels, just as you change outline levels in an ordinary WordPerfect document.

To end a definition list, press Enter ➪ Backspace in Reveal Codes, or select the Normal style from the property bar.

Formatting with Tables

To create a table in the Web editor, click Insert ➪ Table for all the options, or click and drag on the toolbar as you do normally in WordPerfect.

You can insert graphics and other items in HTML tables just as you do in WordPerfect tables.

HTML purists may not approve, but tables sometimes can be a handy way to get around Web formatting limitations when arranging text and graphics on your Web page.

Most of the table editing conveniences found in WordPerfect are still available. You can join cells, change the layout of cells, and perform other operations described in Chapter 16, "Formatting with Columns and Tables." Because you're still in WordPerfect, you can specify numeric formats, define formulas, lock cells, and perform calculations.

Add a Web table example to your Web document (such as the table shown in Figure 11-9).

Figure 11-9: Web table example

Formatting with Columns

To create columns in the Web editor, click the Columns button on the toolbar or click Format ➪ Columns ➪ Format (see Figure 11-10). You can specify the number of columns, their total width in percent or pixels, and the number of pixels between columns.

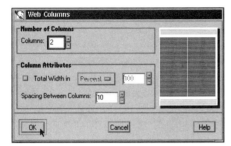

Figure 11-10: Creating Web columns

Caution   Columns are not yet a Web standard, so they are likely to get messed up in non-Netscape browsers. Consider using tables to simulate columns instead.

Adding Preformatted and Monospaced Text

The text in your Web document may not display identically after you convert it to HTML and view it in your Web browser. The browser puts as many characters as possible on a line, based on the font style and screen resolution of each user's display. So line breaks and spacing may differ from browser to browser.

If you want everyone's browser to show the spaces and line breaks of the original (for example, to display program code or figures in an annual report), use the preformatted style:

1. Place the insertion point where you want to begin typing preformatted text (or select the text you want to preformat).

2. Select the Preformatted Text style from the property bar and type your text.

3. Press Enter and select the Normal style (Format ➪ Font ➪ Normal) to resume normal text.

Preformatted text uses a monospaced Courier font, where each character takes up the same amount of space. You can also click the Monospaced button on the property bar to apply the Courier font. What's the difference? Unlike preformatted text, the monospaced text format can vary from browser to browser, because each browser fits as many characters as possible on a line before wrapping to the next line.

Wallpapering Your Room

Ensuring consistent line breaks may be a boring subject, but it couldn't be avoided. Back to the fun stuff. In this section, you create a colorful secondary page and, after that, you link it together with the home page (table of contents) you created. You'll be amazed at how easy it is to exhibit your artistry.

Start by creating a new Web document, such as the document shown in Figure 11-11, with your own title, text, table, and graphics.

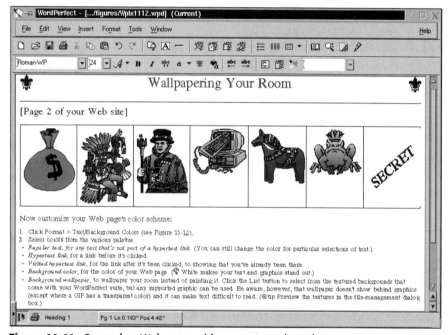

Figure 11-11: Secondary Web page with a custom color scheme

Now, customize your Web page's color scheme:

1. Click Format ⇨ Text/Background Colors (see Figure 11-12).

2. Select colors from the various palettes:

- Regular Text, for any text that's not part of a hypertext link. (You still can change the color for particular sections of text.)

- Hypertext Link, for a link before it's clicked.

- Visited Hypertext Link, for the link after it's been clicked, to show that you've already been there.

Figure 11-12: Customizing your Web page's color scheme

- Active Hypertext Link, for the color that flashes when you click the link.
- Background Color, for the color of your Web page. (White makes your text and graphics stand out.)
- Background Wallpaper, to wallpaper your room instead of painting it (put a graphic in the background, instead of just a color). Click the List button to select from any supported graphic. Be aware, however, that wallpaper doesn't show behind graphics (except where a GIF has a transparent color) and can make text difficult to read.

Adding Hyperlinks

You're now in the final stages of your Web publishing enterprise. You have a home page and a secondary page, both in WordPerfect format. It's time to add some hyperlinks.

Your hyperlinks (hypertext links) let the viewer jump to another location in the current document, to a document on your computer or network, or to a Web page anywhere in the world. Just click the link and off you go! That's what the Web is all about.

You have three ways to display a link (see Figure 11-13):

✦ As underlined, colored text

✦ As a text button

✦ As any graphic turned into a button

You can use the Hyperlink property bar (shown in Figure 11-13) to perform the operations described in Table 11-3.

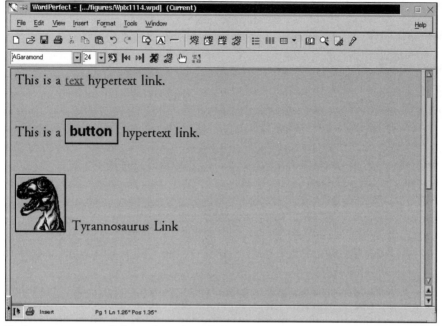

Figure 11-13: Hyperlinks and the Hyperlink property bar

Table 11-3
Hyperlink Property Bar Buttons

Button	Lets You
Hyperlink Perform button	Jump from the link at the insertion point, even when hyperlinks aren't active.
Previous button	Go to the previous link in the document.
Next button	Go to the next link in the document.
Hyperlink Remove button	Remove the current link, leaving the text intact.
Hyperlink Edit button	Edit the properties of the current link.
Hyperlink Active button	Activate or deactivate all hyperlinks.
Hyperlink Style button	Edit the style of text links (WordPerfect only, not for Web documents).

Creating links within a document

Return to your home page (the table of contents) in the Web editor to create its internal hyperlinks. The home page should have a bulleted list of topics.

First, create a bookmark for each place in the document to which you want to jump. Here's how:

1. Go to the top of your first location, such as the "Web Definitions" heading. (In a Web browser, unlike WordPerfect, the hypertext link positions at the top of the screen.)

2. Click the Web Hyperlink button in the toolbar ➪ Insert Bookmark (Tools ➪ Bookmark ➪ Create) and name the bookmark (Figure 11-14).

Figure 11-14: Creating a linked bookmark

3. Create additional bookmarks for the remaining links.

4. Select the text in the Table of Contents for the first link, click the Web Hyperlink button ➪ Create Link (Tools ➪ Hyperlink), then click Go to Bookmark and select the bookmark to which you want to link (Figure 11-15).

Figure 11-15: Selecting the linked bookmark

5. If you want to create a hyperlink button, check "Make text appear as a button."

6. Create links for the remaining items within the document.

For more on creating bookmarks, see Chapter 13, "Editing Techniques."

Linking to another page

Next, you create links between the home page and any secondary pages. To link to another page:

1. Select the text or graphic for the link to the secondary page.

2. Click Tools ➪ Hyperlink, then click Go to Other Document and specify the filename. Specify a filename extension of .HTM (or .HTML). (Leave out the path if you will be putting both pages in the same folder on the server.)

3. Specify a particular bookmark if you want to link to somewhere other than the top of the document. For WordPerfect documents, the list of bookmarks appears automatically.

Providing a way back

While Web browsers have return buttons to let you review the pages you've visited, you should place specific links from a secondary page back to the home page. A return button at the end of a document back to the top is also helpful.

Creating Web links

You may want to provide Web links to other interesting sites. To create Web links:

1. If you're online, go to the location to which you want to link and copy its URL.

2. Return to your WordPerfect document and select the text or graphic to use for the link.

3. Click Tools ➪ Hyperlink, then paste (or type) the full URL (such as http://www.corel.com) in the Go to Other Document box.

4. Click OK, then test the link.

Tip

Web links work in any WordPerfect document—not just documents published to HTML.

Adding e-mail links

To create an e-mail link (so that visitors can leave a message for you or another person):

1. Select the text or graphic to use for the link.

2. Click Tools ➪ Hyperlink.

3. In the Document box, type **mailto:**, followed by (without any spaces) the e-mail address (for example, "mailto:JDoe@anywhere.net").

Links showing Web or e-mail addresses are usually displayed in italics. Use the Address style for this formatting. (If you don't want the whole paragraph to be in italics, use the italic font attribute instead of the Address style.)

Inserting QuickLinks as you type

When you type text beginning with "www", "ftp", "http", or "mailto", WordPerfect's QuickLinks feature turns your text into a hyperlink automatically.

You can also have any other word or phrase turn into a hyperlink automatically, as follows:

1. Click Tools ⇨ QuickCorrect ⇨ QuickLinks.

2. Type the link word or phrase and the link location (see Figure 11-16).

3. To turn QuickLinks on (or off), check "Format words as hyperlinks when you type them."

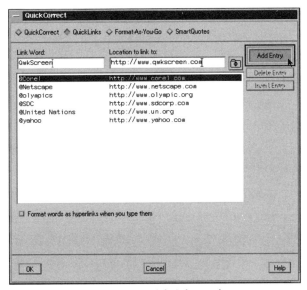

Figure 11-16: Defining a QuickLink word

Your QuickLink entry is given the "@" prefix automatically to distinguish it from an actual name. The prefix is removed from your text as it converts to a link.

Tip When QuickLinks is off, you can select an entry in the QuickLink dialog box and click Insert Entry to create a link.

Editing a hyperlink's properties

To edit a hyperlink's properties, position the insertion point on the link with the arrow keys (don't click) and click the Hyperlink Edit button on the toolbar. (You can also right-click the link and click Edit Hyperlink.)

Editing a hyperlink's text

To edit a hyperlink's text, position the insertion point on the link (don't click) and edit the text.

Deactivating a hyperlink

To deactivate a text hyperlink (without deleting the text), position the insertion point on the link (don't click) and click the Hyperlink Remove button.

You can also go into Reveal Codes and delete one of the hypertext codes.

Roll the Press!

Once your Web pages are finished, just publish them to HTML using the instructions in the preceding "Creating Web Documents in WordPerfect" section.

Your Web site is now complete. Post your site with the help of your site supervisor or network administrator, and you're in business!

For More Information . . .

On	*See*
Adding clip art and pictures	Chapter 9
Formatting and editing tables	Chapter 16
Inserting bookmarks	Chapter 13

✦   ✦   ✦

Writing with
WordPerfect

Writer's Lib

As a crafter of words, you're only as good as your tools. And while the WordPerfect writing tools work great out of the box, this chapter shows you how to add more power to the writing process.

Writing is work. No program can think for you, and there's no substitute for your own eye and ear for language. However, WordPerfect's superlative writing tools can speed up your work and deliver a lively document free from spelling and grammar mistakes. You'll be amazed at how freely your thoughts flow once the program is looking after the mechanics. The great part, as you saw in Chapter 2, "Writing a Letter," is that basic error correction is now fully automatic with:

+ Spell-As-You-Go

+ Grammar-As-You Go

+ Prompt-As-You Go

+ QuickCorrect

+ Automatic typo correction

You also have Formatting-As-You-Go (Chapter 4, "Becoming an Instant WordPerfect Expert") for automatic sentence corrections, instant bullets, and other conveniences.

This chapter covers QuickCorrect tricks in more detail.

Using Spell Checker

Spell checking is the most indispensable writing tool. It's hard not to love Spell-As-You-Go, which even catches duplicate words as you type. Spell Checker enables you to correct your whole document at once, customize your replacement lists, and, in moments of moral laxity, cheat on a crossword puzzle.

✦ ✦ ✦ ✦

In This Chapter

Spell-check your document

Use QuickCorrect to make your typing fly

Find a better word with the Thesaurus

Proofread your documents

Use abbreviations to insert text

Write in other languages

✦ ✦ ✦ ✦

Understanding Word Lists

Spell Checker and Grammatik (including their Spell-As-You-Go and Grammar-As-You-Go tools) match the words in your document against three types of word lists:

✦ *Main dictionaries* (word lists) that come with the program. You can chain as many as ten compatible dictionaries. (See "Adding and removing dictionaries" later in this chapter.)

✦ *Supplementary dictionaries* (user word lists) containing your personal skip and replacement words. A default user word list (containing QuickCorrect entries) comes with the program. You can add to that list, or create and chain additional lists.

✦ *Document dictionaries* (built-in word lists) in which you can place skip and replacement words just for that document.

Lists are searched in reverse order to check a word (from document to personal to main).

Spell-As-You-Go can add skip words to the default user list.

Checking Your Spelling

To spell-check text:

1. Click the Spell button on the toolbar. (You can also click Tools ➪ Spell Check, or right-click a WordPerfect document and click Spell Check.)

   Spell Checker normally checks your entire document (including headers, footers, footnotes, and endnotes) or a text selection. When it stops at a word, you can click the Check list to select other elements to check, such as the current page.

2. When Spell Checker finds a word it doesn't recognize (see Figure 12-1), click one of the following:

   • *Replace* to swap the word in your document with the "Replace with" word. You can edit the suggestion, or click another word in the Suggestions list.

Tip   If Spell Checker can't find a replacement suggestion, clear the "Replace with" box and start typing the misspelled word from the beginning. You'll often find the word after the first few letters.

   • *Skip Once* to remove the marking and keep your spelling of the word.

   • *Skip Always* to add the word to the document list so it's no longer flagged in this document.

- *Add* to put the flagged word in the user word list, so it will be skipped in all your documents.
- *Suggest* to display more replacement suggestions.
- *Resume* to go back to checking your spelling (if you've clicked outside of the Spell Checker to edit your text).

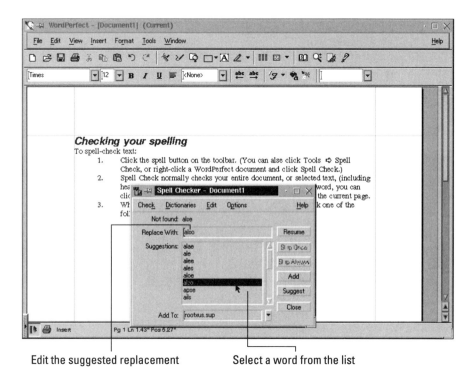

Edit the suggested replacement   Select a word from the list

Figure 12-1: Checking your spelling

Checking Part of Your Document

Click Tools ➪ Spell Check ➪ Check, and click the portion of the document to check, such as the current paragraph or page. Better yet, try either of these tricks before you start the spell check:

✦ Select a portion of your document to check.

✦ Place the insertion point on a misspelled word to check from the insertion point forward.

Selecting Spell Check Options

To select spell check options, click the Spelling button (Tools ➪ Spell Check), then click the Options menu (see Figure 12-2) and check or uncheck the checking and notification options described in Table 12-1.

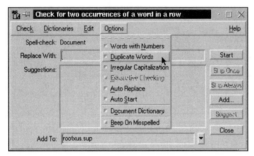

Figure 12-2: Selecting Spell Check options

Table 12-1	
Spell Checker Options	
Option	**_Lets You_**
Words With Numbers	Flag certain words with numbers as possible errors ("4c" but not "32nd").
Duplicate Words	Prompt for deletion of the second occurrence of duplicate words (such as "of of").
Irregular Capitalization	Flag words with irregular capitalization, such as "JULY" and "helP" as possible errors. "GOOD" is okay.
Exhaustive Checking	Expand the number of possible replacement selections in certain languages. (This option is disabled in English and other languages where it doesn't apply.)
Auto Replace	Swap words automatically that have entries in the user word list with replacement words from the list.
Auto Start	Start spell-checking immediately when you select Spell Check. (You can still change options as soon as you stop at a misspelled word.)
Beep on Misspelled	Sound a warning at each word not found.

Adding and Removing Dictionaries

As noted earlier, you can check your spelling and grammar against as many as ten main dictionaries (word lists). You might want to have Spell Check chain two or more main dictionaries if, for example, your document contains both English and Spanish words, or it includes specialized medical or legal terms.

The lists are searched in the order you specify, and the chain must begin with the main dictionary (.LEX file) for the language you're using, such as wpus.lex for US English.

You can also chain as many as ten supplementary dictionaries (user word lists) for various specialized uses or projects. These supplementary dictionaries are used by QuickCorrect, Spell Check, and Grammatik. The chain begins with the default supplementary dictionary, which is rootus.sup for US English.

To add, remove, or select a list in the main or supplementary dictionary search order:

1. Click Tools ⇨ Spell Check, then click the Dictionary menu.

2. Click Main to add or remove main dictionaries in other languages or specialties.

3. Click User Word Lists to create, select, and edit custom user word lists. (Click the first blank line, or the line below where you want the list to appear in the search order.)

Note that removing a dictionary from the search order does not delete the dictionary from your hard drive.

Using Spell Check to Look Up a Word

You can look up words by typing in the Spell Check's "Replace with" box. The more letters you type, the shorter the list becomes. When you type "this," for example, you are left with "this," "thistle," "thistledown," "thistles," and "thistly."

You can use the (?) and (*) wildcards in your lookup to substitute a single character or any number of characters, respectively.

Speed Typing with QuickCorrect

How do you describe QuickCorrect? It's fast. It's accurate. It's automatic. It's habit-forming.

Fixing Typos on the Fly

Click Tools ➪ QuickCorrect in WordPerfect, and you'll see a "Correct other mistyped words when possible" option (see Figure 12-3). Check this feature to fix most typographical errors (typos) automatically where the word is five characters or more and lowercase, and there's only one replacement word close to what you typed.

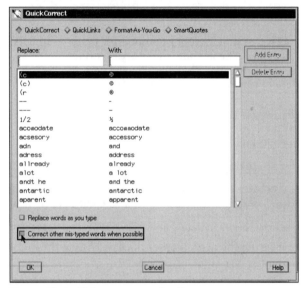

Figure 12-3: Fixing typos on the fly

This feature is turned on by default, which may be confusing because (1) it's so quick and automatic that most users won't know what's happening, and (2) it can, on occasion, make a fix that you hadn't intended. But unless you use lots of scientific, technical, or foreign words that aren't in the dictionary, you'll love the way QuickCorrect fixes mistakes as fast as you make them.

Replacing Words As You Type

QuickCorrect keeps an extensive list of commonly mistyped words (such as "antarctic" and "aparent") that it fixes on the fly. To speed your typing, you can also create abbreviations for words you use often (such as "cl" for "Corel"). Just check the "Replace words as you type" option to correct or expand your entries automatically.

QuickCorrect changes "adn" to "and" the moment you press the spacebar, Enter, Tab, or Indent. Your entry is replaced even if it has quotation marks, an apostrophe, or punctuation attached. For example, if you have a "cl" entry for "Corel," "cl's" followed by a space expands to "Corel's".

Tip If QuickCorrect fixes something that you want to let stand (such as switching a lowercase "i" in quotation marks to "I"), you don't have to turn off QuickCorrect to put it back. Type another word or two, go back and change the text, then slip away by using the arrow key.

Creating QuickCorrect Entries

QuickCorrect entries are a snap to create. If you find yourself repeating a particular typing mistake (such as "comming" instead of "coming"), Spell-As-You-Go can usually create the entry for you. If you find yourself typing a long word or phrase over and over, create a QuickCorrect abbreviation (such as "ilu" for "I love you"). Once you add a few personal entries to the QuickCorrect list, you'll be amazed at the efficiency gained from QuickCorrect.

To add a QuickCorrect entry:

1. Click Tools ➪ QuickCorrect.

2. Type your mistake or abbreviation in the Replace box, then type the replacement word or phrase in the With box (see Figure 12-4).

3. Click Add Entry.

To delete a QuickCorrect entry, type or click the entry, then click Delete Entry. To revise an entry, type or click the entry, type your revision in the With box, then click Replace Entry.

Caution Don't type an actual word in the Replace box. If you set up an abbreviation to replace "win" with "Windows," for example, you may end up typing "I hope you Windows the prize." You could use "wi" or "wn" for the abbreviation instead. Use your judgment when it comes to uncommon words (such as replacing "cant" with "can't").

You can't create multiple QuickCorrect entries for different cases (such as "dt," "Dt," and "DT" for different forms of "document"). However, a single "dt" (for "document") expands in various ways, depending on how you type it:

Typing	Expands to
dt or dT	document
Dt	Document
DT	DOCUMENT

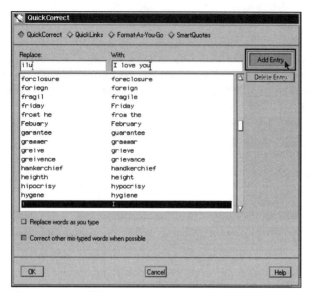

Figure 12-4: Adding a QuickCorrect entry

Note that the case sensitivity for the replacement entries extends from lowercase to uppercase, not the reverse. If you create a "DT" entry for "DOCUMENT," for example, you'll still get "DOCUMENT" when you type "dt."

If you use a term in both its abbreviated (WP) and expanded (WordPerfect) forms, use a variation of the abbreviation for your expanded entry ("ww" for WordPerfect).

You can create variations of QuickCorrect entries to cover plural, possessive, or other forms. For example, you can use "dts" for "documents," "dtg" for "documenting," and "wws" for "WordPerfect's." Frequently used contractions are excellent candidates. Use "dont" for "don't," "im" for "I'm," and so forth. Why bother with the Shift key? Set up capitalized entries for names you type, such as "lorraine" for "Lorraine" and "becky" for "Becky".

Press Ctrl+W to use any special character or symbol in the With box. For example, you can replace "ra" with ⇨ automatically or put the accents on names and words such as "René" and "cliché."

And try this: replace two periods (..) with one (.) for automatic correction in case you type two periods at the end of a sentence accidentally.

Finding a Better Word

If you're looking for a better word, look no further than WordPerfect's Thesaurus.

Looking Up a Word in the Thesaurus

To select a replacement (synonym) for a word, click the word, then click the Prompt-As-You-Go list on the property bar to select the word you want. For an in-depth search of synonyms, click on the word, then click Tools ➪ Thesaurus. From the list of replacement words (see Figure 12-5), you can:

✦ Click any word in the list to display its synonyms.

✦ Type any word in the "Word" box, then click Look Up to find its synonyms.

✦ Click a replacement for your original word, then click Replace.

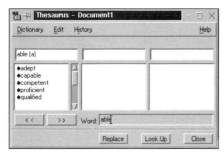

Figure 12-5: Looking for a better word in the Thesaurus

For example, if you don't like any of the replacements offered for "proficient," you can double-click "competent" or any other word to display a secondary list. You may scroll this list and find the word "skilled" more to your liking. Click "skilled" (see Figure 12-6), then click Replace to swap it for "proficient."

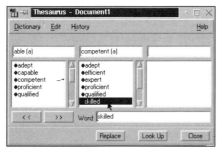

Figure 12-6: Selecting a replacement word from the next column

You can cascade as many lists as you want. Click the back "<<" and forward ">" scroll buttons when you have more than three lists.

Checking Your Grammar

While Grammatik's Grammar-As-You-Go does a great job of catching many common errors of usage and punctuation, proofreading your work with a separate run of Grammatik can perform a more thorough check of grammar, usage, and style. It can also find word roots, examine sentence parts, and check sentence and paragraph construction.

Proofreading a Document

To proofread a document:

1. Click Tools ➪ Grammatik.

2. For each problem encountered (see Figure 12-7), do one of the following:

   - Click a replacement suggestion and click Replace.

   - Click your text to edit it directly, then click Resume to continue.

   - Click Skip to tell Grammatik you don't want to change the highlighted text, or Ignore Word or Ignore Phrase to ignore this word or phrase for the rest of the session.

   - Click Add to put the flagged word in the user list, so it will be skipped in all your documents.

   - Click Next Sentence to continue with the next sentence.

   - Uncheck the rule class to ignore all errors associated with the rule for the rest of the session.

To get a detailed explanation of a flagged problem (including helpful examples), click the name of the error rule class displayed. You can also click any underlined hypertext term in Grammatik's suggestion.

Grammatik normally checks your entire document or selected text. If you turn off the "Start Checking Immediately" option, you can also select To End of Document to check from the insertion point forward. You can also click and scroll your document during a session to change the current checking location.

Grammatik's pretty amazing, but it's not perfect. So don't be afraid to skip its advice.

Selecting Grammatik Options

While Grammatik works fine from the start, take a look at its options. Click Tools ➪ Grammatik ➪ Options, then check the options you want (see Figure 12-8), as described in Table 12-2.

Error class   Possible problem text

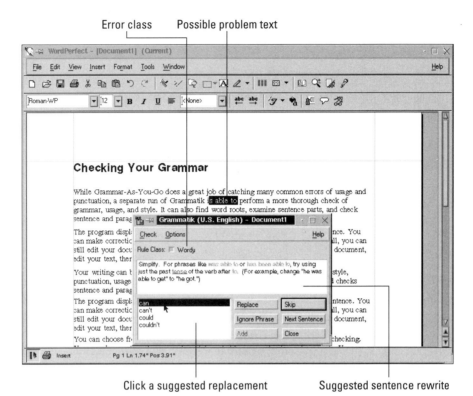

Click a suggested replacement   Suggested sentence rewrite

Figure 12-7: Proofreading a document with Grammatik

Figure 12-8: Selecting Grammatik options

Table 12-2
Grammatik Options

Option	Lets You
Writing Styles	Select and customize writing styles.
Checking Options	Enable or disable the following options:
	Check for Paragraph Errors: Check for a correct use of para-graphs.
	Ignore Periods within Words: Use periods in words.
	Suggest Spelling Replacements: Select a suggested replace-ment for a flagged word.
	Start Checking Immediately: Start proofreading immediately, from the top of your document, if you haven't selected text.
Restore Rule Classes	Reactivate rules you've suspended during this session.
Show Spelling Errors	Use Grammatik to find spelling errors.
Grammar, Mechanics and Style	Use Grammatik to check grammar, mechanics and style. This is the default setting.
Grammar and Mechanics	Use Grammatik to check grammar and mechanics only (not style). See the following section for more information about writing styles and Grammatik.
Statistics	Provide information about the kinds and numbers of words in your document.

Selecting a Writing Style

Grammatik flags various types of possible errors, depending on the writing style you select. Different styles set different thresholds (such as for the length of a long sentence) and turn on different style, grammar, and mechanical rule classes. Each writing style also has a formality level—informal, standard, or formal—according to how strictly it follows the rule classes of usage and diction.

Click Tools ➪ Grammatik ➪ Options ➪ Writing Styles, then select one of the predefined styles shown in Figure 12-9 and described in Table 12-3.

Figure 12-9: Selecting a writing style

Writing Style	Use it For
Table 12-3 **Writing Styles**	
Writing Style	_Use it For_
General	Business writing for a general audience
Advertising	Short, less formal documents
Business Letter	Formal business correspondence
Documentation	Manuals and instructions for a general audience
Fiction	Any writing that does not have to follow strict grammar rules
Journalism	Articles, magazines, newspapers
Memo	Less formal business correspondence
Proposal	Formal documents that follow strict grammar rules
Report	Formal business reports and academic papers
Technical	Technical and scientific reports

The formality level can be adjusted for each writing style. If none of the writing styles is appropriate, edit one of the three custom styles shown in Figure 12-10.

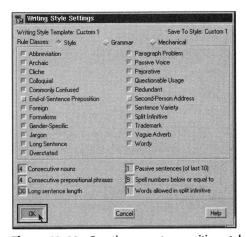

Figure 12-10: Creating a custom writing style

Writing in Other Languages

WordPerfect is an international program, with versions in a number of languages. Whatever your package language, you can still type documents in other languages by using the accents and punctuation marks particular to each. You can also use another language's conventions for date, time, thousands separator, footnote continuation, and so forth. You can even use a non-Roman alphabet (Greek, Cyrillic, Japanese, or Arabic) included in your character sets.

Using the Writing Tools for Another Language

If you're doing extensive writing in another language, use the available language modules (see Chapter 1, "Getting Up and Running") and use the tools for Spell Check, Thesaurus, hyphenation, and Grammatik for that particular language.

To change the language for the screen and keyboard, as well as for the writing tools, you must use the `-lang <language>` parameter when launching WordPerfect, as described in Chapter 1, "Getting Up and Running." For instance, start WordPerfect with the startup option `-lang NL` to start WordPerfect with the Dutch user interface and the Dutch writing tools enabled by default.

Tip   You can create your own foreign language keyboard definition by assigning characters you use frequently in that language to particular keys (see Chapter 27, "Customizing Toolbars and Keyboards").

Using Another Language in the Current Document

To specify another language to use for all or part of your current document (but not for the entire WordPerfect session):

1. Click where you want to start using the conventions for another language, or select the text to which you want to apply the conventions.

2. Click Tools ➪ Language ➪ Settings.

3. Select the language you want to use (see Figure 12-11).

4. To turn off the writing tools temporarily (for example, if you're writing a passage in a language for which you have no tools), check "Disable writing tools in this portion of the text."

Figure 12-11: Using another language in the current document

When you specify a language other than your package language, WordPerfect inserts a language code [Lang:*xx*] (or a pair of language codes around selected text) in your document, where *xx* represents the code for the language (such as GR for Greek).

For More Information . . .

On	See
Spell-As-You-Go	Chapter 2
Grammar-As-You-Go	Chapter 2
Prompt-As-You-Go	Chapter 2
Inserting QuickLinks	Chapter 11
Formatting-As-You-Go	Chapter 4
Inserting SmartQuotes	Chapter 4
Running macros	Chapter 29
Customizing keyboards	Chapter 27
Comparing documents	Chapter 13

✦　　✦　　✦

Editing Techniques

For its incredible range of features, WordPerfect's central function is to provide a better way to enter and edit text. This chapter shows how to use the chapter's text-selection tricks and turn on the power of Find and Replace. You'll also see how to insert bookmarks, make comparisons, and insert comments. As for hidden text — just wait and see!

Selecting (Blocking) Text

Selecting text is usually the first step in editing. To italicize the title of a book, for example, go back and select the title, then put your selected text in italics. In Chapter 2, "Writing a Letter," you saw the basic ways to select text by using the keyboard or dragging the mouse. This section contains a selection technique to suit every taste.

Mastering Mouse Selection Tricks

Normally, you select text with the mouse by dragging. Here are a few more mouse selection tricks:

To select	Do this
A word	Double-click the word.
A sentence	Triple-click the sentence, or click once in the left margin.
A paragraph	Quadruple-click the paragraph or double-click in the left margin.
From the insertion point to the shadow cursor (or I-beam)	Shift+click.

To select multiple words, hold down the mouse button on the second click, and drag the mouse to select word by word. Single or double-click in the left margin, then hold and drag to select sentence-by-sentence, or paragraph-by-paragraph.

Adjusting a Selection with the Mouse

To adjust the selection with a mouse, hold down the Shift key and do one of the following:

✦ Click to extend the selection to the I-beam.

✦ Drag to expand or shrink the selection.

You can adjust the selection in either direction.

Using the Edit Menu or QuickMenu to Select Text

Another way to select text at the insertion point is to click Edit ➪ Select, then click what you want to select. Here's an easier method: right-click in the left margin and select from the QuickMenu (see Figure 13-1).

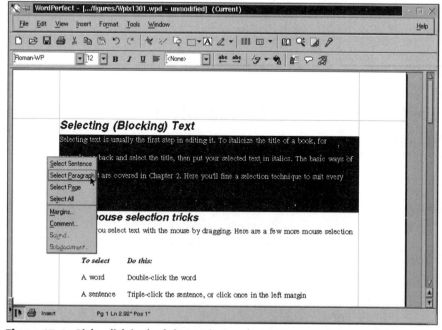

Figure 13-1: Right-click in the left margin to select text

Using Keystroke Selection Tricks

To select your entire document in a hurry (for example, to copy it to the Clipboard), press Ctrl+A (Ctrl+Shift+A with a DOS keyboard).

For lesser amounts of text, you can press F8 (F12 on a DOS keyboard) and use the arrow keys to select the text you want.

You can also press F8 (F12 for DOS) or hold Shift, and use one of the keystroke selection tricks shown in Table 13-1.

Table 13-1
Keystroke Selection Tricks

X/CUA Keystrokes	DOS Keystrokes	To Select (with Select On or While Holding Shift)
The left arrow/the right arrow	The left arrow/the right arrow	One character to the left/right
Ctrl+the left arrow/the right arrow	Ctrl+the left arrow/the right arrow	One word to the left/right
The up arrow/the down arrow	The up arrow/the down arrow	One line up or down
Ctrl+the up arrow/the down arrow	Ctrl+the up arrow/the down arrow	One paragraph up or down
End	End	To the end of the line
Home	Home, Home, the left arrow	To the beginning of the line
Home, Home	Home, Home, Home, the left arrow	To the beginning of the line (before codes)
PgUp	Home, the up arrow (not with Shift)	To the top of the screen
PgDn	Home, the down arrow	To the bottom of the screen
Alt+PgUp	PgUp	To the first line of the previous page
Alt+PgDn	PgDn	To the first line of the next page
Ctrl+Home	Home, Home, the up arrow	To the beginning of the document
Ctrl+Home, Ctrl+Home	Home, Home, Home, the up arrow	To the beginning of the document (before codes)
Ctrl+End	Home, Home, the down arrow	To the end of the document

Selecting from the insertion point to a character

To select from the insertion point to a character, turn on select by pressing F8 (F12 on a DOS keyboard), then type the character through which to select (it can be a lowercase or uppercase character, a space, or a tab). Pressing the key again extends the selection to the next occurrence of that character.

Tip   Press a period to extend your keyboard selection to next period, or press Enter to extend it to the hard return at end of the paragraph.

Selecting Text in Columns and Rectangles

Wait! You're not finished. What about selecting text in tabular columns, even rectangles of screen text?

To select a tabular column with the mouse, point to a corner of the text, hold down the Shift key, then hold down the *right* mouse button and drag to select the text (see Figure 13-2).

Figure 13-2: Selecting a tabular column by right-button dragging

After the column is selected, you can cut or copy it, then paste it in a new location. You can also drag it to a new location.

Caution Save your document before performing columnar surgery. Not all operations are successful!

You can select any rectangle of text, whether it is lined up with tabs or indents. However, the text is not likely to format neatly if you move or copy it to another location.

To select tabular columns or a rectangular block via the Edit menu:

1. Select from the first character of the column you want to the last character of the last column, such as the beginning to the end of the Last Name column in Figure 13-3.

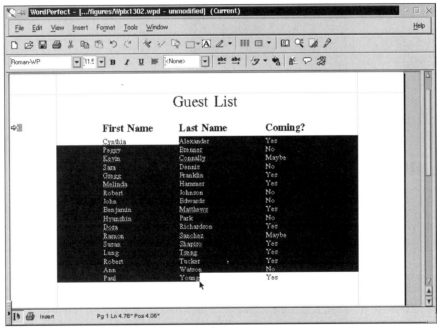

Figure 13-3: Selecting the beginning to end of the Last Name column

2. Click Edit ⇨ Select ⇨ Tabular Column. The Last Name column is now the only text selected (see Figure 13-4). If you had chosen Rectangle instead of Tabular Column, the beginning and end of your selection would be opposite corners of the final rectangular selection.

For more on columns, see Chapter 16, "Formatting with Columns and Tables."

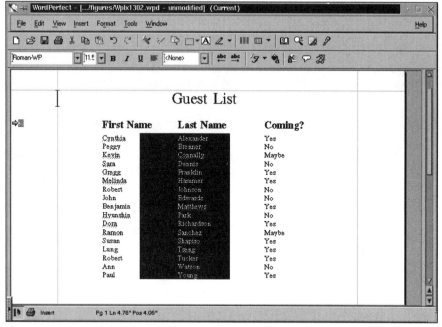

Figure 13-4: Resulting tabular column selection

Finding and Replacing

The more you use Find and Replace, the more you'll find it to be a powerful and versatile editing tool. Selectable find actions and other options discussed in the following sections remain in effect for the duration of the current WordPerfect session.

Finding a Word or Phrase

There's no need to strain your eyeballs when searching for a word or phrase:

1. Press F2 (Edit ➪ Find and Replace).

2. Type the word or phrase in the Find box. (Press Ctrl+W to find a symbol.)

3. Click Find Next, or Find Previous (see Figure 13-5).

Find Next searches down from the insertion point, while Find Previous searches up from the insertion point.

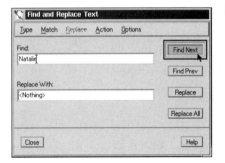

Figure 13-5: Finding a word or phrase

QuickFinding the Next Occurrence

Use the QuickFind buttons on the property bar to find the next or previous occurrence of existing text quickly. Click the word (or select the text), then click the QuickFind Next button or the QuickFind Previous button.

QuickFind matches on whole words only.

Selecting Find Actions

The normal Find and Replace action is Select Match (see Figure 13-6), which enables you to see and edit the found text.

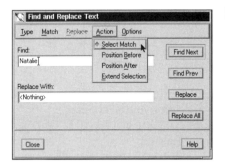

Figure 13-6: Selecting Find actions

Position Before or Position After on the Action menu puts the insertion point in front of or after the text, without selecting it. It will be hard to see the location of your found text, however, because it isn't highlighted, and you won't even see the insertion point until you exit Find and Replace.

Extend Selection lets you extend the current selection to the specified word, phrase, or code.

Finding and Replacing Text or Codes

You can replace automatically the text (or codes) you find. For example, if you were updating instructions you wrote for WordPerfect 7, you could change all occurrences of "WordPerfect 7" to "WordPerfect 8."

To find and replace text:

1. Press F2 (Edit ➪ Find and Replace).

2. Type the search word or phrase, or click the drop-down list to select from the last ten entries.

Tip   Select text, or a code in Reveal Codes, before starting your search to have it appear in the field automatically.

3. Type your replacement text in the "Replace with" box (see Figure 13-7).

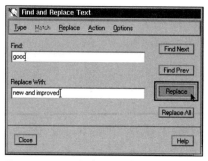

Figure 13-7: Finding and replacing text

4. Select any options you want to change from the Find and Replace menu bar. (See the "More Find and Replace Tricks" section in this chapter.)

5. Click the following buttons, as needed:

Click	*In Order To*
Find Next	Find the next occurrence of your search term with the option of replacing it.
Find Prev	Find the previous occurrence.
Replace	Replace the found item and search for the next. (To delete found text, leave the "Replace with" box empty or showing <Nothing>.)
Replace All	Replace all found items without stopping.

Tip   To use the ? and * wildcard codes in your text searches, click Match ⇨ Codes, then double-click the code to insert it (typed codes won't work). For example, a search on wild*d finds "wildcard" or "wildcatted." However, unless you selected the Whole Word option from the Match menu, there's no need for wildcards at the beginning or end of your search text.

Finding and Replacing Specific Codes

To locate and replace formatting codes, open the Find and Replace dialog box, then click Type ⇨ Specific Codes to find particular codes for margins, justification, fonts, and so forth (as shown in Figure 13-8).

Figure 13-8: Finding and replacing specific codes

Select the code type you want, then click OK, whereupon the appropriate Find and Replace code selections appear. You can, for example, search for a line spacing of 2 and replace it with a line spacing of 1.5, as shown in Figure 13-9. You can replace a font size of 15 with one of 18. To delete a code instead of replacing it, check "Replace with Nothing."

Tip   To see the codes you find, you must be in Reveal Codes.

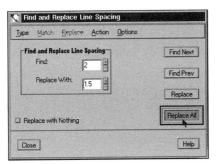

Figure 13-9: Changing line spacing by using Find and Replace

More Find and Replace Tricks

Find and Replace can perform every trick in the book. The follow sections explore these tricks by going through each menu in the Find and Replace dialog box.

The Match Menu

The Match menu, shown in Figure 13-10, presents the following options:

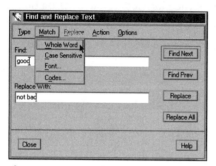

Figure 13-10: Find Match options

✦ *Whole Word* matches only on separate words. For example, it finds the three-letter word "tip", but not "tipsy" or "multiple". When replacing "dog" with "cat", only a pedigree dog is replaced — you won't end up with "catmatic" or an "undercat."

✦ *Case Sensitive* matches on the exact capitalization. When you type Help in the Find box, you get a match for "Help" or "Helps", but not for "help". Case is especially useful when you are searching for a product name such as "Windows" or a personal name such as "Gates."

✦ *Font* lets you search for text of a specific size, font, or other attribute (see Figure 13-11). You can, for example, limit your search to those occurrences of "Windows" that are in large type, as in a heading.

✦ *Codes* lets you search for a code regardless of its value (see Figure 13-12). You can, for example, search for a [Graph Line] code to find and edit a graphics line. Check "Display merge codes only" to select merge codes instead of WordPerfect codes.

The Replace Menu

The Replace menu presents the following options:

✦ *Case Sensitive* to replace text exactly as entered in the "Replace with" box — not with the case of the found text in your document.

Figure 13-11: Matching text with a specific font and size

Figure 13-12: Finding a [Graph Line] code

✦ *Font* to specify the font, size, and appearance of the replacement text.

✦ *Codes* to specify codes as described earlier in "Finding and replacing specific codes."

Tip   Enter the same text in both the "Find" and "Replace with" boxes to change only its characteristics, such as font or font size.

The Options Menu

Normally, you search in all parts of your document, starting from the insertion point, going to the end of the document, and stopping there. Click Options to select from other search possibilities (see Figure 13-13), as shown in Table 13-2.

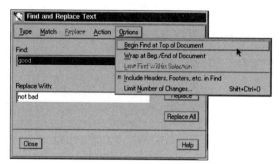

Figure 13-13: Search options

Table 13-2 Search Options	
Option	**Enables You to**
Begin Find at Top of Document	Start each search from the beginning, regardless of your location in the document.
Wrap at Beg./End of Document	Search the entire document, starting and ending at the insertion point.
Limit Find Within Selection	Search only selected text (automatic when a text block has been selected).
Include Headers, Footers, etc. in Find	Search all parts of your document, not just the body of your text (default).
Limit Number of Changes...	Specify how many items can be replaced.

When you don't specify an automatic wrap search, WordPerfect asks if you want to continue searching when it reaches the beginning or end of your document.

Inserting and Finding Bookmarks

You saw how to use the "stick-it-in-the-page-to-keep-your-place" QuickMark in Chapter 4, "Becoming an Instant WordPerfect Expert." Bookmarks are similar to the QuickMark, except that you can place as many bookmarks as you want in a single document, and it takes three quick steps to access the marked place, instead of one. Bookmarks are especially useful for creating hypertext links to jump from place to place.

Creating a Bookmark

To create a bookmark:

1. Click where you want the bookmark.

2. Click Tools ⇨ Bookmark ⇨ Create.

3. Change the text that is picked up automatically to whatever name you like (see Figure 13-14).

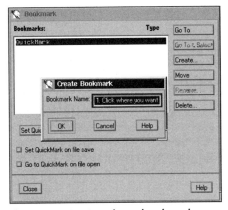

Figure 13-14: Creating a bookmark

Marking Selected Text with a Bookmark

You can drag to select the text for your bookmark name before creating the bookmark. Selected text is also surrounded by a pair of bookmark codes. You can select the text automatically again when you find the bookmark.

Finding a Bookmark

To find a bookmark, click Tools ➪ Bookmark, then select the bookmark and click Go To (or Go To & Select for a bookmark around selected text).

Moving a Bookmark

To move a bookmark (such as when you must change the place of a hypertext link):

1. Click (or select the text) where you want to move the bookmark.
2. Click Tools ➪ Bookmark.
3. Select the bookmark, then click Move.

Note   When you move a selected text bookmark, only the bookmark is moved, not the text.

Renaming or Deleting a Bookmark

To rename or delete a bookmark, click Tools ➪ Bookmark, select the bookmark, then click Rename or Delete.

Comparing Two Versions of a Document

At times, you may want to compare the current screen document with an earlier version on disk. Suppose you're editing a paper, and you realize that some of the old wording may be better than the new version. With Document Compare, you can compare the versions, then keep the best sections from each version. The feature adds redlined text in the current document that is different from the compare document and strikes through text in the current document that is not in the old document.

Comparing Two Documents

To compare the current document with one on disk:

1. Click File ➪ Document ➪ Add Compare Markings.
2. Type the name of the document with which you want to compare the current document.
3. Select whether you want to add comparison markings by the Word, Phrase, Sentence, or Paragraph, and click OK to add compare markings to the current document (see Figure 13-15).

Figure 13-15: Compare two documents

4. WordPerfect adds Compare markings to the current document, as shown in Figure 13-16.

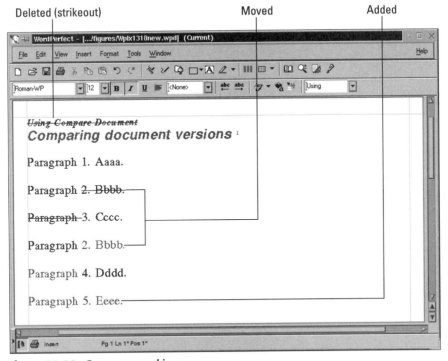

Figure 13-16: Compare markings

Removing Compare Markings

To remove compare markings from the current screen, click File ➪ Document ➪ Remove Compare Markings. You can remove the redline and strikeout marking, or the strikeout only (see Figure 13-17).

Figure 13-17: Removing compare markings

To change the redlining method used for marking text when comparing documents, see Chapter 26, "Fine-Tuning WordPerfect."

Inserting Nonprinting Comments

You can insert comments in a document with your name, initials, and color. Comments can be used for reviewers to provide notes on your work, but can also serve as personal reminders. They neither print nor affect page numbering.

Creating Comments

To add one or more comments to a line of text:

1. Click where you want the comment, then click Insert ➪ Comment ➪ Create. This sequence opens a blank comment screen that looks like a new document screen.

2. Click to insert your initials, your name, the date, or the time.

Click Preferences ➪ Environment in the WordPerfect Program Window to change your name, initials, or comment color.

3. Type the comment, which can include tables, graphics, and other document elements (see Figure 13-18 for a sample).

4. Click the Next button or the Previous button to see or edit other comments, or click the Close button to return to your document.

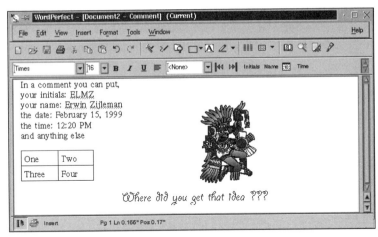

Figure 13-18: Creating a comment

Converting Document Text to a Comment

If you want to print or distribute an unfinished document, you can convert rough notes or other unfinished text to a comment. As a comment, it won't print until you've edited it into its finished form and converted it back to text:

1. Select the text.

2. Click the Comment button on the toolbar (Insert ➪ Comment ➪ Create).

Viewing and Hiding Comments

Comments display as shaded text in Draft view. In Page or Two Page view, click the icon (the author's initials or a miniature text bubble) to display a comment, as shown in Figure 13-19. Click outside the comment to hide it again.

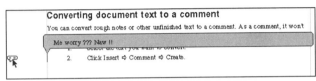

Figure 13-19: Displaying a comment in Page view

If there is more than one comment on a line in Page view, click the multiple-comment icon, then click the icon for the particular comment you want to view.

Editing or Deleting a Comment

To edit a comment, such as to expand a note into full-blown text:

1. Double-click the comment icon (or the comment in Draft view).

2. Edit the comment, then click the Close button.

You can also right-click a comment (or comment icon) to cut, copy, delete, or edit the comment.

Converting a Comment to Text

Once you edit and expand your comment notes, you can convert them into regular document text. Afterward, you may need to edit the punctuation and format to blend the notes into the existing content.

To convert a displayed comment to text and make it a full part of your document, right-click the comment, then click Convert to Text. (In Draft view, click the comment, then right-click the bubble.)

Moving or Copying a Comment

To move or copy a comment, right-click the comment icon (or the comment in Draft view), then click Cut (to move it) or Copy (to copy it), and paste it in the new location.

To delete all comments from the insertion point on, click Edit ⇨ Find and Replace, click Match ⇨ Codes, then double-click the Comment code. Leave the "Replace with" box empty, and click Replace All.

Printing a Comment

To print a comment, double-click the icon (or the comment in Draft view), then click File ⇨ Print ⇨ Print.

Using Hidden Text

You can think of hidden text as an "invisible ink" font attribute. Like a comment, it can either be hidden or displayed. However, don't use hidden text for group review or to post notes to yourself, because it affects page numbering and prints when it's not hidden. Use it to include questions, notes, or comments in your document that you can alternately hide, or display and print. For example, you could use hidden text to hide the answers to a quiz on the copy you print and give to students.

Hidden text is indistinguishable from regular text when displayed, so it can be printed without conversion. Hidden text expands into view when you want to see it (it even affects page numbers) and shrinks to nothing when you don't want to see it. In its normal hidden state, hidden text doesn't even leave an icon behind, as with comments. (Open Reveal Codes and place the insertion point on the right of a Hidden code to view its text.)

Creating Hidden Text

To create hidden text:

1. Click the View menu and make sure that Hidden Text is checked (so that you see the text as you create it).

2. Place the insertion point where you want to create the hidden text (or select the text you want to hide).

3. Click Format ⇨ Font, then check Hidden in the Appearance group.

4. To resume typing normal text, press the right-arrow key to jump past the Hidden code, or repeat Step 3, removing the check.

At this point, your hidden text is still displayed. To hide it, click the View menu and remove the check from Hidden Text.

Tip   To include hidden text in Spell Check, Grammar Check, Find, and other operations, including page counts, be sure that Hidden Text is checked in the View menu.

Converting and Deleting Hidden Text

When hidden text is displayed (checked on the View menu), you can edit and delete it, just as you would ordinary text. You can convert hidden text to regular text by going into Reveal Codes and deleting one of the surrounding Hidden codes.

When hidden text is not displayed, deleting a Hidden code deletes the text as well, so be careful (see Figure 13-20).

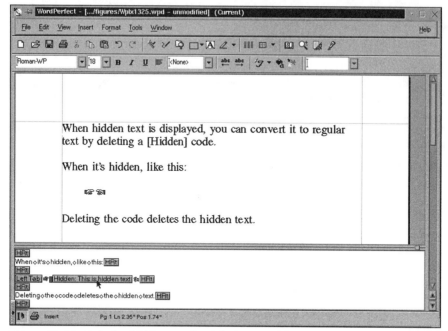

Figure 13-20: Deleting hidden text by deleting a Hidden code (when the text is not displayed)

For More Information . . .

On	See
Basic text selection	Chapter 2
Setting tabs	Chapter 15
Using columns	Chapter 16
Setting QuickMarks	Chapter 4
Creating hypertext links	Chapter 11
Using Corel Versions	Chapter 6

✦   ✦   ✦

Controlling Text and Numbering Pages

✦ ✦ ✦ ✦

In This Chapter

Hyphenate text automatically

Insert page breaks

Keep paragraphs and lines together

Number pages

Create custom numbering formats

Force an odd, even, or new page

Suppress page numbers

✦ ✦ ✦ ✦

Using a word processor can be akin to riding a wild stallion — exhilarating power and speed with an unnerving lack of control. How do you rein in automatic hyphenation for a particular word, or keep a paragraph from breaking across two pages? You certainly don't want to number pages by hand, but what do you do when the automatic page number gets in the way of an illustration or chart? If you're writing a book, how do you ensure that every chapter starts on an odd-numbered page?

Avoid the crude approach. For example, when you want a particular paragraph to start at the top of the next page, the crude approach would push the paragraph by inserting blank lines. As a result, a gaping hole appears on your screen that must shrink or grow if you change your font, use a different printer, or return to edit your text. This chapter shows you neater and simpler ways to position text, break it apart, or keep it together.

Using Hyphenation

Hyphenation divides words at the right margin when the whole word can't fit on the line. Hyphenation can be turned on or off (the default). When it's on, WordPerfect handles hyphenation in one of three ways, depending on the hyphenation prompt option you specify. (See the upcoming section "Selecting the Hyphenation Prompt Option.")

Understanding Hyphens, Dashes, and Hyphenation Codes

WordPerfect's automatic hyphenation requires several types of hyphens, dashes, and hyphenation codes to handle possible situations. When WordPerfect hyphenates a word for you, it inserts an `[Auto Hyphen EOL]` code, instead of the hyphen character. That way, the hyphen disappears automatically if you edit your text so that the hyphenated word is no longer at the end of the line.

Sometimes the program can prompt you to tell it where to place the hyphen. When that happens, a `[- Soft Hyphen]` code normally is inserted permanently, so you won't be prompted again as the word moves back and forth from the margin.

A soft hyphen is only one of many hyphens, dashes, and hyphen codes you can use, as shown in Table 14-1.

Table 14-1
Hyphens, Dashes, and Hyphen Codes

Typed	Code Display	What It Does
Typed Hyphen	[-Hyphen]	Connects two words, as in "good-looking."
Hyphen character or "hard" hyphen	[-]	Like the typed hyphen, except a word with this character will not break across lines when hyphenation is on; the entire word will wrap to the next line.
Automatic hyphenation code	[Auto Hyphen EOL]	Inserted by automatic hyphenation. Disappears when it is no longer needed.
Soft Hyphen	[-Soft Hyphen]	Normally inserted by hyphenation prompt. You can also insert it without being prompted to specify where a word hyphenates. A soft hyphen becomes visible and prints only when it divides the word.
Hyphenation Soft Return	[HyphSRt]	Like the soft hyphen, it specifies where a word divides if it must go across lines, but does not insert a hyphen or space. Useful for words separated by slashes (such as Page Up/Page Down).
Em dash (WP character 4,34)	[:4,34]	Joins two related phrases with a long dash (—). Does not divide text at the right margin when hyphenation is on.

Typed	Code Display	What It Does
En dash (WP character 4,33)	[:4,33]	Indicates a range of numbers (as with page numbers), or separates parts of a phone number. The en dash (–) is shorter than an em dash, but longer than a hyphen. Does not divide text at the right margin when hyphenation is on.
Hyphenation Ignore Word	[Cancel Hyph]	Keeps a word (such as a person's name) from being hyphenated. Instead of dividing at the right margin, the entire word wraps to the next line.

Turning On Hyphenation

By "hyphenation," WordPerfect means automatic, end-of-the-line hyphenation. You can always split words with a hyphen character, em dash, or en dash, whether hyphenation is on or off. To turn on hyphenation:

1. Click the paragraph in which you want hyphenation to begin.
2. Click Tools ⇨ Language ⇨ Hyphenation.
3. Check "Turn hyphenation on" (see Figure 14-1).

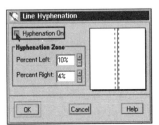

Figure 14-1: Turning on hyphenation

Follow the same procedure, removing the check, to turn hyphenation off later in your document. To eliminate hyphenation from your document entirely, you can go into Reveal Codes and delete the [Hyph: On] code.

Tip Hyphenation is off by default. To turn hyphenation on every time you open a new document, add the [Hyph: On] code to the Initial Document Style (see Chapter 15, "Formatting Your Document").

Selecting the Hyphenation Prompt Option

You can specify the way WordPerfect prompts you when hyphenation is activated:

✦ *Always,* to ask you to position the hyphen every time a word can be hyphenated. This setting is for when you need total control over hyphenation, as in creating advertising copy.

✦ *Never,* to hyphenate words at the right margin without prompting. If the word is not in the main word list, the program uses built-in rules to determine where the hyphen goes.

✦ *When Required* (the default), to position the hyphenation manually only when the program doesn't recognize the word and can't figure out a syllable break.

To change the type of hyphenation prompt, switch to the WordPerfect Program Window and click Preferences ➪ Environment, then click Hyphenation Prompt and select the option you want from the hyphenation prompt list (see Figure 14-2).

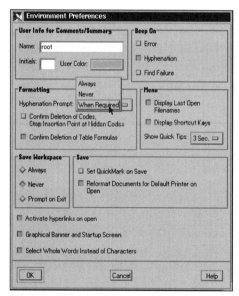

Figure 14-2: Setting the hyphenation prompt option

Answering the Hyphenation Prompt

When hyphenation is activated, WordPerfect tries to hyphenate a word if it spans both boundaries of the hyphenation zone at the right margin. The *hyphenation zone* is a percentage of the line width — the wider the zone, the fewer words hyphenated. When the line is narrow, as in tables or columns, more words are hyphenated. You can adjust the size of this zone with Tools ⇨ Language ⇨ Hyphenation.

If WordPerfect can't find an appropriate hyphenation location, it normally prompts you for assistance (see Figure 14-3). If you set the hyphenation prompt option to Never, WordPerfect wraps the entire word to the next line without prompting.

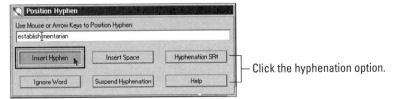
Click the hyphenation option.

Figure 14-3: Answering the hyphenation prompt

When you answer the hyphenation prompt:

1. Position the hyphen within the displayed word by using the arrow keys or by clicking the mouse.

2. Click one of the following hyphenation options:

   • *Insert Hyphen,* to use a soft hyphen to divide the word.

   • *Insert Space,* to use a space to divide the word.

   • *Hyphenation SRt,* to divide the word without using a hyphen or space.

   • *Ignore Word,* to wrap the entire word to the next line by inserting a [Cancel Hyph] code.

   • *Suspend Hyphenation,* to turn off hyphenation temporarily during a spell check or a scrolling command. The word wraps to the next line, but no code is inserted, so you'll be prompted again the next time around.

Manually Inserting Hyphens

To insert various hyphens and hyphenation codes manually, click Format ⇨ Line ⇨ Other Codes, and select the code to insert. You can also use keystrokes to insert several types of hyphens and hyphenation codes, as shown in Table 14-2.

Table 14-2
Keystrokes for Hyphens and Hyphenation Codes

Type of Hyphen or Code	Linux/CUA Keystrokes	DOS Keystrokes
Hyphen	-	-
Hyphen character or hard hyphen	Ctrl+ -	Home, -
Soft hyphen	Ctrl+Shift+ -	Ctrl+ -
Hyphenation soft return	(Click Format ⇨ Line ⇨ Other Codes)	Home, Enter
Cancel hyphenation (immediately before hyphenated word)	Ctrl+/	Ctrl+/

Tip   When manually hyphenating a word at the end of a line, use a soft hyphen. That way, the hyphen will disappear if it's no longer needed.

Inserting an Em Dash or an En Dash

You can use em dashes and en dashes (the width of "M" and "N" characters, respectively) to give your documents the professional look of published books and articles. The long em dash (—) indicates a sudden break in thought that causes an abrupt change in sentence structure, or sets off a parenthetical phrase. The en dash (which is one-half the length of the em dash, but longer than the hyphen) is used primarily to indicate continuing numbers or dates, as in pp. 33–42, 1995–98, or Jan 1998–Mar 1998.

When QuickCorrect or the Format-As-You-Go QuickSymbols is activated, a triple-dash (---) changes automatically to an em dash, and a double-dash (--) becomes an en dash. When these features are deactivated, you can press Ctrl+W, then type **4,34** (em dash) or **4,33** (en dash).

Breaking Text Apart and Keeping It Together

Arranging text on pages is similar to arranging words on lines — just on a larger scale. For example, if the introduction to your paper takes up less than a page, you may want to end the page there and start the main body of your text at the top of page two. What if you want to make sure that a table or list stays on a single page? The following topics show you how to make sections of text behave.

Inserting Page Breaks

Normally, when you reach the bottom of a page, WordPerfect inserts a soft page break. That way, the page break will move when you go back and enter more text. But you can also specify precise page breaks in the following ways.

Inserting hard page breaks

Sometimes, as with the start of a new chapter, you want to set where a page break should fall. In such cases, press Ctrl+Enter to insert a hard page break (you can also click Insert ➪ New Page). No matter how much text you add or delete, the page will always break at the point you set.

The page break appears as a Hard Page code ([HPg]) in Reveal Codes. You can identify a hard page break in Draft view mode by the double solid line across the page. In Page view, a thick black line appears between the pages.

To remove a Hard Page code, place the insertion point just before the page break, then press Delete. You can also go into Reveal Codes to delete the [HPg] code.

Forcing a new page

A variation on the hard page break is forcing a new page. Use it when you want to ensure that a particular paragraph always appears at the top of a page. When you force a new page, a [Force: New] code is inserted at the beginning of the current paragraph. As you edit your document, the code stays attached to the paragraph.

To force a new page:

1. Place the insertion point in the paragraph where you want to force a new page.
2. Click Format ➪ Page ➪ Force Page ➪ New Page (see Figure 14-4).

Figure 14-4: Forcing a new page

To remove a Force New Page code, go into Reveal Codes and delete the [Force: New] code.

Keeping Paragraphs and Lines Together

Up to this point you've used "page surgery" to break the current page apart or start a new page. Now you'll see how to keep lines and paragraphs together on the same page.

Keeping a block of text together

You can block protect a selection of text to keep it from splitting across two pages. To keep a block of text together:

1. Select the text. (To keep table rows together, select the entire row.)

2. Click the Block Protect button. (You can also right-click the block and click Block Protect, or click Format ⇨ Keep Text Together and check "Block Protect.")

The protected block may expand or shrink as you edit it, but the program always tries to keep it together on one page. If the protected block is about to spill over to the next page, the program inserts a soft page break at the beginning of the protected block to move it to the top of the next page.

To remove block protect, open the Reveal Codes window and delete one of the surrounding [Block Pro] codes.

Keeping a number of lines together

You can keep a specified number of lines together with conditional end of page. Use it to prevent a single-line heading from getting stranded, alone, at the bottom of a page. To keep a number of lines together:

1. Place the insertion point on the first of the lines you want to keep together.

2. Click Format ⇨ Keep Text Together, and check "Number of lines to keep together" (see Figure 14-5).

3. Specify the number of lines to keep together (including blank lines).

Figure 14-5: Keeping a number of lines together

This feature inserts a single [Cond] EOP: #] code. Go into Reveal Codes to remove it.

Tip To apply this feature to your headings automatically, add conditional end of page to all your heading styles.

Caring for widows and orphans

Widow/orphan protection prevents one line of a paragraph from getting stranded, alone, at the bottom or top of a page. To enable widow/orphan protection in all or part of your document:

1. Click on the page where you want widow/orphan protection to begin.

2. Click Format ⇨ Keep Text Together, then check "Prevent the first and last lines of paragraphs from being separated across pages" (refer back to Figure 14-5).

This sequence places a single [Wid/Orph] code that can be deleted in Reveal Codes.

Tip To protect every new document, include widow/orphan protection in the Initial Document Style (see Chapter 15, "Formatting Your Document").

Numbering Pages

Page numbering can be as simple as putting a number at the top of the page, or as sophisticated as including chapter and volume numbers, starting each section on an odd page, or designing a custom numbering format.

Numbering Pages in a Standard Position and Format

WordPerfect makes it easy to insert automatic page numbering in standard positions and various formats. To number pages in standard position and format:

1. Place the insertion point on the page where you want the numbering to begin.

2. Click Format ⇨ Page ⇨ Page Numbering ⇨ Numbering.

3. Click the Position list and select a page numbering location (see Figure 14-6). (Use the alternating selections for facing pages, as in a book.)

4. Click options to define the page numbering format (see Figure 14-7). (Use [Pg #] of [Tot Pages #] to display both the current page number and the total number of pages. See the following "Creating Custom Page Numbering Formats" section.)

Figure 14-6: Numbering pages in a standard position

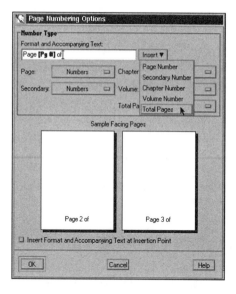

Figure 14-7: Choosing a page numbering format

Inserting a Page Number Anywhere in the Text of Your Document

If you don't want to use a standard page numbering position on a particular page (such as one with a graphic or chart), you can insert an automatic page number anywhere in the text of your document:

1. Click where you want the page number to appear.

2. Click Format ➪ Page ➪ Page Numbering ➪ Insert Page Number.

3. Select the type of page number you want.

4. Click Format ⇨ Page ⇨ Suppress to suspend any standard numbering for the current page.

 Tip   To insert page numbers in headers or footers, click the Page Numbering button on the property bar (see Chapter 15, "Formatting Your Document").

Changing the Appearance of Page Numbers

Page numbers normally appear in your document's default font. To change the font or appearance of your page numbers:

1. Place the insertion point on the page where you want the change in the font or appearance of the page numbers to begin.

2. Click Format ⇨ Page ⇨ Page Numbering ⇨ Numbering.

3. Click Font to select the font face, style, size, color, and shading you want.

Creating Custom Page Numbering Formats

You can create custom numbering formats for practically any conceivable situation. Believe it or not, you can choose from five kinds of page numbers, and these can be displayed in any of five ways, together with any explanatory text. A numbering scheme of "Page iv of 127 in Part C" is not out of the question.

The five kinds of page numbers (refer back to Figure 14-7) are:

✦ *Page numbers* that increment automatically with each new page. In most situations, this number is the only type you'll need.

✦ *Secondary page numbers*, which also increment with each page, are rarer than Elvis sightings. You might use them, for example, if you add 20 pages to the middle of a new edition of a scholarly text, and keep old page numbers along with the new, as in "page 332, old page 312."

✦ *Chapter numbers* and *volume numbers* can identify the location of text in a large work. Use them for any document division, such as Book 3 or Part IV, not just chapters or volumes. These numbers are normally static, so you must adjust them manually when you get to a new division. For example, if the last page of Chapter 3 is "Chapter 3, Page 78," the first page of Chapter 4 will be "Chapter 3, Page 79," unless you change it.

✦ *Total Pages* is the "y" of a "page x of y" format. The *y* refers to the last numbered page of the document, not necessarily the number of physical pages. For example, if a 30-page document is numbered i–x for the first 10 pages, and 1–20 for the last 20, the Total Pages value will be 20, not 30.

Next, you have a choice of ways to display page numbers:

✦ Standard *Arabic numbers* (1, 2, 3).

✦ Lowercase or uppercase *Roman numerals* (i, ii, iii or I, II, III)

✦ Lowercase or uppercase *letters* (a, b, c or A, B, C)

You can mix and match the number types and displays, then add any text to accommodate the most esoteric of page numbering schemes.

To create a custom page numbering format:

1. Place the insertion point on the page where you want the custom format to begin.

2. Click Format ➪ Page ➪ Page Numbering ➪ Numbering ➪ Options.

3. Type any accompanying text, such as "Volume" or "Page", in the "Format and accompanying text" box.

4. Select the display methods for the kind of number you want, then click "Insert" and select the code to insert the code (see Figure 14-8).

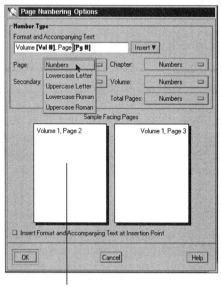

Preview your custom format

Figure 14-8: Creating a custom page-numbering format

5. Repeat Steps 3 and 4 for additional codes and text, such as "Volume II, Chapter 6, Page 342." Be sure to include punctuation and spaces. Preview your custom format just below the edit box.

Changing a Page Number's Value and Display

You can reset any type of page number (other than total pages) at any point in your document. If you are using chapter or volume numbers, for example, you'll need to change the number manually at the beginning of each chapter or volume.

You may want to change the number display at the same time that you change the number. For example, if you are numbering the Preface or Introduction to a work in lowercase Roman, you'll probably want to switch to regular Arabic numbers at the beginning of Chapter 1, and reset the page number to 1.

To change a page number's value and display:

1. Place the insertion point on the page where you want to the change to begin.

2. Click Format ➪ Page ➪ Page Numbering ➪ Numbering ➪ Value.

3. Select the type of page number you want to change.

4. Set the page number to the value you want (see Figure 14-9) or increase/decrease the current number.

5. Click OK, then select a new page-numbering format if you also want to change the number display (as from Roman to Arabic).

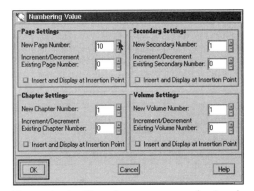

Figure 14-9: Changing a page number's value

Forcing an Odd, Even, or New Page

At times, you may want to be sure that a certain page has an odd or even page number. Or you may want a table of contents, chapter, glossary, or index always to begin on a new page. If your publication is to have facing pages (as in a book), you may want the first page of each section to begin on a new page and have an odd page number.

To force an odd, even, or new page:

1. Place the insertion point in the paragraph where you want to force an odd, even, or new page.

2. Click Format ➪ Page ➪ Force Page.

3. Click "Current Page Odd," "Current Page Even," or "Start New Page" (see Figure 14-10).

Figure 14-10: Forcing an odd, even, or new page

Note   When you force a page, a `[Force: Odd]`, `[Force: Even]`, **or** `[Force: New]` code is inserted at the beginning of the current paragraph at the insertion point. If you force an odd or even page, the program inserts a page break only if necessary.

Suppressing Page Numbers

You may want to suppress page numbering on certain pages (such as the table of contents, chapter title pages, or on a page where a graph appears).

To suppress the page numbering on a particular page, click Format ➪ Page ➪ Suppress, then check "Page numbering," or other items (headers, footers, and watermarks) you want to suppress (see Figure 14-11).

You can also check "Print page number at bottom center on current page," instead of suppressing it, so that it won't interfere with a title or heading.

Figure 14-11: Suppressing a page number

For More Information . . .

On	See
Setting the Initial Document Style	Chapter 15
Placing page numbers in headers and footers	Chapter 15
Inserting numbers anywhere in your text	Chapter 18

✦   ✦   ✦

Formatting Your Document

◆ ◆ ◆ ◆

In This Chapter

Change the default style and font

Fine-tune spacing of letters, words, and lines

Adjust tabs and use different tab types

Justify and advance text

Customize paragraph and page formats

Create headers and footers

Dress up your pages with watermarks

◆ ◆ ◆ ◆

For all the fancy graphs, charts, images, sounds, and other special effects you can employ, most communication is still focused on the written word, packaged by the page.

This chapter takes you on a basic formatting tour, covering the line, paragraph, and page. Other formatting elements (such as columns and tables) are covered in subsequent chapters. Borders and fills are discussed in Chapter 23, "Adding Graphic Lines, Borders, and Fills."

Understanding Your Default Document Settings

Every document uses two default settings you can change:

- ✦ An *Initial Document Style* at the beginning of the document
- ✦ The *default font* for the printer you've selected

When the Initial Document Style is empty, you start with the default format for the language version you've installed. For the U.S. version of WordPerfect, this format is a paper size of $8^{1}/_{2} \cdot 11$ inches, one-inch margins all around, tabs every half inch, single-line spacing, left justification, and so forth.

Any changes that you make while working in your document (such as margin or tab adjustments) take precedence over the default settings.

Note

When you insert another document into the onscreen document, the inserted text is stripped of its original Document Style.

Changing the Document Style

You can't delete the Initial Document Style, but you can edit it to include your personal settings for tabs, margins, justification, and other formatting. You can apply these settings to all new documents you create by saving them to the Document Style in your default template.

Note Every document you create takes its initial formatting from either the Default template or a selected special template for reports, memos, newsletters, and so forth (see Chapter 20, "Working Quickly with ExpressDocs Templates and Styles").

To change the Document Style:

1. Click File ➪ Document ➪ Current Document Style.

2. Be sure that "Reveal codes" is checked in the Styles Editor so that you can see the codes you insert (see Figure 15-1).

3. Select the formatting items you want to change from the Styles Editor menus, just as you would when working in your document.

4. To change the Document Style for all your new documents, check "Use as Default."

Check to change the document style
for all new documents.

Figure 15-1: Changing the current Document Style

Changing the Default Font

When you open a new document, the default font is set for the selected printer. To change the default font for all new documents:

1. Click File ⇨ Document ⇨ Default Font.

2. Select the font face, size, and style you want.

3. To change the default font for all new documents using the current printer, check "Set as Printer Initial Font" (see Figure 15-2).

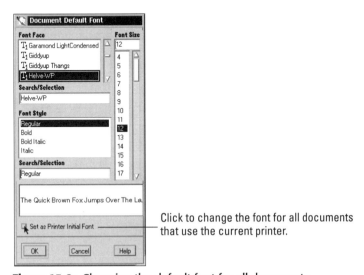

Click to change the font for all documents that use the current printer.

Figure 15-2: Changing the default font for all documents

Fine-Tuning Word and Letter Spacing

WordPerfect lets you customize the formatting of everything from the spacing between two letters to the size of your page. This chapter starts from the small end of the scale and works its way up. You begin by learning how to adjust the space between particular pairs of letters, and refine the word and letter spacing throughout your document.

Adjusting the Space between Letter Pairs

When text is printed, unwanted gaps may appear between certain letter pairs. These gaps are especially apparent between large characters found in advertisements or headlines.

You can use the *automatic kerning* feature to adjust the space between all occurrences of certain letter pairs using instructions built into certain fonts. Use *manual kerning* to adjust the spacing between individual letter pairs, such as to tuck a lowercase *i* under an uppercase *T*.

To set automatic kerning:

1. Place the insertion point where you want kerning to begin, or select the text that you want to kern.

2. Click Format ⇨ Typesetting ⇨ Word/Letter Spacing.

3. Check "Automatic kerning."

To manually adjust the kerning between a specific pair of characters:

1. Place the insertion point between the two characters you want to kern.

2. Click Format ⇨ Typesetting ⇨ Manual Kerning.

3. Adjust the amount of space between the characters (see Figure 15-3).

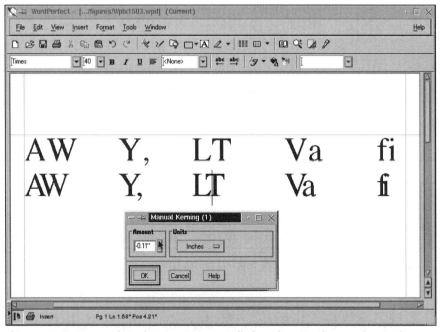

Figure 15-3: You can kern letter pairs manually by adjusting the number in the Amount box

Manual kerning inserts a [Hdav] code, as described in the following "Advancing Text" section.

Inserting Em Spaces, En Spaces, or Small Spaces

You may occasionally need to insert an em space, en space, or small space between characters. While there are no "space" characters in WordPerfect, you can use the following technique:

1. Type an em dash for an em space, a number for an en space, or period for a small space.

2. Select the em dash, number, or period, then click the Font Color button (Format ⇨ Font ⇨ Color) and select the background color (normally white) to make the character invisible.

Adjusting Word Spacing, Letter Spacing, and Justification Limits

As you type, the spacing between letters and words is determined by WordPerfect, based on your current printer and font. While these settings usually provide excellent results, you can use the program's sophisticated typesetting features to adjust these settings manually or use the settings determined by the font manufacturer:

1. Place the insertion point where you want the new word spacing, letter spacing, or justification limits to begin, or select the text you want to adjust.

2. Click Format ⇨ Typesetting ⇨ Word/Letter Spacing.

3. Specify the "Word Spacing" and Letterspacing settings (see Figure 15-4):

   • *Normal* (not the default) uses the font manufacturer's specifications.

   • *Percent of Optimal* enables you to adjust WordPerfect's settings to increase or decrease the spacing between words or letters. You can set the pitch (characters per inch) instead of adjusting the percentage—the greater the pitch, the tighter the spacing.

4. Specify word spacing justification limits (for fully justified text):

   • *Compressed to* specifies how much the spacing between words can be squeezed to fit the words within the margins.

   • *Expanded to* specifies how much the spacing between words can be stretched to fill the space between the margins.

Note   WordPerfect first tries to fit fully justified text to the margins by compressing or expanding the spaces between words, up to the percentage limits. If that technique isn't enough, the spacing between letters is adjusted as well.

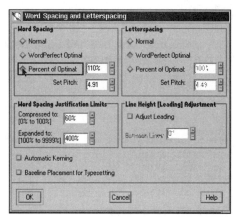

Figure 15-4: Adjusting word spacing, letter spacing, and justification limits

Formatting Lines

You can specify several aspects of the document line, including tab settings, spacing, height, and justification. You can even have numbered lines.

Positioning Text with Tabs

A *tab* moves the insertion point and text to a specific location on the line. Press the Tab key to insert a [Left Tab] code and move to the next tab setting. Press Shift+Tab to insert a [Hd Back Tab] code and move left to the previous tab setting.

Tip If you're in Typeover mode instead of Insert mode, pressing Tab or Shift+Tab only moves the insertion point through existing text. A tab code is inserted only if there is no text. Also, if you press Tab and the insertion point doesn't move, you've probably reached the last tab setting before the margin.

Note Shift+Tab is a reserved key in some X-Window managers. If you can't use Shift+Tab, click Format ➪ Paragraph ➪ Back Tab instead.

By default, WordPerfect sets tabs every half inch relative to the left margin. (Moving the left margin normally shifts the tabs as well.) You can remove and reset tabs to position text precisely. For example, you can remove all but two tabs to create two tabular columns.

Tip You can also use columns or tables to line up your text. In particular, see the discussion of various types of columns (including tabular columns) in Chapter 16, "Formatting with Columns and Tables."

Understanding Tab Types

WordPerfect provides eight types of tabs to align your text. Left tabs are the default, which is why a [Left Tab] code is normally inserted when you press Tab.

Examine the types of tabs in Figure 15-5. A *left tab* stays to the left of your text, so the text you type moves to the right of the tab. A *right tab* stays to the right of your text, so the text you type moves to the left. Text centers around a *center tab*, and a *decimal tab* lines up your text on the decimal point (or another character you designate).

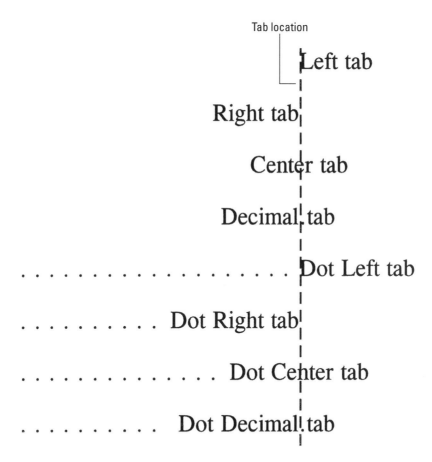

Figure 15-5: How text positions around different types of tabs

When you use a *dot leader tab*, a row of dots (or whatever character you specify) appears from the insertion point to your tab-aligned text.

When you change the tab type, existing tab codes that follow your settings are converted (other than hard tabs, which discussed in the following "Inserting Hard Tabs" section).

Setting Tabs

You can change tab settings from the current paragraph through the rest of a document or a block of selected text. Tabs can be set on the ruler or in the Tabs dialog box.

Setting tabs with the ruler

The ruler is a handy tool for setting tabs, because you can visualize the tabs as you set them. Click View ➪ Ruler to display the ruler (or press Alt+Shift+F3). The tab settings for the paragraph at the insertion point appear as various shaped triangles on the ruler.

You can click a tab marker, then drag it to a new position, or drag it down off the ruler to remove it (see Figure 15-6). To set a new tab, click the bottom of the ruler at the desired position.

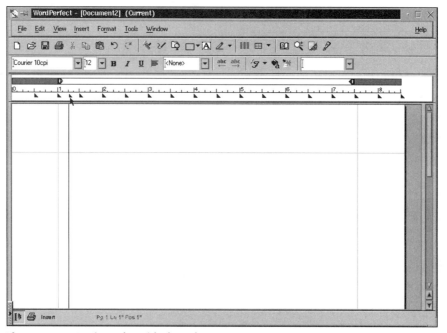

Figure 15-6: Setting tabs with the ruler

Normally, when you set a tab by using the ruler, it snaps to the nearest invisible grid line, located every $1/16$ of an inch or every millimeter. You can turn off the ruler grid to drag a tab to any location. (Right-click the ruler, click Preferences, then uncheck "Tabs snap to Ruler grid.")

Changing the new tab type

When you click the bottom of the ruler to set a new (additional) tab, the tab is of the default type, normally a left tab. To change the new tab type, right-click anywhere along the lower edge of the ruler and select the type of tab you want, as shown in Figure 15-7. To change an existing tab's type, right-click its icon on the ruler.

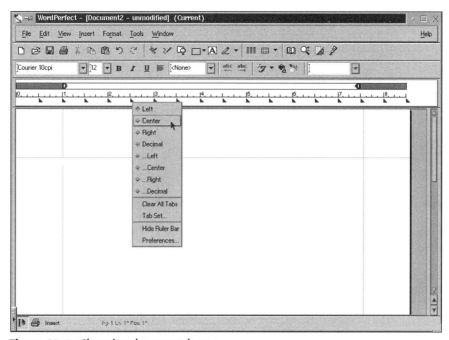

Figure 15-7: Changing the new tab type

Tab settings affect text from the paragraph at the insertion point through the rest of document.

Clearing all tabs

To clear all existing tabs, click the paragraph in which you want to clear the tabs, right-click the lower edge of the ruler, then click Clear All Tabs. Click Tab Set ➪ Default to return to the defaults.

Setting multiple options by using the Tabs dialog box

For heavy-duty tab setting, place the insertion point where you want to change the settings, then click Format ➪ Line ➪ Tab Set to call the Tabs dialog box shown in

Figure 15-8. You can set multiple tab options at once in this box. (You can also right-click the ruler and click Tab Set.)

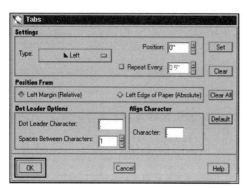

Figure 15-8: Set multiple options by using the Tabs dialog box

Specifying a tab's type and position

You can set both of these tab attributes at once in the Tabs dialog box. Select the type of tab you want from the "Type" list in the Tabs dialog box. Specify where you want to place each tab in the "Position" box. (You can type decimals or fractions.)

Normally, tabs position from "Left Margin (Relative)." You can click "Left Edge of Paper (Absolute)" to specify tabs that stay put as you adjust the left margin.

You must click the Set button for each tab you specify. (The new tab appears on the ruler.)

To place tabs like your new one at regular intervals, click Clear All to remove all current tabs, then check "Repeat every," specify an interval, and click Set.

Clearing tabs and restoring tab settings

The Clear button in the Tabs dialog box lets you delete the individual tabs you specify in the Position box, though the ruler is better suited to that purpose. You can clear all the tabs with the Clear All button, then specify your settings for new repeating tabs, as described in a preceding section, or click Default to return to the default tab settings.

Changing dot leaders and the align character

Dot leaders are the dotted lines that lead the eye across tabular columns, as in an index or table of contents. You can change the character used for dot leader tabs in the "Dot Leader Character" box. To create the line of scissors in Figure 15-9, press Ctrl+W to insert the iconic symbol 5,33. You can also specify the number of spaces between dot leader characters.

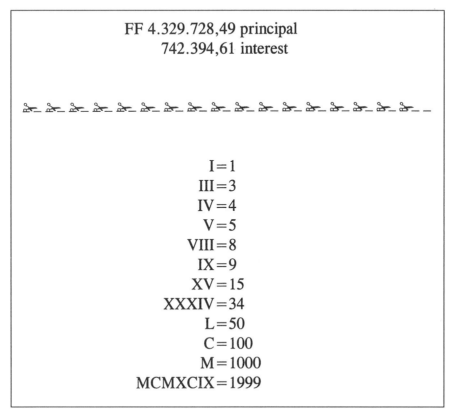

Figure 15-9: Custom dot leader and align characters

When you use a decimal or dot decimal tab, your entries normally align on the decimal point for U.S. English. You can change this alignment character as well. Figure 15-9 illustrates decimal tabs aligned on commas (above the line of scissors) and equal signs (below the scissors).

Inserting Hard Tabs

Suppose you want to use a right tab or a decimal tab instead of a left tab in a particular line of text, without changing the tab type for the remainder of your document. Insert a *hard tab* of the desired type for one-time use. Hard tabs stay as the type you specify, even if you change the type in the rest of your document.

To place a hard tab, click Format ➪ Line ➪ Other Codes, then click the type of tab you want and click Insert. (To insert a hard back tab, press Shift+Tab, or click Format ➪ Paragraph ➪ Back Tab.)

Indenting

Tabs shift text on a single line. To move all the lines in a paragraph to the next tab setting, use an indent instead of tabbing each line.

The easiest way to indent your text is to press F7 (F4 for a DOS-compatible keyboard). You can also right-click and click Indent, or click Format ⇨ Paragraph ⇨ Indent. The text that you type (until you press Enter) indents to the next tab stop.

When you indent existing text (by selecting it and pressing F7), all text from the insertion point to the end of the paragraph is indented to the next tab stop.

When you click Format ⇨ Paragraph, you have a choice of indent styles:

✦ *Indent* moves all lines of a paragraph one tab stop to the right.

✦ *Hanging Indent* (sometimes called an *outdent*) moves all lines — except the first line — one tab stop to the right.

✦ *Double Indent* moves text one tab stop inward from both margins.

✦ *Back Tab* moves the first line of a paragraph one tab stop to the left.

Normally, you want to indent from the beginning of a paragraph, not from the middle of a line. Figure 15-10 illustrates the indent types.

> TAB indents the first line of a paragraph. To indent the first line of all your paragraphs, click Format ⇨ Paragraph ⇨ Format and specify the amount of your first line indent.
>
> INDENT moves all the lines of a paragraph one tab stop to the right.
>
> DOUBLE INDENT moves text one tab stop inward from both margins.
>
> BACK TAB moves the first line of a paragraph one tab stop to the left.
>
> HANGING INDENT moves all lines except the first line one tab stop to the right.

Figure 15-10: Various ways to indent a paragraph

For more on formatting paragraphs, see the following "Customizing the Paragraph" section.

Centering a Line of Text

You can *center* a single line of text (or even part of a line) between the left and right margins (such as for a title or heading). To center a line of text:

1. In an existing line of text, right-click at the beginning of the text you want to center, then click Center (or click the location and click Format ➪ Line ➪ Center).

2. To create a new line of centered text, click Format ➪ Line ➪ Center, type your text, then press Enter. (You can also click the center of your screen with the shadow cursor.)

You can center text in columns just as with ordinary lines.

If you select two or more lines of text and then click Format ➪ Line ➪ Center, the entire block is center-justified, rather than each individual line.

Using Flush Right

Use *flush right* to align a single line of text — or a part of a line — with the right margin. You can also use this alignment to insert dot leaders all the way to the right margin:

✦ In an existing line of text, right-click the location where you want the right alignment to begin, then click Flush Right (or click the location and click Format ➪ Line ➪ Flush Right).

✦ For a new line of text, click Format ➪ Line ➪ Flush Right, type your text, then Press Enter. (You can also click the right margin with your shadow cursor.)

When you align two or more lines of selected text with the right margin, they are right-justified instead.

Using Justification

To *justify* (align) lines of text:

1. Select the lines of text, or click the paragraph where you want justification to begin.

2. Click the Justification button (Format ➪ Justification), then choose Left, Right, Center, Full, and All to create the various types of justification shown in Figure 15-11.

The choice of All fully justifies all the lines of text, including short lines at the ends of paragraphs that aren't normally spread across the page with full justification. (Use All to space the characters in a title across the page, as in a circus poster.)

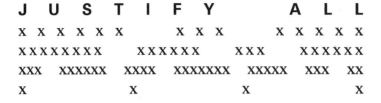

Figure 15-11: Types of justification

Justification is always paragraph by paragraph, not line by line. The Justification button on the property bar indicates the justification type used at the insertion point.

Advancing Text

To position text precisely, as when you're designing a letterhead or filling out a preprinted form, click Format ➪ Typesetting ➪ Advance, then specify the distance and direction you want to advance your text, either from the insertion point, the left edge of the page, or the top of the page (see Figure 15-12). An Advance code is placed at the insertion point to move your text.

Figure 15-12: Advancing text

To place the text *below* a vertical position from the top of the page, rather than above it, click "From Top of Page," then click "Text Above Position" to remove the check. To delete an Advance code, drag it out of the Reveal Codes area.

Adjusting Line Spacing, Line Height, and Leading

Line height, line spacing, and leading are interrelated terms used in controlling the distance between lines of text.

✦ *Line height* is the distance between the top of one (single-spaced) line of text and the top of the next, which includes some white space above the print, as shown in Figure 15-13.

✦ *Line spacing* specifies the number of line heights from one printed line to the next — such as double-spacing or one-and-a-half spacing.

✦ *Leading* (pronounced "ledding") is the white space placed between lines of text.

Tip Double-spacing more than doubles the white space between lines, because you're doubling the total line height, not just the leading.

Line height   Leading

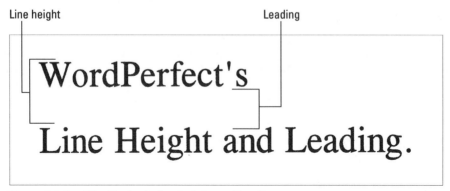

Figure 15-13: WordPerfect's line height and leading

When you change the font face or size, WordPerfect adjusts the line height automatically to accommodate.

Changing line spacing

To change line spacing:

    1. Click where you want the new line spacing to begin, or select a block of text.

    2. Click Format ➪ Line ➪ Spacing, then specify the spacing you want (see Figure 15-14).

Figure 15-14: Changing line spacing

Tip

To change the line spacing between paragraphs (instead of between all lines), see "Changing the Paragraph Format" later in this chapter.

Adjusting the line height

To adjust the line height:

    1. Click the paragraph in which you want the new line height to begin, or select the paragraphs you want to change.

2. Click Format ➪ Line ➪ Height, then click:

- *Auto*, to use the default height for the font you're using.
- *Fixed*, to specify the line height you want (see Figure 15-15).

Figure 15-15: Adjusting the line height

Adjusting line leading

The leading adjustment specifies the amount of space to add or subtract from the total line height. Leading is an exact adjustment, in inches, points, or another unit of measurement. (To adjust spacing by a percentage, rather than by a fixed amount, adjust the line spacing instead.)

To adjust line leading:

1. Click the paragraph in which you want the new setting to begin, or select the lines of text that you want to adjust.

2. Click Format ➪ Typesetting ➪ Word/Letter Spacing.

3. Check "Adjust Leading" (see Figure 15-16), then specify the amount of space you want to add between the lines. (You can type your entry in points, such as **3p**.)

You can specify a negative leading adjustment to close up your lines, but beware of entangling the lowercase *descenders* (like the bottom half of a *p*) that extend below the baseline with the characters in the line below.

Numbering lines

Some documents (such as legal documents, contracts, and instructions) use line numbers for reference. To number the lines in your document:

1. Click the paragraph in which you want the line numbering to begin, or select the paragraphs you want to line number.

2. Click Format ➪ Line ➪ Numbering.

3. Specify the line numbering options you want, as described in Table 15-1.

4. Check "Turn Line Numbering On" (see Figure 15-17) and click OK.

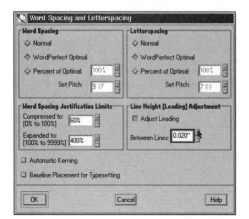

Figure 15-16: Adjusting the leading between lines

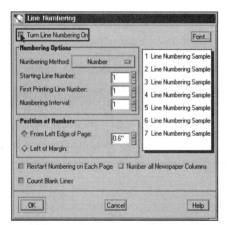

Figure 15-17: Numbering lines

Table 15-1	
Line Numbering Options	
Line Numbering Option	**Enables You to**
Numbering method	Specify numbers, letters, or Roman numerals.
Starting line number	Specify the number assigned to the first line.
First printing line number	Specify the first line number to print.
Numbering interval	Specify how often to print line numbers.

Line Numbering Option	Enables You to
From left edge of page	Position the numbers a specified distance from the edge of the page (or from the center of the space between columns).
Left of margin	Position numbers a specified distance outside the left margin.
Restart numbering on each page	Begin with the starting line number at the top of each page.
Count blank lines	Include blank lines in your line count.
Number all newspaper columns	Number lines in every column.
Font	Specify a particular font face, style, size, color, or other attribute for the line numbers.

Footnotes, endnotes, headers, and footers are not included when numbering lines. When numbering newspaper columns, click "Left of margin" to specify where the line numbers will appear in each column. Keep the distance small enough to fit the numbers within the left margins.

To change your line numbering options, click the line in which you want your new options to begin, then click Format ➪ Line ➪ Numbering.

To turn off line numbering, click the first paragraph you don't want to be numbered, then click Format ➪ Line ➪ Numbering and remove the check from "Turn line numbering on."

You can reactivate line numbering later in your document to start a new line numbering sequence, beginning with the number you specify.

Customizing the Paragraph

As you write, you express your thoughts in sentences and arrange groups of thoughts in paragraphs. Long paragraphs can overwhelm the reader, while very short paragraphs can make your text choppy and hard to follow. The length of your paragraphs may vary, depending on content and audience. For example, paragraphs in a two-page memo or a children's story are normally shorter than those in a scientific paper.

The format of your paragraphs is a major part of your document's appearance. This section shows you several ways to customize your paragraphs. You can also number your paragraphs (see Chapter 17, "Organizing with Bullets and Outlines") or dress them up with borders and fills (see Chapter 23, "Adding Graphic Lines, Borders, and Fills").

What's a Paragraph?

First, how does WordPerfect identify a paragraph? You signal the end of a paragraph every time you press Enter. This action places a hard return code in your document, takes you to the next line, and starts a new paragraph. A hard page break (Ctrl+Enter) also signals the end of a paragraph.

Changing the Paragraph Format

To change your paragraph format (spacing, margins, indent, and so forth):

1. Click where you want the new paragraph format to begin, or select the paragraphs you want to change.

2. Click Format ➪ Paragraph ➪ Format, then specify the settings that you want to change (see Figure 15-18):

   - *First Line Indent* to indent the first paragraph line a specified amount automatically.

   - *Spacing Between Paragraphs* to adjust the spacing between paragraphs. (Try this technique instead of pressing Enter twice.)

   - *Left Margin Adjustment* to adjust the left paragraph margin relative to the current page margin. A negative amount outdents the paragraph.

   - *Right Margin Adjustment* to adjust the right paragraph margin relative to the current page margin.

Tip   When adjusting the number of lines, the number is a multiple of the line spacing. If line spacing is 2 and paragraph spacing is 1.5 lines, you end up with triple spacing between paragraphs (2 · 1.5).

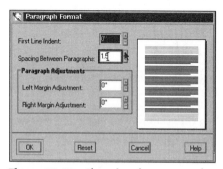

Figure 15-18: Changing the paragraph format

Returning to the default paragraph format settings

Changes to the paragraph format (unless you applied them to selected paragraphs) remain in effect until you reset the format. To return to the default paragraph indent, spacing, and margin settings:

1. Click the paragraph in which you want to return to the default settings.

2. Click Format ➪ Paragraph ➪ Format ➪ Reset.

Deleting paragraph settings

If you don't like your new paragraph settings, go into Reveal Codes and delete the offending code. (You can adjust separate codes for first-line indent, paragraph spacing, left margin adjustment, and right margin adjustment.)

Reusing Paragraph Attributes and Styles

Suppose you just created a nice paragraph format that you want to use in future documents. You may want, for example, to publish a regular sales brochure or issue standard invoices or reports that have a consistent, professional appearance. You can accomplish this task by saving the format, fonts, and attributes of existing paragraphs, including headings, as styles that you can use over and over again.

Chapter 4, "Becoming an Instant WordPerfect Expert," shows you how easy it is to save and apply paragraph styles by using the QuickFormat and QuickStyle features. Chapter 20, "Working Quickly with ExpressDocs Templates and Styles," shows you how to set up style libraries.

Customizing Your Pages

Page appearances can be critical in getting your message across. You can adjust margins, add headers or footers, display a watermark, number the pages, and add borders. You can even create a custom paper size.

You don't have to use the same page format throughout your document. You can create a title page using a large, decorative font with a border, then use a more subdued format for the body of the document.

The following sections show you many ways in which you can customize your page. Page borders and fills are covered in Chapter 23, "Adding Graphic Lines, Borders, and Fills." Page numbering options are described in Chapter 14, "Controlling Text and Numbering Pages."

Adjusting Page Margins

Page margins are the white spaces to the right, left, above, and below the text on the printed page. The default U.S. settings are one inch all around.

When you adjust the left and right margin settings, you affect current and subsequent paragraphs. When you adjust the top and bottom margins, you affect current and subsequent pages. The settings remain in effect until you change them again.

To adjust your page margins:

1. Click the paragraph (for left or right margins) or page (for top or bottom margins) where you want the margin change to begin.

2. Click Format ➪ Margins, and specify your new settings (see Figure 15-19).

Figure 15-19: Adjusting page margins

Adjusting a margin by using the mouse

To adjust a margin by using the mouse, drag its guideline, as described in Chapter 4, "Becoming an Instant WordPerfect Expert."

Deleting page margin settings

If you don't like your new page margins, you can reverse your changes immediately by pressing Ctrl+Z (Undo). Later, you can go into Reveal Codes and delete the individual margin codes.

Changing your default page margins

To change the page margins for all your new documents, choose page margin options while editing the Document Style (see the preceding section "Changing the Document Style").

Centering Text on the Page

Although you can center any line or paragraph horizontally between the left and right margins, you must center the page to have the text centered vertically from the top to the bottom. Figure 15-20 shows a book title page with the text centered on the page. The graphics box with the horse was added after the text was typed.

How to Stay Alive Around Thoroughbreds

by

Ima Goode Jumper

Figure 15-20: Text centered vertically on the page

To center text on the page:

1. Click the page to be centered or the page in which you want centering to begin.

2. Click Format ➪ Page ➪ Center.

3. Click to center the "Current Page" or "Current and Subsequent Pages" (see Figure 15-21).

Figure 15-21: Centering text on the page

To preview how your centered text will print, zoom to Full Page from Page View.

To turn off page centering, click the page in which you want centering to end, then click Format ➪ Page ➪ Center ➪ No Centering (refer to Figure 15-21).

Selecting a Page Size and Orientation

The page size in your document should match the paper on which you're printing. WordPerfect supplies standard page definitions from which to choose, but you can create your own definition for any size paper your printer can handle.

The default page size for the U.S. version of WordPerfect is $8^{1}/_{2}$ by 11 inches. The default orientation is *portrait,* with lines of text across the width of the paper (like this page). The other orientation is *landscape,* which prints the text along the length of the paper.

To select another page size or orientation:

1. Click where you want the new page setting to begin.

2. Click File ➪ Page Setup ➪ Page Size, or Format ➪ Page ➪ Page Setup ➪ Page Size.

3. Select the page size definition and orientation you want (see Figure 15-22).

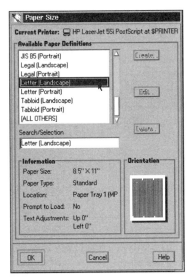

Figure 15-22: Click a definition to change the page size or orientation; information about the new size appears in the box below

Creating a Custom Page Definition

If the paper size you want is not on the list of predefined sizes for your printer, create a custom paper definition:

1. Click File ➪ Page Setup ➪ Page Size ➪ Create, and give your definition a name (see Figure 15-23).

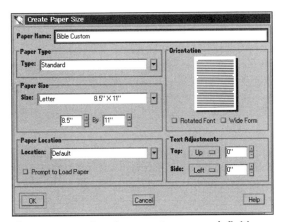

Figure 15-23: Creating a custom page definition

2. Select a paper type (such as standard, letterhead, labels, or envelope).

3. Select a paper size or specify a custom width and height.

4. Select the paper location. Most desktop printers have only one source, so the setting should normally be left as Default. Select Manual Feed if you're defining an envelope or special form that must be fed one sheet at a time.

5. Select a font orientation of Portrait, Landscape, or Both. (Most printers rotate the font rather than the paper to print landscape; if this is the case, select the Both orientation.)

6. Specify printing adjustments to shift your text away from the unprintable zone on your printer — either up, down, left, or right. (Normally, it makes more sense to adjust your document's text, if needed, rather than the page definition.)

To use your custom page definition as the default for all your new documents, select your page definition while editing the Document Style (see the preceding "Changing the Document Style" section in this chapter).

Editing or Deleting a Page Definition

To edit or delete a page definition, click File ➪ Page Setup ➪ Page Size, select the definition, then click Edit or Delete.

Creating Headers, Footers, and Watermarks

Headers and *footers* print at the top or bottom of every page, or on alternate odd or even pages. In a book, they usually include the page number, along with the book title, chapter title, or section title. In papers or reports, headers and footers are a handy place for such information as the revision date, author, company name, or filename (Insert ➪ Other ➪ Filename).

Watermarks are shaded graphics or text images that appear to print behind your document text. They can add a customized elegance to your printed page, or display an arresting element such as "TOP SECRET." A watermark can consist of a company logo, text (usually a decorative font in a large size), or any other graphic. (The watermark in Figure 15-24 uses a clip art image.) Like headers and footers, you can place watermarks on every page, or on alternating odd or even pages.

At any location in your document, you can have two active definitions for headers, footers, and watermarks: A and B. You can print them both on the same page, but the general idea is that you can have distinct displays for the facing odd and even pages, as in a book. Definitions take effect from the current page forward, so you can define different headers, footers, and watermarks in different parts of your document.

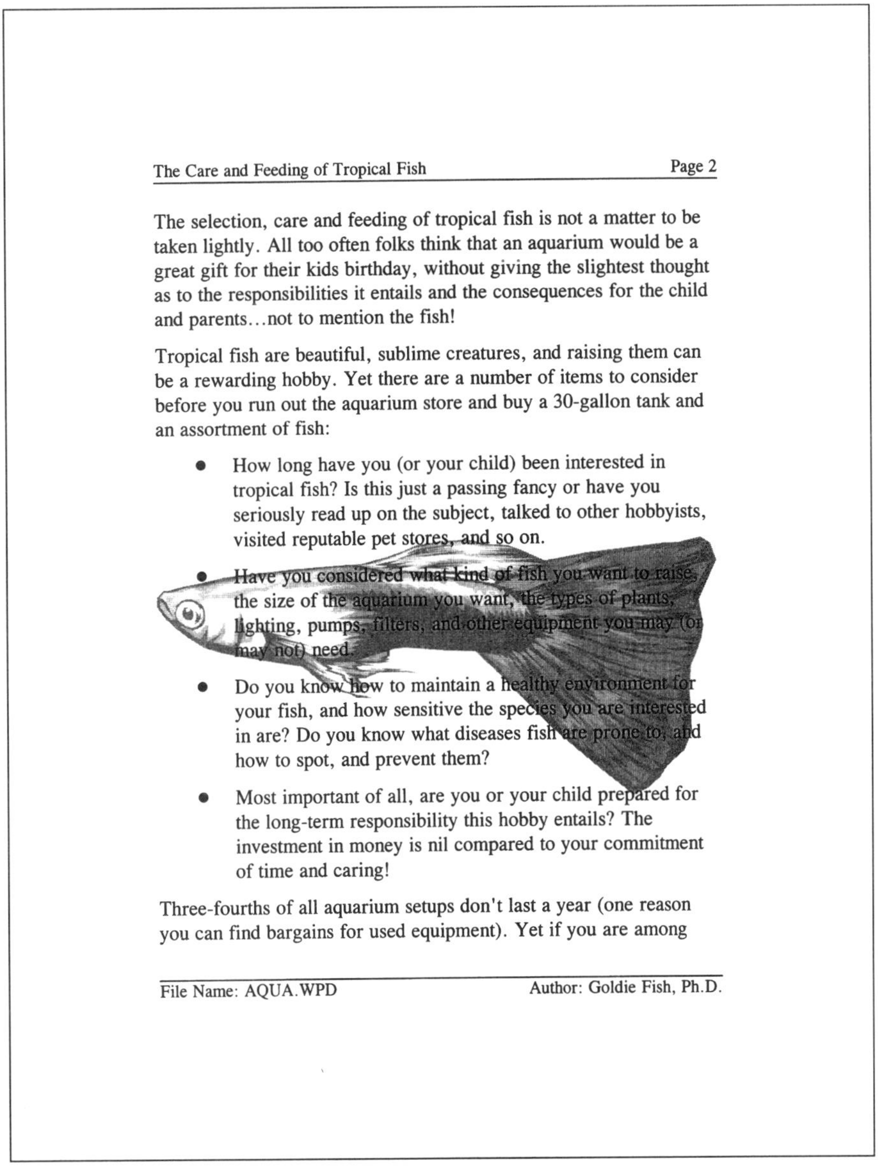

The Care and Feeding of Tropical Fish   Page 2

The selection, care and feeding of tropical fish is not a matter to be
taken lightly. All too often folks think that an aquarium would be a
great gift for their kids birthday, without giving the slightest thought
as to the responsibilities it entails and the consequences for the child
and parents…not to mention the fish!

Tropical fish are beautiful, sublime creatures, and raising them can
be a rewarding hobby. Yet there are a number of items to consider
before you run out the aquarium store and buy a 30-gallon tank and
an assortment of fish:

- How long have you (or your child) been interested in
  tropical fish? Is this just a passing fancy or have you
  seriously read up on the subject, talked to other hobbyists,
  visited reputable pet stores, and so on.

- Have you considered what kind of fish you want to raise,
  the size of the aquarium you want, the types of plants,
  lighting, pumps, filters, and other equipment you may (or
  may not) need.

- Do you know how to maintain a healthy environment for
  your fish, and how sensitive the species you are interested
  in are? Do you know what diseases fish are prone to, and
  how to spot, and prevent them?

- Most important of all, are you or your child prepared for
  the long-term responsibility this hobby entails? The
  investment in money is nil compared to your commitment
  of time and caring!

Three-fourths of all aquarium setups don't last a year (one reason
you can find bargains for used equipment). Yet if you are among

File Name: AQUA.WPD   Author: Goldie Fish, Ph.D.

Figure 15-24: Page with a header, footer, and watermark

When replacing a header, footer, or watermark, specify the same letter for the
replacement. For example, only another header A can replace a header A—not a
header B. You can turn off any or all headers, footers, and watermarks at any time.

Creating a Header or Footer

To create a header or footer:

1. Click the first page in which you want your header or footer to appear.

2. Click Insert ➪ Header/Footer. (In Page or Two Page view, you can also right-click the top or bottom margin.)

3. Click the header or footer you want to create, then click Create (see Figure 15-25). (If you're working in Page view, you proceed directly to the header or footer; if you're working in Draft view, a header or footer window opens. This view looks much like a blank document window.)

Figure 15-25: Creating a header or footer

4. Add any text, graphics, and formatting, and make any property bar selections:

   • The Page Numbering button to insert the page, secondary, chapter, volume, or total page number (see Chapter 14, "Controlling Text and Numbering Pages").

   • The Horizontal Line button to set off your header or footer with a horizontal line (see Chapter 23, "Adding Graphic Lines, Borders, and Fills").

   • The Header Placement button to specify display placement on odd/even pages or on every page.

   • The Header Distance button to set the distance between the text and the header or footer. (The default is one blank line, and you can specify spacing in points. For example, type **18p** for a spacing of 1¹/₂ lines when using a 12-point font.)

   • The Previous button or the Next button to go to the previous or next header/footer.

   • The Close button to exit the property bar. (In Page view, simply click outside of the header or footer.)

To change the header or footer for subsequent pages, create a new header or footer using the same letter as the header or footer you're replacing.

Creating a Watermark

To create a watermark:

1. Click the first page in which you want your watermark to appear.

2. Click Insert ⇨ Watermark, click watermark A or B, then click Create (see Figure 15-26). A new WordPerfect document window opens.

3. Click the Insert Clip Art button or the Insert File button to insert a graphic or text.

   You can type any text in the watermark layer and apply any font or formatting.

Note   If you're using a generic driver for your video card and your watermark consists of a pixel file, your screen may refresh more slowly. This situation will become less of a problem as more video drivers become available for Linux.

Figure 15-26: Creating a watermark

4. Make any other property bar selections:

   • The Watermark Placement button to specify display placement on odd, even, or every page.

   • The Watermark Shading button to adjust the default 25% shading for graphics or text (see Figure 15-27).

   • The Previous button or the Next button to go to the previous or next watermark.

   • The Close button to exit the feature bar.

Figure 15-27: Adjusting watermark shading

Tip   The WATERMRK.WCM macro that comes with WordPerfect helps you create a watermark from a graphic or text, though the options are limited.

Editing Headers, Footers, and Watermarks

To edit a header, footer, or watermark, click any page in which it is in effect, click Insert, click Header/Footer or Watermark, click the item, then click Edit.

In Page view, you can click a header or footer to edit the text directly, or right-click the page and click Watermark to edit a watermark. To change the watermark image, just delete the old one and replace it with the new picture.

 Tip   Editing a header, footer, or watermark changes it all the way back to the first page on which it was created. To specify a different header, footer, or watermark from a certain page forward, create a replacement new element of the same letter (A or B).

Ending or Suppressing Headers, Footers, and Watermarks

You can discontinue headers, footers, and watermarks at any point. You may also want to suppress these items on certain pages, such as title pages or on a page where a graph appears.

To discontinue a header, footer, or watermark from the current page forward, click Header/Footer or Watermark from the Insert menu, then click Discontinue.

To suppress headers, footers, or watermarks on a particular page, click Format ➪ Page ➪ Suppress, then check the items you want to suppress.

To delete a header, footer, or watermark, you can drag its associated code out of the Reveal Codes window, or use Find and Replace, replacing the code with nothing (see Chapter 13, "Editing Techniques").

Using Predefined Watermarks

When you insert clip art in creating a watermark, WordPerfect provides an extensive library of predefined watermark images. Use them to create customized stationery, or stamp your documents with DO NOT COPY, SECRET, or other furtive messages, as shown in Figure 15-28.

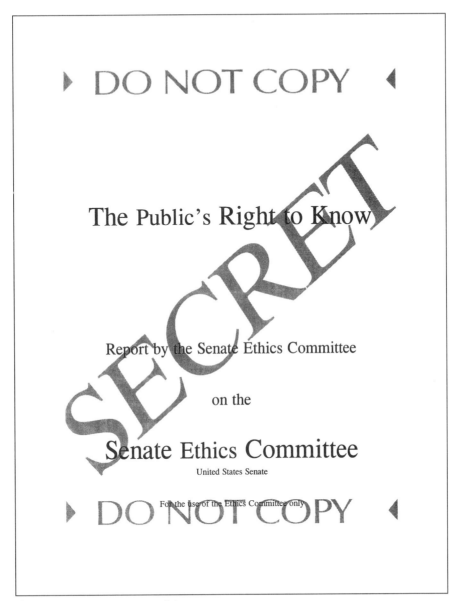

Figure 15-28: Two watermark images you can use

Creating Custom Watermarks

Any graphics image can be used as a watermark. You may need to change the image to black-and-white and adjust the shading to achieve the desired effect (see Chapter 9, "Working with Graphics").

For More Information . . .

On	See
Formatting with the shadow cursor	Chapter 4
Applying paragraph and page borders	Chapter 23
Using document templates	Chapter 20
Formatting with columns and tables	Chapter 16
Numbering paragraphs	Chapter 17
Applying QuickFormats and QuickStyles	Chapter 4
Setting up style libraries	Chapter 20
Numbering pages	Chapter 14
Dragging margin guidelines	Chapter 4
Finding and replacing formatting codes	Chapter 13
Modifying graphics	Chapter 9
Creating labels	Chapter 28

✦   ✦   ✦

Formatting with Columns and Tables

While information is usually displayed from margin to margin (with an occasional tab, indent, or graphic thrown in), columns and tables provide you with other powerful, easy-to-use formatting tools. This chapter gives you all the tips and tricks for using these features.

Presenting Information in Columns

Columns are a handy way to view many types of information, such as an address book, an inventory list, or a restaurant menu. Columns are also useful when writing a script with stage directions or publishing a newsletter with many separate articles.

In WordPerfect, you can specify up to 24 columns across the page and define custom widths and spacing. You can set tabs within columns and justify text. Almost anything that can go on a page can go in a column, including graphics and tables.

Columns come in two basic flavors: *newspaper* (up and down) and *parallel* (across). Each type has several variations and options.

Newspaper Columns

Columns are a must for newspapers, in which the page is far too wide for the reader's eye to grasp. The *standard newspaper columns* in Figure 16-1 read from top to bottom, then jump to the top of the next column upon reaching the end of the page or a column break.

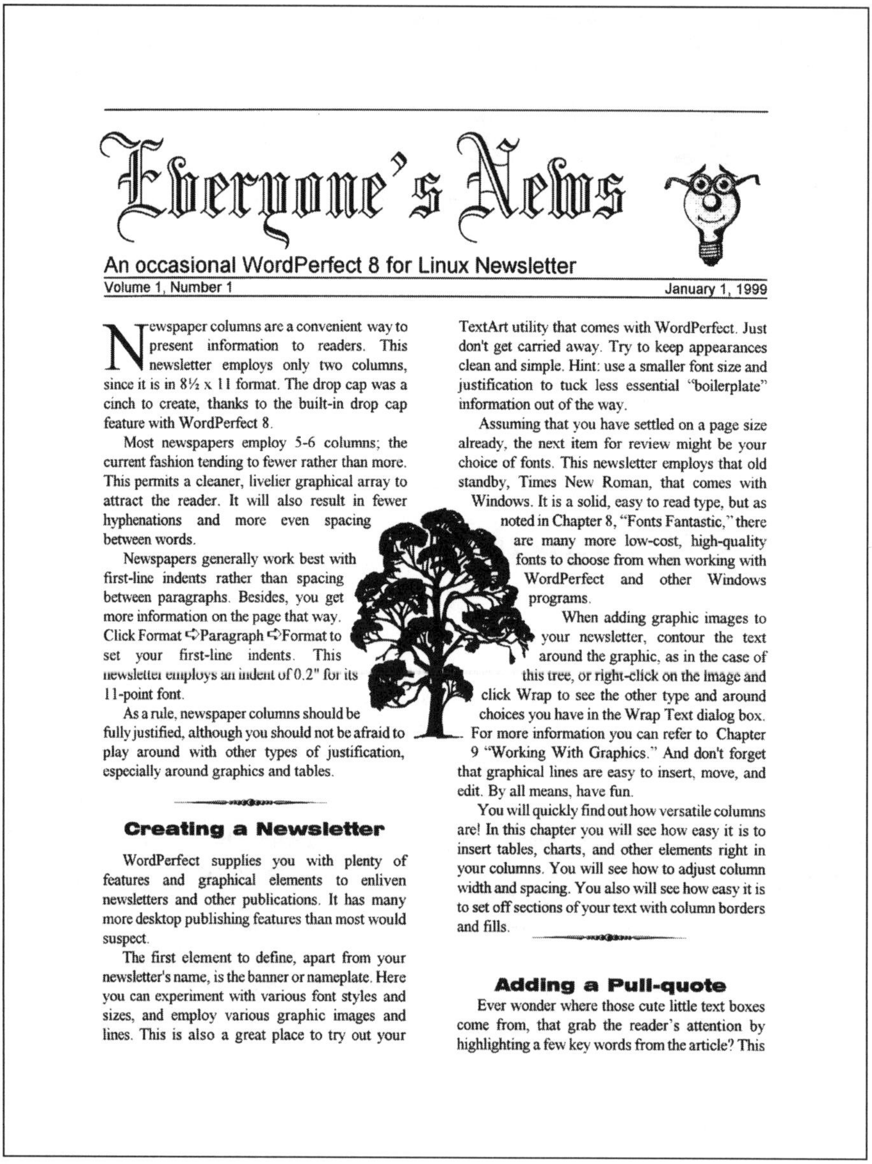

Figure 16-1: Standard newspaper columns

The *balanced newspaper columns* in Figure 16-2 are especially useful if you have a short text passage that you want to display across the page.

Everyone's News

An occasional WordPerfect 8 for Linux Newsletter

Volume 1, Number 1   January 1, 1999

Newspaper columns are a convenient way to present information to readers. This newsletter employs only two columns, since it is in 8½ x 11 format. The drop cap was a cinch to create, thanks to the built-in drop cap feature with WordPerfect 8.

Most newspapers employ 5-6 columns; the current fashion tending to fewer rather than more. This permits a cleaner, livelier graphical array to attract the reader. It will also result in fewer hyphenations and more even spacing.

Newspapers generally work best with first-line indents rather than spacing between paragraphs. Besides, you get more information on the page that way. Click Format ⇨Paragraph ⇨Format to set your first-line indents. This newsletter employs an indent of 0.2" for its 11-point font.

As a rule, newspaper columns should be fully justified, although you should not be afraid to play around with other types of justification, especially around graphics and tables.

Creating a Newsletter

WordPerfect supplies you with plenty of features and graphical elements to enliven newsletters and other publications. It has many more desktop publishing features than most would suspect.

The first element to define, apart from your newsletter's name, is the banner or nameplate. Here you can experiment with various font styles and sizes, and also a great place to try out your TextArt don't get carried away. Try to keep smaller font size and justification to tuck out of the way.

Assuming that you have settled for review might be your choice of old standby, Times New Roman, solid, easy to read type, but as noted there are many more low-cost, high-working with WordPerfect and other

employ various graphic images and lines. This is a utility that comes with WordPerfect. Just appearances clean and simple. Hint: use a less essential "boilerplate" information

on a page size already, the next item fonts. This newsletter employs that that comes with Windows. It is a in Chapter 8 on "Fonts Fantastic," quality fonts to choose from when Windows programs.

When adding graphic images to around the graphic, as in the case of Wrap to see the other type and around more information you can refer to Chapter 9 graphical lines are easy to insert, move, and edit.

your newsletter, you can contour the text this tree, or right-click on the image and click choices you have in the Wrap Text dialog box. For "Working With Graphics." And don't forget that By all means, have fun.

You will quickly find out how versatile columns are! In this chapter you will see how easy it is to insert tables, charts, and other elements right in your columns. You will see how to adjust column width and spacing.

Figure 16-2: Balanced newspaper columns

Parallel Columns

Parallel columns grouped across the page in rows can be seen in Figure 16-3. The first column in the next row starts below the longest column in the row above. Parallel columns are especially useful in résumés, scripts, lists, and other documents in which information is arrayed across the page.

Figure 16-3: Parallel columns

Alternatives to the Column Feature

You can also create columns just by setting tabs, as with the address list in Figure 16-4. See Chapter 15, "Formatting Your Document," for details on setting tabs.

Sonya Brown	789 Farm Road	Los Gatos	CA	95030
Dr. Helen Wang	2305 Mountain Drive	Boulder	CO	80301
Mathew Chapin	362 Meadow Oak Lane	Manchester	CT	06040
Elizabeth Somner	1795 South Street	Winsted	CT	06098
Nancy Morgan	2532 Chapman Drive, N.W.	Washington	DC	20036
Brian Nelson	15 Federal Street	Middlefield	MA	01243
Judy Davis	375 Hamlet Avenue	Brooklyn	NY	11225
Miranda Sanchez	426 President Street	Westlake	OH	44145
George O'Connor	47 Grove Street	Dallas	TX	75235

Figure 16-4: Tabular column alternative

As explained in a following section, multicolumn tables are an easy-to-use alternative to parallel columns with a number of powerful features. You can remove the lines from the table to make it appear like columnar text.

Defining Columns

To define columns, place the insertion point where you want the columns to begin. Then use either the toolbar or the Columns dialog box to define your columns.

Using the Toolbar

The quickest way to define newspaper columns is to click the Columns button in the toolbar, then click the number of columns you want (see Figure 16-5).

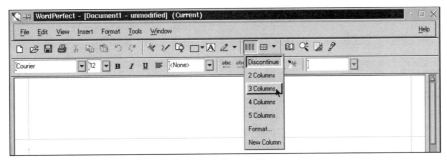

Figure 16-5: Defining columns by using the toolbar

Using the Columns Dialog Box

To access the full range of column features and types:

1. Click Format ➪ Columns, or click the Columns button on the toolbar and click Format.

2. Specify the number of columns you want (see Figure 16-6).

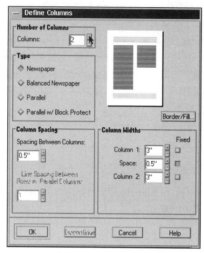

Figure 16-6: Using the Columns dialog box

3. Specify the column type:

   - *Newspaper*, to wrap text from the bottom of one column to the top of the next.

   - *Balanced Newspaper*, to adjust the columns to an equal length.

   - *Parallel*, to jump text from column to column with each text break, with the next row beginning below the longest block.

   - *Parallel w/ Block Protect*, to bump the entire last row to the next page if it doesn't fit, instead of splitting it.

4. Specify any of the following options:

   - *Space Between Columns*, to set the default space between columns.

   - *Line Spacing Between Rows in Parallel Columns*, to adjust the number of blank lines between rows of parallel columns.

- *Column Widths*, to adjust the widths of individual columns (and spaces between columns) to suit the information they contain. Notice that when you change the width of one column, the others adjust in the opposite direction to fit the page margins.

- *Fixed*, to keep the width of the checked column or space constant when you adjust other columns or spaces. (For a column layout of less than the page width, check Fixed for all the widths and spaces.)

- *Border/Fill*, to apply a graphic border or fill to your columns (see Chapter 23, "Adding Graphic Lines, Borders and Fills").

Converting Regular Text into Columns

To convert existing text to columns, place the insertion point in the paragraph where you want your columns to begin, or select a block of text. Then define the columns.

Deleting Column Definitions

To remove columns you have created, go into Reveal Codes and delete the [Col Def:] code. Any column breaks you entered now act as hard page breaks (with the code [HCol-Spg] in Reveal Codes), so delete them as well.

Working in Columns

As soon as you create your columns, you can start entering text, graphics, and anything else. To end a column before the bottom of the page, press Ctrl+Enter to insert a column break. (You can also click the Columns button on the toolbar and click New Column.)

Tip   To insert a page break while in columns, you must press Ctrl+Shift+Enter, because Ctrl+Enter is used for the column break. You can also click Insert ⇨ New Page.

As you enter text in standard newspaper columns, the text fills up the first column, then flows to the next column, as shown in Figure 16-7. With balanced newspaper columns, text moves backward across the column break to keep the columns in balance, as shown in Figure 16-8.

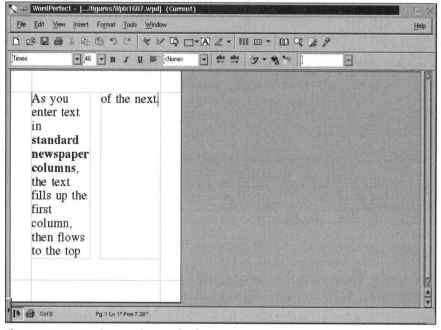

Figure 16-7: Entering text in standard newspaper columns

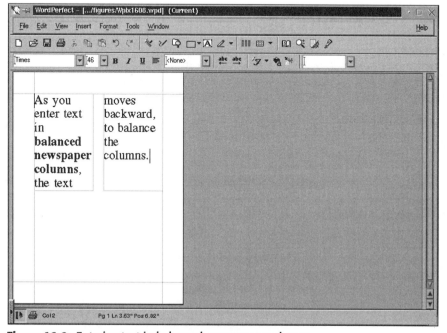

Figure 16-8: Entering text in balanced newspaper columns

As you type in parallel columns, text flows down the current column until you press Ctrl+Enter to jump to the next column. A column break in the last column ends the row, and the row assumes the width of the tallest section.

Discontinuing Columns

To discontinue (turn off) columns:

1. Click where you want the columns to end.
2. Click Format ➪ Columns ➪ Discontinue (or click the Columns button in the toolbar and click Discontinue).

Clicking and Typing in Columns

When the shadow cursor is on (click the Shadow Cursor button on the application bar, if necessary), working in columns is wonderfully intuitive. Simply click wherever you want and begin typing. You can justify text in columns and snap to tabs or indents, just as you do on the page (see Chapter 3, "Mastering the WordPerfect Interface").

To switch columns, point the shadow cursor and click. To turn off columns, point the shadow cursor and click beneath them. (The only thing the shadow cursor can't do is start a new row of columns across the page.)

Formatting and Customizing Columns

You can use the same formatting features within columns that you use in normal document text. You can adjust column widths, set tabs within columns, add line numbers, or apply borders and fills. Three useful features to apply to text within columns follow:

✦ *Full justification* (Format ➪ Justification ➪ Full)

✦ *First-line indent* (Format ➪ Paragraph ➪ Format)

✦ *Hyphenation* (Tools ➪ Language ➪ Hyphenation)

Tip When using tabs to indent within columns, keep the setting small (such as 0.25 inch) to keep your indents in proportion to the column width.

The surest way to adjust column widths and spacing between columns, as described in the preceding section on creating columns, is to click Format ➪ Columns and specify precise widths for your columns and *gutters* (the spaces between columns). The easiest way, as discussed in the following section, is to drag the guidelines.

Dragging Column Guidelines

To adjust the width of a column right on the screen, drag a guideline, as shown in Figure 16-9. (If you don't see the guidelines, click View ➪ Guidelines, then check Columns to put them on display.)

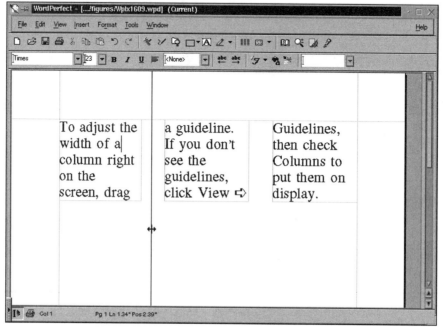

Figure 16-9: Dragging a column guideline

When you drag a guideline, the space between the columns increases or decreases. To adjust adjacent columns without changing the space in-between, drag the column gutter, as shown in Figure 16-10.

Using the Ruler to Adjust Columns

You can change the tabs within columns, the column margins, and the column widths by clicking and dragging the appropriate ruler bar marker, as described in Chapter 15, "Formatting Your Document." (Sketch your column widths and margins by using the ruler bar, then call up the Columns dialog box to make your final adjustments.)

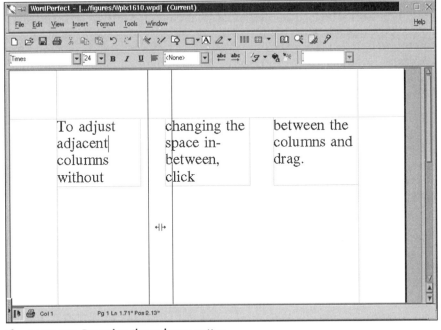

Figure 16-10: Dragging the column gutter

Adding Line Numbers

To add line numbers to newspaper and balanced newspaper columns:

1. Click Format ➪ Line ➪ Numbering.
2. Check "Turn line numbering on."
3. Uncheck "Restart numbering on each page."
4. Check "Number all newspaper columns."

The numbers are placed outside the left margins of numbered columns.

Presenting Information in Tables

A picture may be worth a thousand words, but tables are the best way to present many types of information. Report cards, phone bills, baseball standings, and stock listings are only a few of the everyday tables you use. Many charts and graphs (such as the five-day weather forecast on the television screen) are tabular data in disguise.

What is a table? A *table* is an arrangement of information in horizontal *rows* and vertical *columns*. The intersection of a row and column is a specific *cell* of information. Columns are labeled alphabetically from left to right. Rows are numbered from top to bottom. The *address* of a cell refers to the row and column to which it belongs, as shown in Figure 16-11. Cells can contain numbers, formulas, and graphics in addition to text.

		Column C	
Row 2		Cell C2	

Figure 16-11: Table row, column, and cell addresses

While you can arrange information in a tabular form by using tabs or columns, tables offer many formatting advantages, including header rows that repeat from page to page. You can also assign data types to cells and perform calculations, just as in a spreadsheet program. (see Chapter 21, "Doing Calculations in WordPerfect").

Creating a Table

Chapter 4, "Becoming an Instant WordPerfect Expert," showed you an easy way to create and polish a table: Click the Tables button on the toolbar, drag to create the table, QuickFill the headings, then apply a SpeedFormat style. However, the Create Table dialog box makes it easy to specify an exact number of rows and columns.

Using the Create Table Dialog Box

To open the dialog box, click Insert ➪ Table, then specify the number of columns and rows (see Figure 16-12).

Figure 16-12: Using the Create Table dialog box

Creating a Floating Cell

You can also create a *floating cell*—a one-cell table with no lines—from the Create Table dialog box. Use a floating cell to perform calculations right in your document's text, using the same number formats and formulas as tables (see Chapter 21, "Doing Calculations in WordPerfect").

Creating a Table-In-A-Box

You can draw a table-in-a-box (an unofficial name) and drag it to any location:

1. Click Insert ⇨ Table and specify the number of columns and rows you want.

2. Check "Drag to create a new table," click OK, then drag to the desired table size.

Text flows around the table you draw, as with any graphics box, and there's even a space for a caption, as shown in Figure 16-13.

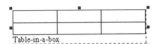

Figure 16-13: Table-in-a-box, with caption below table

Caution To return to creating tables that do not reside in a box, you must remove the check from "Drag to create a new table."

You can format and edit the table within the box. (Editing the contents of a graphics box is easier in Page view.) The height of the box adjusts as you add or delete rows, or change their heights. The width of the box, however, remains fixed as you add or delete columns.

When you resize the width of the box with a mouse, the width of the columns adjusts. However, don't change the height of the box by dragging. The height of the rows will not change, and the box height will also stop adjusting automatically (until you set it back to "maintain proportions").

Creating a Table with the Shadow Cursor

It's even easier to create a table-in-a-box with the shadow cursor. Click and drag a rectangle, then click Table. By using this technique, you'll never have to check the "Drag to create a new table" box. As a result, your next table won't be in a box automatically.

Converting Tabular Text or Parallel Columns to a Table

You can convert text in tabbed or parallel columns to a table. Select the text you want to convert, click the Tables button on the toolbar, and click Tabular Column or Parallel Column (depending on the current format). Figure 16-14 shows a table created from the tabular text.

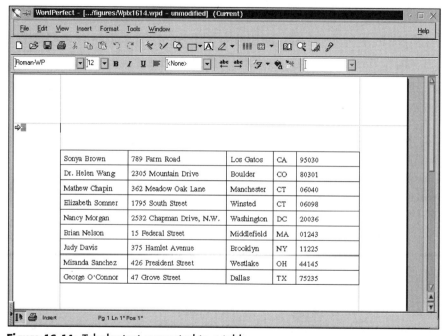

Sonya Brown	789 Farm Road	Los Gatos	CA	95030
Dr. Helen Wang	2305 Mountain Drive	Boulder	CO	80301
Mathew Chapin	362 Meadow Oak Lane	Manchester	CT	06040
Elizabeth Somner	1795 South Street	Winsted	CT	06098
Nancy Morgan	2532 Chapman Drive, N.W.	Washington	DC	20036
Brian Nelson	15 Federal Street	Middlefield	MA	01243
Judy Davis	375 Hamlet Avenue	Brooklyn	NY	11225
Miranda Sanchez	426 President Street	Westlake	OH	44145
George O'Connor	47 Grove Street	Dallas	TX	75235

Figure 16-14: Tabular text converted to a table

Tip   Be sure that the tabular text you're converting has single tabs between items, or you'll get blank columns in your table. (To line up tabular text without inserting extra tabs, display the tab bar or ruler bar, then drag the settings you don't need off the bar and position the remainder.)

Getting Around in Tables

The easiest way to get around in a table is to click the cell you want or use the tab and arrow keys. (Tab at the end of the table to start a new row.)

Because the tab key moves you from cell to cell, you must press Ctrl+Tab to tab within a cell. (Press F7 to tab if Ctrl+Tab is used by your Linux desktop.)

Making Property Bar and Menu Selections

The Table property bar has buttons for commonly used features, such as selecting the current column or row. Other property bars appear when you select cells or select the entire table.

The complete set of table selections can be found on the Table menu on the property bar (see Figure 16-15).

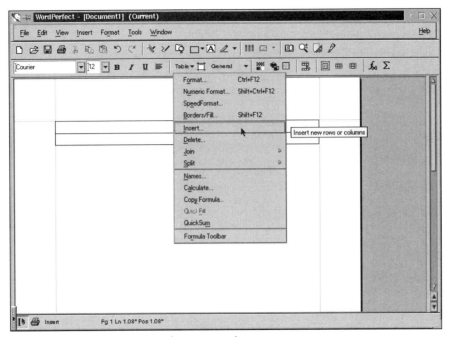

Figure 16-15: Table menu on the property bar

You can also right-click the table to make selections from the QuickMenu.

Using the Selection Arrow

When you point to the upper boundary or left boundary of a cell, a selection arrow appears, as shown in Figure 16-16. Click to select the cell, or click and drag to select a group of cells. (Double-click an upward-pointing arrow to select a column, or double-click a left-pointing arrow to select a row.)

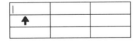

Figure 16-16: Selection arrow

Creating Title and Header Rows

You can use the top table row for the table's title, then designate one or more descriptive rows at the top of a table as header rows that repeat when the table flows to the next page:

1. Click the Select Row button on the property bar to select the top row, then right-click the table and click Join Cells. The top row should now be a single cell, that you can use for the table's title.

2. Click anywhere in the second row (or select one or more cells from the rows you want to use for your table headings).

3. Click the Table menu on the property bar and click Format.

4. Click Row, then check "Header Row" (see Figure 16-17).

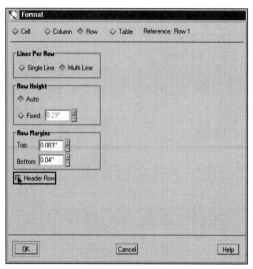

Figure 16-17: Designating header rows that repeat on each page

Your header rows (but not the title) now repeat when the table flows to the next page.

Note that when the insertion point is in a header row, an asterisk (*) appears in the application bar after the cell address.

Creating a Greeting Card List

To put the table features discussed so far to practical use (and preview some others), create the greeting card list in Figure 16-18:

1. Open a new blank document.

2. Click the Tables button on the toolbar bar, then drag to create a 5 · 8 table (5 columns by 8 rows).

3. Click the Select Row button on the property bar to select the top row, then right-click the table and click Join Cells. The top row should now be a single cell.

4. Drag to select the first two rows. Click the Justification button on the property bar and click Center.

5. Type the text in the top two rows, tabbing from cell to cell.

6. Select the first two rows again. Click the Bold button on the property bar. Then right-click, click Format, check "Header row," and click OK. The first two rows of your table are now designated as column header rows that repeat if your list expands to the next page.

7. Put some people on your greeting card list, then save the list as `Greeting Cards.wpd`. You use the file in a following section.

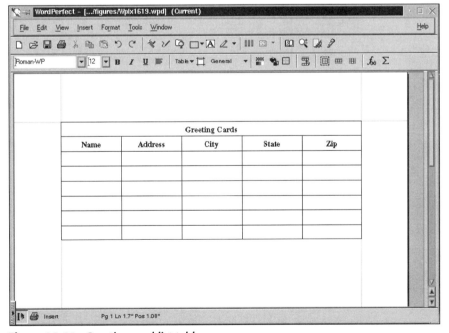

Figure 16-18: Greeting card list table

Changing a Table's Structure

Thanks to the context-sensitive property bar and other features, changing a table's structure to fit your information is easy. Just use the mouse to adjust your table properties.

Adjusting Columns with the Mouse or Keystrokes

You can drag a table's sides and columns to change their dimensions, as shown in Figure 16-19.

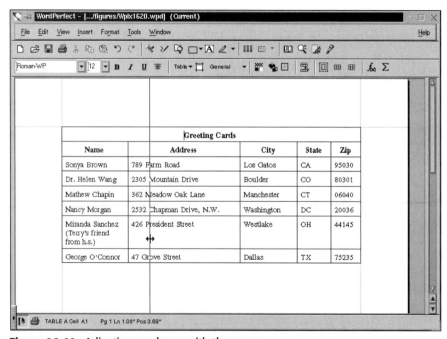

Figure 16-19: Adjusting a column with the mouse

Tip   Hold the Ctrl key to click and drag all the lines from the pointer rightward at once, while retaining the column widths.

Sizing Columns with the Ruler

You can drag the column indicators on the ruler to adjust the width of your columns. You can snap them to grid locations with this method (see Chapter 15, "Formatting Your Document").

Inserting Columns and Rows

To insert one or more columns or rows at the insertion point, click Table ➪ Insert, specify the number of columns or rows to add, then click either Before or After placement (see Figure 16-20).

Figure 16-20: Inserting columns or rows

Inserting a column divides the current column in two. Added columns or rows retain the formatting attributes of the row or column at the insertion point.

Now practice by adding a column for miscellaneous notes to the right of your greeting card list:

1. Right-click the last column of the table and click Insert. Specify one column, click After, then click OK.

2. Type **Notes** in the column header as shown in Figure 16-21.

3. Select the title row and join the two cells.

4. Adjust the column widths, if necessary, to accommodate the new column.

Joining or Splitting Cells, Columns, and Rows

To join a group of cells (such as the top row of the greeting card list), select the cells you want to combine, then right-click and click Join Cells. The resulting cell has the formatting features of the top-left cell of the original group.

To split a cell, place the insertion point in the cell, then click Table ➪ Split ➪ Cell, and specify the number of columns or rows (see Figure 16-22). (Text in a cell can affect the way it splits.) You can also split several selected cells at once.

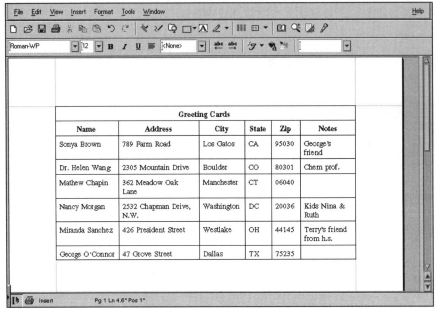

Figure 16-21: Greeting card list with added Notes column

Figure 16-22: Splitting a cell

Deleting Columns, Rows, or Cell Contents

Deleting columns or rows is similar to inserting, except that you also have the option to delete only the cell contents. To delete columns, rows, or cell contents:

1. Select the cell, or any part of the columns or rows.

2. Click the Table menu on the property bar (or right-click),then click Delete.

3. Click Columns, Rows, or "Cell Contents" only (see Figure 16-23).

Figure 16-23: Deleting columns, rows, or cell contents

Using Keystrokes to Insert, Delete, and Add Rows

You can use the following keystrokes to insert and delete rows, or add rows to the end of a table:

Table Keystroke	What It Does
Alt+Insert	Inserts a row above the insertion point.
Alt+Delete	Deletes the current row.
Tab	Adds a row to the bottom of the table (when the insertion point is at the end of the table).

Moving or Copying Cells, Columns, or Rows

To move (cut and paste) or copy (copy and paste) parts of your table or its contents:

1. Select the cells, rows, or columns you want to cut or copy.

2. Right-click and click Cut or Copy.

3. Click one of the following (see Figure 16-24):

   - *Selection*, to cut or copy the contents of your selection.

   - *Row* or *Column*, to cut or copy selected rows or columns and their contents.

   - *Cell*, to copy the contents of a single, unjoined cell. To copy the cell's contents to several adjacent cells, specify the number of cells down or to the right to copy to, and skip Step 4. To copy the cell elsewhere, click "Cell."

Figure 16-24: Moving or copying cells, columns, or rows

4. Click OK, then place the insertion point where you want to move or copy your selection, right-click, and click Paste. You can paste the selection to another table or into your document's text.

Caution   When copying selected contents to another table location, be sure that there's enough room to the right and below the target cell to hold the whole block. Otherwise, your pasted information will be truncated.

When you move or copy a selection to another table, table formatting (such as line styles, fills, and text appearance) is moved or copied as well. When you paste into the body of your document, a table structure is created, even for a single cell.

Now it's time for you to practice this delicate operation. Follow these steps to copy three lines from your greeting card list:

1. Drag to select the top three rows of names in your list.

2. Right-click and click Copy ⇨ OK.

3. Place the insertion point somewhere below the table in your document. (Press Enter a few times to create some space.)

4. Right-click and click Paste. Your page should be similar to Figure 16-25.

Using the Mouse to Move or Copy

You can also use the mouse to move or copy table contents and structure. Select the cells, rows, or columns, then drag the table elements where you want them. (Hold down the Ctrl key or drag with the right mouse button to copy the information instead of moving it). You can also select and drag the entire table.

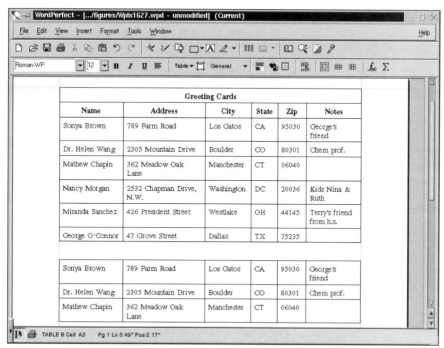

Figure 16-25: Copied table selection

Accessing All Formatting Features for Tables

WordPerfect's extensive formatting features can be applied to the text in tables and table elements. For example, to change the size or appearance of text in part of a table, select the text, then use the toolbar, property bar, and Font dialog box as you would for text anywhere else.

Certain formatting features, however, apply to tables exclusively (such as center vertical alignment of text in a cell or a fixed height to a row). Others (such as column margins) may not be exclusive to tables, but they don't apply to general document text. All of these features reside in the Properties for Table Format dialog box, under the Cell, Column, Row, and Table tabs.

Tip   You'll find buttons on the property bar for such table formatting features as justification, vertical alignment, and rotating cell contents.

When you apply table formatting, the order of precedence in which the elements apply is as follows:

✦ Cell formatting takes precedence over any other settings.

✦ Column or row formatting takes precedence over table format settings.

✦ Table formatting, the most general element, is the same as the underlying document unless you specify otherwise.

Try this exercise. Create a small table, then click a cell and apply right justification by using the property bar. Next, select the entire table and click Format ➪ Justification ➪ Center. The cell you right-justified is not centered, because cell formatting takes precedence over the table format.

To avoid these surprises when you design your table, follow the format order from general-to-specific by establishing the overall format first, then changing specific columns or rows, and finally formatting single cells or small groups of cells.

To format all or part of a table:

1. Place the insertion point in the cell, column, or row you want to format, or select the table elements you want to format.

2. Click the Table menu on the property bar and click Format (or right-click and click Format).

3. Select from the available formatting options for cells, columns, rows, or the entire table, as described in the following sections.

Cells

When using the Format dialog box cell options shown in Figure 16-26, apply any of the features described in Table 16-1.

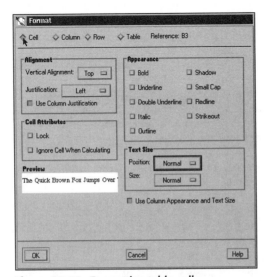

Figure 16-26: Formatting table cells

Table 16-1	
Cell Formatting Features	
Feature	*Enables You to*
Vertical Alignment	Align cell contents at the top, bottom, or center of cells. (Displays as mixed when various cells in a selection are aligned differently.)
Justification	Align cell contents relative to cell margins (left, right, center, full, all, or decimal).
Use Column Justification	Check to have cell alignment default to the justification for the column.
Lock	Prevent information in the cell from being changed.
Ignore Cell When Calculating	Skip the cell when performing calculations.
Appearance	Change the appearance (Bold, Underline, Italic, and so forth) of the text used in the selected cells.
Text Size	Change the position (Normal, Superscript, Subscript) and size of the text in the selected cells.

Columns

When using the Format dialog box column options shown in Figure 16-27, apply any of the following:

✦ *Justification*, to align contents for columns of cells.

✦ *Digits after decimal* or *Position from right*, to either set the number of decimal digits when using decimal alignment or specify where the decimal is placed.

✦ *Column Margins*, to adjust the left and right margins for a column of cells.

✦ *Appearance*, to change the appearance (Bold, Underline, Italic, and so forth) of the text used in the column(s).

✦ *Text Size,* to change the position (Normal, Superscript, Subscript) and size of the text in the column(s).

✦ *Column Width*, to adjust the column width (the combined column widths can't exceed the width of the page). Check *Fixed Width* to keep the column width from changing when you adjust adjacent columns by using the Format dialog box. (You can still drag a fixed-width column to adjust it.)

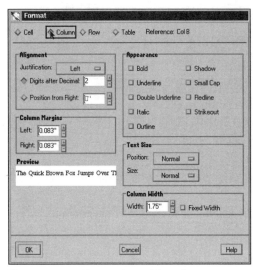

Figure 16-27: Formatting table columns

Rows

When using the Format dialog box row options shown in Figure 16-28, apply any of the following:

✦ *Lines Per Row*, to limit the display of information in the row to a single line (additional lines are converted to hidden text). With the multiline default, the row height expands to accommodate additional lines.

✦ *Row Height*, to set rows to a specific fixed height. Text that doesn't fit in a fixed row is converted to hidden text. (You can drag the bottom edge of a row to enlarge it.)

✦ *Row Margins*, to adjust the top and bottom margins for cells within rows.

✦ *Header Row*, to designate rows that repeat at the top of the table when the table spans across pages.

The table in Figure 16-29 shows how text can be hidden when you specify "Single line only" or a fixed line height. When the contents of the cells are copied into the document below the table, you see the entire text.

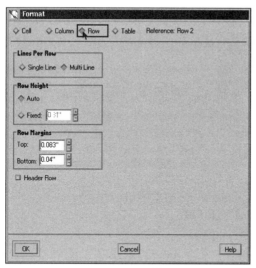

Figure 16-28: Formatting table rows

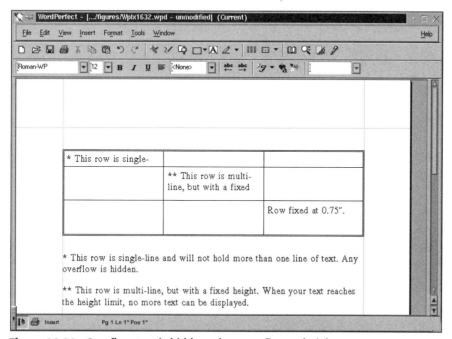

Figure 16-29: Overflow text is hidden when you fix row heights

Table

When using the Format dialog box table options shown in Figure 16-30, apply any of the column options, plus the following:

✦ *Table Position*, to specify the position of the table horizontally within the document: left, right, center, full (the default), or at a specific distance from the left edge of the page.

✦ *Disable Cell Locks*, to unlock all cells temporarily for editing or updating. (Remove the check when you're finished in order to protect the table's contents.)

Figure 16-30: Formatting the table as a whole

Joining and Splitting Tables

You can join and split tables much as you join and split cells, columns, and rows — well, it's a little trickier.

Joining Two Tables

Joining tables is not as simple as joining cells. To join two tables into one, the last row in the first table and the first row in the second must have the same number of columns.

To join two tables:

1. Remove any text and spacing between the two tables, as shown in Figure 16-31.

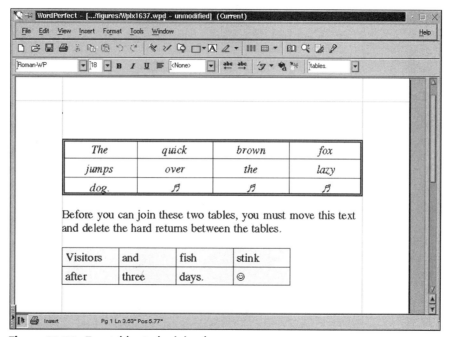

Figure 16-31: Two tables to be joined

2. Click the top table, as shown in Figure 16-32, then click Table ➪ Join ➪ Table.

When the tables are joined as in Figure 16-33, the cells in the lower table assume the table-level formatting of the upper table — but formatting applied to particular cells is retained, as with the cell in the lower-right of the figure.

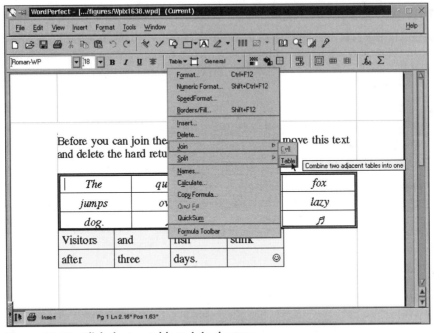

Figure 16-32: Click the top table to join the two

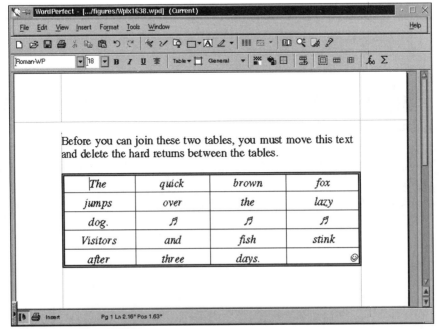

Figure 16-33: Two tables joined together

Splitting a Table

Splitting a table is a little easier than joining. To split a table:

1. Click the row that is to become the top row of the new table, as shown in Figure 16-34.

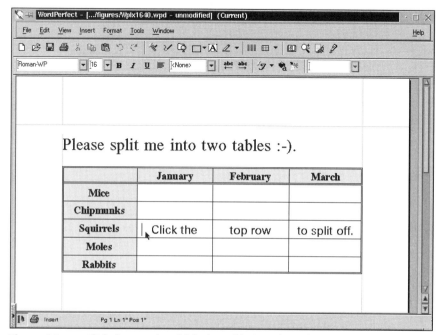

Figure 16-34: Click the row in which the table is to be split off

2. Click Table ⇨ Split ⇨ Table.

3. Use the left-arrow key to place the insertion point between the tables, then hit Enter a couple of times to place some distance between the tables, as shown in Figure 16-35.

Note how the resulting tables retain the formatting features of the original.

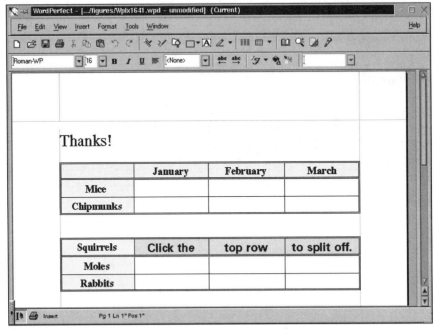

Figure 16-35: Putting some distance between the tables

Deleting or Converting a Table

Table deletion offers several options for deleting or converting a table, including conversion to tabular text:

1. Select the entire table and press the Delete key, or click Table ⇨ Delete.

2. Select from the following deletion options, as shown in Figure 16-36:

   - *Entire Table*, to delete the contents and structure.

   - *Table Contents*, to delete the contents only, leaving the structure intact.

   - *Table Structure (leave text)*, to delete the structure only, leaving the contents as tabular text. (Adjust the tabs if you need to straighten the columns of text.)

   - *Convert to Merge Data File*, to turn the table into a merge data file.

   - *Convert to Merge Data File (first row becomes field names)*, to turn the table into a merge data file, converting the first (column header) row to field names instead of a merge record.

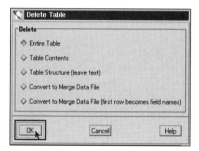

Figure 16-36: Deleting or converting a table

Editing Table Lines, Borders, and Fills

If none of the table SpeedFormat styles described in Chapter 4 ("Becoming an Instant WordPerfect Expert") suits your needs, you can edit table lines, borders, and fills as separate graphical elements. You can then save your formatting as a custom SpeedFormat style.

Applying Lines, Borders, and Fills

A table has no border or fill when you create it, and cells are enclosed in single lines. You can click various property bar buttons to change the inside or outside lines for a selected group of cells (you don't have to select a single cell). Select the entire table to apply a border, as shown in Figure 16-37.

Table	with	a
thick	border	➪
and	a	fill

Figure 16-37: Table with a thick border and a fill

You can also click Table ➪ Borders/Fill to apply lines, borders, and fills to selected cells or the entire table, as shown in Figure 16-38.

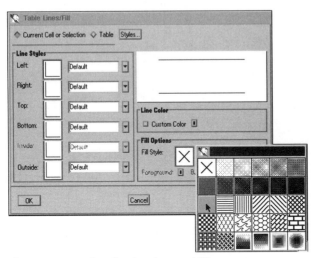

Figure 16-38:: Creating borders and fills

For more on using graphic lines, borders, and fills, see Chapter 23, "Adding Graphic Lines, Borders, and Fills."

For More Information . . .

On	See
Setting tabs	Chapter 15
Using the Shadow Cursor	Chapter 3
Applying graphic lines, borders, and fills	Chapter 23
Creating a chart from a table	Chapter 25
Using the ruler bar	Chapter 15
SpeedFormatting a table	Chapter 4
Doing spreadsheet calculations in WordPerfect	Chapter 21

✦   ✦   ✦

Working with Large Documents

Organizing with Bullets and Outlines

W ordPerfect makes it easy to organize and present your ideas with bullets, numbered paragraph lists, outlines, and headings. You can make your points with WordPerfect's Bullets & Numbering feature, or use WordPerfect's outlining tools to organize your ideas and turn them into a polished document.

Creating Bulleted or Numbered Lists

Use bullets or paragraph numbers to set off a list of items or sequence of instructions. Use one of the following methods for this approach:

✦ Use the Format-As-You-Go QuickBullets

✦ Insert single-level bullets and numbering styles

Using QuickBullets

To create a QuickBullet list:

1. On a new line, type preceding tabs if you want to indent the QuickBullets.

2. Type any of the following:

   • **o**, *****, **O**, **^**, **>**, **+**, or **-** for a bulleted list (press Ctrl+W to use any other symbol, as shown in Figure 17-1)

  - A number followed by **.**, **)**, or **-** for a numbered list (type **i** or **I** for Roman numerals)
  - A letter followed by **.**, **)**, or **-** for an alphabetical list

3. Press Tab, type your text, then press Enter to create the next QuickBullet.

4. Press Enter ➪ Backspace to end the list.

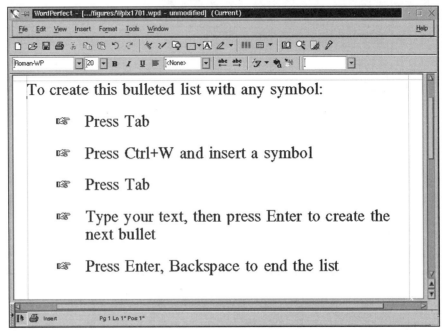

Figure 17-1: QuickBullets employing a WordPerfect character

Tip   Adjust tab settings and paragraph spacing to position the bullets and space the list just right. If QuickBullets isn't working, click Tools ➪ QuickCorrect ➪ Format-As-You-Go to be sure that it is checked.

Using Bullets & Numbering

Use Bullets & Numbering to apply bullets to existing text, or to create a bulleted or numbered list from scratch:

1. Type preceding tabs if you want to indent the list. (You can also select paragraphs of existing text.)

2. Click Insert ➪ Bullets & Numbering (see Figure 17-2) and select the layout you want. (Click "Edit" to use a different symbol.)

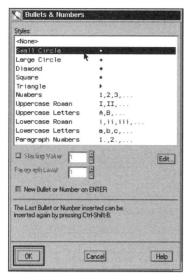

Figure 17-2: Selecting a bullet layout

3. Type your text, then press Enter to create the next bullet. (To put a blank line between your bullets, press Enter before typing any text.)

4. Press Enter ➪ Backspace to end the list.

You can save bullet style changes to your style library (see Chapter 20, "Working Quickly with ExpressDocs Templates and Styles") and use them in future documents.

Changing List Numbers

When you create a lettered or numbered list, WordPerfect increments the list automatically. When you end a list of items and then start a new list later in your document, WordPerfect normally resumes numbering where you stopped. To start from scratch, click Insert ➪ Bullets & Numbering, then set the Starting value to 1.

What's an Outline?

When you're writing a paper, book, or anything in-between, a multilevel outline helps to arrange your ideas. An outline is a powerful aid to the reader as well. This book's table of contents, after all, is really just an outline of parts, chapters, and headings.

For occasional outlines, don't feel obligated to master the outlining tools. However, if you write large documents, WordPerfect's outlining facilities offer powerful assistance.

Understanding Outlining Terms

The following terms are used with WordPerfect's tools to create a full-fledged outline (see Figure 17-3 for an illustration):

✦ An *outline* is a hierarchical list of "parent" headings and "child" subheadings.

✦ The *outline level* refers to an item's position in the tab-stop hierarchy. Each level can have a distinct numbering type or appearance.

✦ *Outline text* is what you type after a number.

✦ *Body text* is the normal document text that you type on separate lines, between the outline items.

✦ *Outline family* is an outline item at any level, and everything under it until the next item on the same or higher level.

✦ A *level definition* specifies the style applied to a particular outline level, including indents, table of contents markers, and text attributes (such as bold or italic).

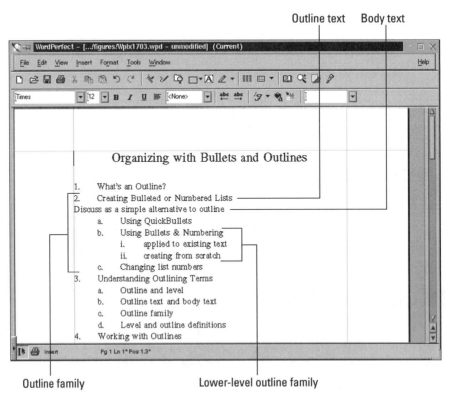

Figure 17-3: Illustration of outlining terms

By putting related level definitions together, you get one of the outline layouts described in Table 17-1.

	Table 17-1	
	Outline and List Layouts	
Layout	*Type*	*Description*
Paragraph	Numbers and styles	The default definition with a sequence of indented levels of 1., a., i., (1), (a), (i), 1), and *a)*.
Outline	Numbers and styles	Another common definition, with a sequence of indented levels of I., A., 1., a., (1), (a), i), and a).
Numbers	Numbers only	Similar to the paragraph layout, but with paragraph numbers only (no styles).
Bullets	Numbers and styles	The levels are set off with various bullet styles (see Figure 17-4).
Headings	Numbers and styles	Instead of letters or numbers, your text is organized into ready-made headings marked for the table of contents (see Figure 17-4).
Definitions	Styles only	Plain Web-publishing style of progressive indentations from the left margin.
Quotations	Styles only	Plain Web-publishing style of progressive indentations from both margins.
Legal	Numbers and styles	Levels are sequenced 1, 1.1, 1.1.1, and so forth for legal documents.
Legal 2	Numbers and styles	Another legal-style with levels of 1, 1.01, 1.01.01, and so forth.

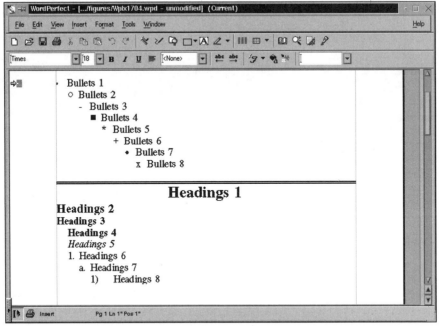

Figure 17-4: Bullets and headings outline levels

Working with Outlines

WordPerfect's outlining tools give you a sharp-looking outline with level numbers maintained automatically as you rearrange your document.

Creating an Outline and Changing Levels

The best way to learn outlining is to use it. You can try the fancier features after you create your basic outline. Use the headings in this chapter to create an outline for practice or create your own. To create an outline:

1. Click Tools ➪ Define Outline, select the outline definition you want, check "Start New Outline" and click OK. This sequence starts the outline and displays the outline tools on the property bar (see Figure 17-5).

Figure 17-5: Outline tools

2. Type the text for the first item, then press Enter and continue adding several items. (Items you add are always the same level as the previous level.)

3. Click the Outline Left Arrow button or the Outline Right Arrow button to change the level of the current item.

4. Click the Outline Up Arrow button or the Outline Down Arrow button to move the current item up or down a line (its level won't change, but numbers readjust automatically).

5. To add body text, press Enter twice, then type on the line between the outline numbers or bullets. (To go back and add text under an item, click the end of the item, then press Enter ⇨ Backspace.)

6. To end the outline, press Enter ⇨ Backspace.

To change your outline's layout at any point in the outline, click Tools ⇨ Define Outline and select the type you want.

Converting Text to an Outline and Back

To create an outline from existing text, select the text, then click Tools ⇨ Define Outline and select the outline definition you want. The outline level for each paragraph is based on the number of preceding tabs or indents.

To convert outline text to body text, click at the beginning of the outline text, then press Backspace.

Hiding Levels and Text

One of the handiest outlining features is the ability to hide outline levels or body text in order to work on your outline in different ways:

✦ Click the Outline Hide Body Text button to show or hide the body text. (Note that the Outline Hide Body Text button remains depressed on the toolbar when body text is hidden.)

✦ Click the Outline Hide Family button to hide the family of an outline item and the Outline Show Family button to show it again. (Hide a family to move it as a single line.)

✦ Click the Outline Show Levels button to pick how many levels (1–8) you want to display. Select <None> to hide the entire outline, other than the body text.

Collapsed (or hidden) information doesn't print. As a result, you can print your outline to any level, with or without the body text.

Level Icon Tricks

Click the Outline Display Icons button to display outline level icons in the left margin. The hollow numbers from 1 to 9 indicate the level of an outline item and its associated text (with a hollow "T"). A plus sign (+) indicates that subordinate items are hidden; a minus sign (-) indicates that the entire family is showing.

> **Tip** Double-clicking an icon alternately hides and shows the subordinate items and text for that family.

When you point to an outline level icon, a double arrow appears. You can then click to select that item's family and drag it to a new location. A horizontal line indicates where the family will be inserted, as shown in Figure 17-6.

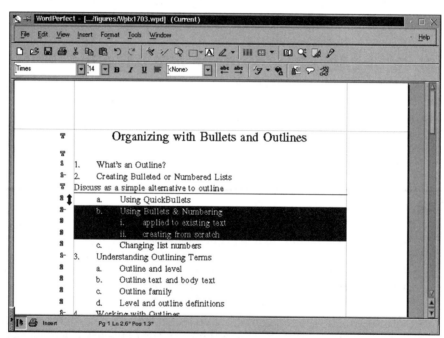

Figure 17-6: Dragging a family to another location

Changing an Outline Item's Number

To change the number of the current and subsequent items in an outline family, click the Outline Set Paragraph Number button, and type Arabic numbers separated by commas to indicate the new number (see Figure 17-7). For example, to set an item to 2.b.iv, type **2,2,4**. Better yet, use question mark wildcards for all but the last number (for example **?,?,4**), so that the item number updates if the preceding numbers change.

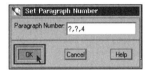

Figure 17-7: Changing an outline item's number

Converting Outline Level Items to Headings

After your document has been completed by fleshing out your outline, you can convert the outline level items to formatted document headings, premarked for the table of contents. Go to the beginning of your outline, click Tools ➪ Define Outline, and select the Headings layout.

Inserting Paragraph Numbers Anywhere in Your Text

WordPerfect lets you insert a paragraph number anywhere in your document, without upsetting the current numbering format:

1. Click View ➪ Toolbars to display the Outline Tools toolbar, then click the Paragraph Numbers button.

2. Specify the outline level, start value, and number type (refer to Figure 17-7).

Customizing Outline Layouts and Styles

You can customize an outline's layout or styles (or create new layouts or styles), then save them to your default template so that they can be used in other documents.

Styles Associated with Outline Layouts

Each of the outline layouts (aside from Numbers) employs particular paragraph styles for each of the eight levels contained. (Definitions and Quotations outlines are for Web page formatting, not outlining.)

The six outline layouts use three sets of outline paragraph styles, as shown in Table 17-2. Because the Paragraph, Outline, and Bullets outlines use the same styles (with different numbers or bullets), changing the styles for one layout changes the other styles as well. Likewise, a change to the Legal definition styles affects Legal 2. Only the Headings layout has unique styles.

Table 17-2 Outline Layouts with Their Associated Styles	
Outline Layout	**Associated Styles**
Paragraph	Level styles 1 through 8
Outline	Level styles 1 through 8
Bullets	Level styles 1 through 8
Legal	Legal styles 1 through 8
Legal 2	Legal styles 1 through 8
Headings	Heading styles 1 through 8

Customizing an Outline Layout

You can change the delivered outline layouts and styles, but you should leave the originals alone and create custom layouts and styles for your particular needs. For example, you may create a custom headings layout called "MyBook," with its own level styles, to use in writing books or reports.

To create or edit outline layouts and styles:

1. Click Tools ➪ Define Outline.

2. Click Create to create a new layout, or select a layout and click Edit.

3. If you're creating a new layout, give it a name and description (see Figure 17-8).

4. Specify numbers or bullets for each level and select styles for each level. You can create new styles for various levels of your definition, rather than edit the shipped styles.

 Caution   Remember, changes to shipped styles affect other outline definitions using the same styles.

Using Custom Outline Layouts and Styles in Other Documents

Normally, the changes you make to outline layouts or styles (and the new ones you create) affect only the current document. To use a new or modified layout in other documents, click Tools ➪ Define Outline, select the layout, click Options ➪ Copy, then copy it to your personal style library (or shared library when you're on a network). See Chapter 20, "Working Quickly with ExpressDocs Templates and Styles," for more details on using styles.

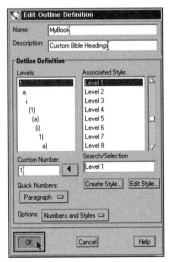

Figure 17-8: Naming and describing a new layout

For More Information . . .

On	See
Customizing a keyboard	Chapter 27
Numbering lines	Chapter 15
Working with styles	Chapter 20
Generating a table of contents	Chapter 18

✦   ✦   ✦

Adding Document References

If you haven't pounded away at a typewriter until five in
the morning, adding footnotes to your term paper before
the ten o'clock class, you've missed one of life's memorable
experiences. You'll never know what it was like to stop in the
middle of a page, roll the typewriter carriage back and forth,
mark the margin with a pencil to reserve space at the bottom,
then type more text, then the separator line, and finally the
footnote, only to realize that you left out a vital note three
pages back.

Footnotes and endnotes are easy to insert in WordPerfect.
The program is also adept at other document references
such as lists of captions, cross-references, and index entries.
You can even mark your text to generate a table of contents
automatically. Short of the final printing and binding, you
can almost publish a book using WordPerfect alone.

Document references can be classed into two types:

   ✦ Notes (including footnotes, endnotes, and citations)

   ✦ Tabulations (such as lists, cross-references, indexes,
     tables of contents, and tables of authorities)

Inserting Footnotes and Endnotes

Three types of notes are used for document references:

   ✦ A *footnote* inserts a reference number or other pointer
     in your text, then places the explanatory notes, citation
     sources, or comments at the bottom of the page, as
     shown in Figure 18-1.

Reference numbers

With WordPerfect footnotes are so easy they're almost fun, as are such document references as endnotes, lists of captions, cross-references, and index entries. You can even mark your text to automatically generate a table of contents. Short of the final printing and binding, you can almost publish a book by using WordPerfect alone.

Document references can be classed into two types:

✔ Notes (including footnotes, endnotes, and in-text citations)

✔ Tabulations (such as lists, cross-references, indexes, tables of contents, and tables of authorities)

This chapter shows you how to add notes to your papers, books, and reports, and mark tabulation entries. Chapter 25 shows you how to generate the table of contents, index, and other tabulations.

Using Footnotes and Endnotes

Three types of notes are used for document references:

✔ A *footnote* inserts a reference number or other pointer in your text, then places the explanatory notes, citation sources, or comments at the bottom of the page (see Figure 24-1). A separator line is placed between the text and your footnotes.

✔ An *endnote* is similar to a footnote, except that your notes are assembled together at the end of a paper, chapter, or other part of your work, rather than on the pages where the citations occur.

✔ An *in-text citation* places the author and page of a cited work in parenthesis in the text, such as "(Kant, 156)," instead of a reference number. The reader turns to the bibliography at the end of the work to find the remainder of the reference (such as the title, publisher, and date). WordPerfect doesn't provide an in-text citation feature.[1]

The choice between footnotes and endnotes is primarily one of aesthetics and convenience. Endnotes may present a cleaner appearance, but the reader must flip back and forth to read the notes and to check references. In the typewriter days, endnotes were easier to create, since all the notes could be typed at once, and there was no fussing with separator lines and spacing at the bottom of the page. With a word processor, however, footnotes are just as easy to create, and they save you the work of setting up the endnote page.[2]

---

[1] Use QwkScreen's In-text Citation feature to create citations that conform to standard styles.

[2] So keep in mind that footnotes are the easiest to create with WordPerfect, with endnotes a close second, and in-text citations a distant third. However, if you are writing for a

Separator line

Figure 18-1: A reference number is inserted for each footnote you create

✦ *Endnotes*, as their name implies, are assembled at the end of a paper, chapter, or other part of your work, rather than on the pages where the citations occur.

✦ An *in-text citation* places the author and page of a cited work in parentheses in the text, such as "(Kant, 156)," instead of a reference number. The reader turns to the bibliography at the end of the work to find the remainder of the reference, such as the title, publisher, and date. (There's no in-text citation feature — they're easy to type.)

Endnotes may give the main document a cleaner appearance, but the reader must flip back and forth to read the notes or check references. Where you have a choice, footnotes are just as easy to create and save you the work of setting up the endnotes page(s).

Creating a Footnote or Endnote

You can add footnotes and endnotes as you type your text, or you can go back to insert them later:

1. Place the insertion point where you want the reference to appear.

2. Click Insert ➪ Footnote ➪ Create.

3. Type the note, as shown in Figure 18-2, then click the Close button on the toolbar. (Or, click outside of your notes when you're in Page view.)

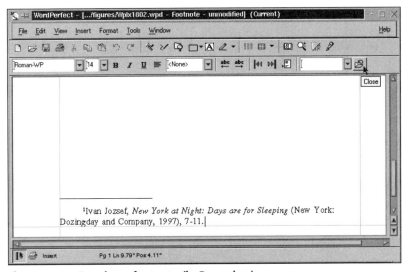

Figure 18-2: Creating a footnote (in Page view)

Tip   WordPerfect provides spacing between the notes automatically. Don't press Enter at the end of a note, or you'll get an extra blank line.

WordPerfect numbers or renumbers automatically the notes you insert. When a footnote can't fit entirely on a page, it carries over to the next.

Caution   A note's number is part of the footnote or endnote style that includes a Footnote (or Endnote) Number Display code for automatic numbering. If you delete the number accidentally, use Undo (Ctrl+Z) to restore it. Don't retype it.

Viewing Footnotes and Endnotes

In Draft view, footnotes and endnotes are kept out of sight (as are headers and footers) to help you focus on the body of your text. Switch to Page view (View ➪ Page) if you want to see your notes.

Editing a Footnote or Endnote

Simply click a footnote or endnote in Page view to edit it, then click back in your text when you're done (or click the Close button on the toolbar). In either Draft or Page view, you can also click Insert ➪ Footnote (or Endnote) ➪ Edit, then specify the note number and click OK.

Moving Text with Footnotes or Endnotes

When you move document text, accompanying footnotes and endnotes move with it (be sure to include the reference number). When you change the order of your notes, their numbers adjust automatically.

Deleting a Footnote or Endnote

Footnotes and endnotes are deleted when you delete the text in which their references are contained. To delete only the note, simply delete the reference number.

Resetting Footnote or Endnote Numbering

At certain points in your document, you may want to reset your note numbering — back to 1 at the beginning of each chapter, for example. To reset footnote or endnote numbering:

1. Click where you want to start renumbering your notes.

2. Click Insert ➪ Footnote (or Endnote) ➪ New Number.

3. Type a new number, or click Increase or Decrease to change it by one (see Figure 18-3).

Tip   You can also reset endnote numbers when you specify their placement, as described in the following section.

Figure 18-3: Resetting a note's number

Specifying Endnote Placement

Normally, endnotes are placed at the end of your document. If your document has an index, however, you probably want to place your endnotes before the end. If you're writing a book or journal, you may want to place endnotes at the end of each chapter or article.

To specify endnote placement:

1. Click where you want the endnotes to appear.

2. Click Insert ⇨ Endnote ⇨ Placement.

3. To restart subsequent endnotes at number 1, click "Insert Endnotes at Insertion Point and Restart Numbering" (see Figure 18-4).

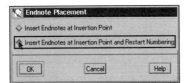

Figure 18-4: Specifying endnote placement

WordPerfect inserts an Endnote Placement code (which displays as a graphic in Draft view), followed by a hard page break to separate your endnotes from the next page of text.

Tip   To start your endnotes on a new page, press Ctrl+Enter to insert a hard page break and type a heading for your endnotes just before the placement code.

Endnotes inserted before the placement code appear at the code. Endnotes inserted after the placement code appear at the next placement code, or at the end of your document.

Changing the Footnote Line Separator

To change the length, style, spacing, and position of the line separator between your text and footnotes:

1. Click the page where you want your line separator changes to begin.

2. Click Insert ➪ Footnote ➪ Options ➪ Separator, then specify any of the options shown in Figure 18-5 and described in Table 18-1.

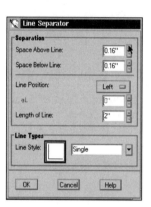

Figure 18-5: Changing the footnote line separator

Table 18-1	
Line Separator Options	
Option	*Enables You to*
Space Above Line	Change the amount of space between the line and the text above it
Space Below Line	Change the amount of space between the line and the footnote below it
Line Position	Place the line in the left margin, from margin to margin (full), centered between the margins, in the right margin, or at a set position from the left edge of the page
Length of Line	Change the length of the line
Line Style	Select a different line style from the palette

Setting Advanced Footnote and Endnote Options

To set advanced footnote and endnote options:

1. Click where you want the options to take effect.

2. Click Insert ➪ Footnote (or Endnote) ➪ Options.

3. Specify any of the options shown in Table 18-2 for footnotes (see Figure 18-6) or endnotes (see Figure 18-7).

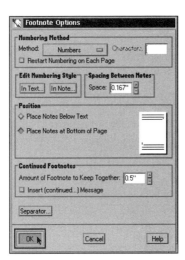

Figure 18-6: Setting advanced footnote options

Figure 18-7: Setting advanced endnote options

Table 18-2
Advanced Footnote and Endnote Options

Option	Enables You to
Numbering Method	Choose from Arabic numbers, uppercase or lowercase letters or Roman numerals, or characters.
Characters	Specify (when using characters) one to five characters, separated with commas, to use for your notes. (Press Ctrl+W to use symbols.) Each character is used in turn, then doubled (**), tripled (***), and so forth as needed for additional notes. (One accepted sequence of symbols is *, †, ‡, §, |.)
Restart Numbering on Each Page (footnotes only)	Restart footnote numbers on each page. (This option is useful when using characters for your numbering.)
Edit Numbering Style	Change the style of your in-text note numbers (In Text) or the number and style of the notes themselves (In Note). See "Editing Footnote and Endnote Styles" later in this chapter.
Position (footnotes only)	Place footnotes at the bottom of the page (the default) or immediately following your text.
Spacing Between Notes	Adjust the amount of space between footnotes or endnotes. (Books often simply indent footnotes, without any spacing between them.)
Amount of Footnote (or Endnote) to Keep Together	Specify, when there's not enough room to print the entire note, how much of your note must print on the current page before splitting the note to print the remainder on the next page. Without sufficient space (the default is about three lines), the entire note gets bumped to the next page.
Insert (continued...) Message (footnotes only)	Print a "(continued...)" message when footnotes split across pages.

Changing Footnote and Endnote Settings for All New Documents

To change footnote settings (other than styles) for all new documents:

1. Click File ➪ Document ➪ Current Document Style and check "Use as Default."

2. Select the options you want from the Styles Editor Insert menu (see Figure 18-8).

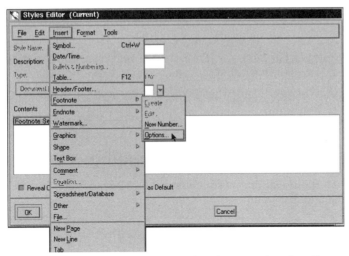

Figure 18-8: Changing footnote and endnote settings for all new documents

Editing Footnote and Endnote Styles

You can edit the system styles of your footnotes and endnotes, for example, to print your notes in a different font or smaller font size. Changing the format or font of your notes won't affect your document's text, and vice versa.

You may also want to edit the footnote style so that footnote text lines up after the number. (With Reveal Codes checked in the styles editor, delete the tab code in the footnote style, and place an indent after the note number instead.) The endnote style simply prints the number, so you may want to add a tab or indent after it. (For notes with tabs or indents, move the tab setting closer to the number so the space between the number and the text is not too large.)

To change the styles of footnotes or endnotes in your document, click Insert ➪ Footnote (or Endnote) ➪ Options ➪ In Note. For more on editing styles, see Chapter 20, "Working Quickly with ExpressDoc Templates and Styles."

Changing Footnote and Endnote Styles for All New Documents

Changes to your footnote and endnote styles normally affect only your current document. To change the styles for all your new documents, you must save the styles to your personal or shared styles library (see Chapter 20, "Working Quickly with ExpressDoc Templates and Styles"):

1. Click Format ➾ Styles.

2. Click Options ➾ Setup and make sure "System Styles" is checked.

3. Select the note style ([Footnote] or [Endnote]) or reference number style ([Ftn#inDoc] or [Endn#inDoc]) that you want to edit, then click Edit.

4. Edit the tabs, font, margins, and other aspects of the style, then click OK.

5. Click Options ➾ Copy ➾ Personal Library (or Shared Library) ➾ OK.

Footnote and Endnote Tips and Techniques

This section provides additional tips and techniques for special footnote and endnote situations you may encounter.

Using both footnotes and endnotes in a document

Some heavily documented works employ a dual system of notes: endnotes for citations and footnotes for substantive notes, definitions of terms, or translations of foreign words and phrases. To distinguish the in-text references, change the footnote numbering to Characters, as described in preceding "Setting Advanced Footnote and Endnote Options" section.

Aligning endnotes

When you type endnote numbers 1 through 9, they line up nicely, one right under the other. When you get to number 10, however, that extra digit shifts the decimal point to the right. To line up those decimal points:

1. Click Insert ➾ Endnote ➾ Options ➾ In Note.

2. Without moving the insertion point, click Format ➾ Line ➾ Tab Set.

3. Select Decimal from the Tab type list and specify 0.25 inches (0.63 cm) in the Tab position box (see Figure 18-9). This setting flushes the endnote numbers right against the decimal, and allows for the width of a standard 12-point character. (You may need to experiment with the width, or double the amount if your endnotes run to three digits.)

4. Click Set, then click OK to return to the Styles Editor.

5. Click Insert ➾ Tab from the Styles Editor menu bar to insert the decimal tab (see Figure 18-10).

To use this endnote style in all your new documents, see the preceding "Changing Footnote and Endnote Styles for All New Documents" section.

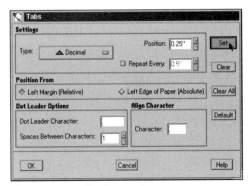

Figure 18-9: Aligning endnotes

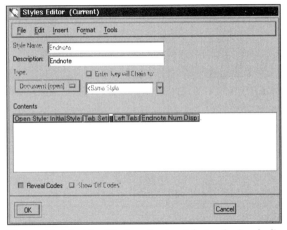

Figure 18-10: Modified endnote style to decimal-align your endnotes

Inserting footnotes in tables and columns

You can place footnotes in newspaper columns, but not in parallel columns. You can also place footnotes in tables, but footnotes placed in table header rows are changed to endnotes.

Converting footnotes and endnotes

Suppose that you just completed a 28-page paper with 50 footnotes, only to realize that you should have used endnotes instead! Don't panic. Simply click Tools ➪ Macro ➪ Play (Alt+F10) and run the Footend macro that comes with the program to convert the footnotes to endnotes automatically. There's also an Endfoot macro to convert endnotes to footnotes.

Making Lists

Lists are a common form of document reference. For example, a list in the front of a book indicates where figures, illustrations, charts, graphs, and other exhibits can be found, as shown in Figure 18-11. The "In This Chapter" sections in this book are lists.

Charts and Tables

World Demand for Nonrenewable Resources 23

Estimated Productivity of the Ocean by Region 41

Millions of US Employed, by Sector, 1950-2000 72

Patterns of International Trade 84

Domestic and Global Income Distribution 107

Federal, State, and local Taxation and Spending 124

Shifting Patterns of Debt 146

Emerging Growth Industries 159

Figure 18-11: Typical list

Creating a list is a three-step process in which you:

✦ Define the list and specify its placement.

✦ Mark the text to include in the list.

✦ Generate the list.

You can mark the text before you specify the list placement, but you must always begin by defining the list. When listing graphics boxes, you don't have to mark the caption text.

Defining a List and Specifying Its Placement

To define a list and specify its placement in your document:

1. Click where you want the list to appear.

2. If you want the list to start at the top of a new page, press Ctrl+Enter to insert a page break.

3. Type and format the title for the list, then press Enter at least twice to put some space between the title and the list.

4. Click Tools ➪ Reference ➪ List, then click Define on the List toolbar (see Figure 18-12).

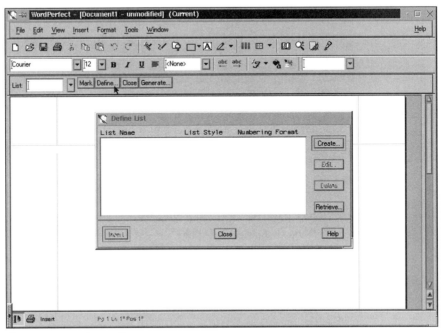

Figure 18-12: List toolbar

5. Click the Create button in the Define List dialog box, and give the list a name (see Figure 18-13).

Figure 18-13: Defining a list

Tip The name of the list is used for marking list items and generating the list. The name doesn't print in your document.

6. Specify any of the following:

- *Position*, to specify how the page number for each list item is displayed and its position in relation to the text. You can also choose not to print page numbers.

- *Styles*, to edit the default hanging indent list style. You may want to leave the default style and then create a custom style to use with your lists. For more on styles, see Chapter 20.

- *Page Numbering*, to specify a page numbering format different from that for the rest of your document. For more on page numbering, see Chapter 14.

- *Auto Reference Box Captions*, to list captions for graphics boxes using the caption type you select, such as Table, Figure, or Text.

7. Click OK, select the definition, then click Insert. A non-printing comment, << List will generate here >, appears in your document.

Tip To define a list instantly, type its name in the List box of the List toolbar, then mark a text item to include in the list. Your list is assigned the default style, which you can edit later.

Deleting a List Definition

To delete a list definition in a document, click Tools ➪ Reference ➪ List, then click Define. Select the list's name, then click Delete.

Retrieving List Definitions from Another Document

To retrieve list definitions from another document into the current document:

1. Click Tools ➪ Reference ➪ List ➪ Define ➪ Retrieve.

2. Specify the name and path of the document with the list definitions you want, click OK, then select the list name you want to retrieve (see Figure 18-14).

Marking Text to Include in a List

To mark the items of text to include in a list:

1. Click Tools ➪ Reference ➪ List, then select the name of the list in the text box on the toolbar.

2. Select the text for the list item, then click Mark.

Repeat Step 2 to add other items to the list.

Figure 18-14: Retrieving list definitions from another document

Unmarking List Items

In Reveal Codes, you can see that each item marked for a list is surrounded by a pair of [Mrk Txt List] codes. If you position the insertion point to the left of a code, you also see the name of the list for which the item is marked. To unmark an item, simply delete one of its surrounding codes.

Making a List of Graphics Box Captions

You don't need to mark graphics box captions to include them in a list. Select the appropriate caption type in Step 6 of the preceding "Defining a List and Specifying Its Placement" section.

Generating Lists

Lists are generated along with other document references, including the table of contents, cross-references, and the index. To generate your references at any time, click Tools ➪ Reference ➪ Generate. You can also click Generate on the List toolbar. (Be sure to regenerate your lists when you finish editing your document. This step ensures that the lists contain the final page numbers for the marked items.)

The list definition must be inserted into your document text in order for the list to generate.

When you generate a list in a master document, text marked in any subdocuments is included. See Chapter 19, "Assembling Multipart Documents," for information on generating master documents.

Creating a Table of Contents

Various types of document references differ more in name than in substance. A table of contents (such as Figure 18-15) is simply a special type of list. Like lists, the table of contents updates page numbers automatically each time it's generated.

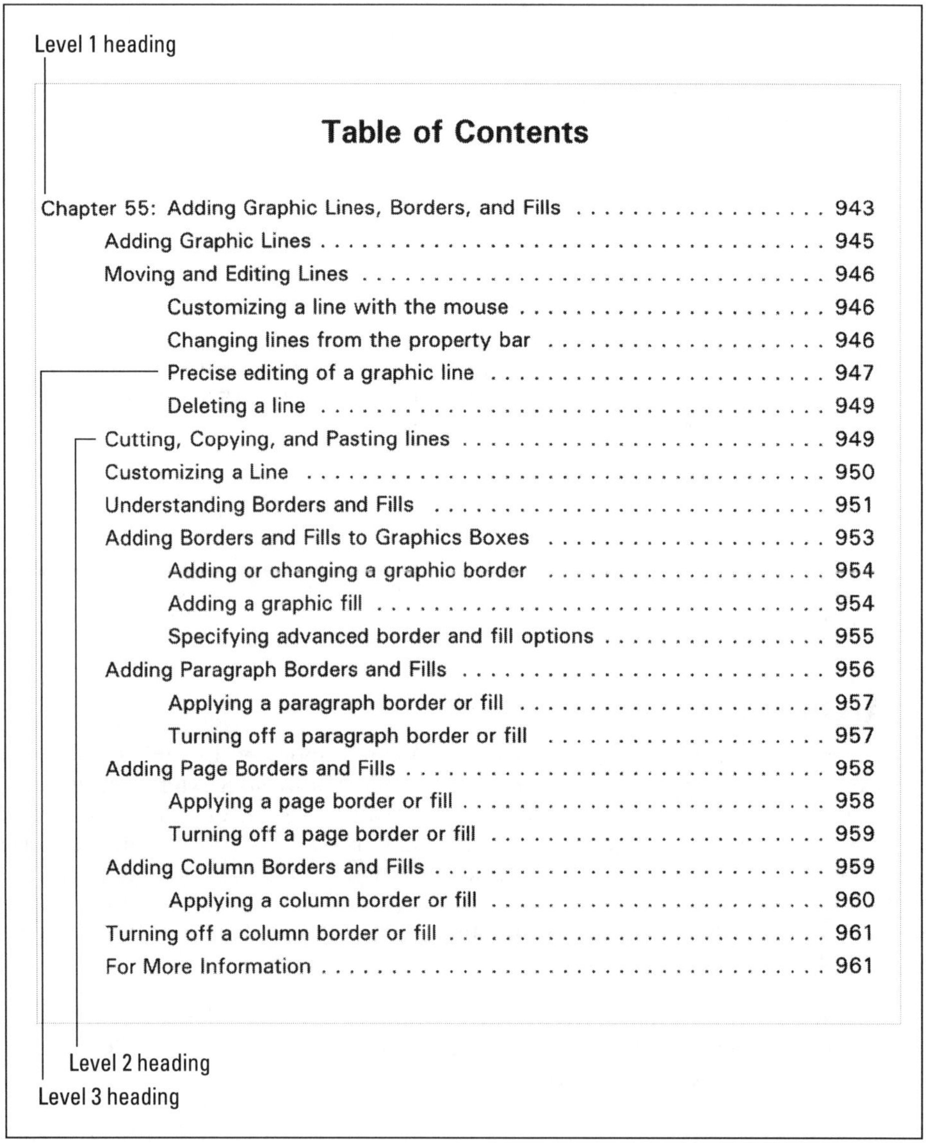
Level 1 heading
Level 2 heading
Level 3 heading

Table of Contents

Chapter 55: Adding Graphic Lines, Borders, and Fills 943
Adding Graphic Lines 945
Moving and Editing Lines 946
Customizing a line with the mouse 946
Changing lines from the property bar 946
Precise editing of a graphic line 947
Deleting a line 949
Cutting, Copying, and Pasting lines 949
Customizing a Line 950
Understanding Borders and Fills 951
Adding Borders and Fills to Graphics Boxes 953
Adding or changing a graphic border 954
Adding a graphic fill 954
Specifying advanced border and fill options 955
Adding Paragraph Borders and Fills 956
Applying a paragraph border or fill 957
Turning off a paragraph border or fill 957
Adding Page Borders and Fills 958
Applying a page border or fill 958
Turning off a page border or fill 959
Adding Column Borders and Fills 959
Applying a column border or fill 960
Turning off a column border or fill 961
For More Information 961

Figure 18-15: Table of contents

A table of contents can have up to five levels of headings (for parts, chapters, sections, and so forth). As with outlines, each level can have a different style.

Creating a table of contents is a three-step process:

✦ Mark the text to include in various levels of the table.

✦ Define the appearance and insert the definition.

✦ Generate the table of contents.

Normally, you mark your text as you go along and define the table of contents when you're nearly finished with your document. You can, however, define the table of contents at any time and continue to mark entries.

Marking Text Automatically by Using Heading Styles

Items in a table of contents usually include the major divisions of a work, such as chapters, sections, and headings. The table of contents can also contain items from the front and the back of the work, such as the preface, introduction, glossary, bibliography, appendices, and index.

If you apply the built-in heading styles 1–5 to the various levels of titles and headings, your text is marked automatically for levels 1–5 of the table of contents. The rest is easy. (For more on styles, see Chapter 20, "Working Quickly with ExpressDoc Templates and Styles.")

When you create a document from an outline that uses the Headings outline definition, heading levels 1–5 are marked automatically for the corresponding level in the table of contents.

Marking Table of Contents Text Manually

You can also mark text manually for inclusion in the table of contents:

1. Click Tools ➪ Reference ➪ Table of Contents to display the Table of Contents toolbar (see Figure 18-16).

Figure 18-16: Table of Contents toolbar

2. Select the text for your table of contents entry.

Tip

The appearance and size of the selected text are retained in the table of contents, as are other formatting codes (such as [HRt]). If you don't want attributes and codes to carry over to the table of contents, turn on Reveal Codes and select the text without its accompanying codes.

3. Click the appropriate Mark button from the toolbar, depending on the level (1–5) on which you want the entry to appear.

4. Repeat Steps 2 and 3 for each of the items you want to include.

Unmarking Table of Contents Items

In Reveal Codes, you can see that each item marked for inclusion in the table of contents is surrounded by a pair of [Mrk Txt ToC] codes. (If you position the insertion point to the left of the code, the code's level is shown.) To unmark an item, simply delete one of the surrounding codes.

Defining the Table of Contents

To specify the appearance of the table of contents and insert its definition:

1. Click where you want the table of contents to appear.

2. To start at the top of a new page, press Ctrl+Enter to insert a page break.

3. Type and format the title for the table of contents. Press Enter at least twice to put some space between the title and the table.

4. Click Tools ⇨ Reference ⇨ Table of Contents, then click Define and specify the number of levels (1–5) you want to include (see Figure 18-17). Text marked for a lower level won't appear in the table of contents.

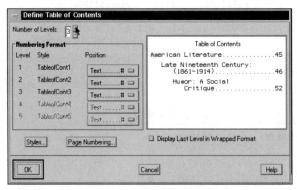

Figure 18-17: Specifying the number of levels for your table of contents

5. Select any of the following options:

- *Position*, to specify how the page number is displayed for each level and its position in relation to the text. You can also choose not to print page numbers (for the top-level part numbers in a larger work, for example).

- *Styles*, to edit the level styles or define custom styles. See the following "Customizing Table of Contents Level Styles" section.

- *Page Numbering*, to specify a page numbering format different from that for the remainder of your document. See Chapter 14, "Controlling Text and Numbering Pages," for more on numbering pages.

- *Display Last Level in Wrapped Format*, to let the text for the last level wrap to the left margin instead of using the hanging indent style. This option is especially useful when your table of contents has three or more levels, and you want to use the last level to list minor topics in a compact form. (Don't use the flush right page numbering position on the wrapped level, because that setting defeats the purpose of wrapping.)

6. Click OK. A nonprinting comment, << Table of Contents will generate here >, displays in your document.

7. If you want the table of contents to be on a page by itself, press Ctrl+Enter to insert a page break.

8. If you want a new page number to begin after the table of contents (for example, if the table of contents is on page v, and you want the next page to be page 1), set a new number for the page that follows the table of contents (see Chapter 14, "Controlling Text and Numbering Pages").

Caution WordPerfect generates a table of contents in each place it finds a definition. If you end up with two or more definitions in your document accidentally, go into Reveal Codes and delete the [Def Mark] codes you don't want.

Customizing Table of Contents Level Styles

You can modify the table of contents level styles that come with WordPerfect, but a safer approach leaves the original definitions alone and uses them as the basis for creating custom definitions and styles suited to your particular needs. You may, for example, want to create custom level styles TableofCont1a, TableofCont2a, and so forth.

Creating and editing table of contents level styles

To create custom table of contents level styles or to edit level styles:

1. Click Tools ⇨ Reference ⇨ Table of Contents.

2. Click Define, then click Styles, and select the level for the style you want to create or edit (see Figure 18-18).

Figure 18-18: Selecting the level for the style you want to create or edit

3. Do one or more of the following:

- Select the style you want to associate with the level.

- Click Edit, then edit the style.

- Click Create, then create a new style for the level.

Using custom table of contents level styles in other documents

Normally, when you create or edit a table of contents level style, your changes apply only to that document. To use your changes in other documents, you must copy them to the personal or shared styles library. For more on styles, see Chapter 20, "Working Quickly with ExpressDoc Templates and Styles."

Generating a Table of Contents

The table of contents is generated along with other document references, including lists, cross-references, and the index. To generate your references at any time, click Tools ➪ Reference ➪ Generate. You can also click Generate on the Table of Contents toolbar.

When you generate a table of contents for a master document, text marked in any subdocuments is included. See Chapter 19, "Assembling Multipart Documents," for information on master documents and subdocuments.

Editing the Table of Contents

You can edit a table of contents after it has been generated, but keep in mind that any errors you correct in the table of contents — rather than at the source where the text is marked — reappear the next time you generate document references. As a result, you should edit the document text, then regenerate the references.

Creating a Table of Authorities

A *table of authorities* is a list of the cases and statutes cited in a legal brief, as shown in Figure 18-19. The table can be divided into sections (such as for cases, constitutional provisions, statutes, and regulations) that are sorted alphabetically. Citations can occur anywhere in your document, including footnotes and endnotes — not just in the body of your text.

TABLE OF AUTHORITIES

CASES

Alan MacWeeney, Inc. v. Esquire Associates, Inc., Nos. 43849-43850, Decision of September 26, 1991 . . . . 41, 42

Blakemore v. Coleman, 701 F.2d 967, (D.C. Cir. 1983) 36

Castorina v. Rosen, 290 N.Y. 445 (1943) 27

Crosby v. 20 Fifth Avenue Hotel Co., 172 Misc. 595, 173 Misc. 604 19

Dearmyer v. Clark, 71 A.D.2d 807, 419 N.Y.S.2d 361 (4th Dep't 1979) 15, 22

E.F. Hutton Group, Inc. v. United States Postal Service, 723 F. Supp. 951 (S.D.N.Y. 1989) 34, 35

General Motors Acceptance Corp. v. Grafinger, 61 Misc. 2d 670, 306 N.Y.S.2d 606 (N.Y.C. Civ. Ct., N.Y. Cty 1969) 19

Girard Studio Group. Inc. v. Young & Rubican, Inc. 147 S.D. 2d 357 (1st Dept. 1989)

. . . . 38, 39

Goldstein v. Pullman Co., 220 N.Y. 549 (1917) 29

Guild v. Atlantic-Third Corporation, 18 Misc. 2d 635, 186 N.Y.S.2d 77 (App. Term, 2d Dep't 1959) 15, 22

Hoffman v. Portogallo. Inc. (Supreme Court, New York County, Index No. 19102/85) June 25, 1987 38

Hunter Trucking Co., Inc. v. Glatzer, 285 App. Div. 314, 136 N.Y.S.2d 857 (1st Dep't 1955) 22, 25, 26

Figure 18-19: Table of authorities

Each section of a table of authorities is actually a single-level table defined and inserted on its own, with its own text citations. There is no definition for the table of authorities as a whole.

Creating a table of authorities involves four steps in which you:

✦ Decide what sections you need.

✦ Mark the text to include in the various sections of the table.

✦ Define the sections.

✦ Generate the table.

Deciding What Sections You Need

The first step in creating a table of authorities is to decide what sections you need for grouping your citations. You may want to sketch the sections on a piece of paper before you begin.

Marking Legal Citations Manually

Marking text for a table of authorities is different from marking text for a list or a table of contents. The various cases, statutes, and other items in the table are often cited repeatedly, perhaps with different wordings. To be sure that the citations for the same source are alike, you define the citation the first time it is encountered, then insert the same citation in your text at each subsequent encounter.

The way you mark text for a table of authorities, therefore, depends on whether the citation is a first occurrence or subsequent occurrence:

✦ On the first occurrence, you define both a *Full Form* for the citation (the way you want the citation to appear in the table) and a *Short Form* (the name by which you look it up when you mark subsequent occurrences).

✦ On subsequent occurrences, you look up the Short Form from the Table of Authorities toolbar and mark the text.

Creating the first citation of an item

To mark the first citation of a table of authorities item:

1. Click Tools ⇨ Reference ⇨ Table of Authorities, if necessary, to display the Table of Authorities toolbar (see Figure 18-20).

Figure 18-20: Table of Authorities toolbar

2. Select the text for the citation and click Create Full Form.

3. Type the section of the table in which you want the citation to appear, or select a section from the list.

4. Edit the Short Form text the way you want it to display on the toolbar (see Figure 18-21). (The text doesn't appear in the table.)

Figure 18-21: Creating the first citation of an item

5. Click OK, edit the Full Form text the way you want it to appear in the table, then click Close.

Revising a citation's Full Form text

To revise a citation's Full Form text, click Edit Full Form on the Table of Authorities toolbar. Next, select the item, click OK, edit the text, then click Close.

Marking subsequent occurrences of a citation

To mark subsequent citations of a table of authorities item:

1. Click Tools ➪ Reference ➪ Table of Authorities, if necessary, to display the Table of Authorities toolbar.

2. Click where you want to mark the item.

3. Select the item's Short Form name from the list (or type it in the text box), then click Mark.

4. Repeat Step 3 to mark subsequent occurrences.

Unmarking table of authorities items

When you mark an item of text for inclusion in the table of authorities, a [TOA] code is inserted in your document. When displayed in detail in Reveal Codes (if the code is not displayed in detail, place the insertion point to the left of the code), the code for the first citation of an item is in the form of [TOA: section name, short form name, Full Form]. The codes for subsequent markings read [TOA: short form name].

To delete a table of authorities citation, go into Reveal Codes and delete the code. If you delete the Full Form code and leave subsequent markings for the item in your text, you get a warning during the generation process that WordPerfect can't find the Full Form text. The program substitutes the Short Form text in your table of authorities, preceded by an asterisk.

Defining the Table of Authorities

Defining a table of authorities is a three-step process in which you:

✦ Type the headings for the table of authorities and its various sections in your document.

✦ Mark where you want the various sections to appear.

✦ Define the format of each section.

To define a table of authorities:

1. Click where you want the table of authorities to appear.

2. Type **Table of Authorities** (or whatever title you use) and format the title.

3. Type the heading of the first section (such as "Cases" or "Constitutional Provisions"), then press Enter at least twice to put some space between the heading and the citations to be generated.

4. Click Tools ➪ Reference ➪ Table of Authorities, if necessary, to display the Table of Authorities toolbar.

5. Click Define, then Create, Edit, or Retrieve a Definition for a Section of the Table. (See the following "Creating or Editing Sections of the Table of Authorities" or "Retrieving Table of Authorities Section Definitions" sections.)

6. Select the section you want, then click Insert. A nonprinting comment, << Table of Authorities will generate here >, displays in your document. (You can only see the section name in Reveal Codes, but it does generate.)

7. Repeat Steps 3 through 6 for each section you want in the table. (Each section can have its own format.)

8. If you want the table of authorities to be on a page by itself, press Ctrl+Enter to insert a page break.

9. If you want new page numbers to begin after the table of authorities (for example, if the table of authorities is on page v, and you want the next page to be page 1), set a new number for the page that follows the table of authorities (see Chapter 14, "Controlling Text and Numbering Pages").

Creating or Editing Table of Authorities Sections

You define a table of authorities section automatically by typing a new section name when you create the first citation of a table of authorities item. You can then go back to edit its format. You can also define a section before you create any entries for it.

To create or edit a table of authorities section:

1. Click Tools ⇨ Reference ⇨ Table of Authorities, if necessary, to display the Table of Authorities toolbar.

2. Click Define, then either click Create and type a name for the section, or select the section you want to edit and click Edit.

3. Specify any of the options in shown in Figure 18-22 and described in Table 18-3.

Table 18-3	
Table of Authorities Editing Options	
Option	*Enables You to*
Position	Specify how the page number is displayed (or choose no page numbering).
Styles	Edit the default table of authorities style (for editing styles, see Chapter 20, "Working Quickly with ExpressDoc Templates and Styles").
Page Numbering	Specify a page numbering format different from that for the rest of your document (see Chapter 14, "Controlling Text and Numbering Pages").
Underlining Allowed	Allow citation underlining in the table as well.
Use Dash to Show Consecutive Pages	Combine groups of sequential page numbers (7–11) rather than list them separately (7, 8, 9, 10, 11).

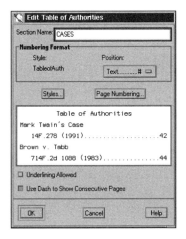

Figure 18-22: Creating or editing a TOA section definition

Retrieving Table of Authorities Section Definitions

To retrieve table of authorities section definitions from another document, such as one that has the standard formats for your office, use the following steps:

1. Click Tools ⇨ Reference ⇨ Table of Authorities ⇨ Define ⇨ Retrieve.

2. Specify the name and path of the document with the definitions you want, then click OK.

3. Click the window and check the definitions you want to retrieve (see Figure 18-23).

Figure 18-23: Retrieving Table of Authorities section definitions from another document

Deleting a Table of Authorities Section Definition

To delete a table of authorities section definition in a document, click Tools ⇨ Reference ⇨ Table of Authorities ⇨ Define. Select the definition you want to delete, then click Delete. (Any markings for the section remain in your text.)

Generating the Table of Authorities

The table of authorities is generated along with other document references (including lists, cross-references, and the index). To generate your references, click Tools ⇨ Reference ⇨ Generate. You can also click Generate on the Table of Authorities toolbar.

When you generate a table of authorities for a master document, text marked in any subdocuments is included (see Chapter 19, "Assembling Multipart Documents").

Editing the Table of Authorities

You can edit a table of authorities after it has been generated, but keep in mind that any errors you correct in the table of authorities — rather than at the source where you defined your entries and marked the text — reappears the next time you generate your document references. As a result, you should edit the document text, then regenerate document references.

Creating Indexes

A well-planned, thorough index enhances the accessibility of a book or other large document. The time and care spent in creating an index will be rewarded by the reader's appreciation and loyalty. Creating an index is a personal and mechanical process. No computer program can match your judgment in defining entries. While creating an index takes imagination and patience, WordPerfect's indexing tools can help you get the job done quickly and accurately. In particular, you can create a *concordance file* — a list of index terms and phrases — then let the program search and list every occurrence of each item.

An index can include both headings and subheadings, as shown in Figure 18-24. You can also define the format for your index entries.

Creating an index is a three-step process in which you:

✦ Mark the entries in your text (or add them to a concordance file).

✦ Define the appearance and placement of the index.

✦ Generate the index.

Understanding Indexes

An index should enable the reader to find every statement pertinent to the topic at hand. An index often includes names of persons as well as subjects. Some scholarly or complex works have additional indexes for authors or titles. A poetry anthology may have an index of first lines. (See "Creating more than one index for a document" later in this chapter.)

The three components of an index follow:

✦ *Heading*. The heading is the principle subdivision of an index, and is normally a noun ("files") or noun phrase ("file preferences").

✦ *Subheading*. When a heading has a large number of page references, you should break it down into topical subheadings, with specific page numbers. (Leave out the heading page number if the subheadings are scattered widely throughout your work.) Some books have indexes with three or more levels, but WordPerfect can generate only two.

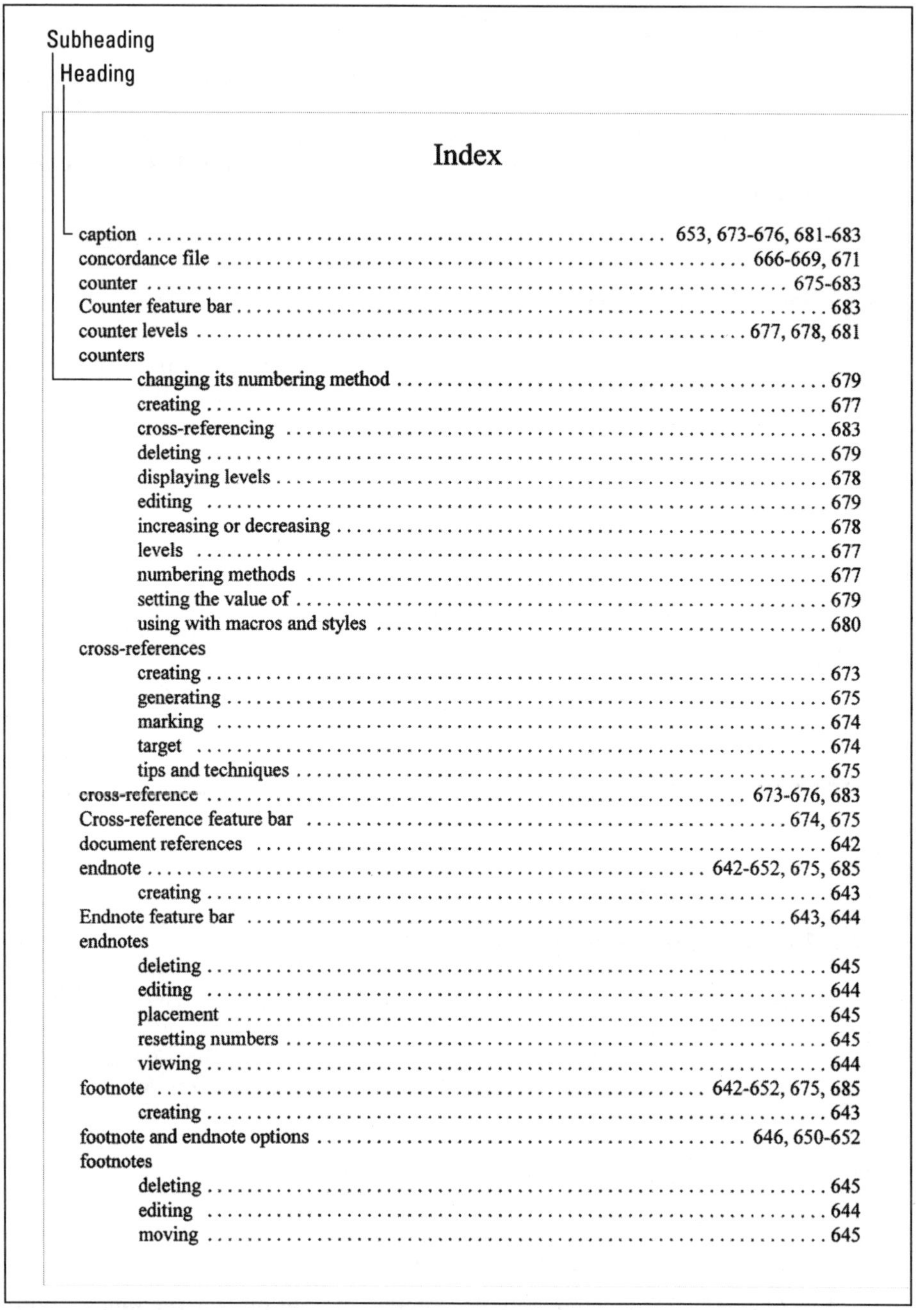

Subheading
Heading

Index

Figure 18-24: Index with headings and subheadings in the standard format

✦ *Cross-reference*. Many indexes have cross-references, which refer to items by different names or point the reader to additional related information. See "Adding cross-references to indexes" later in this chapter.

Marking Individual Index Entries in Your Text

You can manually mark each index entry in your text, or use a concordance file to automatically list every occurrence of a word or phrase. You can also combine both methods by putting some items in the concordance file and manually marking others.

To mark individual index entries:

1. Click Tools ➪ Reference ➪ Index to display the Index toolbar (see Figure 18-25).

Figure 18-25: Index toolbar

2. Select the word or phrase you want to index.

3. Click the Heading box to display the text you selected. You can edit the text to how you want it to appear in the index, or select a previous heading from your list. (The index heading can be different from the actual words in your document.)

Be sure to click the Heading box before you mark the entry. Otherwise, the item is indexed under the previous entry's heading.

4. If this entry is a subheading, press the Tab key (or click Subheading box) and edit the subheading text to your liking. For example, if your selected text is "individual index entries", you may want to have a heading of "index" and a subheading of "individual entries." You can also select a subheading from the list.

5. Click Mark. (An [Index] code is placed before your selection.)

You can mark the same text selection more than once. For example, you can have the Page Layout command appear under both "Printing" and "Formatting" headings. You can also mark an item twice (heading only and heading plus subheading) if you want its page number to appear under both the heading and subheading.

6. Repeat Steps 2 through 5 to mark additional entries.

Unmarking Index Entries

To unmark an index entry, go into Reveal Codes and delete the [Index] code preceding the item. To revise an entry, delete the code and mark the text again. Your index will reflect the changes in its next iteration.

Creating a Concordance File

For efficient indexing of large documents, nothing beats the concordance file. It also spares you the painful process of manually reindexing a large document with extensive revisions.

The concept of the concordance file is straightforward. You create a list of words and phrases, then have the program search out the words and create an index entry for every match. When you define your index, you specify where the concordance file is found.

To use concordance files effectively, keep these points in mind:

✦ Mark the entries in the concordance file just as you mark individual entries in the document text. That way, your generated index contains the precise headings and subheadings you want.

✦ An unmarked concordance entry produces a heading index entry when it finds a match.

✦ Capitalization appears in the index as you type it in the concordance file, not as it's found in the document text. (However, matching is not case-sensitive.)

✦ Matching is on whole word and exact spelling ("drag" doesn't match on "drags" or "dragging").

✦ You don't have to sort (alphabetize) the concordance file, but the index generates faster if you do. (See Chapter 22, "Sorting Information," for more about sorting.)

To create a concordance file:

1. Open a new blank document and save it to the name you want.

2. Click Tools ➪ Reference ➪ Index to display the Index toolbar.

3. Type an entry for the index.

Tip: Tile your document and the concordance file on your screen, then drag items from the document while holding Ctrl to copy them to the concordance file.

4. If desired, enter a custom heading and subheading, then click Mark, as described in the preceding "Marking Individual Index Entries in Your Text" section. (Mark the item twice if you want page numbers at both the heading and subheading levels.)

5. Press Enter, then repeat Steps 3 and 4 to create additional items (see Figure 18-26).

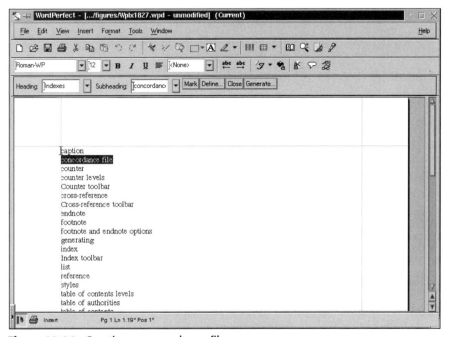

Figure 18-26: Creating a concordance file

Defining an Index

Now that you've marked index entries in your text and created a concordance file, let's define the index:

1. Click where you want the index to appear.

2. If you want the index to start at the top of a new page, press Ctrl+Enter to insert a page break.

3. Type and format the title for the index. Press Enter at least twice to put some space between the title and the index.

4. Click Tools ⇨ Reference ⇨ Index ⇨ Define.

5. Specify any of the options shown in Figure 18-27 and described in Table 18-4 .

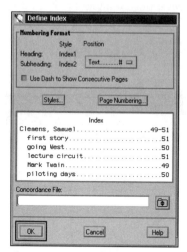

Figure 18-27: Defining an index

6. Click OK. A nonprinting comment, << Index will generate here >, displays in your document.

Table 18-4 **Index Editing Options**	
Option	**Enables You to**
Position	Specify how the page number is displayed in the index and its position in relation to the text.
Use Dash to Show Consecutive Pages	Combine groups of sequential page numbers (7–11) rather than list each page separately (7, 8, 9, 10, 11).
Styles	Edit the styles for the index headings and subheadings. (See the following section, "Customizing Index Heading and Subheading Styles.")
Page Numbering	Specify a page numbering format different from that for the rest of your document (see Chapter 14, "Controlling Text and Numbering Pages").
Concordance File	Specify the name and path of the concordance file you want to use for this index.

Caution WordPerfect generates an index at each place it finds a definition code. If you end up with two or more definition codes in your document accidentally, go into Reveal Codes and delete the [Def Mark] codes you don't want.

Customizing Index Heading and Subheading Styles

You can customize index heading and subheading styles (Index1 and Index2), or create new styles or definitions, to suit your particular needs:

1. Click Tools ➪ Reference ➪ Index ➪ Define ➪ Styles.

2. Select the level style you want to change (see Figure 18-28).

Figure 18-28: Customizing index heading and subheading styles

3. Do one or more of the following:

  • Select the style you want to associate with the level.

  • Click Create to create a style.

  • Click Edit to edit the style.

Using Custom Index Level Styles in Other Documents

You can save your custom index styles and definitions to your personal or shared styles library for use in other documents. For more on styles and templates, see Chapter 20, "Working Quickly with ExpressDoc Templates and Styles."

Generating an Index

The index is generated along with your other document references, including the table of contents, lists, and cross-references. To generate your references, click Tools ➪ Reference ➪ Generate. You can also click Generate on the Index toolbar.

When you generate an index for a master document, text marked in any subdocuments is included (see Chapter 19, "Assembling Multipart Documents").

Editing an Index

You can edit an index after it has been generated. Keep in mind, however, that any errors you correct in the index—rather than at the source where you marked the text or in the concordance file—reappear the next time you generate the document references. As a result, you should change the text in the document and then regenerate the index.

Indexing Tips and Techniques

The indexing topics covered thus far should take care of most of your needs. However, if you are indexing a large, complex document, you may want to use these additional tips and techniques.

Creating more than one index for a document

Some scholarly or complex works have more than one index. You can create multiple indexes in either of two ways.

The first method groups all the items for your second index (such as authors and titles) under a single index heading, with each particular item marked as a subheading. After your index is generated, create your second index heading manually, move the collection of subheadings to that location, and edit formatting codes (deleting the style codes may do the trick). This method may sound crude, but it can be simple and effective. Secondary indexes usually require only one heading level, so upgrading all the items from subheading to heading status should give you a second index.

A second and more elegant strategy creates a second concordance file that contains the entries for your secondary index. You can then place a second index definition in your document, specifying the name of your second concordance file. A drawback to this method is that if you have marked individual index entries in your text (in addition to using concordance files), these items generate in both indexes and must be deleted from one index manually.

Displaying an index in multiple columns

Indexes usually are displayed in multiple columns, for the reader's convenience and in the interests of conserving space. Indexes in multiple columns usually read better if, when you define your index, you change the default page number position (flush right, preceded by a line of dots, or a "dot leader") to one that follows the text immediately (such as, "*Text*, #").

You can define columns for your index either before or after it is generated. Simply place the insertion point before the index definition (if you go into Reveal Codes, you see the Index Definition code), and click the Columns button on the toolbar to select the number of newspaper style columns you want. You can also select the entire index, then apply the columns definition. For more on formatting with columns, see Chapter 16, "Formatting with Columns and Tables."

Creating alpha breaks in an index

Most large indexes are broken into alphabetical sections as a convenience to the reader. At minimum, a blank line is inserted before the introduction of the next letter. Usually, large capital letters are used to introduce each section, and the breaks sometimes include horizontal bars, reversed text, or other embellishments. These features can be added by editing the generated index manually.

Adding first and last index entries to the tops of pages

There is no automatic way to have the page headers show the first and last index entries for the pages in view. If you want to place these locators in your page headers after the index is generated, edit the header manually for each index page. Alternately create and discontinue Header A and Header B with each page. Be careful to type the heading text, even if the locator points to a subheading item. For example, if you're referring to the "creating" item under "footnotes," you should type **footnotes** in the page header. For more on page headers, see Chapter 15, "Formatting Your Document."

Adding cross-references to indexes

Most good indexes contain *cross-references* to aid the reader in finding information on various topics. Index cross-references come in two flavors: *see* (such as "Leaving, see Exiting"), when the topic is indexed under more than one heading; and *see also* (such as "Fonts 93–105, see also TextArt"), to point the reader to a related topic.

Don't confuse index cross-references with the document cross-references discussed in the following section. Index cross-references are simple alphabetic entries with no page numbers of their own — not dynamic links to the document text.

Unfortunately, there is no WordPerfect feature to help you add cross-reference items to your index. You must type these items manually after the index is generated. To be safe, keep a list of the cross-references for your index in a separate document; if you regenerate your document references, the cross-references are wiped out and must be re-created.

Inserting Document Cross-References

Document cross-references are another convenience for the reader of large documents. A *document cross-reference* points to another part of a document closely linked to the current discussion. For example, you may be discussing a table or figure and want to add a reference to the page on which the item actually appears.

Cross-references are simple to create in WordPerfect, and their page numbers update automatically each time your document's references are generated.

Understanding Cross-Reference Terms

You need to know the following cross-reference terms:

✦ The *reference* is the item placed in your text (such as "see page 37") to refer the reader to another document location.

✦ The *target* is where the reader can find the item (the "page 37" in the reference).

✦ The *target name* is the link between the reference and the target. It enables WordPerfect to place the target page number in the reference automatically during the generation process. In most cases, you need a unique target name for each reference-target pair. (The target name doesn't print.)

In addition to the page number, a cross-reference can display chapter, volume, caption, and other numbers.

Creating Cross-References

Creating a cross-reference is a three-step process in which you:

✦ Mark the reference.

✦ Mark the target.

✦ Generate the cross references.

Marking a reference

To mark a reference:

1. Type the text and punctuation to accompany the reference (such as "(see page)") with a space where the number is to appear.

2. With the insertion point in the space, click Tools ➪ Reference ➪ Cross-Reference to display the Cross-Reference toolbar in Figure 18-29.

3. If you're not creating a page reference, click Reference and select the reference type you want (see Figure 18-29). The Caption Number reference includes the caption text, such as "Figure 7."

Figure 18-29: Selecting a cross-reference type

4. Click the Target box and type the target name you want, or select a target name from the list. (Each target name you create is added to the list.) If you type in a name, remember it: you must use the same name when you mark the target. If the name you indicate here and the target name don't match, the reference doesn't generate.

5. Click Mark Reference to insert the reference code in your document.

A question mark (?) appears where you defined the reference until you mark the target and generate your document references.

Marking a target

To mark a cross-reference target:

1. Click within the text you're referencing. (That way, if the text is moved, the target goes with it.)

If you're targeting a footnote or endnote, click in the footnote or endnote, not the document text. If your reference is to a caption number, counter, paragraph number, or outline number, place the insertion point to the immediate right of the targeted item. (When targeting a graphics box, use Reveal Codes to place the insertion point immediately to the right of the graphics box code.)

2. Click Tools ➪ Reference ➪ Cross-Reference, if necessary, to display the toolbar.

3. Click the Target box and type the target name you want, or select the target name from the list.

4. Click Mark Target to insert the target code.

Unmarking references and targets

To unmark a reference or target, go into Reveal Codes and delete the Ref Pg (reference) or Target code. To revise an entry, delete the code and mark the item again. Your cross-references reflect the changes with the next iteration.

Generating cross-references

Your cross-references are generated along with all your other generated document references, including the table of contents, lists, and index. To generate your references, click Tools ➪ Reference ➪ Generate. You can also click Generate on the Cross-Reference toolbar.

If a marked reference still has a question mark (?) after your document is generated, no target by the same name was found in your document. You may have forgotten to mark the target or marked the target by the wrong name (capitalization doesn't matter, but the spelling must be exact). If the name is wrong, delete the target code and mark the target again. Another possible reason for a matching failure: you marked the target item as a reference instead of a target.

When you generate cross-references for a master document, text marked in any subdocuments is included (see Chapter 19, "Assembling Multipart Documents").

Cross-Referencing Tips and Techniques

Sometimes you may want to depart from the one-reference-one-target theme when creating cross-references. Use the following tips and techniques in these situations.

One target with more than one reference

In some cases, you may want to cross-reference a target with more than one type of reference. For example, you may want to create a reference in the form of "(Figure 4, page 37)." In this case, create two references using the same target name — one for the caption number, the other for the page number. Because both references use the same target name, you only need to mark the target once.

Multiple targets for one reference

One reference can have multiple targets. An example: "(see pages 2, 14, 50)." In this case, mark the reference once, then mark each target separately, using the same target name. When you generate the cross-references, commas and spaces are added automatically.

Using Counters

Counters are one of those features that you rarely (if ever) adjust. Once you understand how counters work, however, you'll discover the cool tricks you can do with them.

Understanding Counters

WordPerfect has several built-in features that count and display the number of pages, chapters, paragraphs, lines, footnotes, figures, and other items in your document. The program also provides two types of *counters* to keep track of anything else:

✦ *User-defined counters* for anything not counted automatically (such as sections, exhibits, examples, or problems). You can mark the things you want to count, and manipulate and display counter values at will.

✦ Five *system counters* to count various types of graphics boxes in your document automatically. These counters explain why the default captions for graphics boxes display with the likes of "Figure 1," "Figure 2," and so forth. System counters increment automatically, yet they can be edited and set in the same manner as user-defined counters (you just can't edit their names).

Employing user-defined counters is a three-step process in which you:

✦ Create the counter.

✦ Specify where you want the numbers to increase or decrease.

✦ Specify where you want to display the numbers.

The important thing to remember is that user-defined counters are not automatic. You must place a code in your document each time you want to change or display the counter value.

Counter levels and numbering methods

You can create counters with one to five levels by using a variety of numbering methods (such as "I, i, a, 1"). Each level of a counter must be set, increased, or decreased individually. You can display the levels individually as well. You can almost think of each level number as a counter unto itself. The only exception is that when you increase or decrease a counter level, all the levels below it are reset to 1. If you don't want this to happen, set individual levels to particular values (see the following "Setting a Counter Value or Changing Its Numbering Method" section).

Suppose you have a four-level counter set to "II, ii, g, 6". If you increase the second level to "iii," the new value for the counter is "II, iii, a, 1."

This process only works from higher to lower, not from the bottom up. When you increment the third level in this example beyond "z," it does not reset to "a" and push the second level from "iii" to "iv." Instead, the third level moves to "aa, bb, cc," and beyond.

The initial value of a new counter is 1. It can be decreased or set to 0.

Creating a Counter

To create a counter for your document:

1. Click Insert ➪ Other ➪ Counter.

2. Click Create, then type a name for the counter.

3. To use more than one numbering level, specify the number of levels you want (see Figure 18-30).

4. Click the "Numbering Method" lists to specify the numbering method for various levels.

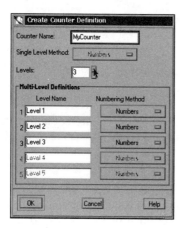

Figure 18-30: Creating a counter

Increasing or Decreasing a Counter

Once a counter is defined, you can specify the places in your document where you want its value to increase or decrease (typically with each new section, exhibit, example, or other item that you're counting). While inserting the counter increase or decrease codes is a manual process, the actual count is maintained automatically.

To increase or decrease a counter:

1. Click where you want to increase (or decrease) the counter number.

2. Click Insert ⇨ Other ⇨ Counter.

3. Select the counter (or level for a multilevel counter) you want to increase or decrease (see Figure 18-31).

User-defined counter System counters

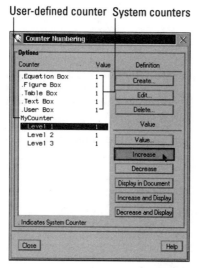

Figure 18-31: Selecting the counter to increase or decrease

4. Click Increase or Decrease.

Displaying Counter Levels

You don't display the counters themselves, but the individual levels of which they are composed. For example, if you have a two-level counter in the form of "22.13" for displaying chapter and figure numbers, you must display the chapter number (22) and the figure number (13) in two separate operations by using two separate counter display codes.

To display a counter level in your document:

1. Click where you want to display the counter level, then click Insert ⇨ Other ⇨ Counter.
2. Select the counter (or level for a multilevel counter) you want to display (refer to Figure 18-31).
3. Click Display in Document.

Increasing or Decreasing and Displaying Counters in One Operation

You can both increase or decrease a counter (or a counter level of a multilevel counter) and display its value in one operation:

1. Click where you want to increase or decrease and display the counter level.
2. Click Insert ⇨ Other ⇨ Counter.
3. Select the counter (or level for a multilevel counter) you want to increase or decrease and display (refer to Figure 18-31).
4. Click Increase and Display, or Decrease and Display.

If you go into Reveal Codes, you see that you have inserted two codes in your document, one to increase (or decrease) the counter's value and the other to display it.

Setting a Counter Value or Changing Its Numbering Method

Instead of increasing or decreasing the value of a counter by 1, you can set a counter to a particular value at any point in your document. You can also change a counter's numbering method:

1. Click where you want to set the value of a counter or change its numbering method (the numbers and values before the insertion point are not affected).

2. Click Insert ➪ Other ➪ Counter and select the counter.

3. Click Value, then specify the new value for the counter or various levels for a multilevel counter (Figure 18-32). You can click the lists to change the numbering method at the same time.

Figure 18-32: Setting a counter value or changing its numbering method

Deleting a Counter

To delete a counter, click Insert ➪ Other ➪ Counter, select the counter you want to delete, then click Delete.

Editing a Counter Definition

You can edit an existing counter in the same way that you define a new one. Follow the steps described in the preceding "Creating a Counter" section, but this time select an existing counter and click Edit. You may want to edit a system counter in the current document (this edit doesn't change the system default), as described in the following "Displaying multilevel numbering in captions" section. You cannot change a system counter's name.

Counter Tips and Techniques

Here are some tips for using counters and examples of how they can be applied.

Using copy and paste for repetitive counter operations

Counter applications tend to be repetitive by nature. Suppose you are using counters to number problems and solutions in an instructional document. When it comes to numbering the second problem, you can type some text and insert counter increase and display codes (such as "Problem 2").

Instead of repeating this process for the third problem, simply select the text and codes for the second problem, then copy and paste them in your document to get "Problem 3." You can then repeat the pasting process as many times as necessary; each time the counter display increases automatically by one.

Using counters with macros and styles

If you repeat a particular counter operation frequently, consider incorporating it into a custom macro or style. One example creates interrogatory statements that take the form of "Question 1:" and "Answer 1:." Each succeeding pair of questions and answers increase in value by one. To automate this process:

1. Click Insert ⇨ Other ⇨ Counter, then click Create. Give the counter a name of **Interrogatory** and click OK. Click Decrease to initialize the counter to 0.

2. Click Format ⇨ Styles, then click Create and give the style a name of **Question**. Click the Contents box and type **Question**, followed by a space. Click Insert ⇨ Other ⇨ Counter from the Styles dialog box, select the Interrogatory counter, and click Increase and Display. Then type the colon (:), followed by another space.

3. Click OK to return to the Style List dialog box, then click Create again to create a style named **Answer.** Type **Answer** followed by a space in the Contents box. Click Insert ⇨ Other ⇨ Counter from the Styles dialog box, select the Interrogatory counter, and click Display in Document. Type a colon (:) and a space.

4. If you want to add a blank line between the answer and the next question, check "Show 'off codes.'" Place the insertion point after the [Codes to the left are ON — Codes to the right are OFF] code and press Shift+Enter to insert a Hard Return [HRt] code.

5. To chain the Answer style to the Question style, check the "Enter key will chain to:" box, select Question from the drop-down list, then click OK. Next, select the Question style, click Edit, and chain the Question style to the Answer style.

Wherever you want to use the Question-and-Answer styles sequence, click Format ⇨ Styles, select the Question style, then click Apply. Type the text for the first question, press Enter, type the answer, then press Enter to go to the second question, and so forth. To break out of the styles chain and resume normal text, click Format ⇨ Styles and select the <None> style.

Displaying multilevel numbering in captions

Another common counter operation displays multilevel numbers in the captions for figures, tables, exhibits, and other document elements (such as "Table 22.3"). You can define a multilevel counter for this purpose, then increment and display your counter in the captions.

To display multilevel numbers in graphics box captions, modify the program's automatic system counters to assign the number of levels you want. The program increments the lowest level of the system counter when you create a graphics box. However, the default caption styles display only the highest level of the system counter. Therefore, to display multiple counter levels by using the built-in captions, you must modify the caption style as well.

In the following exercise, the system styles are left intact, and new styles are created to display multilevel captions for custom Image or Figure boxes:

1. Click Format ⇨ Graphics Styles.

2. Select the style you want to customize, click Options, Copy, give the new style a name (such as "Two-Level Caption Box"), and click OK.

3. With the new style selected, click Edit ⇨ Caption, then click the "Number style" Change button.

4. Click Create in the Style List dialog box, give the new caption style a name (such as "2-level Cptn"), and change the style Type to Document (open).

5. Turn on any formatting codes you need (such as Ctrl+B for bold), and type the text you want (such as "Figure"), followed by a space.

6. Click Insert ⇨ Other ⇨ Counter. Then click Create and give a name to the new counter definition (such as "Two-level").

7. Specify the number of levels you want for the counter (such as 2 or more), then click OK.

8. Select Level 1 of your new definitions, then click Display in Document. (This sequence inserts a [Count Disp] code in your style.)

9. Type any punctuation separating the level displays (such as a period or a hyphen), then click Insert ⇨ Other ⇨ Counter, select Level 2 of your counter, and click Display in Document. Repeat this process for any remaining levels.

10. Turn off any formatting codes that you turned on in Step 4 (for example, press Ctrl+B to turn off bold).

11. Click OK to return to the Style List dialog box. With your new style selected, click Apply.

12. Click the Change button for Counter, select the counter definition you created in Step 5 (such as Two-level), click Select, then click OK ⇨ OK Close.

You can now use the graphics box style you created in any document. Click Insert ⇨ Graphics ⇨ Custom Box, select the style you created, and click OK. If you right-click the graphics box and click Create Caption, the correct number of levels should appear.

After inserting custom graphics boxes in your document, you may want to set the first levels of the counter you created to number your boxes with the likes of 14.1, 14.2, and so forth. To do so, place the insertion point before the first graphics box code, then click Insert ⇨ Other ⇨ Counter, select the counter, and click Value to set it.

Note   In addition to creating a new caption style, you have to create a new graphics box style and a new counter style to get multilevel numbering to work. That's because all components of the graphics box are based on styles.

Cross-referencing counters

To include a counter in a cross-reference, click Reference on the Cross-Reference toolbar, then select Counter (see the preceding "Marking a Reference" section). If the counter has multiple levels, there will be a period between each level (4.2).

If you are cross-referencing a figure with a multi-level caption number created with counters (see the preceding "Displaying Multilevel Numbering in Captions" section), reference the counters instead of the figure box caption.

For More Information . . .

On	See
Creating and editing styles	Chapter 20
Numbering pages	Chapter 14
Generating document references	Chapter 19
Using templates	Chapter 20
Assembling multipart documents	Chapter 19
Creating hyperlinks	Chapter 11
Formatting with columns	Chapter 16
Creating page headers	Chapter 15

✦   ✦   ✦

Assembling Multipart Documents

In writing a book or other large work, it's easier to work on one chapter or part at a time, rather than write the entire document at once. With this strategy, you and your coworkers can focus on manageable tasks without becoming overwhelmed by the magnitude of the project. In addition, you can edit and check your work easily, as well as send out chunks for criticism and review.

WordPerfect's Master Document feature lets you edit large documents in manageable chunks, then assemble the pieces at publication time. This chapter shows you how easy it is to use this function.

How Master Documents and Subdocuments Work

A *master document* is nothing more than an ordinary document with links to pull in *subdocuments* (other ordinary documents) when it expands, as shown in Figure 19-1. That way, everyone can work on the particular subdocuments, then assemble the whole document at publication time.

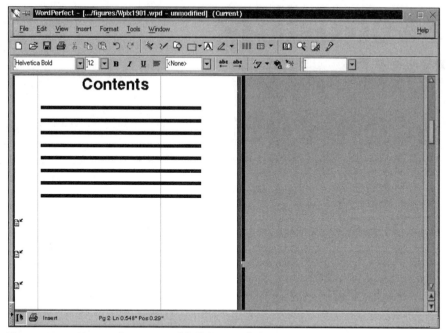

Figure 19-1: Master document with links to subdocuments

Put the items that pertain to your document as a whole in the master document, such as a title page, the table of contents, and the index. Other candidates for the master document are a dedication, acknowledgments, credits, a list of charts and tables, and other text too short to merit an individual document.

You can expand the master (either temporarily or permanently) to display or print the entire document, and generate the table of contents, index, lists, and other document references automatically (see Chapter 18, "Adding Document References").

Sometimes advantages accrue from editing your expanded master, especially when the document as a whole is nearly complete. For example, you can find and replace a particular word or phrase throughout the entire work. Spell checking and grammar checking also can be more efficient, especially when you want to skip particular words or rule classes.

Tip   When you make changes at the master document level, be sure to save them to the subdocuments, as explained in the following "Condensing the Master Document" section in this chapter. Otherwise, you'll lose your master document changes the next time you expand it.

Assembling a Master Document

With these concepts and cautions in mind, you're ready to assemble a master document. This process can involve:

✦ Creating subdocuments

✦ Creating the master

✦ Expanding the master

✦ Generating references

✦ Printing the master document

✦ Condensing the master document

Tip   The Reference toolbar (see Figure 19-2) is especially handy when working with master documents. Right-click the toolbar and click Reference to display it. (Right-click the Reference toolbar and uncheck Reference to dismiss the toolbar when you no longer need it.)

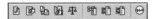

Figure 19-2: Reference toolbar, with handy buttons for master document tasks

Creating the Master Document and Subdocuments

Wherever possible, styles and codes should reside in the master document (see the following "Using Formatting Codes and Styles" section in this chapter). You may find, however, that certain features belong in the subdocument, rather than in the master. For example, if the header or footer for each subdocument contains the name of that chapter or section, then the codes for the header or footer must be placed in each subdocument.

The only essential master document items are the subdocument codes. In practice, as noted previously, you're likely to include the contents, index, and other features as well. To create a master document:

1. Open a new or existing document to use as your master.

2. Create pages for your cover, title, copyright notice, table of contents, and other front matter (such as a list of illustrations). Insert a hard page break (Ctrl+Enter) between each page. (For more on creating a table of contents and lists, see Chapter 18, "Adding Document References.")

3. Add any formatting codes that you want to use for the entire document (such as for the base font, margins, spacing, page numbering, and headers).

4. Place the insertion point where you want to insert a subdocument link. To begin the subdocument on a separate page, press Ctrl+Enter to insert a hard page break. To begin each subdocument on an odd page (as with chapters in a book), click Format ⇨ Page ⇨ Force Page ⇨ "Current page odd."

5. Click the Subdocument button on the Reference toolbar (File ⇨ Document ⇨ Subdocument). You can also right-click the left margin and click Subdocument.

6. Select the file you want to link, then click Include (see Figure 19-3). You can specify a filename that doesn't exist (the default path will be the same directory as the master) and create the subdocument later.

Figure 19-3: Inserting a subdocument link

7. Repeat Steps 4 through 6 for other subdocuments you want to link.

8. Create a page for your index or other matter for the back of your document. (For more on creating an index, see Chapter 18, "Adding Document References.")

Tip

When your master and subdocuments reside in your default document directory (click Preferences ⇨ Files in the WordPerfect Program window to set the default document directory), the subdocument link contains only the filename, without the path. This arrangement makes it easier to transfer files to another location. See the following "Transferring Master Documents to Another Location" section in this chapter.

Viewing subdocument links

The way subdocument links display on the screen depends upon your view mode, as shown in Figure 19-4. In Draft view, a link displays as shaded comment text. In Page or Two Page view, a link appears as an icon that you can click to display the path and filename.

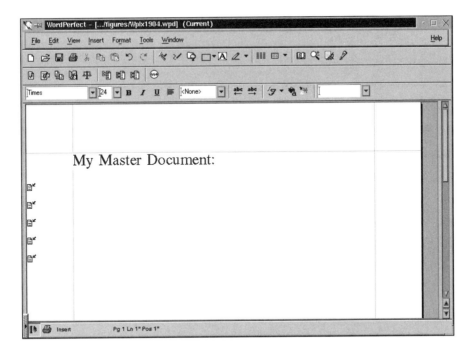

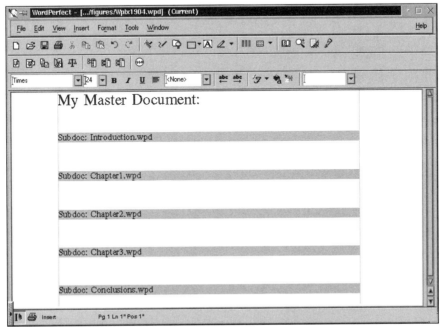

Figure 19-4: Subdocument links displayed in Draft and Page view

Moving and deleting subdocument links

By going into Reveal Codes, you can cut and paste the link codes in a condensed master to rearrange the subdocuments.

If you no longer want to include a subdocument in the master, simply go into Reveal Codes and delete its [Subdocument] link code.

Tip Delete the [Subdocument] link code when the master is in its compressed form. Otherwise, you must delete the [Subdocument Begin] or [Subdocument End] code, and all the expanded text between the codes.

Caution Deleting a [Subdocument Begin] or [Subdocument End] code in an expanded master breaks the subdocument link and the remaining text no longer will condense. Restore it immediately with Undo (Ctrl+Z).

Expanding the Master Document

Once your master document is defined, you can expand all or part of it:

1. Click the Master Document Expand button on the Reference toolbar, or click File ➪ Document ➪ Expand Master.

2. Uncheck the subdocuments you don't want to expand, then click OK (see Figure 19-5). You can also click Mark/Clear, then click Mark All or Clear All.

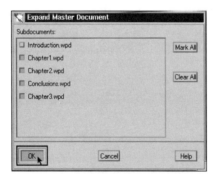

Figure 19-5: Expanding the master document

The expanded subdocuments appear between a pair of [Subdocument Begin] and [Subdocument End] codes.

When the program can't find a subdocument, a Subdocument Error dialog box appears (see Figure 19-6). You can then specify the correct path and filename, click

Cancel to stop the expansion process, or click Skip to bypass that document and
expand the remaining subdocuments.

Figure 19-6: Dialog box that appears when
a subdocument can't be found

If a subdocument has a password, you are prompted to enter the password when
you expand the master.

Caution Close any open subdocuments before you expand the master. Otherwise, you can
end up with one version of a subdocument on screen, and another in your
expanded master.

Generating Master Document References

Many master documents contain definitions for generated references, such as the
table of contents, lists, cross-references, and index. You can mark text in the
subdocuments, then generate the references for the document as a whole.
Reference definitions in particular subdocuments, such as a list of figures at the
beginning of a chapter, generate at the same time.

You can generate references when a master is condensed (for example, to print the
table of contents and the index, but not the remainder of the document). When you
generate references, WordPerfect expands the master temporarily, generates the
references, then returns the master to its condensed state automatically.

To generate references for a master document:

1. Click the Master Document Generate button on the Reference toolbar
   (Tools ➪ Reference ➪ Generate).

2. Click Options, then check any of the following:

   • *Save Subdocuments* to save generated changes to your subdocuments
     (see Figure 19-7).

   • *Build Hypertext Links* to create and generate any hyperlinks to marked
     text. (For more on hyperlinks, see Chapter 11, "Web Writing and
     Publishing.")

Figure 19-7: Generating master document references

Printing the Master Document

When the master document is expanded, the subdocuments are formatted for the master document's printer. This process ensures that even if several people with different printers work on various parts of the document, the final assemblage will have a consistent look and feel. Fonts and other settings may not appear as they did in the original subdocuments.

Condensing the Master Document

When you condense an expanded master, you choose which subdocuments to condense and whether to save changes to them:

1. Click the Master Document Condense button on the Reference toolbar (File ⇨ Document ⇨ Condense Master).

2. Each subdocument is listed twice — once to be condensed and once to be saved. Uncheck those subdocuments you don't want to condense or save. To act on all the subdocuments at once, click the Mark/Clear and click Condense All, Clear Condense, Save All, or Clear Save (see Figure 19-8).

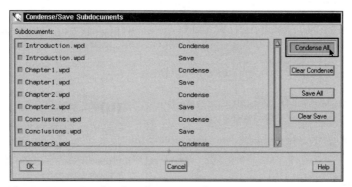

Figure 19-8: Condensing the master document

If you don't want to save any subdocument changes, click Clear Save.

Saving the Master Document

When you save an expanded master, you are prompted automatically as to whether you want to condense the master first (see Figure 19-9).

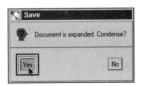

Figure 19-9: Prompt when saving an expanded master

To save your master document in its expanded form, especially when it is assembled, polished, and ready to print, click No. (You can still condense it later.) Otherwise, click Yes to condense the master, then choose whether to save changes to the subdocuments, as explained in the preceding "Condensing the Master Document" section.

Master Document Tips and Techniques

Here are some tips and techniques to making the most of the master documents.

Placing Subdocuments within Subdocuments

One interesting technique turns subdocuments into lower-level masters by placing subdocuments within them. This process creates a master pyramid, chaining three or more levels, to handle a very large document with a complex structure. You might do this placement with a book that has multiple parts and several chapters within each part. When you expand a master that contains lower-level masters, the lower-level masters expand automatically as well.

Restarting Footnote and Endnote Numbers

In many large documents, such as scholarly journals or anthologies, you may want to restart your footnote or endnote numbering at the beginning of each subdocument. Unfortunately, with footnote numbering, WordPerfect is too clever for its own good. The program figures that there's no need to restart your footnote numbers until after you have created your first footnote, so it won't let you set the footnote number at the beginning of each subdocument. Therefore, you must first expand your master, then reset the numbering at the beginning of each expanded subdocument. (Click Insert ⇨ Footnote ⇨ New Number, and specify a new number of 1.)

You don't have this problem with endnotes, because when you specify endnote placement in a subdocument, you have the option to restart numbering.

Restarting Page Numbers in Subdocuments

If you want to restart page numbering in each subdocument, you encounter the same problem with footnote numbers — you can't set the page number to 1 until after the first page. In this case, you can usually work around the problem without expanding the master. The trick: place a hard page break and reset the page numbering (Format ⇨ Page ⇨ Page Numbering ⇨ Numbering ⇨ Value) *before* each subdocument code.

Converting Subdocuments from Other Formats

Subdocuments in another format are converted to the default WordPerfect format when they're pulled into the master. Files from WordPerfect 5.0 and up are converted automatically. Otherwise, WordPerfect tries to determine the format and prompts you for confirmation (see Chapter 7, "Managing Your Files").

Using Formatting Codes and Styles

Whenever possible, formatting codes and styles should be placed in the master, not the individual subdocument. When you expand a master, subdocument formatting codes and styles are pulled in along with the text — and in WordPerfect, codes are on until you turn them off.

For example, consider a book of ten chapters (subdocuments) that you want to print entirely in the Helvetica font. Suppose the last page of Chapter 3 is composed inadvertently in the Times New Roman font. When you expand your master, everything from the last page of Chapter 3 to the end of the book (or up to the next font code) will be composed in Times New Roman.

To correct this type of problem, locate and delete the offending code. (Delete it in the subdocument as well, so it doesn't reappear.)

If special formatting is required within a particular subdocument (such as for margins or tabs), you should first select the text before you apply the formatting. That way, your special formatting will be turned off before the end of the subdocument, so as not to affect the formatting of subsequent text within the expanded master.

When you expand a master, then condense it and save the subdocuments, you may see changes to your subdocuments, even when no change is made to the expanded master itself. The possible reasons follow:

✦ The Initial Document Style (see Chapter 15, "Formatting Your Document") of the master replaces that of each subdocument. (Don't put any codes in subdocument Document Styles for this reason.)

✦ Similarly, named styles in the master, or a preceding subdocument, override styles with the same name in succeeding subdocuments. (The styles currently in effect are saved with the subdocuments.)

✦ WordPerfect's auto code placement feature deletes codes it considers to be redundant. For example, if a double-space code is already active in your expanded document, the auto code placement feature deletes a similar code in a subdocument.

✦ A subdocument has a different character map from that of the master (its map gets replaced by the master's map).

Using Headers and Footers in Master Documents and Subdocuments

Headers and footers can be defined in either the master document or in subdocuments, depending on how they're used. For example, you may have a header displayed on the even pages (such as the title of a book) that stays the same throughout your expanded document. In that case, define the header as Header A in your master. You may also have a Header B that displays the title of each subdocument, or chapter, on the odd pages. Define the Header B at the beginning of each subdocument. For more on headers and footers, see Chapter 15, "Formatting Your Document."

Transferring Master Documents to Another Location

If the subdocument links in your master document contain only the filenames, without the paths, it will be easier to transfer the master and its subdocuments to another location on your computer or to another computer.

The trick: have your subdocuments in your default document directory when you create the links and when you expand your master. To specify your default document directory, switch to the WordPerfect Program window and click Preferences ➪ Files.

For More Information . . .

On	See
Defining and marking document references	Chapter 18
Creating an index or table of contents	Chapter 18
Inserting hyperlinks	Chapter 11
Converting documents	Chapter 7
Changing the Initial Document Style	Chapter 15
Creating headers and footers	Chapter 15

✦   ✦   ✦

Honing Your Skills

✦　✦　✦　✦

✦　✦　✦　✦

Working Quickly with ExpressDoc Templates and Styles

Nothing beats mass production when it comes to turning out CDs, ballpoint pens, or WordPerfect documents. This chapter looks at features to produce and update all or part of a document quickly:

✦ *Templates (ExpressDocs)*, to apply format, content, and features automatically.

✦ *Styles*, to give similar types of text (such as headings and lists) a consistent, easy-to-update appearance.

Understanding ExpressDoc Templates

Can you imagine making holiday cookies by cutting the dough painstakingly to form each gingerbread man or tree? Of course not — most likely you'd use a cookie cutter for quick, consistent results.

WordPerfect's document cookie cutters are called *ExpressDoc templates* in WordPerfect for Linux (they're called plain *templates* in the Windows and DOS versions of WordPerfect). These cookie cutters are named "ExpressDoc templates" or "templates" for the remainder of this chapter.

Dozens of fill-in-the-blanks templates create calendars, newsletters, business cards, memos, term papers, and other types of documents. These templates have the filename extension .WPT found in the wpexpdocs directory.

There's nothing mysterious about how templates work. In fact, every time you open a blank document, you call the Default template with its styles, toolbars, keyboards, and other parts of your working environment. Without this template, you'd have to specify margins, tabs, justification, spacing, and other formatting every time you opened a document.

You can even try your hand at creating your own ExpressDoc templates to automate your personal word-processing tasks. For example, you can create a template that displays your company letterhead and prompts you for the name and address of the recipient.

Using ExpressDoc Templates

When you click File ⇨ Open, you open a blank document based on the Default template. To use a specialized template instead:

1. Click File ⇨ ExpressDocs.

2. Select the template you want and click Select (see Figure 20-1).

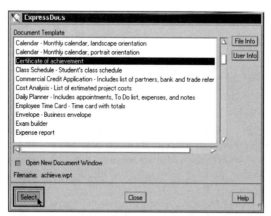

Figure 20-1: Selecting a template-based project on which to work

3. The first time you open a template you have to enter some personal information (see Figure 20-2). This information is added automatically to the templates you open.

Figure 20-2: Adding personal information to your ExpressDoc templates

4. WordPerfect may ask you to customize your document by entering information that will be inserted into the template automatically. For example, you can enter a name and a description for a certificate of achievement (as in Figure 20-3).

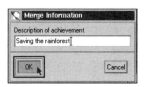

Figure 20-3: WordPerfect prompts you to add a description to your certificate of achievement template.

5. When the template opens, enter your text or data, and make any changes to the document's format, fonts, graphics, and so forth.

6. Click File ⇨ Save and name your document.

Note

To change the personal information you added to the ExpressDoc templates, click File ⇨ ExpressDocs ⇨ User Info.

Creating Your Own ExpressDoc Templates

The ExpressDoc templates that come with WordPerfect may be quite convenient, but why not create your own templates for documents like your company letters or forms? Here's how:

1. Set up a new document exactly the way you want, or clean up a copy of an existing document. Note that templates can also contain graphics, macros, styles, and toolbars.

2. Click File ⇨ Properties ⇨ Document Summary and add a descriptive name.

3. Click File ⇨ Save As and save your document in the ExpressDocs directory with the extension .wpt.

4. The next time you click File ⇨ ExpressDocs, the template you just created shows up in the list (see Figure 20-4). Click File Info to change the descriptive name.

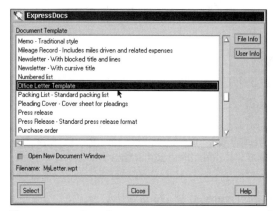

Figure 20-4: Opening your own ExpressDoc template

Tip   You can also insert keyboard merge codes to create templates that prompt the user for input. See Chapter 28, "Mass-Producing with Labels and Merge," for more information on inserting keyboard merge codes.

Applying Styles

Whereas templates format your document as a whole, styles format particular sections of text within documents. Styles save time in two ways:

✦ Once you package your formatting as a style, you can apply the style to similar text in the same and other documents.

✦ When changing an underlying style, you can update every place the style is applied in the document automatically.

Text and Graphics Styles

WordPerfect has two classes of styles:

✦ *Text styles*, composed of formatting codes, which are the subject of this chapter.

✦ *Graphics styles*, composed of graphic elements that define boxes, borders, lines, and fills (see Chapter 9, "Working with Graphics," and Chapter 23, "Adding Graphic Lines, Borders, and Fills").

The plain term "styles" always refers to text styles, which you can think of as bundles of paired or open formatting codes (see Chapter 3, "Mastering the WordPerfect Interface"). The three types of text styles follow:

Type of Style	Paired/Open	What It Does
Character	Paired	Formats text character by character.
Paragraph	Paired	Formats text paragraph by paragraph.
Document	Open	Changes the appearance of text from the insertion point forward.

The Initial Document Style is a special document style found at the beginning of every document. You modify the default tabs, margins, justification, line spacing, and so forth in this style (see Chapter 15, "Formatting Your Document").

Using Automatic Styles

Character and paragraph styles come in standard and automatic flavors. With an automatic style, changing the format of a paragraph or characters in one location changes the style for all paragraphs or characters. The QuickStyles and QuickFormat features create automatic styles.

Where Styles Are Stored

To take full advantage of style features, you must know the following four places where styles can be stored:

✦ *In WordPerfect's system*. These built-in system styles support such features as bullets, outlining, footnotes, headers, footers, watermarks, hypertext, and Web publishing. You can change these features in a document or template, but not in the system. Apart from the styles for Headings 1–5, which are copied to your current document, they're not usually on display.

✦ *In your document*. Normally, styles that you create are stored in your document and are available for use only in that document.

✦ *In an ExpressDoc template*. A style stored in an ExpressDoc template is available to all documents based on that template.

✦ *In a file*. You can save styles to a separate library file, then retrieve them for use in any document. This file can be a personal library or a shared library (on a network).

Applying Styles

Normally, when you open a blank document, only the styles for Headings 1–5 appear in the listings. These styles, used to format titles and various level headings, are premarked to appear automatically in a generated table of contents (see Chapter 18, "Adding Document References," for more about tables of contents).

Try the following experiment to see how the heading styles work:

1. Open a new blank document, type **Heading 1 (Title)**, and then press Enter twice. (Don't make your heading text bold.)

2. Go down the line typing **Heading 2**, **Heading 3**, **Heading 4**, and **Heading 5**.

3. Place the insertion point in each heading in turn, and select its style from the property bar list, as shown in Figure 20-5.

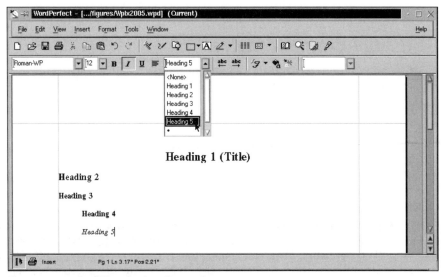

Figure 20-5: Applying the heading styles

 Tip

You can also select each style, then type the text and press Enter. (Because the styles are paired paragraph styles, they terminate when you press Enter.)

You can also apply styles from the Format menu:

1. Do one of the following:

   • *For a character style*, select the text to which you want to apply that style.

   • *For a paragraph style*, click the paragraph.

   • *For a document style*, click where you want the style to begin to take effect.

2. Click Format ⇨ Styles, select the style, and click Apply (see Figure 20-6).
(You can also double-click a style in the list.)

Figure 20-6: Applying a style
from the Style List

Listing Styles

Normally, only your document styles appear in the Style List, but you can display
and select styles from any source, including your personal style libraries and the
system styles. (See the following "Creating Your Own Styles" section to learn about
making and saving your custom styles.) Click Format ⇨ Styles ⇨ Options ⇨ Setup
and check the sources you want to display (see Figure 20-7).

Figure 20-7: Selecting sources
for your style listings

Enter-Key Chaining and Turning Off Styles

The most natural way to turn off a style is by using keystrokes. For a character
style, you can simply press the right-arrow key to move the insertion point outside
of the styled text. The particular keystrokes to turn off a paragraph style depend on
the "chaining" function assigned to the Enter key, as shown in Table 20-1.

	Table 20-1		
Enter-Key Chaining and Off Keystrokes for Paragraph Styles			
Enter Key Chains to	*Result of Pressing Enter*	*Example*	*Keystroke(s) to Turn Off*
<None>	Style turns off	Headings	Enter
<Same Style>	Style turns off, insertion point moves past it, then style turns back on	Bullets	Enter+Backspace
Another style	Style turns off, insertion point moves past it, and the other style turns on	Question-Answer chain (see the following "Chaining Styles" section)	Right arrow or Enter+Backspace
(Deselected)	Hard return within style; doesn't turn the style off		Right-arrow key

When no keystroke is available, as with a document style, you can always turn off a style by selecting <None> from the Style List on the property bar (or click Format ➪ Styles and apply <None>).

Deleting a Style

You can delete a style you applied by removing its code in Reveal Codes.

Creating Your Own Styles

Now you're ready to create your own styles.

Creating styles by example

The easiest way to create styles in a document is by using the QuickStyle or QuickFormat features described in Chapter 4, "Becoming an Instant WordPerfect Expert":

1. Place the insertion point in your formatted text.

2. Do either of the following:

   • Click Format ➪ Styles ➪ QuickStyle, type a name and description, then click either "Character" or "Paragraph."

   • Click the QuickFormat button on the toolbar.

Tip The QuickFormat Characters option lets you copy character attributes, but it doesn't save them as a style. Use QuickStyle to save attributes as a character style.

Using the Styles Editor to create or edit a style

You can also edit a style, or create one from scratch, in the Styles Editor:

1. Click Format ⇨ Styles, then do either of the following:
    - Highlight a style and click Edit.
    - Click Create and type a name and description for the new style.
2. Click the Type pop-up list to select or change a style type. (You can't change the type of a system style.)
3. Add codes and text in the Contents box. You can choose items from the Styles Editor menu, press keystrokes, or type text (see Figure 20-8).

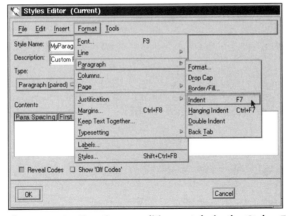

Figure 20-8: Creating or editing a style in the Styles Editor

Tip Click Insert ⇨ Tab to insert a tab code. Make sure that "Reveal Codes" is checked so that you can see the codes you insert.

4. Click OK to save the new or changed style. Existing text based on the edited style is updated automatically.

Creating a New Set of Headings

Suppose you want to create a set of heading styles similar to the system styles, but using an informal, modern font. Use the following steps to copy the set of system headings, then insert the font code in your custom styles:

1. Open a new blank document and click Format ⇨ Styles.

2. Highlight Heading 1 and click Options ⇨ Copy.

3. Click "Current Document," "Personal Library," or "Shared Library," depending on whether you want to use the style for the current document only, or have it available for all your new documents (see Figure 20-9). Save to a shared library when you're on a network and want other users to have access to your styles.

Figure 20-9: Selecting a location for a style copy

4. Click OK and give the style another name of up to 12 characters and spaces, such as "Inf Head 1," as shown in Figure 20-10.

Figure 20-10: Naming the style you're copying

5. Highlight the new style, click Edit ⇨ Format ⇨ Font, select the font you want, then click OK ⇨ OK to save your changes. (Give your new styles a description while you're at it.)

6. Repeat Steps 2 through 5 for the other four heading styles, then close the Style List dialog box.

7. You can now type some text and apply your new styles, as shown in Figure 20-11.

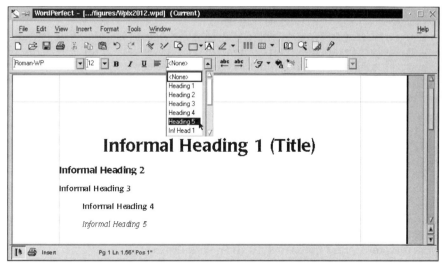

Figure 20-11: Testing your new heading styles

Chaining Styles

If you examine your heading styles in the Styles Editor, you see that the "Enter Key will Chain to" option is checked and set to <None>. This setting means that when you press Enter, the style is turned off and the insertion point moves to the next line.

If you click the Bullets button on the toolbar to insert a bullet, then double-click its style code in Reveal Codes, you see that "Enter Key will Chain to" is set to <Same Style>. This setting means that each time you press Enter, another bullet is created, until you end the list by pressing Enter ⇨ Backspace.

Normally, when you create a style, the "Enter Key will Chain to" is set to <Same Style>, so the style keeps repeating until you turn it off (such as with bullets). If you want your style to behave like a heading, remove the check or have it chain to <None>.

You can also chain one style to another, even to another and back, in a continuous loop. One practical use of this technique creates a two-style Question-Answer sheet in the form of:

Question:

Answer:

Question:

Answer:

To create this Question-Answer style chain:

1. Click Format ⇨ Styles ⇨ Create to create the Question style. Type **Question:** followed by a space in the Contents box of the Styles Editor. Leave the type as Paragraph (paired), but don't set the "Enter Key will Chain to" option yet.

Tip   You can select "Question:" in the Styles Editor and click the Bold button to make it bold, just as you would in a document.

2. Create the Answer style, with a preceding tab (Insert ⇨ Tab). Select Question from the "Enter Key to Chain to" list.

3. Go back and edit the Question style, setting "Enter Key to Chain to" to **Answer**.

To start the chain, select Question from the styles list on the property bar, type some text, and press Enter. You switch to the Answer style automatically. Type some text, then press Enter to start the next question.

To turn off the chain, press Enter ⇨ Backspace or select <None> from the styles list.

Specifying "Off Codes"

With paired styles, you can insert codes to execute after the style ends.

With the styles created in the previous Question-Answer exercise, the answer follows the question on the next line, with no blank line in between.

To skip a line after each question and answer, you can add hard returns as "off codes" following the end of each style:

1. Click Format ⇨ Styles, highlight the Question style, and click Edit.

2. Check "Show 'Off Codes.'"

3. Click after the ON/OFF separator comment, then press Enter to insert a [HRt] code, as shown in Figure 20-12.

Do the same procedure for the Answer style to obtain a blank line after each question and each answer.

Resetting a System Style

To reset a system style that you've edited, click Format ⇨ Styles, select the style, and click Options ⇨ Reset.

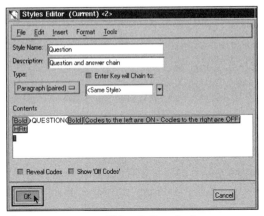

Figure 20-12: Specifying "off codes"

Specifying Where Styles Are Saved

Normally, the styles you create are saved in the current document. However, you can also save these styles in a personal or shared (on a network) library to use them in other documents as well. To specify another location, click Format ⇨ Styles ⇨ Options ⇨ Setup and click another location under Default (see Figure 20-13). The next style you create will be saved in your selected location.

Figure 20-13: Specifying where styles are saved

Saving Styles to a File

You can save styles to any file, not just one designated as your personal or shared library:

1. Click Format ⇨ Styles ⇨ Options ⇨ Save As.

2. Specify a name and location for the file.

3. Click whether you want to save user styles, system styles, or both (see Figure 20-14).

Figure 20-14: Saving styles to a file

The styles are saved in a blank WordPerfect document.

Retrieving Styles from a File

To retrieve styles from a library file into your current document:

1. Click Format ⇨ Styles ⇨ Options ⇨ Retrieve.

2. Go to the folder and select the file.

3. Click whether you want to retrieve user styles, system styles, or both.

If any of the names conflict, you get a warning message to avoid overwriting the existing styles in your document.

Tip   A styles file is simply another document. You can retrieve styles from any document created in WordPerfect 6.1 and up.

Deleting a Style

To delete a (nonsystem) style:

1. Click Format ⇨ Styles and select the style.

2. Click Options ⇨ Delete and select either of the following (see Figure 20-15):

   • *Include Codes*, to delete all occurrences of the style from the document.

   • *Leave Codes*, to delete the style but leave the style's formatting codes in your document.

Figure 20-15: Deleting a style

To remove a style from a section of text, drag the style out of Reveal Codes.

For More Information . . .

On	See
Getting PerfectExpert help	Chapter 5
Using graphics styles	Chapters 9, 23
Using formatting codes	Chapter 4
Customizing the Initial Document Style	Chapter 15
Using QuickStyle and QuickFormat	Chapter 4
Using styles in master documents	Chapter 19

✦   ✦   ✦

Doing Calculations in WordPerfect

✦ ✦ ✦ ✦

In This Chapter

Create floating cells

Customize numeric formats

Name tables, floating cells, and table parts

QuickSum columns and rows

Create formulas

Insert functions and define arguments

Use arithmetic and logical operators

Calculate all or part of a document

✦ ✦ ✦ ✦

While WordPerfect is not the obvious choice for extensive spreadsheet tasks, the program has impressive spreadsheet capabilities for general and occasional use. Calculations can be performed on table cells, rows, and columns (see Figure 21-1), or on floating cells that you can place anywhere in your document. The calculated results can be based on mathematical formulas or a variety of spreadsheet functions.

Understanding Calculations

WordPerfect can calculate the results of any expression for which you can construct a formula. When constructing formulas, you can use over 100 built-in functions, which are grouped under the following categories:

Function Category	Types of Functions
Mathematical	Average, maximum, sine, and sum
Date	Time and date values for minutes, hours, days, months, and years
Financial	Depreciation, payments, rates, and terms
Logical	If, and, or, true, false, and sign
String	Character, currency, length, and trim
Miscellaneous	Cell, block, column, row, index, and match

WordPerfect also has special shortcuts to calculate subtotals, totals, and grand totals down a column.

The "Creating Formulas" section in this chapter demonstrates how to construct formulas by using functions, operators, values, and cell addresses.

Cheese 'N Things
Delicatessen

SOLD TO:
Johnson, Harold V.
1256 W. Country Lane
Beaufort Junction, NV

DATE:
May 21, 1999

Invoice

QTY	Item Description	Code	Price	Amount
2	Quarts Milk	N	$0.76	$1.52
1	Lbs. Cheddar	N	$1.84	$1.84
3	Rolls 36mm film	T	$3.98	$11.94
5	Liters soda	D	$1.29	$6.45
1	Box crackers	N	$1.95	$1.95
12	Cans cat food	T	$0.39	$4.68

Subtotal	$28.38
Sales Tax (7.5%)	$1.25
Deposit (@ 5¢ per item)	$0.25
TOTAL DUE	$29.88

N: Non-taxable
T: Taxable
D: Deposit item

Figure 21-1: Invoice employing WordPerfect tables

Importing or Linking to a Spreadsheet

If you perform lots of number-crunching tasks, you may want to use a full-blown spreadsheet program (like Quattro Pro) that is expressly designed for the job. In this scenario, you can either import all or part of the spreadsheet as a WordPerfect table or create a dynamic link to the spreadsheet, so the changes made in the spreadsheet program will appear automatically in your document.

To import a spreadsheet into WordPerfect or create a spreadsheet link:

1. Click Insert ⇨ Spreadsheet/Database, then do either of the following:

   • Click Import to import a spreadsheet in a WordPerfect table.

   • Click Create Link to create a dynamic link to your spreadsheet.

2. Set the Data type to Spreadsheet, choose to import or link the data as a table, then specify the spreadsheet file and the range that should be imported or linked (see Figure 21-2).

Figure 21-2: Specifying the spreadsheet data to which to import or link

If you link the data, the table is updated every time you click Insert ⇨ Spreadsheet/Database ⇨ Update. You can also click Insert ⇨ Spreadsheet/Database ⇨ Options, then click Update on Retrieve to have the table update automatically every time you open the document (see Figure 21-3).

Figure 21-3: Setting your spreadsheet link to update automatically every time you open the document

Because spreadsheet programs are oriented toward performing calculations, they excel at extensive numeric tasks, rather than formatting text and graphics. However, you can create formulas in WordPerfect to perform simple or complex calculations when necessary. Whether you calculate in WordPerfect or link to a spreadsheet, WordPerfect's formatting features can add a professional polish to your results.

Creating Floating Cells

Occasionally, you may want to perform calculations right in your document's text, rather than in a separate table. You can perform this function by creating *floating cells* that resemble one-celled tables with no formatting. You can place floating cells anywhere in your document, such as in Figure 21-4. Floating cells either calculate a value by referencing data from other tables or floating cells, or hold a value referenced by another table or cell.

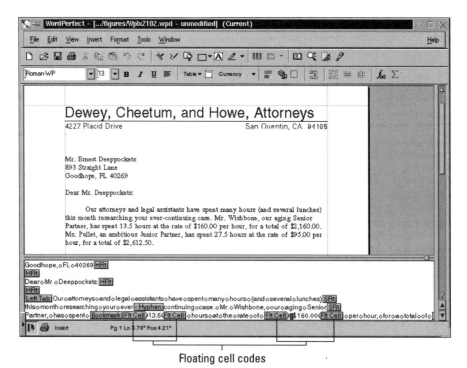

Floating cell codes

Figure 21-4: A floating-cell letter (note the paired [FltCell] codes)

To create a floating cell:

1. Click where you want the floating cell to appear.
2. Click Insert ➪ Table (or double-click the Tables button), then click Floating Cell (see Figure 21-5).

Figure 21-5: Creating a floating cell

Your floating cell is assigned a name, and the Formula toolbar appears (as in Figure 21-6) so you can customize the name and insert formulas, as described in a following section.

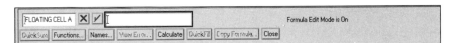

Figure 21-6: Formula toolbar

Using Numbers in Tables

Numbers have many uses in floating cells and tables. You can apply different numeric formats to represent costs, prices, part numbers, temperature readings, barometric pressure, mathematical formulas, addresses, phone numbers, dates, times, percentages, and so forth. You can customize how numbers are displayed in your tables: as decimals to the tenth place, with a currency sign, as short or long dates, or in various other ways, both preset and custom. You can also mix and match different number formats in different table columns or even in different cells. The following sections detail the many options for specifying number formats in tables.

Specifying a Numeric Format

To change the default General number display to a particular format (such as Accounting, Date/Time, Currency, or Scientific):

1. Select the area of the table you want to change, or click the cell, column, or table.

2. Do one of the following:

   • To apply one of the default numeric formats, click the Numeric list on the property bar and select a format described in Table 21-1.

   • To apply a custom numeric format, click Other at the bottom of the Numeric list in the property bar (or click Table ➪ Numeric Format) and continue with the following steps.

3. Choose whether to format cells, columns, or the entire table (see Figure 21-7).

Note   As noted in Chapter 16, "Formatting with Columns and Tables," cell formatting takes precedence over all others, followed by columns and rows, and finally formatting applied to the table as a whole. Therefore, if certain cells are already formatted, they can only be changed again by selecting the cell type.

Figure 21-7: Specifying a numeric format

Tip   You don't have the choice of Row because calculations are usually done within columns. To specify a numeric format for one or more rows, select all the cells in the rows.

4. Click the number type you want (or check "Use Column Type" to have cells adopt the number type of their column).

5. For further customizing options, see the following section, "Customizing a Numeric Format."

Table 21-1
Numeric Formats

Select	To Display
Accounting	Currency aligned with the currency symbol at the left edge of the column.
Commas	Numbers in fixed format with commas as thousands separators and negative numbers in parentheses.
Currency	Numbers with up to 15 decimal places, the currency symbol for the language you're using, thousands separators, and a decimal-align character (decimal point, comma, or other special characters).
Date/Time	Numbers in the specified date and time format.
Fixed	Numbers rounded to up to 15 decimals, and no thousands separator. If the number contains fewer decimals than specified, empty spaces to the right are filled with zeros.
General (default)	Numbers with no thousands separators or trailing digits, rounded to nearest integer (whole number with no decimals).
Integer	Numbers without decimals (rounded).
Percent	Numbers as percentages with a percent sign (%) and the specified number of decimals. For example,"0.67222" displays as "67%."
Scientific	Numbers in exponential notation with the specified number of decimals. For example, with three decimals, the number "23,560,000" displays as "2.356e+07."
Text	Numbers display as you enter them (can't be used in calculations).

Customizing a Numeric Format

After you've applied basic numeric formats and options (see the preceding "Specifying a Numeric Format" section), you may find certain data is still not in the precise format you want. In that case, you can further customize various numeric formats:

1. Select the area of the table you want to customize, then click Table ➪ Numeric Format ➪ Custom.

2. Select various options as shown in Figure 21-8 and described in Table 21-2.

Note that Date and Time formats are customized differently, as shown in the following section.

Figure 21-8: Customizing a numeric format

Table 21-2
Custom Numeric Options

Option	Enables You to
Negative Numbers	Display negative numbers with a minus sign or in parentheses; or display CR/DR to show credits and debits.
Use Currency Symbol	Display currency symbol with numbers.
Align Currency Symbol	Align currency symbol at left edge of cell.
Symbol	Select from the available currency symbols.
Digits after Decimal	Set the number of decimal digits.
Round for Calculation	Round the display of the numbers to the number of decimal places you specify.
Use Commas	Insert commas as thousands separators (does not apply to the Scientific, Date, or Text types).

Selecting a Custom Date/Time Numeric Format

To select a custom date/time numeric format, click Table ⇨ Numeric Format, select Date/Time, then click Custom and select from the list of custom formats (see Figure 21-9).

Figure 21-9: Selecting a custom date/time numeric format

Entering Dates and Times

You enter most table numbers as you would type any number. However, dates and times have a few more rules. After you choose the way you want dates and times to appear, you can enter them in several ways. For example, with the U.S. English defaults, both 12/29/98 and 12-29-1998 become December 29, 1998 when you leave the cell. Plain integer entries are assigned consecutive values starting with January 1, 1900. Thus, 36,525 becomes January 1, 2000.

Enter times using the 24-hour system, with a colon (:) between the hours and minutes. In U.S. English, hours greater than 12 are converted normally to p.m. (14:30 becomes 2:30 p.m.).

Naming Tables, Table Parts, and Floating Cells

Okay, you're saying, now I've decided how I want my numbers to appear. Can we get to the calculations already? Relax. There's one more preliminary item: naming your tables. WordPerfect assigns names to tables and floating cells in sequence (Table A, Table B, Floating Cell A, Floating Cell B, and so forth). You can also give tables and floating cells the names of your choice, for ease of reference in calculations. You can also name cells, selected blocks, rows, and columns.

You can type a cell address in a formula (such as E17) or block coordinates (such as H2:H13) to reference a particular cell or block. However, when you're creating formulas, it's easier to reference cells and blocks by using easy-to-remember names, such as Total Hours, State Tax, or Quarterly Sales. Besides making formulas easy to understand, you're less likely to make a mistake when using names, and the formula will still work if you move the named selection.

Table names can be up to 20 characters long, with any combination of letters, numbers, spaces, or symbols, and must begin with a letter or underscore (_).

Changing the Name of a Table or Floating Cell

To get some practice in naming floating cells, tables, and table parts, open a new document and create a floating cell. Then create a 2 × 9 table similar to the example in Figure 21-10, and enter text in at least two rows of cells.

City	Fare
London	$259
Paris	$295
Madrid	$545
Budapest	$580
Buenos Aires	$569
Milan	$599
New Delhi	$830
Tokyo	$885

Figure 21-10: Table to which you can assign names

Now click Table ➪ Names to see the default names for your floating cell and table (Figure 21-11).

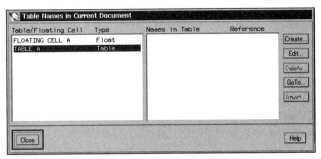

Figure 21-11: Default names for floating cell and table

Tip

When you're in a table or floating cell, its name appears at the bottom of the screen.

To change the name of the current table or floating cell:

1. Click Table ⇨ Names.

2. Click the name, then click Edit and type the new name.

Name the table "Air Fares" to use in a forthcoming exercise.

Naming Table Parts

To name a table cell, selected block, row, or column for easy formula reference:

1. Click the cell, row, or column, or select a range of cells.

2. Click Table ⇨ Names, then click Create.

3. Click Cell/Range, Column, or Row, then type the name (see Figure 21-12). The Reference line shows the address of the part.

Figure 21-12: Naming a cell, row, column, or a range of cells

Using Text in Cells for Names

You can use the text in cells to name columns, rows, the cells below, or adjacent cells:

1. Click the cell or select the cells with the text you want to use.

2. Click Table ⇨ Names ⇨ Create.

3. Click "Use Text from Current Cell to Name" (see Figure 21-13).

Figure 21-13: Using text in cells for names

4. Click Column, Row, Cell Right, or Cell Down.

Now let's practice. Using your Air Fares table, select all the cities in the left column to name all the fare cells to their right as shown in Figure 21-14. (Note that the cell names are sorted automatically in alphabetic order.)

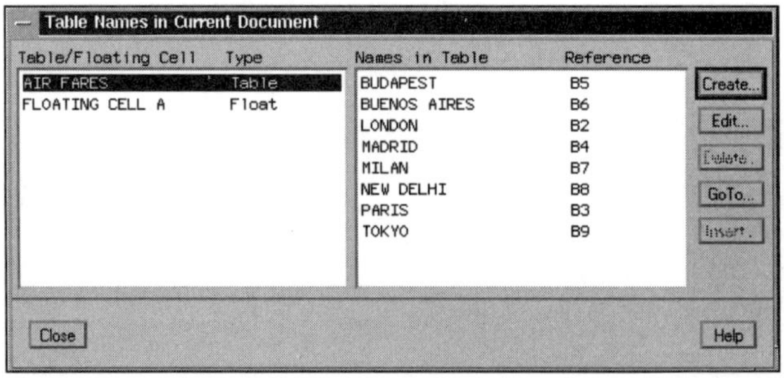

Figure 21-14: Fares in Column B named after the cities in Column A

Editing and Deleting Table Part Names

To edit the name of a table part:

1. Click the table and click Table ➪ Names.

2. Click the name of the table part, then click Edit and type a new name. (To apply the name to a different table part, click the Type list.)

To delete the name of a table part, click the table, click Table ➪ Names, click the name, then click Delete. (You can't delete the name of the entire table or a floating cell.)

Going to a Table by Name

If you're looking for a particular table in a large document, you can search for it by name. Click Edit ➪ Go To (Ctrl+G), to select the table and click OK, as shown in Figure 21-15. You can also go to a floating cell or a named table part.

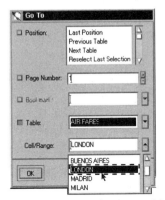

Figure 21-15: Going to a table part by name

Creating Formulas

Now that you know how to name tables and their parts, you're ready to create formulas to be used in calculations.

Understanding Table Formulas

Spreadsheet and floating cell formulas can be as simple as summing a column of numbers, or as complex as computing the Internal Rate of Return or Net Present Value.

Formulas don't have to be mathematical. They can be *logical functions* that are either 1 (true) or 0 (false), or *text functions* that manipulate text strings or return a number (such as the number of characters in a cell).

A table formula can contain any of the following:

✦ *Functions* that perform various arithmetic, calendar, financial, logical, and text operations

✦ *Operators*, of either the arithmetic (+, -, *, /) or logical (=, >, |, &) variety

✦ *Values* (constants) that you enter in the formula (such as 8.5%)

✦ *Cell addresses*, such as B2:C4

Table 21-3 shows some examples of spreadsheet formulas.

Table 21-3 **Spreadsheet Formulas**	
Formula	*What It Does*
+C12	Inserts the value found in cell C12.
=SUM(C12:C16)	Sums the values found in all the cells C12:C16.
=Rate*Balance	Multiplies the value found in the cell named Rate by the value found in the cell named Balance.
=MAX(B2:H2)	Displays the highest value found in the cells of Row 2, from Columns B to H.
=AVE(E2:E12)	Calculates the average of the cell values found in Column E, from Row 2 to Row 12.
AND *list of statements*	Returns 1 (true) if all the statements in the list are true; 0 (false) if not.
=CELL(*col,row*)	Returns the value found in the specified cell.
IF(Tax="T",0.075*Price,0)	Computes 7.5 percent tax if the entry in the cell named Tax contains "T"; returns 0 if it contains anything else.
=LEFT(D4,4)+LEFT(E4,4)	Displays the first four characters of the text in cell D4 together with the first four characters of cell E4.
=LENGTH(D11)+2	Displays the number of characters in cell D11, plus 2.

Entering Table Formulas

Although you can type formulas directly into cells, it's usually easier to use the Formula toolbar, as shown in the following exercises.

1. Click in the table or floating cell in which you want to enter a formula.

Tip

A floating cell is simply a pair of codes. If the floating cell is empty, go into Reveal Codes to place the insertion point between the codes.

2. Click the Formula button. (You can also click Table ➪ Formula Toolbar, or right-click a table and click Formula Toolbar.)

3. Do any of the following in the Formula toolbar (see Figure 21-16):

   • Click Functions to select a predefined function (see the following "Inserting Functions and Defining Arguments" section).

   • Click in the Formula Edit box and type a formula (functions, operators, values, and the cells they address).

   • Click a cell or select a range of cells to insert cell addresses.

   • Click Names, then double-click a name to insert a table or part name.

   • Click QuickSum to sum a number of columns (see the following "Using QuickSum and Simple Formulas" section).

Formula Edit box   Normal editing is suspended

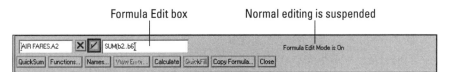

Figure 21-16: Entering a table formula in the Formula Edit box

4. Click the Table Formula Accept button to insert the formula into the current cell, or click the Table Formula Cancel button to cancel the formula changes.

When you select a function from the Formula toolbar or click the Formula Edit box, you go into Formula Edit mode where normal editing and menu functions are suspended (note the "Formula Edit Mode Is On" message in Figure 21-16). Then, when you click a cell or select a range of cells, the address of the cell or range is inserted into your formula.

Using QuickSum and Simple Formulas

To practice entering some simple formulas, create a 4 · 5 Product table as shown in Figure 21-17.

	1998	1999	Total
Product A	1000	2000	
Product B	2000	3000	
Product C	3000	4000	
Total:			

Figure 21-17: Table on which to practice

Summing a column

You don't need the Formula toolbar to add a column of numbers: You can use QuickSum. Simply click the bottom cell of Column B in your Product table, then click the QuickSum button (you can also click Table ➪ QuickSum, or press Ctrl+=).

Tip   In your Product table, the total includes the year. However, if you assign a number type of Text to the top row of the table, the year is ignored.

Calculating sums of table cells

When you QuickSum your column, you place the total "=" function in the bottom cell of Column B. When the insertion point is in the cell, notice that the cell formula, not the sum, displays at the bottom of the screen.

By using the Formula toolbar, you can sum a column, row, or any selected group of cells. Try these techniques on your Product table:

1. Click the last cell in column C (C5).

2. Click the Formula Edit box, type **SUM(C2:C4)**, then click the Table Formula Accept button.

3. Drag to select cells B2 through D2, then click the QuickSum button (Note how the row is totaled and the formula +SUM(B2:C2) appears in the Formula Edit box.)

4. Drag the indicators to select Rows 2 through 5 and click the QuickSum button. Your totals should agree with the totals in Figure 21-18.

	1998	1999	Total
Product A	1000	2000	3000
Product B	2000	3000	5000
Product C	3000	4000	7000
Total:	6000	9000	15000

Figure 21-18: Product table with totals

Tip

The preceding exercise was designed to give you a feel for entering formulas. In practice, you can select the block of cells you want to sum, together with blank cells below and to the right to hold the sums, then click Table ➪ QuickSum to get all your totals at once.

Editing and Deleting Formulas

To edit cell formulas by using the Formula toolbar:

1. Click the cell that contains the formula you want to edit or delete.

2. Click the Formula Edit box, and edit or delete the formula.

3. Click the Formula Check button on the toolbar.

To delete cell formulas:

1. Click the cell (or select the cells) with the formula(s) you want to delete.

2. Click Table ➪ Delete ➪ Cell Contents (see Figure 21-19).

Figure 21-19: Deleting table formulas

Inserting Functions and Defining Arguments

To insert a predefined formula function in a cell:

1. Click the Functions button on the Formula toolbar.

2. Select the function you want, then click Insert (see Figure 21-20). A description of the function appears beneath the list.

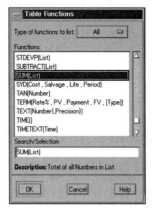

Figure 21-20: Inserting a formula function

By default, all functions are displayed. You can click the "Type of functions to list" button to display only Arithmetic, Calendar, Financial, Logical, Miscellaneous, or Text functions.

Most functions require one or more *arguments*, as indicated by the keyword in parentheses (see Table 21-4). Replace the keywords with values or references to cells. For instance, replace the "Number" in INT(*Number*) with "56.432" to return the integer "56." A more complicated function, MID(*Text, Position, Count*), looks in a text string (Text) and extracts a number of characters (Count) beginning at a certain place (Position) in the text string.

You can also *nest* functions by placing a function within another function. For example, INT(AVE(List)) returns the integer portion of the average of the listed numbers.

Some functions do not require an argument. For example, COL() returns the column number of the cell at the insertion point.

Table 21-4 Common Argument Keywords	
Keyword	*Replace With*
Cell	The address or name of a cell.
Block	The address or name of a range of cells.
Date/Time	A date or time number.
List	Any combination of cell or range references, numbers, formulas, functions, or logical statements. Separate items in the list with commas. In some cases, you can leave an item blank. The order of items is critical to some functions.
Number/Count	Numbers you specify in performing a calculation or repetitive operation.

To practice entering functions and arguments, try the following exercise to calculate the amount of money you need now to provide a specified cash flow in the future (Net Present Value):

1. Create the table as shown in Figure 21-21. In Column B, assign the percent number type to the first cell and the currency number type to the cells below Amount. Enter the annual interest rate of 6.75 percent and the amounts of cash to be paid at the end of each year.

Annual Rate	6.75%
Year	Amount
1	$5,000.00
2	$5,000.00
3	$6,000.00
4	$6,000.00
5	$7,000.00
Net Present Value	

Figure 21-21: Net present value table

2. Click the last cell in column B, then click the Formula button (Table ➪ Formula Toolbar).

3. Click Functions, list the Financial functions, and then select NPV(List, Rate%) and click Insert (see Figure 21-22).

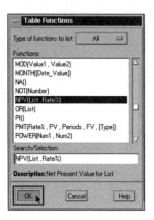

Figure 21-22: Selecting the NPV function

4. With the keyword "List" highlighted as in Figure 21-23, select cells B3 through B7 (the amounts for years 1 through 5) to replace it with the cell range.

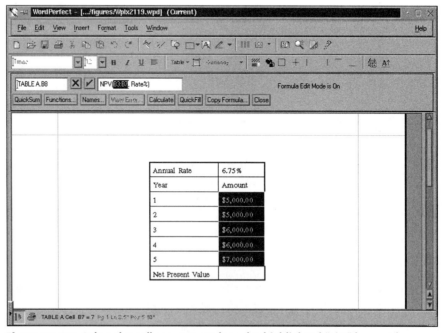

Figure 21-23: Select the cell range to replace the highlighted "List" keyword.

5. Select the argument "Rate%," then click cell B1. B1 replaces the keyword "Rate%."

6. Click the Table Formula Accept button to insert the formula into cell B8, and calculate the Net Present Value (see Figure 21-24).

Annual Rate	6.75%
Year	Amount
1	$5,000.00
2	$5,000.00
3	$6,000.00
4	$6,000.00
5	$7,000.00
Net Present Value	$23,673.81

Figure 21-24: Resulting net present value when you replace keywords "List" and "Rate" by cell addresses

Using Arithmetic and Logical Operators

An *operator* specifies a relationship between two numeric or text values, or two or more logical statements.

The Arithmetic operators Table 21-5 apply only to numbers.

Table 21-5 Arithmetic Operators	
Arithmetic Operator	**What It Does**
+ (addition)	Adds values.
- (subtraction)	Subtracts value on right from value on left.
- (negation)	Changes the sign of the value. For example, -(4) = -4;-(-4) = +4.
* (multiplication)	Multiplies values.
/ (division)	Divides value on left by value on right.
% (percent)	Divides value on the left by 100.
% (remainder)	When between two values, returns the remainder of the value on the left divided by the value on the right. For example, 33%6 displays 3 in the cell because 33 divided by 6 equals 5 with 3 remaining.
^ (exponent)	Raises the value on the left to a power specified by the value on the right. For example, $4^3 = 4*4*4 = 64$.
! (factorial)	Calculates the factorial product of the integer on the left. For example, 3! = 3*2*1= 6.

Caution   When using % to represent percent, be sure to follow the % sign with a separator, such as a space or parenthesis, or another operator. If % is enclosed between two values, it is treated as a remainder operator.

Most *logical operators* compare two or more numeric or text values (see Table 21-6). A logical operator returns 1 if the logical statement is true, and 0 if it is false.

A few of the logical operators evaluate and compare a series of logical statements and return a value of 0 or 1, depending on the outcome of the comparison. Text values are considered in ASCII order, with A being a lower value than Z.

Table 21-6 Logical Operators	
Logical Operator	*What It Means or Does*
=	Equal to.
>	Greater than.
<	Less than.
<> or !=	Not equal to.
>=	Greater than or equal to.
<=	Less than or equal to.
& or (AND)	Connects two or more logical statements. Returns 1 (true) if all statements are true, and 0 (false) if any are false.
! or (NOT)	Returns the inverse of the function or statement. For example, if the statement is true, ! returns 0 (false).
| or (OR)	Connects two or more logical statements. Returns 1 (true) if any of the statements is true, and 0 (false) if all are false.
^^ or (XOR)	Connects two or more logical statements. Returns 1 if one of the two statements is true, but not both. Returns 0 if both are true or both are false. When there are more than two statements, returns 1 if an odd number are true and 0 if an even number are true. Known as *exclusive* OR.

You can use logical operators to determine the alphabetic sequence of text strings. For example, the formula "Armstrong" > "Jones" returns 0 (false) because "Jones" appears later in the alphabet and is considered a higher value.

Understanding the Operator Order of Precedence

WordPerfect follows the traditional mathematical order of precedence in calculating the results of formulas. Table 21-7 shows a list of the order in which operators are calculated, from first to last.

Table 21-7	
Operator Order of Precedence	
Level of Precedence	*Operator(s)*
1	! (factorial), % (percent)
2	! (NOT), - (negation)
3	^ (exponential)
4	*, / , % (remainder)
5	+, - (subtraction)
6	<, <=, >, >=
7	-, <> or !=
8	& (AND)
9	^ ^ (XOR)
10	| (OR)

Operators of the same level of precedence are calculated from left to right. The two exceptions are ! (NOT) and - (negation), which are calculated from right to left.

To change the normal order of precedence, enclose the part of the formula to calculate first in parentheses. For example:

```
2 * 3 + 4 = 10
2 * (3 + 4) = 14
```

Using Logical Functions

Logical functions evaluate numeric or text entries in order to choose a course of action. The Cheese 'N Things invoice shown in Figure 21-1, for example, computes sales taxes and deposit amounts after logically evaluating each product's code.

The logical operation is performed by separate table named TAX+DEP. The table has as many rows as the invoice has line items, so it can compute the applicable taxes and deposits, as in Figure 21-25.

Tax	Deposit
0	0
0	0
0.8955	0
0	0.25
0	0
0.351	0
0	0
0	0
0	0
0	0
1.2465	0.25

Figure 21-25: Tax and deposit table used in computing the invoice

The formula in the second row of the Tax column uses a logical function that tests to see if the item is taxable:

```
If(Invoice.C2="T", .075*E2, 0)
```

In this formula, if cell C2 in the table named INVOICE contains a "T," the total cost in cell E2 is multiplied by .075, or 7.5%. If it is not "T," a 0 is put in this cell. The formula is copied down the column to the other line items.

The Deposit column contains similar formulas:

```
If(Invoice.C2="D", .05*A2, 0).
```

If the item requires a deposit, the number of items is multiplied by .05.

As the line items are entered in the invoice, the tax and deposit amounts for each item are entered automatically in the second table. The cell contents are summed in the bottom cells, then referenced by the Sales Tax and Deposit lines of the invoice. When all items are entered and the document is recalculated, the totals appear on the invoice.

Using Special Summation Functions

Three special functions, not included in the Table Function lists, are shortcuts to calculating subtotals, totals, and grand totals in a column of numbers:

✦ *Plus sign* (+) calculates a subtotal by adding the cells above it until it reaches the top of the column or another cell with a +.

✦ *Equal sign* (=) calculates a total by adding all the subtotal (+) cells above it, until it reaches the top of the column or another cell with an =.

✦ *Asterisk* (*) calculates the grand total of all the total (=) cells above it.

Try this exercise to practice using special functions to calculate subtotals, totals, and grand totals:

1. Create the table shown in Figure 21-26. Don't worry about the formatting niceties, just the amounts in Column B.

2. Click the cell to the right of Subtotal Item A, then click the Formula button to display the Formula toolbar.

Items by Store	Quantity On Hand
Store 1	512
Store 2	135
Subtotal Item A	
Store 1	575
Store 2	389
Subtotal Item B	
Total A+B	
Store 1	1023
Store 2	543
Subtotal Item C	
Store 1	376
Store 2	279
Subtotal Item D	
Total C+D	
Grand Total	

Figure 21-26: Quantity-on-hand table on which to practice

3. Click the Formula Edit box, enter + and click the Table Formula Accept button (see Figure 21-27). The first subtotal is calculated.

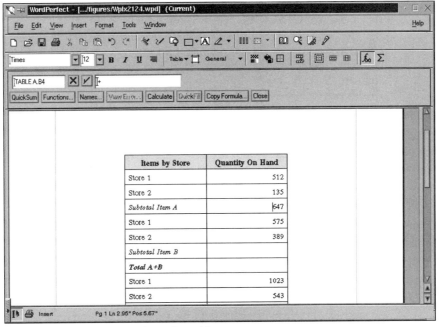

Figure 21-27: Computing the subtotal for Item A

4. Click the other subtotal cells, repeating Step 3.

5. Click the cell to the right of Total A+B, click the Formula Edit box, enter =, and click the Table Formula Accept button.

6. Repeat Step 6 for Total C+D.

7. Click the cell to the right of Grand Total, click the Formula Edit box, enter *, and click the Table Formula Accept button.

8. Click Close to remove the Formula toolbar. Your table should have the totals shown in Figure 21-28.

Items by Store	Quantity On Hand
Store 1	512
Store 2	135
Subtotal Item A	647
Store 1	575
Store 2	389
Subtotal Item B	964
Total A + B	1611
Store 1	1023
Store 2	543
Subtotal Item C	1566
Store 1	376
Store 2	279
Subtotal Item D	655
Total C + D	2221
Grand Total	3832

Figure 21-28: Table with all the totals

Referencing Cells by Column and Row Names

If you've named the columns and rows in your table, you can use their names to reference specific cells. Figure 21-29, for example, shows a table used to tally the weekly occupancy at a local resort. Rows 2 through 5 are named for weeks 1 to 4. Columns B through E are named for the months in the second row.

Instead of referencing the cell for the third week of April by using its address of C5, you can specify the column and row names, April.Week3, separated by a period (.).

Weekly Occupancy - Happy Hollow Hotel				
	March	April	May	June
1				
2				
3		April.Week3		
4				

Figure 21-29: You can reference a cell by its column and row names.

Using Relative, Absolute, and Mixed Cell Addresses

Normally, cell formulas reference *relative* addresses. When you copy a formula from one cell to another (see the following section for more information), the addresses in the formula change to maintain the same position relative to the new cell that they had to the previous cell. If, for example, you enter the formula C5+C9 into cell C10, then copy the formula to cell D10, the new formula will be D5+D9.

If you want to keep the cell references from changing when copying a formula, indicate *absolute* cell addresses with square brackets, as in [C5+C9].

Sometimes you may want either the row or column reference to be absolute, while the other reference remains relative. This strategy is called a *mixed* address. The address [C]4, for example, increments the row number when the formula is copied down a column, but the Column C reference won't change.

Copying a Formula

After you create a formula for a row or column, you can copy that formula to other cells. The invoice in Figure 21-1, for example, computes the total amount for each item purchased in Column E. The formula, If(A2>0, A2*D2, 0), was entered in cell E2, then copied down the nine cells below E2. In cell E3, the formula reads If(A3>0, A3*D3, 0), because the cell references are relative.

To copy a formula:

1. Click the cell that contains the formula you want to copy.

2. Click Copy Formula on the Formula toolbar (or click Table ⇨ Copy Formula.)

3. Click To Cell and enter the address of the cell to which you want to copy the formula, or click Down or Right and enter the number of times to copy the formula (see Figure 21-30).

All relative cell references are updated to keep their relative positions with the new cells. All absolute references remain unchanged.

Figure 21-30: Copying a table formula

QuickFilling Cells

Use QuickFill to fill cells with incrementing values across a row or down a column. The values can be numbers, Roman numerals, days of the week, months, or quarters. To use QuickFill with numbers, you must already have two values entered so that the size of the increments can be calculated. With the other types, only one cell entry is needed to set the pattern.

To QuickFill cells:

1. Select the cell or cells with the starting value(s), plus the cells you want to fill.
2. Click the QuickFill button (Table ⇨ QuickFill).

To practice using Copy Formula and QuickFill, let's create a table to compute the monthly payments for a 30-year mortgage, for two different principal amounts, at 12 different interest rates:

1. Create a table with 15 rows and 3 columns. (The precise headings and formatting are not important.)
2. Select Column A and assign it the Percent numeric format, with three digits after the decimal. Assign the Currency numeric format type to Columns B and C.
3. Enter the principal amounts shown in Figure 21-31. Enter the first two interest rates. (Don't type the percent signs or dollar signs.)
4. Click the Formula button to display the Formula toolbar.
5. Select the interest rate cells to the bottom of Column A, including the two already filled. Click QuickFill on the Table Formula bar.
6. Click Cell B4. Click Functions, select the payment (PMT) financial function, then click Insert.

Monthly Payments for a 30-year Fixed Mortgage		
	Principal	
Rate	$75,000.00	$100,000.00
6.125%		
6.250%		

Figure 21-31: Mortgage payment table to practice Copy Formula and QuickFill

7. Replace the argument keyword, "Rate%," with the formula **[A]4/12**. The A column reference is in brackets to keep it absolute when you copy the formula to Column C. (Because the payments are monthly, the annual interest rate is divided by 12 to find the monthly rate.)

8. Replace the argument keyword, "PV," with the formula **(-[B3])**, the principal amount. (The present value is negative because it is already paid out and the payments increase the value until it is 0.)

9. Replace the argument keyword "Periods" with **360** (30 years times 12 months per year).

10. Replace the argument keyword "FV" (Future Value) with **0** (because the loan will be paid off at the end of 30 years.)

11. Delete the optional keyword "[Type]," including the comma. Click the Table Formula Accept button to compute the monthly payment.

12. Click Cell B4 and click Copy Formula. Click Down, enter **11**, then click OK.

13. With the insertion point in Cell B4, click Copy Formula. Click To Cell, enter **C4**, then click OK.

14. Click Cell C4 and edit the formula in the Formula Edit box. Change the PV argument from "-[B3]" to **-[C3]**. The formula for C4 should read, PMT([A]4/12,-[C3],360,0).

15. Click the Table Formula Accept button to insert the formula into Cell C4. Click Copy Formula, click Down, specify 11, and click OK. The numbers in your table should match Figure 21-32.

Monthly Payments for a 30-year Fixed Mortgage		
	Principal	
Rate	**$75,000.00**	**$100,000.00**
6.125%	$455.71	$607.61
6.250%	$461.79	$615.72
6.375%	$467.90	$623.87
6.500%	$474.05	$632.07
6.625%	$480.23	$640.31
6.750%	$486.45	$648.60
6.875%	$492.70	$656.93
7.000%	$498.98	$665.30
7.125%	$505.29	$673.72
7.250%	$511.63	$682.18
7.375%	$518.01	$690.68
7.500%	$524.41	$699.21

Figure 21-32: Computed payment table

Viewing Formula Errors

If "??" appears in a cell when you insert a formula, the formula is invalid (WordPerfect can't calculate the result). If you see "ERR," it means that the formula references a cell with an invalid formula.

Click View Error on the Formula toolbar to see a brief description of the cause of the error.

Calculating Formulas

Table cells calculate automatically when you insert the formula. Floating cells calculate automatically when you move the insertion point out of the cell. However, if you change the contents of a cell that a formula references, the cell containing the formula is not necessarily recalculated at the same time. You can specify the frequency and extent of automatic recalculation, or turn it off completely.

Tip

If you've changed a referenced cell and formulas haven't been recalculated, the word Calculate appears to the right of the Formula Edit box. The reminder disappears when you click the Calculate button.

Calculating the Current Table or the Entire Document

To calculate the formulas in the current table only, click anywhere in the table, and click Table ➪ Calculate ➪ Calc Table (see Figure 21-33). To calculate all the table formulas in the document, click the Calc Document button instead.

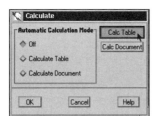

Figure 21-33: Calculating formulas

If Formula toolbar is displayed, you can click the Calculate button to recalculate all the formulas in the document.

Setting Automatic Calculation

When you change a cell that contains a formula, it is always recalculated—but other cells with formulas that contain references to that cell are not necessarily updated. To set the recalculate option, click Table ➪ Calculate, then click one of the following:

✦ *Off* to disable automatic calculation

✦ *Calculate table* to recalculate the entire table whenever the contents of a cell are changed

✦ *Calculate tables in document* to recalculate the entire document when a cell is changed

Locking and Ignoring Cells

To lock cells so their contents can't be changed, select the cells, then click Table ➪ Format ➪ Cell and check Lock.

You can also exclude cells such as text labels from calculations by checking "Ignore cell when calculating."

To practice excluding cells from calculations:

1. Open or re-create the Product table from Figure 21-15. If you formatted the Year row as "Text," reformat it to "General" for this exercise.

2. Select Cells B5 and C5, then click Table ➪ Delete ➪ Cell contents ➪ OK to replace old formulas.

3. Select all cells in columns B, C, and D, then click Table ➪ QuickSum. The calculated totals should include the years in the top row (see Figure 21-34).

	1998	1999	Total
Product A	1000	2000	3000
Product B	2000	3000	5000
Product C	3000	4000	7000
Total:	7998	10999	18997

Figure 21-34: Column totals before the years are excluded

4. Select Cells B1 and C1 (which contain the years), then click Table ➪ Format ➪ Cell, click "Ignore cell when calculating," and click OK.

5. Click Table ➪ Calculate. The totals should exclude the years (see Figure 21-35).

	1998	1999	Total
Product A	1000	2000	3000
Product B	2000	3000	5000
Product C	3000	4000	7000
Total:	6000	9000	15000

Figure 21-35: Column totals after the years are excluded

Tip   When the insertion point is in a cell that is excluded from calculations, the Application Bar displays a double quotation mark (") in front of the cell contents.

For More Information . . .

On	See
Creating tables	Chapter 16
Formatting tables	Chapter 16
Formatting order of precedence	Chapter 16

✦   ✦   ✦

Sorting Information

When searching through a mountain of information, how do you locate your desired data? Fortunately, a great deal of information is sorted. Imagine trying to locate a number in a telephone book without its alphabetic sorting!

The information in your document, spreadsheet, or database is no different. The sorting arrangement can differ according to need. You generally want your list of friends or customers to be in alphabetical order, but sometimes you may want to sort your friends by birth date, a mailing by ZIP code, or your customers by total sales in descending order.

Basic sorts are easy in WordPerfect, and this chapter also shows you how to do some sophisticated sorting and extracting. For example, you learn how to select customers in Illinois with purchases totaling more than $5,000, then sort them according to the last sales call. If you're publishing a newsletter, you can extract the names and addresses for subscriptions that are about to expire. If you're a teacher, you may want a list of students in danger of failing. These sort and extraction techniques are often used when performing a merge (see Chapter 28, "Mass-Producing with Labels and Merge").

Doing Simple Sorts

Before you get to the fancy sorts, let's do an easy regular-type sort.

Sorting Lines of Text

Open a new document and type a list of names in random order, such as in Figure 22-1.

Bill Shakespeare
James Joyce
Franz Kafka
Alice Walker
Kurt Vonnegut
Milan Kundera
Toni Morrison
Colin Dexter

Figure 22-1: List of names to sort

To sort the names:

1. Select the names.

2. Click Tools ➪ Sort, then click Sort By Line and click OK (see Figure 22-2).

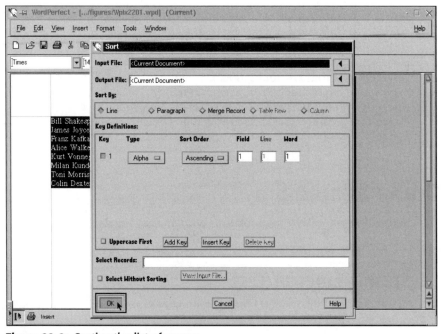

Figure 22-2: Sorting the list of names

Presto! The names are sorted, as shown in Figure 22-3.

> Alice Walker
> Bill Shakespeare
> Colin Dexter
> Franz Kafka
> James Joyce
> Kurt Vonnegut
> Milan Kundera
> Toni Morrison

Figure 22-3: Sorted names

But wait! You want the list sorted by last name, not by first name. That's a little more complicated, but still easy enough. To sort the list by last name:

1. Select the names and click Tools ➪ Sort again, but change the default options.
2. Change the number of the Word parameter in the key to 2, as shown in Figure 22-4, then click OK. This time, the names come out sorted by the second word in the first field (the last name), as shown in Figure 22-5.

Figure 22-4: Sorting on the last name

Figure 22-5: List sorted by last name

Colin Dexter
James Joyce
Franz Kafka
Milan Kundera
Toni Morrison
Bill Shakespeare
Kurt Vonnegut
Alice Walker

Tip   If some of the names contain a middle name or middle initial, you can connect
them with a hard space (Ctrl+Space) to treat them as a single word during sorting.
See the following "Connecting Words to Sort Them As One" section.

Sorting Table Rows

Sorting table rows can be even easier than sorting lines of text. Just click the
column you want to sort, click the Select Column button to select it, then click the
Table Sort button and select the way you want to sort (see Figure 22-6).

You can also select only the cells for the rows you want to sort. (Designated header
rows are excluded automatically from the sort.)

Sophisticated Sorting with Records and Keys

Basic sorts are easy and intuitive in WordPerfect. Once you get the hang of a few
more concepts and features, you will be able to sort any records thrown your way
into whatever order you need.

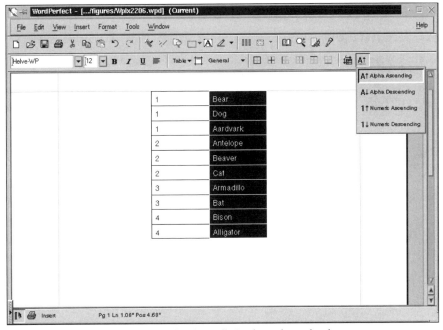

Figure 22-6: Sorting table rows by the cells in the selected column

Sort Records: The Types of Things You Can Sort

Sometimes, sorting all types of information — such as words in a sentence — doesn't help resulting searches. Instead, you want to sort *records*, or related bundles of information (such as telephone book entries) that are easier to find if they're in a particular order. If you're familiar with database managers such as Paradox or Access, you already know that a collection of records (your telephone book, for example) is called a *data file* or *database*. When you talk database language, each distinct item within a record (last name, first name, street, ZIP, and phone number) is called a *field*. Don't be put off by the terminology — there are many collections of sorted records that you use in everyday life. In addition to the telephone book, dictionaries, encyclopedias, recipe files, and checkbook ledgers are all data files. A book's index is nothing but a sorted collection of records, with fields for the heading text and page numbers.

How Sort Records and Their Subdivisions Are Identified

Because WordPerfect is text-based (not record-based, like a full-fledged database system), it uses its standard formatting codes to identify records and their subdivisions, down to individual words in a line. WordPerfect can recognize five types of sort records. Each type of record can, in turn, be subdivided in particular ways:

Record Type	How the Record Is Recognized	Record Subdivisions
Line	Each line ends with a hard return.	field, word
Paragraph	Paragraphs are separated by two or more hard returns.	line, field, word
Merge record	Each record ends with an ENDRECORD code.	field, line, word
Table row	Each row of cells is a record.	column, line, word
Column	Each row of columns is a record.	column, line, word

Line, paragraph, and parallel column records are illustrated in Figure 22-7.

Even though the names of the record subdivisions depend on how they're formatted, the sorts work the same way. When you create or edit a sort for a particular record type, its proper sequence of subdivisions displays automatically.

All you do need to know is how WordPerfect identifies the record subdivisions within your document:

Record Subdivision	How It Is Identified
Field	Tab, indent, center, or flush-right codes separate fields in lines of text. ENDFIELD codes separate fields in merge data files.
Line	Lines are separated by a hard or soft return.
Word	Words for sort purposes are separated by spaces, or the date and time separators (/, hard hyphens, and : for U.S. English). For example, "12/29/02" is three sort words.
Column	Columns in a table row are numbered from left to right, starting with Cell 1. Columns in a row of parallel columns are separated by hard page codes, and are numbered from left to right.

John B. Moseley	420 Seaview Dr.	La Jolla	CA	92037
Nancy Peterson	987 Haight St.	San Francisco	CA	94109
Florence Byrnes	5240 Main St.	Woodbury	CT	06798
Alicia E. Eberhardt	1500 Golden Ave.	Atlanta	GA	30327
William B. Wattson	468 Hereford Rd.	Palestine	TX	75801

Forty-niner   Hybrid Tea   Red
More of a bi-color, with the outside of the petals a creamy yellow and the inside a bright red that turns blue as it ages. Nicely formed buds and a compact, upright bush.

French Lace   Flonbunda   White
Very full-petaled flowers in clusters of six or more open to resemble charming old-fashioned roses. Large, buff-white blooms on spreading plants with dark green foliage. Vigorous and disease resistant.

America   Climber   Pink
Plentiful coral buds open into huge pink blossoms with a silver sheen. Fragrant and disease resistant. Used well when grown as a pillar rose.

Peru	South America	496,222 square miles. Crops include barley, beans, cacao, casava, coca, corn, cotton, grapes, oca and olluco, potatoes, quinua, rice, sugar, sweet potatoes, and wheat.
France	Europe	212,821 square miles. Crops include apples, artichokes, barley, buckwheat, corn, grapes, oats, potatoes, rye, sugar beets, and wheat.
Jamaica	Central America	4,692 square miles. Crops include bananas, cacao, casava, citrus fruit, coffee, copra, corn, ginger, pimentos, rice, sugar cane, and sweet potatos.

Figure 22-7: Line records with tabs between fields, paragraph records separated by two hard returns, and parallel column records

What Are Sort Keys?

The fields on which you sort are known as *sort keys*. When you sorted your list of names by last name, you used the second word in each line as your sort key.

You can specify as many as nine keys in a single sort. The records are first sorted by key 1, then the matching records within key 1 are further sorted by key 2, and so forth. For example, the address list entries in Figure 22-8 were sorted by state (key 1), then by last name (key 2), so that the names within each state are in order.

Last name is key 2   State is key 1

Sonya Brown	789 Farm Road	Los Gatos	CA	95030
Dr. Helen Wang	2305 Mountain Drive	Bolder	CO	80301
Mathew Chapin	362 Meadow Oak Lane	Manchester	CT	06040
Joseph Guss	1207 Spring Road	Sommerville	CT	06072
Elizabeth Somner	1795 South Street	Winsted	CT	06098
Nancy Morgan	2532 Chapman Drive	Washington	DC	20036
Brian Nelson	15 Federal Street	Middlefield	MA	01243
Judy Davis	375 Hamlet Avenue	Brooklyn	NY	11225
Miranda Sanchez	426 President Street	Westlake	OH	44145
George O'Connor	47 Grove Street	Dallas	TX	75235

Figure 22-8: Records sorted by two keys (last name, within state)

Sort keys can be alphanumeric (blanks, followed by symbols, numbers, and letters) or numeric (numbers only). The sort order can be ascending—numbers from negative to positive, or letters from A to Z—or descending (the reverse).

Defining Keys and Performing Sorts

With these sort concepts in hand, you're ready to do some sophisticated sorting. For the exercises that follow, open a new document and create an expanded list of writers, such as the list shown in Figure 22-9. The particular names, dates, countries, and types don't matter, as long as you have a variety of records, including two to three records for some particular countries and types.

You are creating line records, although paragraph, table row, and parallel column records work equally well. Separate the fields in each record with a single tab code, and end each record with a hard return, including the last. Set the tabs (see Chapter 15, "Formatting Your Document") so that the fields are aligned. Save your list when you're finished and make a backup copy, then try out variations on the general sort instructions that follow.

Caution If you begin your lines with a tab or indent, keep in mind that the name following the first tab will actually be field 2.

Amos Oz	1939-	Israeli	novelist
Naguib Mahfouz	1911-	Egyptian	novelist
Ngūgĩ Wa Thiong'o	1938-	Kenyan	novelist
Emily Dickinson	1830-1886	American	poet
Kornel Ujejski	1823-1897	Polish	poet
Heinrich Heine	1797-1856	German	poet
Miguel de Cervantes Saavedra	1547-1616	Spanish	novelist
Anton Chekhov	1860-1904	Russian	playwright
Li Bo	701-762	Chinese	poet
Henrik Ibsen	1828-1906	Norwegian	playwright
Gloria Naylor	1950-	American	novelist
Mario Vargas Llosa	1936-	Peruvian	novelist
Murasaki Shikibu	978?-1026	Japanese	novelist
Honoré de Balzac	1799-1850	French	novelist
William Shakespeare	1564-1616	British	playwright
Sylvia Plath	1932-1963	American	poet

Figure 22-9: List of writers on which to practice

To sort records in a document:

1. Select the records you want to sort, unless you're sorting the entire document. (When sorting table row or parallel column records, select the records you want to sort, or click the table or parallel columns to sort all the records.)

Note To use a document on disk for your sort input or sort output, see the following "Sorting from an Input File or to an Output File" section.

2. Click Tools ⇨ Sort.

3. Click the record type (line, paragraph, merge record, table row, or parallel column) by which you want to sort.

4. For key 1, specify the Type (alpha or numeric), Sort order (ascending or descending), and record subdivision (such as Field 3, Word 1) on which you want to sort.

5. To specify additional keys, click Add Key to add lower-level key definitions at the end of the list (see Figure 22-10), or Insert Key to insert keys before the highlighted key (the key numbers adjust automatically). When your definition has more than one key, you can also click Delete Key to remove the selected key.

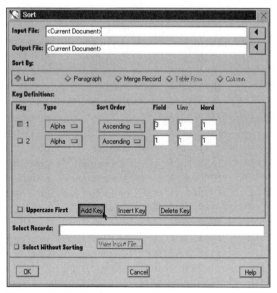

Figure 22-10: Adding a sort key

6. Click OK to run the sort.

Caution   You cannot undo a sort in WordPerfect for Linux. Therefore, make sure to save your changes before you perform a sort.

Use your list of authors to practice sorting in different orders on various record subdivisions. Try sorting by last name (field 1, word 2), date of birth, nationality, and type of writing. Be sure to try multiple keys, such as by nationality (key 1: field 3, word 1), and then by name within nation (key 2: field 1, word 1), as shown in Figure 22-10.

Tip   If some of your writers' names are more than two words (as with Honoré de Balzac), see the following "Sorting by the Last Word" section.

Using Word Sorting Tricks

You can use some tricks when sorting on particular words, including the last word in a row, two words you want to sort as one, and dates.

Sorting by the Last Word

Use negative numbers in your sort keys to designate record subdivisions in reverse order. A common application of this technique is to sort by last name, as with the list of names in Figure 22-11.

Bill Shakespeare
James Joyce
Mario Vargas Llosa
Alice Walker
Honoré de Balzac
Milan Kundera
Toni Morrison
Colin Dexter

Figure 22-11: Use −1 to sort these last names

The last name in the list can be either the second or third word from the left, but it's always the last word on the right (except for Vargas Llosa). By sorting on −1, you get the desired results (see Figure 22-12).

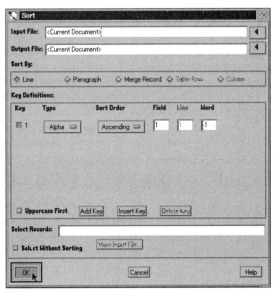

Figure 22-12: Sorting on −1.

Connecting Words to Sort Them as One

Use a hard space (Ctrl+Backspace) between words you want to sort as one. For example, if some names in your list contain middle names or middle initials, you can connect them with a hard space (Ctrl+Space) to treat them as a single word during sorting. For example, with the name Mario Vargas Llosa, put a hard space between Vargas and Llosa so that the last name will sort as "Vargas Llosa" instead of "Llosa."

Sorting Dates

The date and time separators work the same way as spaces in separating words. For example, the dates 2/14/99 or 2-14-99 sort as three words if you are using U.S. English. (The hyphens are hyphen characters, or "hard" hyphens, not the hyphen codes entered when you press the hyphen key.)

When sorting dates in these formats, specify a key for word 3 (the year), then specify keys for words 1 and 2 (the month and day).

Sorting from an Input File or to an Output File

In most cases, you sort the document on your screen. Sometimes, however, you may want to sort from the document to another file on disk. That way, for example, you can keep your address list sorted by name intact, and make a working copy sorted by state. You can also sort from a file on disk without bringing it up to the screen. To specify a sort input or output file on disk:

1. Click Tools ➪ Sort.

2. Click the list button for the "Input File" or "Output File" and specify the file.

3. Specify the sort order as described previously in this chapter, then click OK.

Caution   You must sort tables or parallel columns on the screen. Do not specify an input file or output file for a table or column sort.

Extracting Records with Sort

Sometimes you may not want to use all the records in your list. Say, for example, that you want to notify your clients in a particular state of an upcoming seminar, or you must send out notices to those in your organization whose memberships are about to expire. In such cases, you can use sort to *extract* (select) the particular records you need.

Defining Extraction Statements

Record extraction is a two-part process. You define the keys (the same type of keys you use for sorting), then construct an extraction statement to pick out the records you want. For example, the following statement tells WordPerfect to extract only the records for American poets:

```
key 1=American & key 2=poet
```

This extraction statement makes use of three operators: the greater than or equal to (>=) symbol, the ampersand (&) symbol, and the equals sign (=). Table 22-1 describes the sort-extraction operators you can use.

The space after "key" is optional ("key 1" and "key1" are the same) and values are not case-sensitive ("American" and "american" are the same).

Table 22-1 Sort-Extraction Operators	
Operator	**What It Does**
|(OR)	Selects records that meet either key condition. (You must type the | symbol, not the word OR.) Example: key 1=Johnson | key 3=CA extracts all records with Johnson in key 1, as well as all records with CA in key 3.
& (AND)	Selects records that meet both key conditions. (You must type the & symbol, not the word AND.) Example: key 1=Johnson & key 3=CA extracts records for those Johnsons living in California.
=	Selects records with keys equal to the designated value. Example: key 4=92037 selects records with a 92037 ZIP code.
<>	Selects records with keys not equal to the designated value. Example: key 4<>poet selects records for all non-poets.
>	Selects records with keys greater than the designated value. Example: key 3>Jones selects records for people whose names fall later in the alphabet than Jones, such as Kelly or Randolf, but not Johnson.
<	Selects records with keys less than the designated value. Example: key 2<5000 selects records with values less than 5,000 in key 2.
>=	Selects records with keys greater than or equal to the designated value. Example: key 5>=Kansas selects records for Kansas and states that follow it in the alphabet.
<=	Selects records with keys less than or equal to the designated value. Example: key 5<=Kansas selects records for Kansas and states that precede it in the alphabet.

Extracting Records

When you extract particular records, you normally keep your original list intact, and send your output to a separate file. To extract records:

1. Select the records from which you want to extract, unless you are extracting from the entire document. (When extracting from table row or parallel column records, click anywhere in the table or parallel columns to use all the records.)

2. Click Tools ⇨ Sort.

3. Click the list button to the right of the Output File box, then click Select File and specify the file for your extracted records. (The file is created or updated by the sort.)

Caution

Unless you specify a different output file, the records that do not meet your selection criteria are deleted from the file you're sorting.

4. Specify the key definitions, following Steps 3–5 in the previous "Defining Keys and Performing Sorts" section.

5. Using your key definitions and the selection operators shown in Table 22-1, type the record-selection statement in the Select Records box (see Figure 22-13).

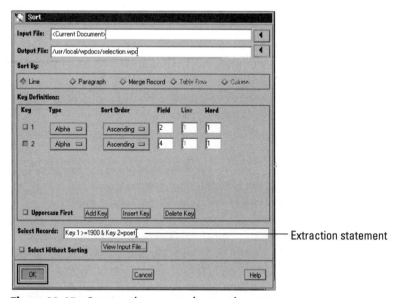

Figure 22-13: Constructing a record-extraction statement

6. To extract the selected records in their original order, check "Select Without Sorting."

7. Click OK to extract the records.

Creating Extraction Statements with Multiple Operators

You can create extraction statements with multiple operators as well as any combination of AND and OR conditions. For example, the following example extracts all French novelists, plus all German writers (novelists or not):

```
key 4=novelist & key 3=French | key 3=German
```

Notice in this example that the operators in the extraction statement read sequentially from left to right. You can modify this order with the help of parentheses. For example, the following statement extracts all novelists from France and Germany:

```
key 4=novelist & (key 3=French | key 3=German)
```

The addition of parentheses causes WordPerfect to read the OR statement in its entirety before activating the AND condition.

Using the Global Extraction Key

You can also use a *global* extraction key (key g) to extract on a word or value, regardless of its location in the record. For example, the following statement extracts all records with the word "Japanese":

```
key g=Japanese
```

Use the global key only with the "=" operator. For example, if you specify "key g>Peruvian" instead, you still get Mario Vargas Llosa's record, because the global key finds that his family name (Vargas) meets the extraction condition. If you specify "g>1800", you extract every record, because numbers come before letters in the alphabetical sort sequence.

For More Information . . .

On	See
Performing merges	Chapter 28
Setting tabs	Chapter 15

✦   ✦   ✦

Adding Graphic Lines, Borders, and Fills

In This Chapter

Set off your document with graphic lines

Edit and maneuver lines

Customize lines

Add borders to graphics boxes, paragraphs, and columns

Add and customize graphic fills

There's no better way to polish your desktop publications than with graphic lines, borders, and fills. The newsletter in Figure 23-1 illustrates how lines and borders can organize text and graphic elements in a professional and aesthetically pleasing way. Fills direct the reader's eye to key information in text boxes, columns, tables, and paragraphs.

Figure 23-1: Illustration of graphic lines, borders, and fills

Adding Graphic Lines

Graphic lines (or rules) were a part of printing prior to the invention of type. WordPerfect's graphic lines come in two directions: horizontal and vertical. (To draw curved or diagonal lines, see Chapter 9, "Working with Graphics.") The default single, black line is 0.013 inches wide and extends from margin to margin, but you can place lines of any length, thickness, color, spacing, or style at any location.

A horizontal line is placed at the text baseline by default; a vertical line is placed at the insertion point (see Figure 23-2). To insert a line:

1. Position the insertion point where you want the line to appear. (The text line can be blank.)

2. Click Insert ⇨ Shape, then click Horizontal Line or Vertical Line.

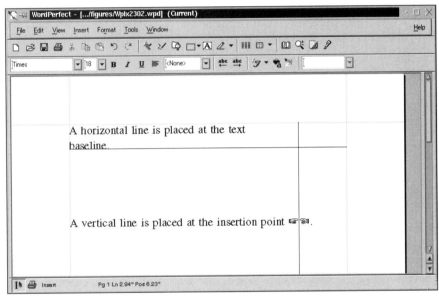

Figure 23-2: Default horizontal and vertical lines

When you place a vertical line at the left or right margin, the line shifts slightly into the margin away from the text.

Tip You can type four or more hyphens (-) or equal signs (=) at the beginning of a line, then press Enter to insert a single or double horizontal line. (For more on Format-As-You-Go options, see Chapter 4, "Becoming an Instant WordPerfect Expert.")

Moving and Editing Lines

Moving and editing graphic lines with a mouse is simple and intuitive. You can also use a dialog box for additional options and more precise control.

Customizing a Line with the Mouse

Click a line to select it. Six resizing handles appear (as shown in Figure 23-3), and you can drag them to change the line's length or width.

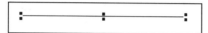

Figure 23-3: Resizing handles on a selected line

Drag the end handles to change the length. To change the width, grab one of the middle handles, as shown in Figure 23-4. When you grab an end handle, it's easy to change the length accidentally. (Thicker lines have a middle handle at the ends that you can drag to adjust the length.)

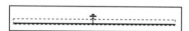

Figure 23-4: Dragging a middle handle to change the thickness of a line

Point to a line and click to drag it to another location.

Changing Lines from the Property Bar

Click a graphic line, then click buttons on the property bar to change its style, thickness, or color, as shown in Figure 23-5. You can also change a horizontal line to vertical, and vice versa.

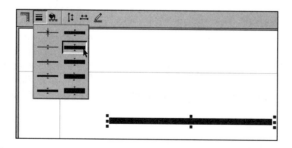

Figure 23-5: Changing the thickness of a line from the property bar

Precise Editing of a Graphic Line

For more precise (if less intuitive) line adjustments, select the line and click the Edit Line button to open the Edit Graphics Line dialog box (shown in Figure 23-6). You can also double-click or right-click a line to edit it.

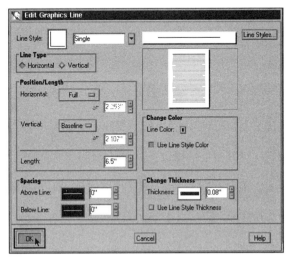

Figure 23-6: Precise editing of a graphic line

Tip   Make your rough adjustments to a graphic line with the mouse. Then, with the line still selected, click the Edit Line button (or double-click the line) to do the fine tuning.

Options for adjusting the line's length and position are discussed in this section. To edit other line attributes, see the following "Customizing a Line" section.

Editing horizontal lines

The default horizontal position for a horizontal line is Full, from margin to margin. Click the Horizontal list to change it to Left, Right, Centered, or Set. Set permits you to specify a precise offset from the left edge of the page (not the left margin). When you switch from Full to Set, WordPerfect adjusts the length of the line automatically as you change the offset.

The default vertical positioning of a horizontal line is the text baseline at the insertion point. You can also select Set from the Vertical list to designate a precise distance (offset) from the top of the page.

A horizontal line set to Full switches automatically to Left when you specify a length.

To create a centered, horizontal, three-inch-long line placed one-third of the way down the page:

1. Click Insert ➪ Shape ➪ Horizontal Line to place a horizontal line at the insertion point.

2. Double-click the line, then click the Horizontal list, click Centered, and specify a length of 3 inches.

3. Click the Vertical list, click Set, then specify an offset of 3.67 inches. The preview window should match Figure 23-7.

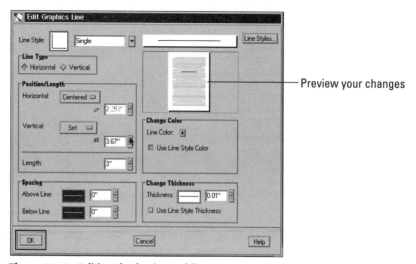

Preview your changes

Figure 23-7: Editing the horizontal line

To edit the same line with the mouse:

1. Click the line and drag it to the desired location.

2. Drag one of the handles at either end of the line to shorten or lengthen the line (see Figure 23-8).

Figure 23-8: Adjusting the line
with a mouse

3. Double-click the line and note how its parameters have changed.

Editing vertical lines

The default vertical position for a vertical line is Full, from the top to bottom margins. You can also select Top, Bottom, Centered, or Set.

Set permits you to specify a precise offset from the top of the page (not the top margin). When you switch from Full to Set, WordPerfect adjusts the length of the line automatically as you change the offset.

You have several horizontal placement options for a vertical line, including Column Aligned, to place vertical lines between columns. When you place a vertical line between columns, you also specify the column after which the line should appear.

A vertical line set to Full switches to Top automatically when you specify a length.

To insert a vertical line midway between the margins, extending from the line at the insertion point down to the bottom margin:

1. Click anywhere in a text line, about one-third of the way down the page, then click Insert ⇨ Shape ⇨ Vertical Line.

2. Point to the line and double-click; then click the Horizontal list and click Centered.

3. Click the Vertical list, click Set, then enter the line position (for example, 4"). The preview window should resemble Figure 23-9.

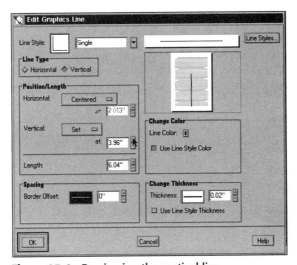

Figure 23-9: Previewing the vertical line

4. Click OK, then click and drag the line to move it around the page. Double-click the line and note how its parameters have changed.

Deleting a Line

To delete a line, click the line to select it, and then press Delete.

Cutting, Copying, and Pasting Lines

You can right-click a line to cut or copy it, then paste it just as you would ordinary text (see Chapter 2, "Writing a Letter").

Creating a Custom Line

You can create a custom line or customize an existing line to specify the style, position, length, spacing, color, and thickness you want. You can even create a custom line style to apply to your lines. The styles you create are listed along with the system styles (see Chapter 20, "Working Quickly with ExpressDoc Templates and Styles"). Whenever you want to apply the customized width, color, pattern, and so forth to another line, simply select your style by name from among the line styles.

To create a custom line or customize an existing line:

1. Click where you want to insert the line, then click Insert Line ➪ Custom Line (or double-click the line you are editing).

2. Click "Horizontal line" or "Vertical line."

3. Specify the horizontal position, vertical position, and length, as described in the preceding "Precise Editing of a Graphic Line" section.

4. Specify any of the Line options described in Table 23-1.

Table 23-1 Custom Line Options	
Option	**Enables You to**
Line color	Change the line's color, or check "Use Line Style Color" to return the line to its default color.
Line Style	Select a line style from the palette (shown in Figure 23-10) or the list. (The list has all the styles, including your custom styles.)
Line thickness	Change the line's thickness. You can also click "Use Line Style Thickness" beneath the preview to return the line to its default thickness.

Option	Enables You to
Spacing above/ below line	For a horizontal line at the default vertical baseline, specify the spacing above and below the line. For a left- or right-aligned vertical line, specify the border offset of the line from the margin (see Figure 23-11).
Line Styles	Select a line style or create a custom style using all the line and pattern options.

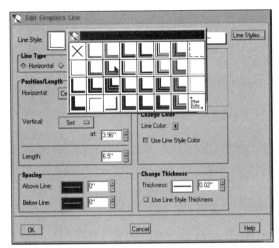

Figure 23-10: Selecting a line style

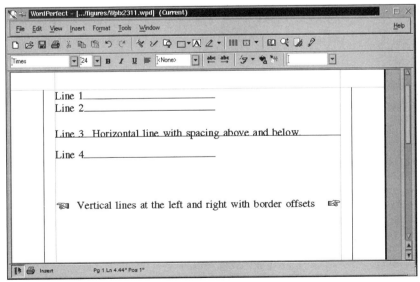

Figure 23-11: Spacing horizontal and vertical lines

Understanding Borders and Fills

Borders and fills (backgrounds) give your paragraphs, pages, columns, and graphics (including drop caps) a distinctive appearance, as shown in Figure 23-12. WordPerfect provides an array of border and fill styles that you can apply automatically to your documents; you can also customize any of the preset styles to fit your needs.

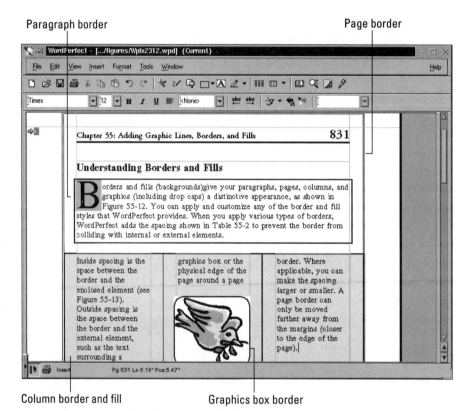

Figure 23-12: Examples of borders and fills

To apply borders, you need to understand the two types of border spacing—*inside spacing* and *outside spacing* (see Figure 23-13). Inside spacing is the space between the border and the enclosed element. Outside spacing is the space between the border and the external element, such as the text surrounding a graphics box or the physical edge of the page around a page border. Where applicable, you can make the spacing larger or smaller. A page border can only be moved farther away from the margins (closer to the edge of the page).

When you apply various types of borders, WordPerfect adds the spacing described in Table 23-2 to prevent the border from colliding with internal or external elements. For example, text in a box needs some internal space, while a graphic can go against the box border.

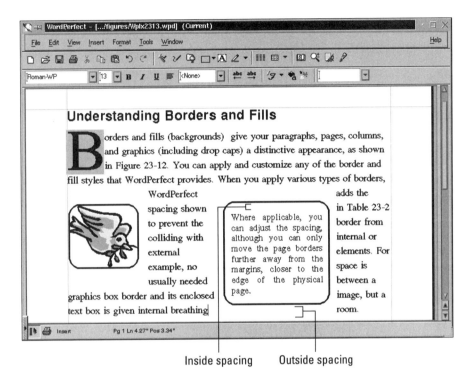

Figure 23-13: Inside and outside border spacing

Table 23-2
Default Inside and Outside Border Spacing

Border Type	Inside Spacing	Outside Spacing
Paragraph	bottom 0"; top/left/right .028"	top 0"; bottom .028"; left/right N/A
Page	N/A	¾ of margin, minus line thickness
Column	top/bottom 0"; left/right (smallest adjacent column space - line thickness) /2	top/bottom 0"; left/right N/A
Graphics box with image	0"	.167"
Graphics box with text	.083"	.167"

Adding Borders and Fills to Graphics Boxes

This section discusses the general options you have when adding borders and fills, illustrated by their application to graphics boxes. The particulars on adding graphic borders and fills to paragraphs, pages, and columns are covered in following sections.

Adding or Changing a Graphic Border

You can click the Graphic Border button to change the border style, thickness, or color of a selected graphics box (see Figure 23-14), or click the Graphic Fill button to add or change its fill. To access all the options, click More on either palette. (You can also right-click a graphic and click Border/Fill.)

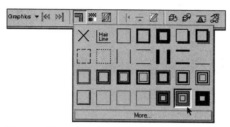

Figure 23-14: Making a selection from the graphic border palette

Graphic borders are similar to graphic lines, with additional drop shadow and rounded corner options that are customized easily (see Figure 23-15).

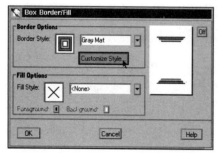

Figure 23-15: Adding a drop shadow to a graphic border with a single line and rounded corner

Applying a Graphic Fill

When applying a graphic fill, you have a variety of solid, patterned, and gradient fills from which to choose (shown in Figure 23-16).

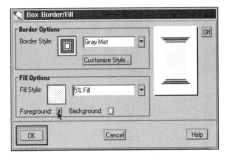

Figure 23-16: Selecting a fill type

You can then click the Foreground color palette to select a foreground color for the fill. With pattern or gradient fills, you can click the Background color palette to pick a background color as well. Click Pattern to select any of the patterns from the palette (shown in Figure 23-17).

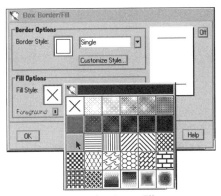

Figure 23-17: Selecting a fill pattern

Specifying Advanced Border, Fill, and Shadow Options

When applying borders and fills to graphics boxes, paragraphs, pages, and columns, you can click the Customize Style button to bring up the dialog box shown in Figure 23-18, then click the tabs to specify various additional options as described in Table 23-3. From here, you can also customize all the other border and fill properties.

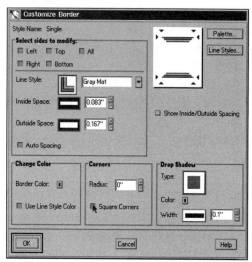

Figure 23-18: Specifying advanced border and fill options

Table 23-3
Border, Fill, and Shadow Options

Option	Enables You to
Spacing	Specify the inside and outside spacing.
Drop Shadow	Specify the color and direction (width and height) of a drop shadow.
Corner radius	Check "Square Corners" or specify a radius. Not applicable to paragraphs and columns. Rounded page borders print, but they don't display onscreen.

Using Paragraph Borders and Fills

Paragraph borders and fills are an excellent way to highlight critical information in your document. They have a powerful visual impact, so use them judiciously.

Applying a Paragraph Border or Fill

You can put a border around a single paragraph or a series of selected paragraphs. You can apply a paragraph border or fill to existing text, or specify a border or fill and continue typing. If you apply a border to a paragraph that extends beyond the bottom of the page, the border is closed at the end of the page and begins anew at the top of the next page.

To apply (or change) a paragraph border or fill:

1. Click where you want the paragraph border or fill to begin, or select a group of paragraphs.

2. Click Format ➪ Paragraph ➪ Border/Fill and select a border style (see Figure 23-19). (Click Customize Style, then check "Show Separator Line" to put a separator line between paragraphs.)

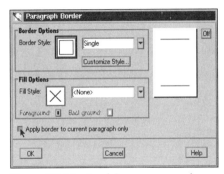

Figure 23-19: Applying a paragraph border or fill

3. Check "Apply border to current paragraph only," or leave the check box empty to let the border (and fill) surround subsequent paragraphs as well.

4. Specify any other border and fill options described in the preceding "Adding Borders and Fills to Graphics Boxes" section.

Turning Off a Paragraph Border or Fill

Click Format ➪ Paragraph ➪ Border/Fill ➪ Off to turn off a paragraph border or fill. To remove the border or fill from all the paragraphs, you can also go to the beginning of the border or fill, open Reveal Codes, then delete the [Para Border] code.

Using Page Borders and Fills

Use page borders and fills to encompass the entire page visually, including headers and footers.

Tip You won't see a page border in Draft view. The best observation point is Page view, at a zoom of Page Width or Full Page.

Applying a Page Border or Fill

To apply (or change) a page border or fill:

1. Click anywhere in the page where you want the border or fill to begin. You can also select any part of several pages to which you want the border to apply.

2. Click Format ⇨ Page ⇨ Border/Fill, and then select a border style (see Figure 23-20).

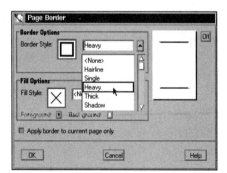

Figure 23-20: Applying a page border

3. Check "Apply border to current page only," or leave the check box empty to let the border (and fill) surround subsequent pages as well.

4. Specify any other border and fill options described in the preceding "Adding Borders and Fills to Graphics Boxes" section.

Turning Off a Page Border or Fill

Click Format ⇨ Page ⇨ Border/Fill ⇨ Off to turn off a page border or fill. To remove the border or fill from all your pages, go to the beginning of the border or fill, open Reveal Codes, then delete the [Pg Border] code.

Using Column Borders and Fills

You can use borders and fills with columns much as you do with paragraphs and pages. Two of the border styles—Column Between and Column All—are designed especially for columns. Column Between draws vertical lines between the columns. If you have three columns, for example, Column Between draws two lines. Column All draws a box around the columns, as well as lines between them.

Applying a Column Border or Fill

When you apply a column border or fill, it surrounds a group of columns, not just the column at the insertion point. You can, as with the Column All border style, include separator lines between the columns. (To apply a border or fill to particular text within a column, select the text and apply a paragraph border instead.)

To apply (or change) a column border or fill:

1. Click anywhere in a column where you want the border or fill to begin.

2. Click Format ➪ Columns ➪ Border/Fill and select a border style (see Figure 23-21).

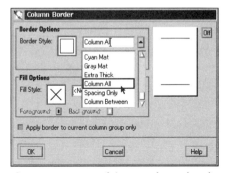

Figure 23-21: Applying a column border

3. Do either of the following:

   • Select "Apply border to current column group only" to apply the border or fill only to the columns you clicked.

   • Leave the selection off to have the border or fill surround all subsequent columns in your document as well.

4. Specify any other border and fill options described in the preceding "Adding Borders and Fills to Graphics Boxes" section.

Note   Don't worry if a column border doesn't look as expected in the document window. Sometimes the lines do not display properly, but print normally.

A fill pattern (such as shading) applies to the whole width of the columns on the page. Parallel columns have spacing between their rows, causing breaks in the borders or fills.

Tip   To place lines between parallel columns, create vertical graphic lines, and position them between the parallel columns, see the preceding "Moving and Editing Lines" section.

Turning Off a Column Border or Fill

Click Format ➪ Column ➪ Border/Fill ➪ Off to turn off a column border or fill. To remove the border or fill from all the columns, you can also go to the beginning of the border, open Reveal Codes, then delete the [Col Border] code.

For More Information . . .

On	*See*
Drawing graphic lines and objects	Chapter 9
Format-As-You-Go	Chapter 4
Cutting, copying, and pasting	Chapter 2
Creating and saving styles	Chapter 20
Working with graphics	Chapter 9
Creating drop caps	Chapter 4

✦   ✦   ✦

Creating Equations

Normally, you enter characters and numbers in lines or columns of text. However, when creating mathematical and scientific equations, you have to break the character-formatting rules. That's where the Equation Editor comes in. As this chapter reveals, WordPerfect is adept at formatting equations used in mathematical and scientific text.

Using the Equation Editor

The Equation Editor builds mathematical or scientific equations and formulas for textbooks, papers, and other documents. It doesn't solve the equations or test their validity, but it does check that your syntax is correct. You can insert the equations you create in the current document, or save them as text or graphics files to be inserted whenever you need them.

As shown in Figure 24-1, there are two equation styles:

✦ *Inline*, to place the equation graphic in your text (the default)

✦ *Standalone*, to place an equation graphic centered on the page, between lines of text

The Equation Editor works the same way for both inline and standalone equations. The difference is in the style of graphics box (placement, size, fill, and so forth) in which the equation is enclosed. You can resize, move, and rotate equation graphics after they are created.

Equations appear in the same font face, style, size, and color as your document's initial font, unless you specify a different font in the Equation Editor. By default, equations are in italics, though you can change the font face or style (see the "Changing the Equation Font" section later in this chapter).

$$x = \frac{-b \pm \sqrt{b^2 - 4ac}}{2a}$$

$$\begin{pmatrix} a_1 a_2 & \cdots & a_r \\ b_1 b_2 & \cdots & b_r \\ c_1 c_2 & \cdots & c_r \end{pmatrix}$$

"My tenure for some H_2O!," cried the scientist in the Sahara.

Did you know that $NH_4NCO \xrightarrow{\text{Heat}} H_2N-\overset{\overset{O}{\|}}{C}-NH_2$?

Figure 24-1: Standalone and inline equations

Creating an Equation

This section first examines the general steps for creating an inline equation. The second section describes the alternate steps to follow when creating a standalone equation.

Creating an Inline Equation

To create an inline equation:

1. Place the insertion point where you want the equation to appear.

2. Click Insert ➪ Graphics ➪ Custom Box, then click Inline Equation and click OK (see Figure 24-2).

3. Type characters and numbers in the editing window of the Equation Editor (see Figure 24-3).

4. Insert commands and symbols from the palette, or type commands directly and insert WordPerfect characters. (See the following "Using the Equation Palette" and "Inserting Commands and Symbols" sections.)

Select the equation palette   Editing window

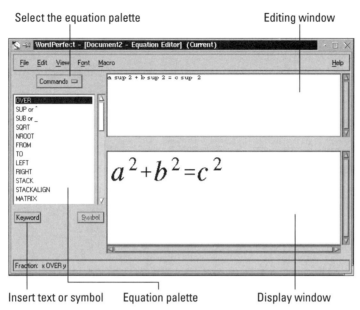

Insert text or symbol   Equation palette   Display window

Figure 24-2: Selecting the Equation box for an inline equation

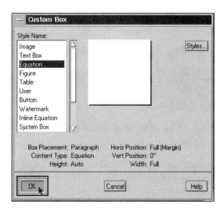

Figure 24-3: Equation Editor screen

5. Click View ➪ Redisplay to see how the equation will appear in your document. (You can also press Ctrl+F3, as long as that keystroke isn't used by your Linux desktop manager to switch to another virtual desktop, as explained in Chapter 3, "Mastering the WordPerfect Interface.")

6. Click File ➪ Close to close the Equation Editor and insert the equation into your document.

Creating a Standalone Equation

To create a standalone equation:

1. Place the insertion point between the lines of text where you want the equation to appear.

2. Click Insert ⇨ Equation, then follow the procedures in Steps 3–6 in the preceding "Creating an Inline Equation" section.

Using the Equation Palettes

You can select various formatting commands and display items from the Equation palettes at the left of the screen (they're actually scrollable lists, not palettes). Click the pop-up list above the current palette to select any of the other palettes described in Table 24-1.

	Table 24-1 **Equation Palettes**
Palette	*Lets You Select*
Commands	Keywords for commands that perform various formatting functions (such as arranging variables or drawing a line)
Large	Mathematical, scientific, bracket, and brace symbols, both large and small
Symbols	Common symbols (such as prime, infinity, approximately equal to, much greater than, and there exists)
Greek	Uppercase and lowercase Greek letters
Arrows	Various types of arrows, as well as hollow and solid figures, such as triangles, squares, and circles
Sets	Symbols, relational operators, Fraktur and hollow letters, and other characters associated with set theory
Other	Diacritical marks (accents) and various types of ellipses
Function	Mathematical functions (such as sin, cos, tan, and log)

Click the buttons underneath the palette to insert the selected command as either a keyword (SUP) or symbol ($^$). You can also double-click an item to insert it.

If you are typing equations directly, without using the palette, you can click View ⇨ Palette to remove the palette from the screen.

Using the Equation Editor Menus and Keyboard

The Equation Editor menu selections, described in Table 24-2, provide the features you need to create and edit equations.

Table 24-2	
Equation Editor Menu Selections	
Click	*In Order to*
File ⇨ Close	Close the Equation Editor and insert the equation in your document.
File ⇨ Save As	Save the equation to a file.
File ⇨ Cancel	Exit the Equation Editor without saving changes.
File ⇨ Insert File	Retrieve an equation file from disk to edit.
View ⇨ Redisplay	Update the display window with your editing changes.
View ⇨ Zoom Display	Adjust the size of the equation in the display window (not the printed size).
View ⇨ Palette	Show or hide the Equation palette.
Font ⇨ Equation Font	Change the font of the current equation, without affecting the document's text.
Font ⇨ Symbol	Insert WordPerfect characters into your equation.

The menu bar has other items you may want to use, including a Macro menu from which you can record and play macros.

The Equation Editor has its own keyboard layout you can use to insert various symbols with Ctrl+alpha keystrokes. To select the keyboard, click Edit ⇨ Settings in the Equation Editor, then click Equation Editor ⇨ Select.

Be sure to switch back to your regular WordPerfect keyboard after you're finished typing equations. You can switch to the WordPerfect program window, then click Preferences ⇨ Keyboard and select your keyboard.

Zooming the Equation Display

Click View ⇨ Zoom Display in the Equation Editor to adjust the size of the equation in the display window (see Figure 24-4). Normally, the equation display is twice its printed size (200 percent). You can specify another zoom percent, or size the equation to the maximum height or width that fits the window. ("Full equation" picks the lesser percentage of the full height and the full width—the maximum zoom at which you can still see the entire equation.)

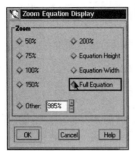

Figure 24-4: Zooming the equation display

Inserting Commands and Symbols

Equations and formulas are made up of variable names, numbers, commands, special symbols, and functions. You can place these items in an equation in three ways:

✦ Select the palette with the item you want and double-click the item (or select the item and click the Keyword or Symbol buttons).

✦ Type the item directly into the editing window.

✦ Insert a special mathematical symbol by using the WordPerfect Characters dialog box.

You can use either text or a symbol for certain items. For example, the keyword SUM and the symbol @sum display and print the same way. (Select a palette item to see its description in the status bar.)

Always place a space before and after command keywords to avoid a syntax error. If you choose Redisplay and nothing happens, you may have a syntax error. Look in the status bar for an error message. If there is an error, the insertion point in the editing window is placed where the error occurred.

Tip   While typing a long, complex equation, press Enter to continue the equation on multiple lines. This formatting doesn't affect the way your equation displays or prints.

Table 24-3 shows a list of the commands on the Equation Command palette with descriptions and examples.

Table 24-3
Equation Commands

Command	What It Does	Example	Result
{ and } (French braces)	Indicates the beginning and ending of a group.	a~+~b over c~+~d # ` # {a~+~b} over {c~+~d} Insert	$a + \dfrac{b}{c} + d$ $\dfrac{a+b}{c+d}$
~ (tilde)	Inserts a full space.	Func {The ~ area ~ of ~ a ~ \circle ~ is:} # pi ` r^2	The area of a circle is: πr^2
` (backward accent)	Inserts a small (one-quarter) space.	Func { ab ` c ` ` d ` ` ` e ` ` ` ` f ~ g }	abcd e f g
& (ampersand)	Separates columns in a matrix or marks horizontal alignment characters in STACKALIGN.	Stackalign {y` =& ` x^2 ` +4x ` + 4 # =& ` (x ` + ` 2) ^2 # ~ =& ` -2}	$y = x^2 + 4x + 4$ $= (x+2)^2$ $= -2$
# (pound sign)	Inserts a hard return in an equation, or indicates a line break in a matrix or stack.	See preceding example.	
. (period)	With LEFT or RIGHT, indicates an omitted opening or closing delimiter.	F_x ` ` = ` ` Left\{stack{` ` - ~ (x <= 0) # ~ x ~ (x>0)} RIGHT.	$F_x = \begin{cases} - & (x \le 0) \\ x & (x>0) \end{cases}$
\ (backslash)	Treats a symbol or command as text.	y ` ` = ` ` \{a ` (b ` ` c) ` + ` 6 ` \}	$y = \{a(b-c)+6\}$
ALIGNC	Aligns information at the center of the subgroup or matrix.	ALIGNC a over {a+b}	$\dfrac{a}{a+b}$

Continued

Table 24-3 (continued)

Command	What It Does	Example	Result
ALIGNL	Aligns information in the subgroup or matrix at the left margin.	ALIGNL a over {a+b}	$\dfrac{a}{a+b}$
ALIGNR	Aligns information in the subgroup or matrix at the right margin.	ALIGNR a over {a+b}	$\dfrac{a}{a+b}$
BINOM	Creates a binomial construction. Parentheses expand to fit the size of the expression.	BINOM n x	$\begin{pmatrix} n \\ x \end{pmatrix}$
BINOMSM	Same as BINOM, in a smaller font.	C~BINOMSM n x	$C\begin{pmatrix} n \\ x \end{pmatrix}$
BOLD	Puts information in bold.	BOLD {E~=~m`'c^2}	$\boldsymbol{E = m\,c^2}$
FROM and TO	Gives the beginning and end limits of a symbol, printed below and above the symbol.	Sum FROM {i=1} TO n x_i	$\displaystyle\sum_{i=1}^{n} x_i$
FUNC	Removes italics from a variable or group enclosed in curly braces.	FUNC{Water~gas ~reaction:}# ~ C`'+`' H_2O`' scalesym 200 `'CO`'+`'H_2	
HORZ	Adjusts horizontal spacing of equation or expression as percentage of font size manually. Positive numbers move information to the right, negative to the left.	Left ({n `'+`' k {vert 90 HORZ -110 n}} over 2 right)	$\left(\dfrac{n+k}{2} \right)$
ITAL	Puts information in italics.	ITAL {a `'=`' F over m}	$a = \dfrac{F}{m}$
LEFT and RIGHT	Together creates parentheses or brackets that expand to fit the information they enclose.	LEFT ({a+b} over {c+d} RIGHT) ^3	$\left(\dfrac{a+b}{c+d} \right)^3$

Command	What It Does	Example	Result
LINESPACE	Adjusts vertical line spacing in a STACK, STACKALIGN, or MATRIX structure.	Left (LINESPACE 150 MATRIX {a_1 & a_2 & a_3 # b_1 & b_2 & b_3} right)	$\begin{pmatrix} a_1 & a_2 & a_3 \\ b_1 & b_2 & b_3 \end{pmatrix}$
LONGDIV	Creates a long-division sign.	23 `` LONGDIV {`` 6729 }	$23\,\overline{)6729}$
LONGDIVS	Same as LONGDIV except uses a square sign.	23 `` LONGDIVS {`` 6729 }	$23\,\overline{)6729}$
MATFORM	Indicates alignment formats within MATRIX columns. The first format applies to the first column, the second to the second, and so forth.	MATRIX {MATFORM {AlignL & AlignC & AlignR} column_1 & column_2 & column_3 # a_1 & a_2 & a_3}	$\begin{matrix} \text{column}_1 & \text{column}_2 & \text{column}_3 \\ a_1 & a_2 & a_3 \end{matrix}$
MATRIX	Creates a matrix. The ampersand (&) separates columns. The pound sign (#) separates rows.	M ~=~ Left (MATRIX {1 & 2 & 3 # -1 & -2 & -3 # 4 & 5 & 6} Right)	$M = \begin{pmatrix} 1 & 2 & 3 \\ -1 & -2 & -3 \\ 4 & 5 & 6 \end{pmatrix}$
NROOT	Creates an *n*th root radical sign.	x ~ = ~ NROOT 5 {0.754}	$x = \sqrt[5]{0.754}$
OVER	Creates fractions.	{a+b} OVER {c+d}	$\dfrac{a+b}{c+d}$
OVERLINE	Draws a line over the expression.	OVERLINE {x+y}	$\overline{x+y}$
OVERSM	Same as OVER, using a smaller font size.	Sum from {x=1} to c {mu^x `` c^-mu} OVERSM {x!}	$\sum_{x=1}^{c} \frac{\mu^x c^{-\mu}}{x!}$
PHANTOM	Inserts invisible characters as placeholders to line up stacked expressions.	{` } _ { { phantom 2 }92 } ^238 Func U	$\begin{matrix} 238 \\ 92 \end{matrix}\text{U}$
SCALESYM	Enlarges or reduces a symbol, letter, number or text. To enlarge or reduce the entire equation, change the equation font size.	SCALESYM 200 int from 0 to 1 ` f	$\int_{0}^{1} f(x)dx$

Continued

Table 24-3 *(continued)*

Command	What It Does	Example	Result
SQRT	Creates a square root radical sign.	SQRT {` a^2 + `` b^2}	$\sqrt{a^2 + b^2}$
STACK	Stacks a set of groups or subgroups vertically.	Left. STACK {a # b # c} Right} ~ = ~ vector ~ p	$\left.\begin{array}{l}a\\b\\c\end{array}\right\} = \textit{vector } p$
STACKALIGN	Aligns a stack of equations or expressions on a specified symbol, indicated by an ampersand (&).	STACKALIGN {1234.&56 # 1.&6789 # 56.&390}	$\begin{array}{r}1234.56\\1.6789\\56.390\end{array}$
SUB or _	Creates a subscript.	3x SUB 1 ~+~ 4x _2	$3x_1 + 4x_2$
SUP or ^	Creates a superscript.	A`` =`` pi r SUP 2	$A = \pi r^2$
UNDERLINE	Underlines information.	Stackalign {$10.&26 # 2.&14} over UNDERLINE {UNDERLINE {$12.40}}	$\begin{array}{r}\$10.26\\2.14\\\underline{\$12.40}\end{array}$
VERT	Adjusts horizontal spacing of equation or expression as percentage of font size manually. Positive numbers move expressions up, negative numbers move down.	Scalesym 200 VERT 50 HORZ -110 x_1	$\boxed{x_1}$

Creating Equation Examples

You can practice using the Equation Editor on two of the examples from Table 24-3. The FROM and TO example is for the sum of all values of the variable *x* from the first value to the *n*th value. The second example uses the NROOT command to display the 5th root of the number 0.754.

To create these two equations:

1. Open a new document and click Insert ➪ Equation.

2. Click the Commands button to display the Equation palette pop-up list, and then click Large. Select the summation symbol at the top of the list and click the Keyword button. The word "SUM" appears in the editing window.

3. Click the Equation palette pop-up list again and switch back to the Commands palette, then double-click FROM.

4. Type {i=1}, press space, then double-click TO in the Commands palette. Type **n**, press space, type **x**, then double-click the command SUB and type **i**. The equation in the editing window should read:

   SUM FROM {i=1} TO n x SUB i

5. To put spacing between the two equations, enter **#** ~ **#** on the second line.

6. On the third line, enter **x = NROOT 5 {0.754}**.

7. Click View ➪ Redisplay to see how the equations will appear when printed.

8. When your equations resemble Figure 24-5, click File ➪ Close to insert them in your document.

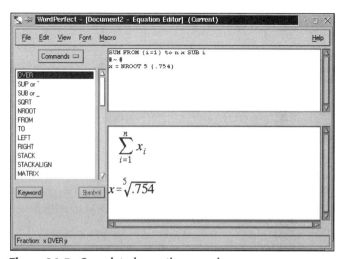

Figure 24-5: Completed equation exercise

Resizing or Moving an Equation Box

Standalone equations are centered horizontally on the page of text. They are enclosed in graphics boxes that span the width of the page. You can shrink the boxes so that you can move the equation toward a side. Resizing the box doesn't change the size of equation itself.

Click near the equation to select the equation box, then click and drag the handles to resize the box. Click anywhere on the box to drag it to a new position. See Chapter 9, "Working with Graphics," for more information on manipulating graphics boxes.

Editing an Equation

To edit an equation, double-click the equation in the document to open the Equation Editor, then change the equation in the editing window. You can also right-click the equation and click Edit Equation.

To edit an equation you saved as a file, click Insert ➪ Equation, then click File ➪ Insert File, specify the name and path of the file, and click Retrieve.

As you work, click View ➪ Redisplay to see the effects of your changes. All text-editing tools are available in the editing window. You can cut, copy, and paste in the equation-editing window just as with regular text. You can also use Undo (Ctrl+Z) to back out your changes, or use Find and Replace to replace certain commands by other commands.

Formatting an Equation

You can format equations to appear exactly the way you want. However, you format equations in a different manner than document text. Pressing space or Enter, for example, does not change your equation's appearance. Instead, use the special equation-formatting tricks as described in the following sections.

Changing the Equation Font

Click Font ➪ Equation Font (or press F4) to change the face, style, size, and color of your current equation, without affecting your document's text (see Figure 24-6). The change affects the entire equation. Click Default to reset the equation's font back to the document initial font.

To change the default font for all your inline equations, click Format ➪ Graphics Styles ➪ Inline Equation ➪ Edit ➪ Settings, and change the font as described above. To change the default font for standalone equations, do the same for the Equation box style.

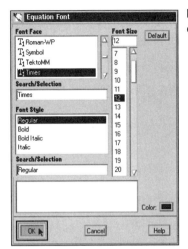

Figure 24-6: Changing the equation font

Starting with Subscript or Superscript

Superscripted and subscripted characters in the body of an equation cause no problems, except when they precede the first variable. You cannot begin an equation with a SUB (_) or SUP (^) command, so begin the equation with a small space (backward accent) in a pair of group delimiters {`}.

To Create the Equation   Type

^{238}U {`}^238 FUNC U

$_nX_m$ {`}_n FUNC X_m

Printing Commands and Symbols As Text

Certain variable names or symbols are used for Equation Editor commands or special symbols. To enter commands (such as FROM) or symbols (such as ±) as literal text, they must be preceded by a backslash (\).

If, for example, you want a curly bracket to appear in the equation and without delimiting a group, type \{. To write out the beta in the Roman alphabet, type **\beta** so that WordPerfect inserts it as plain text, not as ß.

Turning Off Italics

Alphabetic characters in an equation display in italics normally. Use the FUNC command to remove italics from a variable or a group enclosed in curly braces.

Adding Hard Returns

When you press Enter in the editing window, the text you type moves to the next line, but this action has no effect on the equation display. To add a hard return to the equation, use the pound-sign command (#). To add more than one hard return to the equation, use multiple pound signs separated with backward accents (`) or tildes (~).

For example, to put these expressions on two lines

> a+b
>
> c+d

type **a+b # c+d**.

To put double-spacing between the expressions, type **a+b # ` # c+d**.

Adjusting Horizontal Spacing

If you use the spacebar to insert spaces to make the equation in the editing window easier to read, the spaces won't affect the printed results. To add spaces to the printed equation, use the backward accent and tilde instead. The backward accent inserts a quarter-space, while the tilde inserts a whole space. You can use as many as necessary to align the characters and symbols of your equation.

You can also use the PHANTOM command to insert invisible characters as placeholders to align stacked expressions.

Changing an Equation's Position within the Graphics Box

Your equations are normally centered (left to right and top to bottom) within the equation box. To change the position of an equation box's contents, right-click the equation box and click Content. Click the Horizontal Position and Vertical Position pop-up lists to select new positions (see Figure 24-7).

Figure 24-7: Changing an equation's position within the graphics box

Adding Borders and Fills to Equation Boxes

You can add a border or fill to an equation box, just as you can to any other graphics box. Right-click the equation, click Border/Fill, then select the border and fill you want. Figure 24-8 shows a resized equation from the exercise, with a drop-shadow border and a 10 percent fill. See Chapter 23, "Adding Graphic Lines, Borders, and Fills," for more information.

Figure 24-8: Resized equation box with a drop shadow and a 10 percent fill

Adding a Caption

To add a caption to an equation box (as in Figure 24-9), right-click the equation, then click Create Caption and type your caption. The default position of the caption is inside the graphics box, centered at the right. To change the position, right-click the equation box and click Caption.

Figure 24-9: Equation box with a caption

Equation #1

See Chapter 9, "Working with Graphics," for more on adding captions to graphics boxes.

Saving and Retrieving Equations

You can save an equation as a separate file, either as text or as a WordPerfect graphic with a .WPG file extension. A WordPerfect graphic can be rotated, scaled, or moved around a document, but it cannot be edited further in the Equation Editor.

Tip   To treat the equation both as a graphics image and as a text equation, save the original equation twice — once as a WPG file and once as text.

To save an equation apart from the underlying document while you are in the Equation Editor, click File ➪ Save As. (To save only part of a long equation, select the part you want to save first.) Type a name for the file in the Filename box. The default extension for an equation is .EQN.

To save the equation as a graphics file, click File ➪ Save As, then click the Save File as Type drop-down list, and select WordPerfect Graphics 2.0 (or 1.0) format. Name your file with an extension of .WPG.

To retrieve an equation saved as a text file, place the insertion point in the document where you want the equation to appear and click Insert ➪ Equation. Then click File ➪ Insert File, select the file you want, and click Retrieve. You can then edit the equation in the usual manner and insert it in your current document.

Deleting an Equation

To delete an equation from a document, click the equation to select it, then press Delete or backspace. WordPerfect does not ask you to confirm the deletion, but you can restore it with Undo. You can also delete the Equation or Inline Eq box code in Reveal Codes.

For More Information . . .

On	*See*
Working with graphics boxes	Chapter 9
Applying borders and fills	Chapter 23
Adding captions to graphics	Chapter 9

✦   ✦   ✦

Charting Data

Charts and graphs are effective tools for making a point. Suppose you are reporting the five-year growth in earnings for your company or writing on the relationship between smoking and heart disease. A strategically placed chart can give your words clarity and impact.

Creating stunning charts and graphs is a cinch with WordPerfect's charting facilities. This chapter explains the software's charting elements.

Understanding Data Charts

The terms *chart* and *graph* are used interchangeably to mean the graphical representation of data. This chapter uses the term *chart* throughout.

The chart itself can be boiled down into the following two elements:

- ✦ The *chart data*, either entered directly or taken from an existing table or spreadsheet
- ✦ The *style of the chart* (such as bar, pie, or line), plus variations and perspectives

The term *style* sometimes refers to the entire range of formatting options, which you can save as a custom style to apply to charts. Other times, WordPerfect uses *style* in the narrow sense of the three or four variations of a particular chart type.

The following instructions use the charting terms summarized in Table 25-1, most of which are illustrated in Figure 25-1.

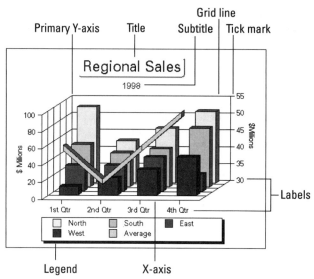

Figure 25-1: Charting terms on display

Table 25-1
Charting Terms

Term	Description
Title	The title and subtitle describing the chart. You can also assign titles to the X and Y axes.
Axes	The horizontal (X) and vertical (Y) dimensions of a chart, usually scaled with tick marks, much like a ruler. The independent variable (such as "time") is displayed along the X axis, with the various series being tracked (such as "millions US $ or percentages) scaled to the primary Y axis on the left or the secondary Y axis on the right.
Grid and Tick	The lines and marks used as visual guides.
Series	A row of the data you're charting, represented graphically by a bar, line, pie segment, or other means.
Legend	The visual key to the chart's series.
Frame	The 3-D box that lets you view the chart from various perspectives.
Labels	Values displayed on the scales and data items.
Layout	The arrangement and shape of bars, lines, and other chart elements.
Perspective	The angle from which the chart is viewed.

Creating a Chart

To create a chart starting with sample data, click Insert ➪ Graphics ➪ Chart. You can then edit the data in the chart to fit your needs.

To create a chart with data from a WordPerfect table, click the table, then click Insert ➪ Graphics ➪ Chart. A default bar chart is created from your table's contents, using the first column and row for the chart's labels and legends. You can edit the chart's appearance, but no built-in link exists between the table and the chart. Therefore, when you change data in the table, you must delete the chart and re-create it or change the data in the chart as well.

A Look at the Chart Editor

A sample chart appears in the WP Draw Chart Editor (see Figure 25-2). If you started from the sample data, the top Chart Editor window contains the chart data in a spreadsheet-like datasheet. The bottom window contains your chart. Use the Options menu to change your chart's properties.

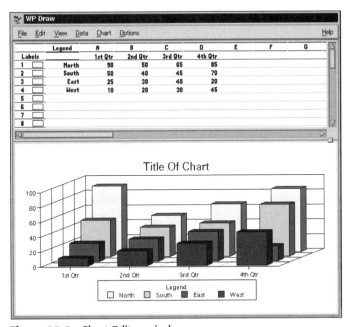

Figure 25-2: Chart Editor window

Click View ⇨ Chart Only to hide the datasheet, click View ⇨ Data Only to hide the chart, and click View ⇨ Data and Chart to display both your data and the chart. Click File ⇨ Exit and Return to Document to go back to your document — the chart will be inserted there, but you can't edit it. Double-click the chart to go back to the Chart Editor and edit your chart.

Selecting the Chart Type

Now enter the Chart Editor and click the Chart menu to select one of the chart types described in Table 25-2.

Table 25-2 Chart Types		
Chart	*What It Does*	*Use It to*
	Connects data for each series in a continuous solid area.	Show the trend for each series and, when stacked, the contribution of each series to the whole.
	Presents data as vertical or horizontal bars of varying height.	Show comparative amounts or trends, and, when stacked, the contribution of each series to the whole.
	Displays connected high and low values, and one or two values in between.	Show daily high and low values for stocks, plus the opening and close.
	Connects data for each series in a continuous line.	Show the trend for each series, normally not its contribution to the whole.
	Serves each item as a slice of a circle. Individual slices can be exploded for emphasis. You can have up to nine pie graphs in one chart.	Show the comparative amount of various items, as well as each item's contribution to the whole.

Chart	What It Does	Use It to
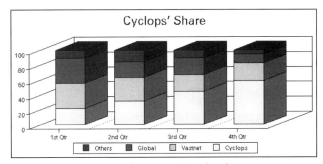 Scatter (XY)	Plots data as the interception points between two values on the X and Y axes.	Show the relationship between two variables (such as age and income).
Mixed	Employs different styles of series in one chart.	Separate different types of data into visual categories.

Tip   You need not specify a mixed chart from the start. You can start with your favorite basic type, then change the type for particular series.

Most chart types come in a number of varieties. The differences between varieties are more than cosmetic. For example, the stacked 100 percent bar chart shown in Figure 25-3 emphasizes a company's increasing market share, rather than its absolute increase or decrease in sales.

Figure 25-3: Pick the chart variation that best conveys your point

All types of charts can be displayed in either two or three dimensions.

Editing a Chart

To edit a chart, double-click the chart, or right-click the chart and click Edit Image. Now edit the datasheet, import other data, or change the appearance of your chart using the available menu options.

Entering, Editing, and Selecting Data

Enter the data for your chart (including labels and legends) in the datasheet. (When creating pie charts, each pair of columns describes an additional pie in the group.)

You edit the datasheet much as with a WordPerfect table or a spreadsheet. You can click (or double-click) cells to revise their contents, and move from cell to cell by using the arrow keys or Tab.

You can click or drag to select cells (see Figure 25-4) and employ any of the standard editing tools (such as cut, copy, paste, and delete). For example, you can select a column or row, then cut and paste to move it to another location. Use any of the selection tricks listed in Table 25-3. (Note that selections do not display on some systems.)

Caution   You cannot undo when editing a chart's data in the datasheet. Before you start, save your document with the chart to another name, so you can recover if things go wrong.

Figure 25-4: Dragging to select a group of datasheet cells

Table 25-3	
Datasheet Selection Tricks	
To Select	*Do This*
A group of cells	Drag from one corner to the other.
Columns or rows	Click or drag the column or row labels.
Entire datasheet (including empty cells)	Click the upper-left label or click Edit ⇨ Select All.

Clearing or Deleting Data

You can clear entries in the datasheet, leaving the columns and rows intact, or you can delete entire columns or rows. To clear the sample data, click the datasheet, click Edit ⇨ Select All, and then Edit ⇨ Clear ⇨ Both.

To clear a cell or selected cells:

1. Select the cell or group of cells you want to clear.

2. Press Delete or click Edit ⇨ Clear.

3. Click one of the following (see Figure 25-5):

   - Data (to clear the data but leave the format intact).

   - Format (to return to the general numeric format, leaving the data intact). (See "Changing the Data Format" later in this chapter.)

   - Both (to clear both the data and the format).

Figure 25-5: Clearing data

To delete columns or rows:

1. Click a cell in the first column or row you want to delete.

2. Click Edit ⇨ Delete.

3. Click Row(s) or Column(s), and then specify the number of rows or columns to delete (see Figure 25-6).

Figure 25-6: Deleting columns or rows

Importing Data

If you want to chart small amounts of data, you can type the data in the datasheet. However, suppose you want to chart large amounts of spreadsheet data? Instead of retyping everything, you can import this data into your datasheet.

Spreadsheet conversions don't always work when importing spreadsheet data into your chart in WordPerfect 8 for Linux. You're more likely to have success if you first export the data from your spreadsheet program as ANSI or ASCII text, then import the text by following these steps:

1. Click the datasheet.

2. Click File ⇨ Import and select the file (spreadsheet text) you want to import.

3. Select from the following options (see Figure 25-7):

    • File format of ANSI or ASCII text

    • Delimiter of tab, comma, or space

    • Clear or keep the current data

    • Transpose data to switch columns and rows

Figure 25-7: Importing data as ANSI or ASCII text

4. Click OK to import the data.

Follow the same procedure to import spreadsheet data directly, rather than the intermediate ANSI or ASCII text. With the direct import approach, you have the additional option to enter a range or a named range of data that should be imported.

Changing How the Datasheet Is Displayed

To change the width of a datasheet column, click Data ⇨ Column Width, then specify the number of digits the column should hold. (Select multiple columns to adjust them all at once.)

You can enter as much information as you want in a cell, regardless of the column width. Numbers too large to display appear in scientific notation or with a greater than sign (>), depending on the number format. For example, the number 5,500,000,000 displays as 5.5E +9. If text is too long to display, it scrolls in the cell.

Redrawing the Chart

In most cases, your chart is redrawn automatically after every change. If not, you can click View ⇨ Redraw (or press Ctrl+F3) to update your chart.

Inserting Rows or Columns in the Datasheet

To insert rows or columns in the datasheet:

1. Click where you want to insert rows or columns (existing data shifts down or to the right).
2. Click Edit ⇨ Insert.
3. Click Row(s) or Column(s), and then specify the number to insert (see Figure 25-8).

Figure 25-8: Inserting rows or columns in the datasheet

Changing the Data Format

To specify a variety of numeric and date formats for the data in your chart:

1. Select the datasheet cells you want to change.
2. Click Data ⇨ Numeric Format or Data ⇨ Date Format.
3. Select the format you want from the list (see Figure 25-9), and then select particular display options.

For an in-depth discussion of numeric and data formats (including custom formats), see Chapter 21, "Doing Calculations in WordPerfect."

Editing the Chart Title or Subtitle

The default chart has a title but no subtitle. To edit the title or create a subtitle:

1. In the Chart Editor, click Options ⇨ Titles, and then click Title or Subtitle.
2. Type the text for your title or subtitle and click Options to adjust the position, box properties, and font properties of the title (see Figure 25-10).

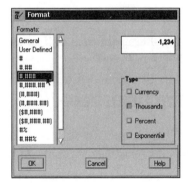

Figure 25-9: Changing the numeric data format

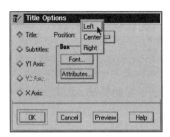

Figure 25-10: Changing the title's properties

See Chapter 23, "Adding Graphic Lines, Borders, and Fills," for more on box borders and fills.

Adding Axis Titles

You can add descriptive titles to the axes, such as "$ millions," "Temperature," "Region," or "Year," as shown in Figure 25-11.

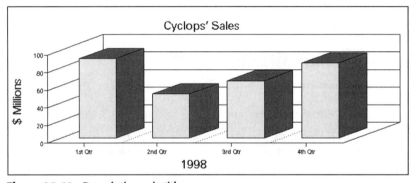

Figure 25-11: Descriptive axis titles

To add axis titles:

1. In the Chart Editor, click Options ➪ Titles and click the axis title you want to add or edit.

2. Click Options ➪ Font to change font properties (see Figure 25-12).

3. Click Options ➪ Position to select a vertical or horizontal orientation.

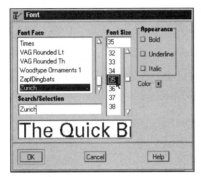

Figure 25-12: Changing the properties of an axis title

Note that to edit the secondary Y axis you must first assign a data series to it. Click Options ➪ Series, select the series you want to assign to the secondary Y axis, and then click Y2 (see Figure 25-13).

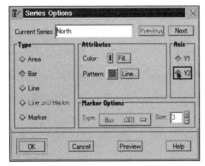

Figure 25-13: Assigning a data series to the secondary Y axis

Changing the Legend Display

The legend provides a visual key to the colors and lines used in your chart. A legend is created automatically when you create a chart; the legend items are displayed in the Legend column on the datasheet. However, you can customize how the legend looks or even delete the legend. To change the legend display:

1. Click Options ➪ Legend (see Figure 25-14).

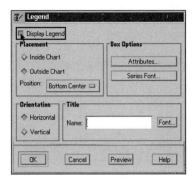

Figure 25-14: Changing the legend display

2. If you don't want a legend, deselect the Display Legend box. Otherwise, decide if you want to place the legend inside or outside your chart. Select from eight possible positions. Finally, click Horizontal or Vertical to specify the orientation of the legend in your chart.

3. Click Series Font to change the font for the legend items. (Edit the legend names in the Legend column of the datasheet.) Click Attributes to change the properties of the legend box.

4. Click the Name box to add a legend title and click Font to specify its font (the title font and the font for the legend items can be different).

Editing Descriptive Labels

Labels from your datasheet are normally displayed along the X and Y axes. You can also specify data labels for particular values displayed in the chart (see Figure 25-15). (Pie charts have unique label features explained in the following section.)

To edit a chart's descriptive labels:

1. Click Options ➪ Labels.

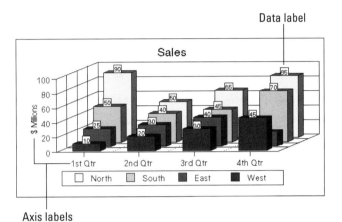

Figure 25-15: Descriptive labels

2. Click the labels you want to change, then specify the font to be used, the box properties, the position (see Figure 25-16), and other options. To turn off specific labels, click the labels you want to remove and uncheck "Display."

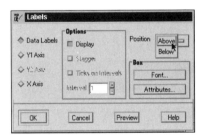

Figure 25-16: Adjusting label properties

You can also specify how frequently the descriptive labels appear. See the following "Changing the X-Axis Label and Tick Display" section.

Changing a pie chart's data labels

Pie charts are a different species when it comes to labels. Because they have no axes, they display segment labels instead (as in Figure 25-17). The following three items can be displayed in the pie chart labels:

✦ The descriptive text from the datasheet

✦ The absolute value of the segment

✦ The percent of the segment in relation to the whole

Only the descriptive text displays by default.

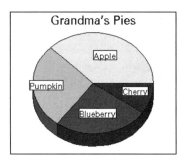

Figure 25-17: Data labels on pie chart segments

To change a pie chart's label display:

1. Click Options ⇨ Labels in the Chart Editor.

2. Click the Value, Percent, and Label pop-up lists to display these items either inside or outside the pie (see Figure 25-18).

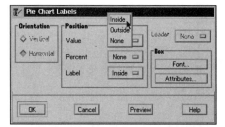

Figure 25-18: Specifying pie chart data labels

3. If two or three items are displayed together, click "Horizontal" or "Vertical" to select their orientation, as shown in Figure 25-19.

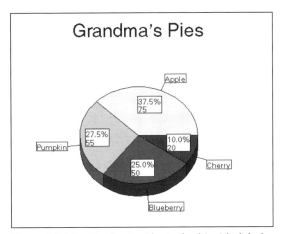

Figure 25-19: Pie chart with stacked inside labels and medium leaders

4. If items are displayed outside the pie, you can click "Leader" to connect them to the segments with short, medium, or long leaders.

Changing a Chart's Appearance

So far, you have learned how to enter data in your chart and define its titles and labels. This section explores the various ways to change the appearance of a chart. (Click View ➪ Chart Only to remove the datasheet from view when editing a chart's appearance.)

Changing the Type or Style of a Chart

To change a chart's type, click the Chart menu or click the buttons at the top part of the floating palette shown in Figure 25-20.

In addition to changing a chart's type, you can also specify style or layout options that change the shape of bars, lines, and other chart elements. Click the layout buttons on the floating palette, or click Options ➪ Layout (see Figure 25-21) to select the style and layout options described in Table 25-4. (Note that pie charts and high/low charts have unique layout features, as described in the following sections.)

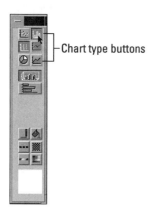

Figure 25-20: Picking a chart type from the palette

—Chart type buttons

Figure 25-21: Changing a chart's layout or style

Table 25-4
Chart Style and Layout Options

Option	Enables You to
Style	Select a style, as displayed in Figure 25-22 and described in Table 25-5. (Note that high/low charts have unique styles, described in a following section.)
3D	Display the chart in 3-D.
Horizontal	Switch from vertical to horizontal display.
Sizes	Adjust the width, depth, overlap, and other aspects of the series on display. Figure 25-23 shows some custom size options applied to a chart.

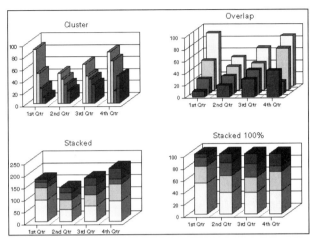

Figure 25-22: Style options for most charts (illustrated with a bar chart)

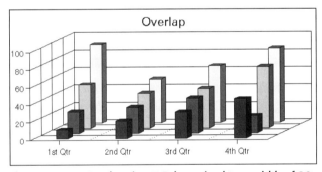

Figure 25-23: Overlapping 3-D bars sized to a width of 20 and a depth of 40

Table 25-5
Chart Layout Styles

Style	*What It Does*
Cluster	Clusters bars by column (bar charts only).
Overlap	Overlaps bars, lines, or areas.
Stacked	Stacks bars, lines, or areas vertically.
Stacked 100%	Stacks bars, lines, or areas vertically to show relative rather than absolute values.

Changing a pie chart's layout

A pie chart has unique layout features. To change a pie chart's layout:

1. In the Chart Editor, click Options ➪ Layout (see Figure 25-24).

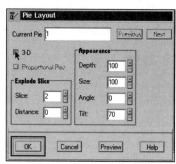

Figure 25-24: Changing a pie chart's layout

2. Up to nine pies can be added to your chart. Click Previous and Next to switch between pies.

3. Specify any of the layout options shown in Table 25-6.

Table 25-6
Pie Chart Layout Options

Option	Enables You to
3D	Switch between two- and three-dimensional display.
Proportional	Display two or more pies as different sizes, based on their absolute values.
Explode slice	Move a slice the distance you specify (see the example in Figure 25-25).
Depth	Change the 3D height from 1 to 100.
Size	Change the size of the pie from 10 to 100.
Angle	Change the counter-clockwise rotation from 0 to 359 degrees.
Tilt	Change the frontal view from 10 to 90 degrees (flat).

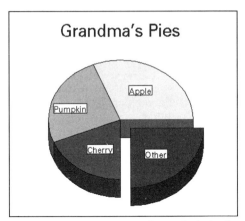

Figure 25-25: Pie chart with "exploded" slice

Changing the layout of a high/low chart

Like pie charts, high/low charts have unique layout features. To adjust a high/low chart's layout, click Options ➪ Layout, then select:

✦ *Style* to display lines, bars and error bars, error bars, or areas (see Figure 25-26).

✦ *Sizes* to change the width, height, and depth of the high/low markers.

Figure 25-26: Changing the layout of a high/low chart

Switching a Chart's Dimensions or Orientation from the Palette

For most types of charts, you can click the 3D button on the floating palette to toggle between two- or three-dimensional display, or click the Horizontal/Vertical button on the floating palette to toggle between vertical and horizontal display.

Taking a Different Perspective

You can change the perspective of a 3D chart to view it from various angles.

To understand perspective, think of a downtown block as a vertical bar chart. Then imagine that you are a passenger in a helicopter flying over and around this block. From high overhead, the buildings look like two-dimensional figures. From outside of the block, you can see both the tops of the buildings and their sides. When you land and get out of the helicopter, you see one or two vertical sides from ground level. The buildings don't change, only your perspective. In changing your chart's perspective, the chart moves while the data remain the same.

To change the perspective of a 3D chart:

1. Click Options ⇨ Perspective, then specify one of the following Angle options:

   • *Right-angle axes*, when checked, provides the conventional display of the X and Y axes at right angles (see Figure 25-27). Remove the check to allow the X axis to follow the horizontal rotation.

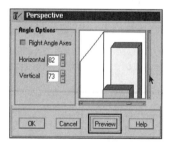

Figure 25-27: Changing a chart's perspective

   • *Horizontal* changes the angle from which you view the X axis from 0 (sideways) to 90 (straight on). Figure 25-28 shows the X axis at a perspective of 70.

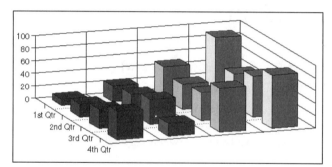

Figure 25-28: Horizontal (X) perspective at 70

Tip   Use the scroll bars next to the preview window to adjust the horizontal and vertical perspectives quickly.

- *Vertical* changes the angle from which you view the Y axis from 0 (directly above) to 90 (directly in front). Figure 25-29 shows the Y axis at a perspective of 50.

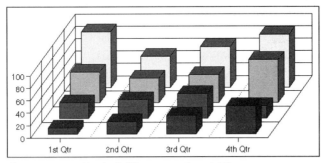

Figure 25-29: Vertical (Y) perspective at 50

2. Click Preview to test your selections on the chart.

3. Click Cancel to return to your original perspective.

To change the perspective of a pie chart, see the preceding "Changing a Pie Chart's Layout" section.

Changing the Properties of a Series

You can specify how each row of data displays as a series on the chart. You can change the type (as from bar to line), color, width, and a number of other display properties. Figure 25-30 shows a mixed chart composed of different types of series.

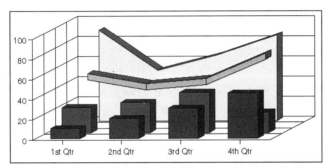

Figure 25-30: Mixed chart with different types of series

To change the properties of a series:

1. Click Options ⇨ Series. Click Previous or Next to switch among series.

2. Select from the series types (see Figure 25-31). The available series types, displayed in Figure 25-32, depend on the chart's type and number of dimensions.

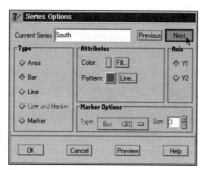

Figure 25-31: Changing the properties of a series

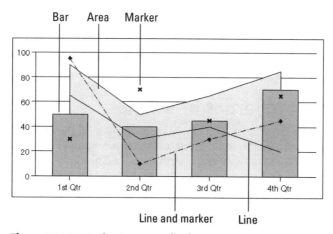

Figure 25-32: Series types on display

3. Specify the color, pattern, fill, width, or style attributes, depending on the type of series you selected.

4. For a series with markers, select from the available marker shapes, then specify a size from 1 to 10.

5. Select the Y axis to which you want the series to be scaled (see the following "Changing Y-Axis Scales and Values" section).

6. Click the arrows at the upper left to edit a different series.

Changing the X-Axis Label and Tick Display

To clean up your X-axis display (with fewer labels and other options):

✦ Click Options ➪ Labels ➪ X axis, then select from the following (see Figure 25-33):

Select	In Order To
Display labels	Display the axis labels.
Stagger	Display the labels with alternating long and short tick marks (as shown in Figure 25-34).
Ticks on Intervals	Specify the number of ticks to skip between labels.

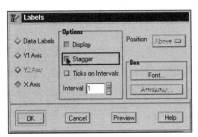

Figure 25-33: Changing the X-axis label and tick display

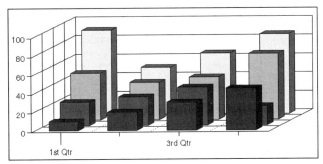

Figure 25-34: Staggered X-axis labels and an interval of two

Changing Y-Axis Scales and Values

The Y axes display *scales* of values, with ticks, by which the series are measured. For example, the primary Y axis in the chart in Figure 25-35 has a scale from $0 to $200 million. If you're displaying two different types of series on the same chart, you can use the secondary Y axis on the right to display a second scale of values (the market share in this case).

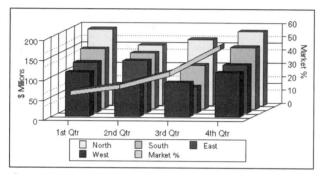

Figure 25-35: Axes scales, values, and ticks

To change Y-axis scales and values:

1. Click Options ➪ Axis in the Chart Editor.

2. Click the Y axis you want to change, as shown in Figure 25-36, and then specify any of the items described in Table 25-7.

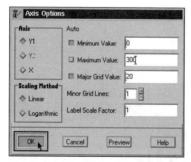

Figure 25-36: Changing Y-axis scales and values

Changing the Grid and Ticks Display

Horizontal grid lines extend the visual scale of the Y axes across the chart. Normally, you do not need vertical grid lines, though they can be specified as well.

Table 25-7
Y-Axis Scale and Value Options

Option	Enables You to
Minimum Value/ Maximum Value	Specify the starting and ending values for the scale or check Automatic to let the program calculate the values for you.
Major Grid Value	Specify the interval between major (usually numbered) grid lines.
Minor Grid Lines	Specify the number of minor grid lines that should be displayed between the major grid lines.
Label Scale Factor	Divide the scale values by a number, to make the scales easier to read. If the scale is from 0 to 50,000, for example, a scale factor of 1,000 changes the scale to 0–50. (Try putting the "Thousands" in the Y-axis title instead.)
Linear	Displays the scale in uniform increments (such as 20, 40, 60, and so forth).
Logarithmic	Displays a logarithmic scale with increments (such as 10, 100, 1,000, and so forth).

Grid and tick lines are either major or minor. Major lines usually have long ticks with labels. Minor lines usually have short ticks (if any) and no labels. Click Options ➪ Grid/Tick in the Chart Editor to change the style and color of major and minor grid lines and the position of tick marks (see Figure 25-37). Figure 25-38 shows a chart of quarterly sales, and the same chart after changing the minimum value and displaying minor grid lines.

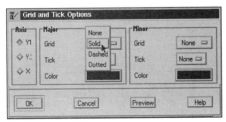

Figure 25-37: Changing the grid and ticks display

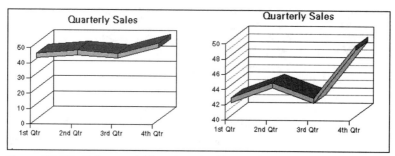

Figure 25-38: Before and after changing the minimum Y-axis value and displaying minor grid lines

When series are assigned to the secondary Y axis, you can also define its grid lines.

Changing the Chart Frame Display

The chart frame consists of the lines and fills around the various sides of the chart. These lines and fills aid the eye in gauging the values of the elements within the chart. Figure 25-39 shows the chart of quarterly sales with a frame around all sides, including the top and bottom.

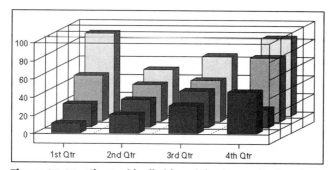

Figure 25-39: Chart with all sides of the frame displayed and a base height of 10

Click Options ➪ Frame in the Chart Editor to select the sides of the frame to display, and then specify the line color, fill, and other options. (A frame can interfere with the general picture, so you may want to hit the Preview button before you apply a frame.)

Customizing the Chart's Graphics Box

When you create a chart, it is placed in a graphics box that can be edited like any other to change its border, fill, size, position, and so forth. See Chapter 23, "Adding Graphic Lines, Borders and Fills" for information on customizing graphics boxes.

Chart Tips and Techniques

This section discusses some special techniques for creating, displaying, and manipulating your charts. You also learn how to save a customized style and apply it to other charts.

Transposing Columns and Rows

To transpose rows into columns (or columns into rows) in the datasheet:

1. Select the datasheet columns or rows you want to transpose.

2. Click Cut or Copy from the Edit menu.

3. Select the columns or rows where you want the transposed data to be placed, or click the upper-left cell at the new location. (The transposed data is placed in the selected cell, as well as in those cells below it or to the right.) Transposed data replaces any existing data.

4. Click Edit ➪ Paste Transposed.

Excluding Columns and Rows

You can exclude datasheet rows or columns that you don't want to appear in your chart.

To exclude columns or rows in the datasheet:

1. Select any cells with data in the rows or columns you want to exclude.

2. Click Data ➪ Exclude Row/Col, and then click Row(s) or Column(s).

The excluded columns or rows appear dim and don't display on the chart. To restore any or all of the excluded columns or rows, select the cells as before, and click Data ➪ Include Row/Col.

This feature is useful particularly when you want to chart only a portion of a dataset.

Creating Custom Chart Styles

To save the layout of a customized chart as a style that you can apply to new charts you create:

1. Click File ⇨ Save Style in the Chart Editor.

2. Give your custom style a name (use the default extension of .CHS) and specify its folder and path.

To apply your custom style to a new chart, click File ⇨ Retrieve Style and select the style.

For More Information . . .

On	See
Working with graphics	Chapter 9
Changing numeric and date formats	Chapter 21
Applying graphic box borders and fills	Chapter 23
Working with custom styles	Chapter 20

✦   ✦   ✦

Customizing and Automating

◆ ◆ ◆ ◆

◆ ◆ ◆ ◆

Fine-Tuning WordPerfect

CHAPTER

26

Thanks to usability tests and an enhanced graphical interface, WordPerfect is easier than ever to use, and is an efficient environment for everyday tasks. Still, your needs are unique, and you have a particular way of getting things done.

WordPerfect provides a number of ways to "arrange the furniture" in your working environment and screen display. A little time spent exploring the possibilities can make your work more pleasurable and efficient for years to come. The idea here is to experiment — to find what works best for you. Remember, however, that an incredible amount of work went into designing the WordPerfect environment, so don't feel compelled to change anything.

Understanding WordPerfect's Settings

To understand settings properly, we need to answer the three following questions:

- ✦ What's a setting?
- ✦ Where do you set them?
- ✦ Where are they stored?

What's a Setting?

A setting is any element in your working environment that stays put from session to session. A custom style or macro is not a setting, because it is only applied when called. Even a change to your Document Style is not a setting, as it affects only the current document. However, a change to the Initial

Document Style (see Chapter 15, "Formatting Your Document") is a setting because it affects all future documents. A custom toolbar or keyboard is also a setting, as it stays put until you change it again.

Where Do You Set Them?

While most user settings are found in the Preferences dialog box of the WordPerfect program window (the focus of this chapter), important exceptions include your QuickCorrect options, your guideline display, your Undo history, and your printer's Default Font. Appendix A provides a quick reference to all your user settings.

Where Are Your Settings Stored?

All settings are stored in the directory /root/.wprc. This directory contains your general settings, the printers you installed, the changes you made to WordPerfect system styles, the supplementary dictionary, your Grammatik settings, and your QuickList and QuickFinder indexes.

Your Settings Control Center

Click Preferences in the WordPerfect program window to display your settings control center (Figure 26-1). From there, you can click the particular icon for nearly all of the settings discussed in this chapter.

Figure 26-1: Your settings control center

Setting Up Your Display

Display Preferences (see Figure 26-2) has six items in the top part of the dialog box for specifying the various settings discussed in the next six sections.

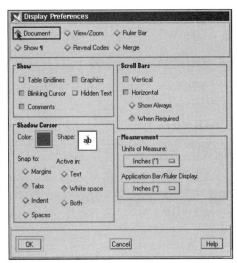

Figure 26-2: Document section of Display Preferences

Setting Your Document Display

Click Document in Display Preferences to set the document display settings described in Table 26-1.

Setting Your Symbols Display

Suppose you're cleaning up a document written by someone who used spaces rather than tabs, and used hard returns to end lines in the middle of a paragraph. To save yourself the bother of looking into Reveal Codes, click the Show (paragraph symbol) item in Display Preferences and check the particular symbols you want to see. Then click View ⇨ Show (paragraph symbol) to toggle your symbols display.

You can also select Show Symbols on New and Current Document if you always want symbols to appear.

Table 26-1
Document Display Settings

Setting	Enables You to
Show section	
Table Gridlines	Speed your display when checked by turning off shaded fills and showing non-graphic dotted lines in place of the normal table lines. (Leave unchecked and turn on Table Gridlines from the View menu when you need them.)
Blinking Cursor	Display a blinking cursor or a non-blinking cursor.
Comments	Display or hide comments.
Graphics	Hide graphics when unchecked to speed your display when editing text. (Leave checked and turn off graphics from the View menu when necessary.)
Hidden Text	Display hidden text when checked. (Leave off and use View menu when you want to see it.)
Scroll Bars section	
Vertical	Display the vertical scroll bar.
Horizontal	Display the horizontal scroll bar. You can choose to show the horizontal scroll bar all the time or display it only when required. (If you use the horizontal scroll bar rarely, you can uncheck the setting to give yourself more screen space.)
Shadow Cursor section	
Color	Click the palette to change the color of your shadow cursor.
Shape	Click the palette to pick a different shape for when you point to text.
Snap to	Pick whether you want the shadow cursor to snap to (and insert formatting codes for) margins, tabs, indents, or spaces. (Margins, which includes the ability to center text, is normally enough and avoids accidental insertion of tabs, indents, and spaces.)
Active in	Choose to have the shadow cursor appear when your pointer is in text (active in text), in white space, or both.

Setting	Enables You to
Measurement section	
Units of Measure	Select the units of measure for setting margins, line spacing, paper size, and so forth.
Application Bar/ Ruler Display	Select the unit of measure to display on the application bar and ruler.

Setting Your View and Zoom

Chapter 3, "Mastering the WordPerfect Interface," describes how the view and zoom settings affect your visual comfort and the ease with which you edit your text. Click the View/Zoom item in Display Preferences to change your default view or zoom.

Setting Your Reveal Codes Display

Tired of squinting at small, black-on-gray text in Reveal Codes? Click the Reveal Codes item in Display Preferences to specify a new font size, font color, or several other display options (see Figure 26-3) described in Table 26-2.

Tip   When codes are displayed, you can right-click the Reveal Codes window and click Preferences to change the display options.

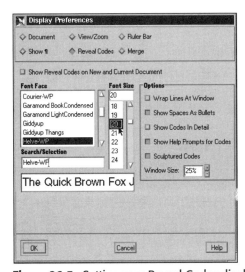

Figure 26-3: Setting your Reveal Codes display

Table 26-2
Reveal Codes Display Preferences

Setting	Enables You to
Show Reveal Codes on New and Current Document	Have your Reveal Codes window open by default (not a likely choice).
Font Face	Pick a display font. Clarity is the only objective. (In most cases, the default font works well.)
Font Size	Use a large size to make your codes stand out, as shown in Figure 26-4. (This feature is especially useful for the visually impaired.)
Wrap Lines at Window	Wrap the lines in the Reveal Codes window so that you can see all the codes without scrolling (handy when using a larger Reveal Codes font size).
Show Spaces as Bullets	Display spaces as bullets to make them easier to count.
Show Codes in Detail	See the formatting details associated with each code. (Otherwise, you must position the insertion point to the left of the code to see the details.)
Show Help Prompt for Codes	Display help information when you position the mouse pointer on a code.
Sculptured Codes	Give the codes a 3D look.
Window Size	Adjust the default size of the Reveal Codes window (normally 25 percent of the document window).

Setting Up Your Ruler

Click the Ruler Bar item in Display Preferences to select the ruler display settings described in Table 26-3. (You can also right-click the ruler, when displayed, and click Preferences.)

Setting Your Merge Codes Display

Click the Merge item in Display Preferences to display your merge codes in full (the default) or as markers to make your document more readable. You can also choose not to display your merge codes.

When working with a particular merge file you can always change the merge code display from the Merge toolbar (see Chapter 28, "Mass Producing with Labels and Merge").

Table 26-3 **Ruler Settings**	
Setting	**Enables You to**
Show Ruler Bar on New and Current Document	Display a ruler bar by default.
Tabs Snap to Ruler Grid	Have the tabs snap to the nearest invisible grid line, located every 1/16 of an inch or every millimeter. You can turn off the ruler grid to drag a tab to any location. However, it's much easier to set tabs at precise off-grid locations in the Tab Set dialog box (see Chapter 15, "Formatting Your Document") than by dragging.
Show Ruler Guides	Have a vertical dotted line display on your screen to indicate the new tab location.

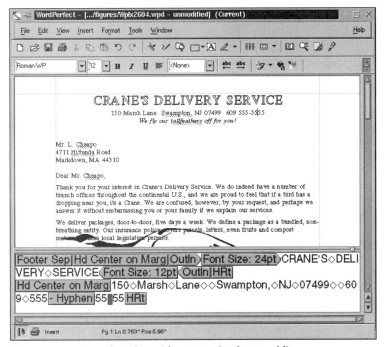

Figure 26-4: Reveal Codes with a 20-point font and line wrap

Setting Up Your Environment

The Environment Preferences dialog box (see Figure 26-5) contains various settings discussed in the next three sections.

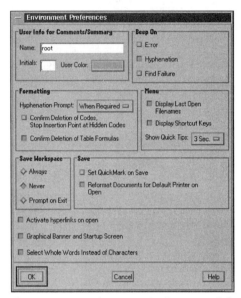

Figure 26-5: Environment Preferences dialog box

General Environment Setup

Table 26-4 describes the general settings you'll find in Environment Preferences.

Table 26-4	
General Environment Settings	
Setting	**Enables You to**
User name, initials, and color	Insert your name and initials automatically when you create a document summary or insert a comment. (Select a distinctive color for your comments or document review.)

Setting	Enables You to
Activate hyperlinks on open	Turn on hyperlinks in documents you receive or create. (Documents without hypertext are not affected.)
Select Whole Words Instead of Characters	Select word-by-word rather than character-by-character when you drag the mouse.
Save QuickMark on Save	Insert a QuickMark at the insertion point when you save a document. This setting enables you to return to the point where you stopped editing the last time you opened the document.
Reformat Documents for Default Printer on Open	Reformat documents composed on a different printer automatically when you open them. If not checked, WordPerfect looks for the document's printer among your list of available printers. If it finds the printer, the program switches to that printer to edit the document. If the document's printer is not found, however, WordPerfect still reformats the document for the current printer. (Check a reformatted document to see that the pages still look good and the paragraphs, tables, and other elements don't break at awkward places.)

Setting Up Your Interface

Table 26-5 describes the interface settings in Environment Preferences.

Table 26-5 Interface Settings	
Setting	Enables You to
Graphical Banner and Startup Screen	Display the splash screen and the image on the WordPerfect Program window.
Items to display on menus	
Display Last Open Filenames	Display or hide the names of the last nine open files in the WordPerfect Program window.
Display Shortcut Keys	Show the keyboard shortcuts on the menus.
Show Quick Tips	Display pop-up descriptions when you point to toolbar and menu items, and set the number of seconds they remain on the screen.

Continued

Table 26-5 (*continued*)	
Setting	*Enables You to*
Save Workspace (documents and window layout)	
Always	Saves the currently displayed document window. The next time you start WordPerfect, your document reopens and you return to where you left off.
Never	Never save your workspace.
Prompt on Exit	Choose whether to save your workspace when you exit WordPerfect.

Setting Prompts and Beeps

Table 26-6 describes the prompt and beep settings in Environment Preferences.

Table 26-6 Prompt and Beep Settings	
Setting	*Enables You to*
Prompts	
Hyphenation Prompt	Select the hyphenation prompt setting discussed in Chapter 14, "Controlling Text and Numbering Pages." (If in doubt, stick to When Required, the default.)
Confirm Deletion of Codes, Stop Insertion Point at Hidden Codes	Be prompted when you're about to delete a code while editing character-by-character.
Confirm Deletion of Table Formulas	Receive a warning when you're about to type over a formula in a table cell or floating cell. (You can't see the formulas, so leave this protection activated.)
Beeps	
Error	Hear a warning when an error occurs (off by default).
Hyphenation	Hear a beep when you're prompted to set the hyphenation point (on by default).
Find Failure	Hear a beep when what you're looking for in your document can't be found (off by default).

Setting Up Your Files

Files Preferences (see Figure 26-6) tells WordPerfect where your documents, macros, graphics, and other files are stored. Default directories are specified when you install WordPerfect, but you can change defaults or specify additional directories for various items (such as a separate directory for the macros you write).

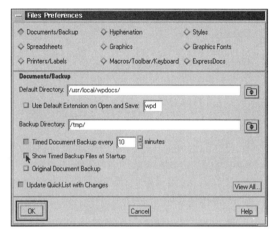

Figure 26-6: Files Preferences, showing the Documents/Backup settings

Updating Your QuickList

All the Files Preferences items have an "Update QuickList with Changes" selection to update your QuickList automatically when you change any of the default directories. You may want to uncheck this item to assume direct control over what appears in your QuickList and keep it from becoming cluttered with items you seldom use. (A change to this setting for one item is reflected for all the others.) For tips on setting up a QuickList, see Chapter 7, "Managing Your Files."

Selecting Document File Settings

Click the Documents/Backup Item in Files Preferences to select the general document and backup file settings described in Table 26-7.

Table 26-7
General Document File Settings

Setting	Enables You to
Default Directory	Specify the initial open or save directory for a WordPerfect session. After the selection, you always return to the last directory accessed. (Specify your most common directory.)
Use Default Extension on Open and Save	Specify the extension that's added automatically to the filename when you open or save a document. Normally, leave the check and the extension as "wpd" so programs recognize your files as WordPerfect documents.
Backup Directory	Specify where your timed document backups are stored.
every *x* minutes	Have WordPerfect make timed backups of your screen documents at the interval you specify.
Show Timed Backup Files at Startup	Display all the timed-backup files WordPerfect finds after starting the program.
Original Document Backup	Have WordPerfect create a backup copy each time you save a document, with the same filename and a .BAK extension. (This setting sounds great, because you'll always have two versions of a document. However, it also means that your hard drive will fill up in half the time, and you will have to sort through all those .BAK files. See Chapter 6, "Working without Worries," for more on backup techniques.)

Specifying Your Hyphenation File Locations

Click the Hyphenation item in Files Preferences to specify the default directory to store hyphenation files.

Specifying Your Style Libraries

Click the Styles item in Files Preferences to specify your default and additional style libraries (see Figure 26-7). You can only specify a shared library when you're on a network.

You have to start WordPerfect with the -adm startup option (see the following "Starting WordPerfect with Custom Options" section) to specify a shared style library.

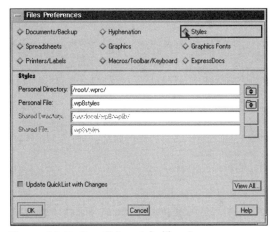

Figure 26-7: Specifying style libraries

Specifying Spreadsheet File Locations

Click the Spreadsheets item in Files Preferences to specify your default and supplemental directory for spreadsheet files — the files you want to share or import, not the programs themselves.

Specifying Your Graphics and Font File Locations

Click the Graphics Fonts item in Files Preferences to specify the location of your graphics and font files. The installation sets up a default graphics folder containing a small clip art selection, plus you can designate a supplemental folder.

You have to start WordPerfect with the -adm startup option (see the following "Starting WordPerfect with Custom Options" section) to change the default directory for Type 1 fonts.

Specifying Printer and Label File Locations

Click the Printers/Labels item in Files Preferences to specify the location of your printer drivers, your default label file, and the label types to show (see Figure 26-8). (See Chapter 10, "Printing Documents Booklets, and Envelopes," and Chapter 28, "Mass-Producing with Labels and Merge" for more about printing and labels).

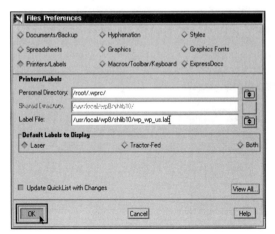

Figure 26-8: Specifying printer and label file locations

Specifying the Macro/Toolbar/Keyboard File Location

Click the Macros/Toolbar/Keyboard item in Files Preferences (see Figure 26-9) to specify the directory for storing macros, toolbars and keyboard definitions. The supplemental directory holds the WordPerfect macros described in Chapter 29, "Automating with Macros." You should store your own macros in a separate directory.

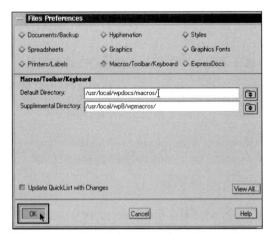

Figure 26-9: Specifying macro, toolbar, and keyboard locations

Specifying Your ExpressDocs File Location

Click the ExpressDocs item in Files Preferences to specify the location of ExpressDoc templates. The default directory holds the ExpressDocs that come with WordPerfect, so you should only change this setting if you want to use your own ExpressDocs.

Viewing All Your File Locations at Once

Click the View All button in any of the Files Preferences dialog boxes for a comprehensive look at all your file settings, as in Figure 26-10.

Figure 26-10: Viewing all your file locations at once

Setting Up Your Document Summaries

Document Summary Preferences shown in Figure 26-11 let you automate various tasks, as described in Table 26-8.

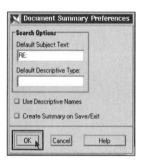

Figure 26-11: Setting up your document summaries

Table 26-8
Document Summary Settings

Setting	Enables You to
Default Subject Text	Tell the program what text to search for when filling the subject field automatically. For example, you can have WordPerfect search for "RE:" or "Subject:" in your memos, then extract the text immediately following to fill in the Subject field of the document summaries.
Default Descriptive Type	Specify text for the Descriptive Type field, such as "Report" or "Memo," to be filled in automatically when you create a document summary. (Leave it blank if you have a diversity of types.)
Use Descriptive Names	Display descriptive filenames in file management dialog boxes (such as Open and Save) and on the WordPerfect title bar.
Create Summary on Save/Exit	Be prompted to create a document summary when you save a document that doesn't yet have one.

Customizing Your Application Bar

The WordPerfect developers gave careful thought into putting the most useful features on the application bar. From left to right, you have the Shadow Cursor switch and printer details. Next, you have the General Status that displays Insert or Typewrite when you're editing text, and special information on tables, columns, macros, merges, and styles at other times. Your combined position display is the rightmost item.

Still, you can customize your application bar if necessary. For example, you may want to add the date and time to the application bar. You can then click these buttons to insert the date or time in your document. To customize your application bar:

1. Click Application Bar in the Preferences dialog box or right-click the application bar and choose Settings.

2. Check or uncheck the features you want from the list of available items (see Figure 26-12).

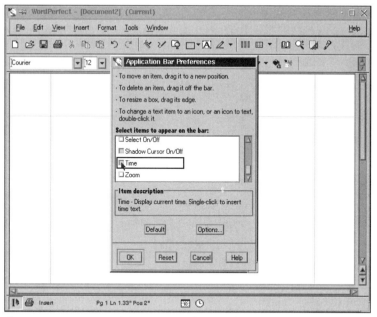

Figure 26-12: Customizing your application bar

3. Follow the dialog box instructions to move, delete, or resize an item, or switch it between text and icon display.

4. Click Options to change the font face and size.

5. Click OK to keep your new settings, or click Reset to restore the application bar to its default settings.

Customizing Keyboards

You can select different keyboards (such as WordPerfect for DOS or WordPerfect for Windows) and customize keyboards to activate a feature, run a macro, play keystrokes, or launch a program. See Chapter 27, "Customizing Toolbars, Menus, and Keyboards," for details.

Changing the Redline Method and Relative Font Sizes

Click Fonts in the Preferences dialog box to change the redline method and relative font sizes (see Figure 26-13).

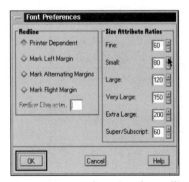

Figure 26-13: Changing the redline method and relative font sizes

Changing the Redline Method

Select the redlining method used for marking text when comparing documents:

✦ *Printer Dependent* to use your printer's redline method (usually a shaded background).

✦ *Mark Left (or Right) Margin* to put the redline character in the left/right margin of lines with new text.

✦ *Mark Alternating Margins* to put the redline indicator in the left margin of even pages and the right margin of odd pages.

If you are not using the Printer Dependent setting, you can click the Redline Character box and press Ctrl+W to specify a different redline character (normally a vertical bar).

For information on comparing documents, see Chapter 13, "Editing Techniques."

Setting Relative Font-Size Percentages

The relative size attribute ratios are especially handy for titles, headings, footnotes, indented quotes, and so forth, where you want those parts of your text to maintain a consistent appearance relative to the base font used for regular text. The percentages apply in certain styles, such as footnotes and headings, and when you select a relative font size from the Font dialog box (see Chapter 8, "Fonts Fantastic").

Specify any size attribute ratios that you want to change. To restore the original settings, refer to Figure 26-13.

Specifying Conversion Settings

Click Convert in the Preferences dialog box to change the conversion settings, as shown in Figure 26-14 and described in Table 26-9. Normally, you won't have to change these settings, which specify how graphics, ASCII-delimited text records, and documents from other word processors are imported into WordPerfect. However, you may want to adjust these settings when importing database records during a WordPerfect merge, because all programs do not export records with the same delimiters.

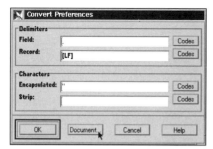

Figure 26-14: Specifying conversion settings

Table 26-9 Conversion Settings	
Setting	*Enables You to*
Delimiters	
Field	Specify the character or code used to separate fields when importing a spreadsheet or database as ASCII-delimited text.
Record	Specify the character or code used to separate records.
Characters	
Encapsulated	Specify the character (such as a double quotation mark) used to enclose each field or mark the place for a field that is not being used.
Strip	Tell WordPerfect the characters you want to remove from the file you're converting.

Click Document to specify document conversion preferences for underlining, margins, paper size alignment character, and language (see Figure 26-15). These settings are used when importing documents from WordPerfect 4.2, DCA, DisplayWrite, and certain other formats.

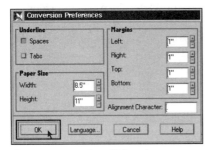

Figure 26-15: Specifying document conversion settings

Changing Your Color Scheme

Click Colors in the Preferences dialog box to change the color scheme for your document windows (see Figure 26-16). You can select another color scheme from the list, then click OK.

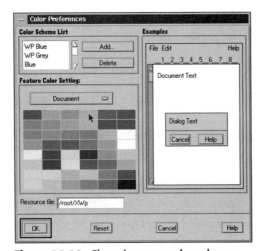

Figure 26-16: Changing your color scheme

You can also design your own color scheme:

1. Click a screen element in the Examples panel (such as document text or a dialog box), then click the color you want. (You can also select elements from the listing above the color palette.)

2. Repeat Step 1 for each element you want to change, then click Add, and give your color scheme a name.

3. Click OK until you save your color scheme to your resource file, which is normally XWp.

Your color scheme selection takes effect the next time you start WordPerfect. You can click Reset to return to the default settings.

Specifying Default Print Settings

Click Print in the Preferences dialog box to change the default print settings for your documents (see Figure 26-17). See Chapter 10, "Printing Documents, Booklets, and Envelopes," for more information on print settings.

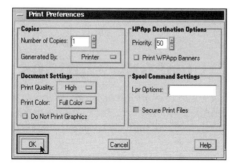

Figure 26-17: Specifying default print settings

Specifying Administrator Settings

If you start WordPerfect with the -adm startup option, you can also change administrator settings from the Preferences dialog box (see Figure 26-18):

✦ Click the Administrator button to add or remove other WordPerfect administrators.

✦ Click the Print Restrictions button to prevent various users or groups from performing certain functions, such as creating and controlling printers or setting maximum print priority.

✦ Click the File Locking button to enable or disable file locking. File locking prevents two users on a network from editing the same file at the same time and overwriting each other's changes.

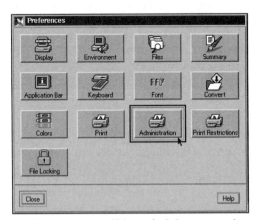

Figure 26-18: Specifying administrator settings

Starting WordPerfect with Custom Options

When launching WordPerfect, you can also make use of one or more of the *startup options*, described in Table 26-10, to customize your WordPerfect environment. See Chapter 1, "Getting Up and Running," for instructions on how to use these options.

Table 26-10 WordPerfect's Startup Options		
Option	*Enables You to*	*Example*
filename	Open a particular file automatically. Include the path if it's not in your default document directory.	Letterhead.wpd
filename /bk-bookmark name	Open a particular file and move to the specified bookmark.	Letterhead.wpd /bk-Address

Option	Enables You to	Example
-adm	Start WordPerfect with administrator access. This enables you to set system default Preferences, set printer preferences, install fonts, and perform other administrator functions. You must log in as root to Linux and X-Windows to be able to start WordPerfect with administrator access. (The administrator can then give other users administrative access, as described in the preceding "Specifying Administrator Settings" section.)	
-docGeometry	Specify the geometry (in pixels) of the document window.	-docGeometry 600 · 400
-faceName "fontface"	Change the text in the program windows and dialog boxes to the specified font typeface.	
-fastGraph	Use faster (but in some cases inaccurate) graphics rendering.	
-fontSize size	Change the text in the program windows and dialog boxes to the specified font point size.	
-help	List all the available startup options.	
-ignore	Start WordPerfect without using your personal settings. Use this option as a troubleshooting tool when you can't start WordPerfect.	

Continued

Table 26-10 (*continued*)

Option	*Enables You to*	*Example*
-lang language	Start WordPerfect in the language indicated by the two-letter language code.	-lang nl
-lowmem	Minimize WordPerfect's memory usage. Use this option as a troubleshooting tool.	
-lownet	Minimize WordPerfect's network traffic. Use this option as a troubleshooting tool.	
-macro macroname	Run the specified macro when you start WordPerfect. If the macro is not in the default or supplemental macro directory, you must include the full pathname.	-macro endfoot.wcm
-maxColors 216/125/16/2	Limit WordPerfect to using the number of colors you specify.	-maxColors 16
-noauto	Disable the auto code placement feature of WordPerfect.	
-nobackup	Disable timed backups and original document backups.	
-printer "printer name"	Use the specified printer as your default printer for the current session. (The printer must be installed.)	-printer hpdj540c.prs
-recover	Attempt to repair documents that are not functioning properly. Use this option as a troubleshooting tool.	
-restore	Delete your personal settings and restore the default settings.	
-setup path	Specify the directory where the settings files are stored.	-setup /usr/local/settings/

Option	Enables You to	Example
-temp path	Specify the directory where WordPerfect stores its temporary files.	-temp /tmp
-useISOFonts	Use ISO-Latin 1 X fonts instead of WordPerfect X fonts.	

When using a startup option, you need to provide only enough characters to make it unique. For example, -m is sufficient to specify the -macro startup option, but -rec is needed to differentiate -recover from -restore.

For More Information . . .

On	See
Changing the Initial Document Style	Chapter 15
Locating your settings	Appendix A
Inserting comments	Chapter 13
Configuring the shadow cursor	Chapter 4
Changing the default font	Chapter 15
Setting tabs	Chapter 15
Changing the merge code display	Chapter 28
Using other languages	Chapter 12
Selecting the hyphenation prompt option	Chapter 14
Setting up QuickList	Chapter 7
Selecting backup options	Chapter 6
Using ExpressDocs	Chapter 20
Playing the installed macros	Chapter 29
Using labels	Chapter 28
Customizing toolbars and application bars	Chapter 27
Importing files	Chapter 7
Restoring a document	Chapter 6

✦ ✦ ✦

Customizing Toolbars, Menus, and Keyboards

♦ ♦ ♦ ♦

In This Chapter

Display and hide
toolbars

Change your toolbar
display

Customize toolbars
and property bars

Customize QuickTips

Customize your
keyboard shortcuts

♦ ♦ ♦ ♦

As the previous chapter demonstrated, WordPerfect provides an efficient environment that can be adjusted to the way you work. Do you need even more flexibility? No problem. This chapter goes into more detail on tweaking the elements of WordPerfect's user interface to create an environment in which you feel most comfortable.

What You Can Customize

You can think of toolbars, menus, and keyboards as alternate paths to getting things done. Toolbars and keyboards can be customized to activate a feature, run a macro, play keystrokes, or launch a program. *Toolbars* include two specialized variants, the context-sensitive *property bar* and the informative and responsive *application bar*. For more information on customizing the WordPerfect application bar, see Chapter 26, "Fine-Tuning WordPerfect." WordPerfect toolbars can also be customized for particular ExpressDocs (see Chapter 20, "Working Quickly with ExpressDoc Templates and Styles"). For example, you can create a special toolbar for a specific publishing project.

Displaying and Hiding Toolbars

By default, WordPerfect displays one toolbar, plus the property bar and application bar. You can always display extra toolbars, such as a custom toolbar designed for a particular task. Click View ➪ Toolbars and check the toolbars you want to display (see Figure 27-1). You can also right-click a toolbar to choose additional toolbars from the menu that appears.

Figure 27-1: Check the toolbars you want to display

To hide a toolbar, right-click the toolbar (or click View ➪ Toolbars) and remove the check from its name.

Changing Your Toolbar Display

To change several toolbar display options:

1. Right-click any toolbar, then click Settings.

2. Click Options, then select any of the options, as shown in Figure 27-2 and described in Table 27-1.

Table 27-1	
Toolbar Display Options	
Option	**Enables You to**
Font Face	Select the font used if you're displaying text buttons.
Font Size	Change the font size if you're displaying text buttons. A larger font results in wider buttons.
Appearance	Choose whether to display buttons as Text Only, Picture Only, or Picture and Text. (Picture Only provides room for many more buttons, and you can always point to a button to see its QuickTip text.)
Maximum number of rows/columns to show	Display two or three rows of buttons if they cannot all fit on a single row. (Leave this setting at 1 to preserve screen space. WordPerfect displays a scroll bar to the right of the toolbar when there are more buttons than can be displayed.)

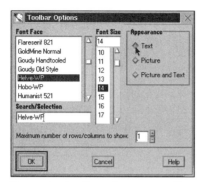

Figure 27-2: Changing your toolbar display

Customizing Toolbars

You can create your own toolbars, modify existing toolbars, and modify property bars.

To create a custom toolbar or customize an existing toolbar:

1. Right-click the toolbar, then click Settings.

2. Select a toolbar (see Figure 27-3), then click:

   • Create to start a new toolbar from scratch

   • Edit to modify a toolbar (see the following section for further instructions on editing toolbars)

   • Rename to change the name of a custom toolbar

   • Reset to return to the default settings of a system toolbar you edited

   • Delete to remove a custom toolbar

Figure 27-3: Selecting a toolbar to customize

Because property bars are specific to various program features, you can neither change how they're invoked nor create a custom one. You can only edit or reset them.

Editing a Toolbar

After clicking the Edit option, as described in the previous section, you're located in the Toolbar or Property Bar Editor (see Figure 27-4), where you can complete any of the following tasks:

- Click *Activate a Feature* to select a feature from any of the categories, then click Add Button to add a feature to the toolbar or property bar.

- Click *Play a Keyboard Script* to type the keystrokes you want to execute when you click the button, then click Add Script.

Tip QuickCorrect abbreviations are generally handier than toolbar buttons for inserting scripts.

- Click *Launch a Program*, click Select File, and select an executable (for example, you may want to add a calculator to the Tables property bar).

- Click *Play a Macro*, click Add Macro, and select the macro you want to run.

Note When you add a macro to a toolbar or keyboard, you are asked if you want to save the macro with its full path. If you click Yes, the program first looks in that directory to find the macro. If it doesn't find it there, it then looks in your default macro directory and finally in your supplemental macro directory. If you click No, the program looks only in your default and supplemental macro directories.

3. Move a button by dragging it to a new location.

4. Delete a button by dragging it off the toolbar.

5. Click Separator to add a space between groups of buttons.

Customizing a Button's Text and QuickTip

You can customize the text that appears on a button and the QuickTip that displays when you point to it:

1. Right-click the toolbar, click Edit, then double-click the button you want to customize.

2. Type the button text and the QuickTip prompt for the button (see Figure 27-5).

Figure 27-4: Editing a toolbar

Figure 27-5: Customizing a button's text and QuickTip

Customizing Keyboard Shortcuts

For all the glamour of the WordPerfect screen, the keyboard is still the most flexible and responsive input device. You should not overlook its possibilities.

In most cases, the default keyboard is the best choice. However, if you're more comfortable with the WordPerfect DOS keyboard or the WordPerfect Windows keyboard, there's no need to apologize. You can even create a combination of X-Windows, DOS, and Windows keystrokes, combining the best of all worlds. Anyway, it's your keyboard. You can modify WordPerfect's system keyboards to incorporate your own favorite shortcuts. You can also create custom keyboards, either from scratch or from a copy of an original. To modify a system keyboard or create a custom one:

1. Switch to the WordPerfect Program window and click Preferences ➪ Keyboard.

2. Select a keyboard (see Figure 27-6), then click:

- *Create* to start a new keyboard from scratch

- *Edit* to modify a keyboard (see the following section for further instructions)

- *Delete* to remove a keyboard

- *Copy* to create a custom duplicate under a new name, which you can then edit. Use this strategy when modifying the standard keyboards.

Figure 27-6: Selecting a keyboard to customize

Editing Keyboard Shortcuts

After clicking the Edit option as described in the preceding section, you're located in the Keyboard Editor (see Figure 27-7). Highlight the key you want to change by scrolling the list or pressing the keystrokes, then do any of the following:

- Click *Activate a Feature* to select a feature from any of the categories, then click Assign Feature.

- Click *Play a Keyboard Script* to type the keystrokes you want the shortcut key to execute, then click Assign Script.

- Click *Launch a Program*, click Select File, and select an executable.

- Click *Play a Macro*, click Assign Macro, and select the macro you want to run. (See the note on macro paths in the preceding "Editing a Toolbar" section.)

Tip

Instead of assigning a macro to a keystroke, you can name a macro for a Ctrl or Ctrl+Shift keystroke so that you can play it no matter what keyboard you use (see Chapter 29, "Automating with Macros").

Figure 27-7: Editing keyboard shortcuts

Click Unassign to remove the assignment from the selected keystroke.

3. To display the keystroke feature on the corresponding menu item, check "Assignment Appears on Menu."

For More Information . . .

On	See
Customizing WordPerfect's application bar	Chapter 26
Using WordPerfect ExpressDocs	Chapter 20
Using WordPerfect's shortcut keys	Chapter 4
Creating control key macros	Chapter 29

✦   ✦   ✦

Mass Producing with Labels and Merge

CHAPTER

28

Say you want to mail all your customers a holiday letter or a notice about a great new product. Do you print multiple copies addressed "Dear Valued Customer"?

To send a personal message to each of your clients, try merging your customer list with a form instead. While you're at it, enclose a business card that you created by using the label facilities.

When it comes to mass-produced labels and customized documents, WordPerfect has the tools you need.

Producing Labels

WordPerfect helps you bring order to this complex world by sticking labels on things — envelopes, file folders, diskettes, cassettes, name tags, cards, spice jars, merchandise, children, pets, and anything else. You can also use the label facilities to print stuff that doesn't stick, like tent cards, note cards, rotary cards, business cards, and other perforated forms.

You start by defining and printing labels on their own. Later in this chapter, you generate labels during a merge.

Creating Labels

You can create labels by using any of WordPerfect's predefined formats, including most of the commercially available sheet-fed and tractor-fed styles. To create labels:

1. Open a blank document or place the insertion point in the page where you want to start your labels.

2. Click Format ➪ Labels, then click the type of labels you want to display: Laser, Tractor-fed, or Both. (Laser labels are sheet labels used with various types of printers, including inkjets.)

3. Scroll the list to find the definition you want, then click OK (see Figure 28-1).

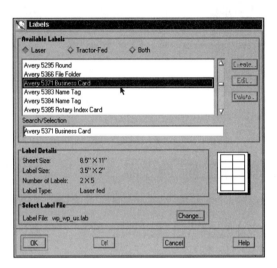

Figure 28-1: Selecting a label definition

Filling in Your Labels

You can type label text, add graphics, and use any of WordPerfect's editing or formatting features just as with any other WordPerfect page. (To center label text vertically, click Format ➪ Page ➪ Center and select "Current and subsequent pages.")

When you're finished with one label, press Ctrl+Enter (or click Insert ➪ New Page) to insert a [HPg] code and go on to the next label (see Figure 28-2).

Each label on a physical sheet is a logical page, as you can see from their numbers on the application bar. If a label overflows, WordPerfect issues a soft page break to start the next label, as with any other page.

When you display labels in Draft view, only the unformatted label texts are displayed, one after the other, separated by page breaks (see Figure 28-3). Note the [Labels Form] and [Paper Sz/Typ] codes used to define and print the labels, and the [HPg] codes between labels.

Point and click to maneuver among labels. Click the Previous Page and Next Page icons at the bottom of the vertical scroll bar to jump between physical pages (sheets) of labels. Using the keyboard, you can Page Up and Down, or use Go To (Ctrl+G) to maneuver among logical label pages.

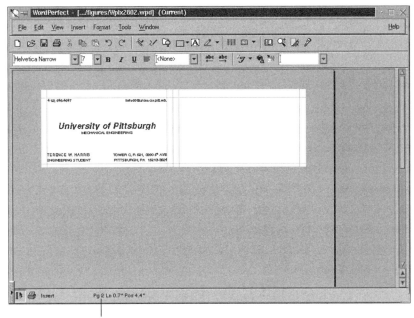

Page number—each label on the physical page is one logical page.

Figure 28-2: Press Ctrl+Enter to start the next label

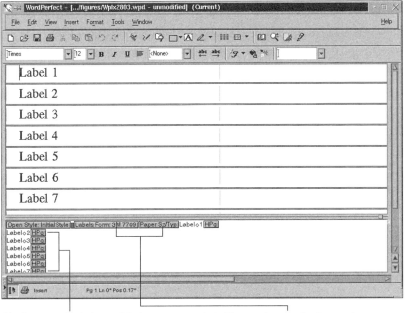

Hard page codes between labels   Label form and paper size/type codes

Figure 28-3: Labels in Draft view

Duplicating Labels

Normally, you use the merge feature to add specific information to a base document, like adding a name and address to copies of the same form letter (following sections in this chapter demonstrate that task). But you can also use the merge feature to duplicate a set of labels. Here's how:

1. Enter the text and graphics for one or more labels. For example, to duplicate two-up labels, complete the first row (logical pages one and two).
2. Click Tools ➪ Merge ➪ Merge.
3. Select Current Document from the Form File list.
4. Select New Document from the Output File list.
5. Click Options, specify the number of copies for each record, then click OK. Click OK again to start the merge.

Turning Off Labels

To stop entering label text, click Format ➪ Labels ➪ Off. (WordPerfect adds blank labels, if necessary, to fill out the sheet.) Note that any page-formatting features you may have selected for the labels (such as centering) remain in effect, even after the labels have been turned off.

Printing Labels

Printing is based on physical pages (sheets) of labels, not logical pages, unless you specify a range of pages:

✦ Print the full document to produce all the labels.
✦ Print the current page to produce the sheet of labels at the insertion point.
✦ Specify a page range to print a range of labels (logical pages).

Click on the toolbar and zoom to Full Page to preview the labels before you print them. Next, print your labels on a blank sheet of paper and hold it up against the labels to make sure that the print lines up correctly. Even then, different paper stock (such as that for business cards) may feed differently, so you may need to adjust the top margin a bit.

If you're printing tractor-fed labels, ensure that the top of the page is aligned properly.

Creating Custom Labels

The default label file for English versions of WordPerfect is WP_WP_US.LAB, and includes label definitions for various Avery products (Avery is the leading label manufacturer). You can add custom definitions to this file, or edit and delete existing entries. You can also create and use other label files with a .LAB filename extension. (Install language modules to add country-specific label definitions.)

As you can see from Figure 28-3, the label definition code is separate from the label form and independent of your printer. Label definitions are not special forms, but special formats for standard page sizes. This setup allows label definitions to be stored in a separate file, and also makes it easy to transfer documents with labels among various systems using different printers.

Creating a label definition

If you have labels that are not defined in the label file, create a new label definition. To add label definitions to the default label file, you must start WordPerfect with the -adm startup option. You can also create a new personal label file (see the following "Creating a new label file" section).

To add a new label definition to the default label file:

1. Open a blank document or click the page in which you want to start your labels.

2. Click Format ⇨ Labels.

3. Select an existing definition similar to your desired template, then click Create.

Type a Label description (see Figure 28-4), then click Change if you want to change the label sheet size. This sequence takes you to the Edit Page Size dialog box, with the options explained in the section, "Creating a Custom Page Definition," in Chapter 15, "Formatting Your Document." (The page type of "Labels" can't be changed.)

Tip

In some cases, the option to change the label sheet size is grayed out after creating a label definition. Just save the new label definition and edit it to change the label sheet size.

4. Specify the placement of labels on the page. Preview the resulting label layout as you define the following label arrangement options:

   • *Label Size*, to specify the height and width of a single label.

   • *Labels Per Page*, to specify the number of labels across and down the page.

   • *Top Left Label*, to specify the position of top-left label, measured from the paper edges to label edges.

   • *Distance Between Labels*, to specify the horizontal distance between columns and vertical distance between rows.

   • *Label Margins*, to specify the margins for information within each label.

   • *Label Type*, to specify whether the definition is for laser printers, tractor-fed printers, or both.

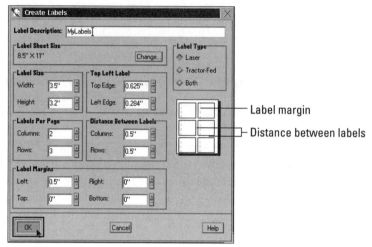

Figure 28-4: Creating a custom label definition

5. Click OK to return to the Labels dialog box. If you get a message that your labels can't fit on the page, go back and adjust your specifications.

6. To use the label definition now, highlight it and click OK. To use it later, click Cancel.

Editing and deleting label definitions

To edit or delete a definition in a label file:

1. Click Format ⇨ Labels, then select the label definition you want to edit or delete.

2. To delete the label definition, click Delete. To edit the definition, click Edit, then specify the options described in Steps 4 through 7 in the preceding "Creating a label definition" section.

Creating a new label file

Rather than alter the installed label file, you can store your custom label definitions in a separate file:

1. Start WordPerfect with the -adm startup option, as described in Chapter 1, "Getting Up and Running."

2. Click Format ⇨ Labels, then click Change under "Select label file."

3. Specify the folder for your label file, if necessary, then click Create, type a filename and description, and click OK (see Figure 28-5). The .LAB filename extension is added automatically.

4. To switch to your new label file, highlight it in the Label File dialog box, then click OK.

Figure 28-5: Creating a new label file

Because it's easier to customize label descriptions than create new ones, copy an existing file to a new name, rather than start a new file from scratch. Then select the file you copied in the Label File dialog box and click Edit to give it your own description (such as "Custom Label File"). Finally, select the new file and customize it by editing and deleting the label descriptions.

Deleting a label file

To delete a label file, click Format ➪ Labels ➪ Change, select the file you want to delete, then click Delete.

You can't delete the label file currently in use. If the file is currently selected when you open the Label File dialog box, highlight another label file, click Select, then go back and delete the file you no longer want.

Mass Producing with Merge

You, too, can create mass mailings that begin "Congratulations, Jane Doe, you're a Grand Prize finalist in our Million Dollar Sweepstakes!" Presumably, you have better uses for the Merge feature, such as sending notices or invoices to your clients or mailing holiday letters to your friends.

The standard merge combines a data source with a form document to produce the merged documents (see Figure 28-6).

Data source   Merged documents

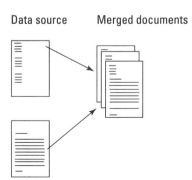

Figure 28-6: Combining a data source with a form document to produce the merged documents

Form document

The *data source* contains the information that changes from letter to letter, such as names and addresses. Your data source can be:

✦ A WordPerfect *data file* (document in text or table format)

✦ A file in a format recognized by WordPerfect (such as a spreadsheet or a database)

✦ A text file, in a specific format, from another word processor, database, or spreadsheet program

You can also supply keyboard information during a merge.

The *form document* is a standard WordPerfect document that contains your letter, invoice, label, flyer, or other text common to each merged document. The form file can also contain commands to control the merge process.

Note Merging files (Tools ➪ Merge) is not the same as combining two documents into one with Insert ➪ File.

Setting Up the Data File

The first step in performing a merge is to set up the data file with *records* (such as telephone book entries) for every friend, client, CD, or your own object. Each record, in turn, contains all the fields of variable information that gets plugged into the merged document.

Tip If you set up the data file first, it is easy to specify the name and place for each field when you create the form document. (The names in the form document must match the names from the data file precisely, or the data won't be found.)

A WordPerfect data file can be either text or a table. A table can be easier to edit, particularly when you have more than a handful of fields to a record or when some records have blank fields.

Note A data file can have up to 65,535 records (if they can fit into your computer's memory). Each record can have up to 255 fields in a text file or 64 columns in a table.

For the exercises in this book, you create a data file of at least three records with these seven fields for each record:

✦ First Name

✦ Last Name

✦ Address

✦ City

✦ State/Prov

✦ Zip

✦ Greeting

Tip Breaking the name and address into several fields gives you added flexibility.

To create the data file:

1. Open a new blank document.

Tip If you're creating a table, a landscape layout (click File ➪ Page Setup ➪ Page Size and select Landscape) with narrow margins and a smaller font lets you fit more columns across the page.

2. Click Tools ➪ Merge. To create a data table (instead of a text data file), check "Place records in a table." Click Data. If the current document isn't blank, click "New Document Window" and click OK (see Figure 28-7).

Figure 28-7: Creating a merge data file

3. Type **First Name** in the "Name a Field" box, then press Enter or click Add (see Figure 28-8).

Figure 28-8: Naming fields for the data file

4. Repeat Step 3 for the Last Name, Address, City, State/Prov, Zip, and Greeting fields, then click OK. (You can arrange fields with the Move Up and Move Down buttons.)

5. Click OK and type the first record in the Quick Data Entry dialog box (see Figure 28-9):

First Name	**Fred**
Last Name	**Jones**
Address	**P.O. Box 112**
City	**Middlewood**
State/Prov	**MA**
Zip	**12345**
Greeting	**Mr. Jones**

Press Tab or Enter, click Next Field to go to the next field, or click any field. (Press Ctrl+Enter to place multiple lines in a field without jumping to the next field.)

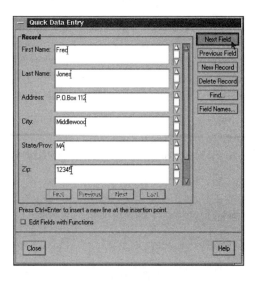

Figure 28-9: Filling in the first record

6. Click New Record and enter the second record:

First Name	**Alice**
Last Name	**Parker, M.D.**
Address	**151 Maple Street**
City	**Cottontown**
State/Prov	**KY**
Zip	**98765**
Greeting	**Dr. Parker**

7. Click New Record and enter the third record:

First Name	**George**
Last Name	**Alton**
Address	**1086 Main Street**
City	**East Tangerine**
State/Prov	**NJ**
Zip	**76530**
Greeting	**George**

8. Click Close, then click Yes, and provide a name and path for the file.

Your finished data should resemble Figure 28-10, if the file is in text format, or Figure 28-11, if the file is a table. If it doesn't look right, you can correct the screen document or try again from the beginning.

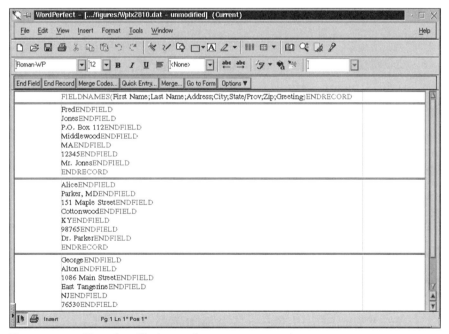

Figure 28-10: Your data file in text format

Resist the impulse to reformat the text within the cells of a table, as it will unwrap just fine when you merge the data. You may, however, adjust the width of the columns according to the information they contain, just as you would any other table (see Chapter 16, "Formatting with Columns and Tables").

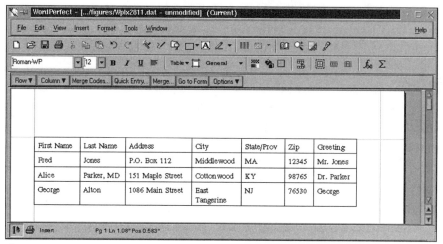

Figure 28-11: Your data file in table format

Examining Your Data

You can see three types of codes in a text data file:

 ✦ *FIELDNAMES* specifies the fields in the data file

 ✦ *ENDFIELD* indicates the end of each field

 ✦ *ENDRECORD* indicates the end of each record (including the field names record)

For easier viewing, each field begins on a new line and each record begins on a new page.

A data table doesn't need special codes, because the header row is used for the field names, and each of the following rows is a separate record.

Creating the Form Document

Now that your data is defined, you can create the form document with your boilerplate text. Your form document can include codes to control the merge process. However, the initial form for this exercise needs only the DATE code, plus FIELD codes to show where information from the data file gets inserted in the text.

To create the form document:

   1. Open a new blank document (If you're in the data document, click "Go to Form" and follow the prompts).

2. Click Tools ⇨ Merge ⇨ Form. (If you skip Step 1 and your document isn't blank, click "New document window" and click OK.)

3. Enter the name and path of your data file and click OK (see Figure 28-12).

4. Click Date on the Merge bar to insert a date code, then move down a couple of lines, click Insert Field, and click Insert to place the First Name field in your document (see Figure 28-13).

Figure 28-12: Associating a data file with your form document

Figure 28-13: Inserting an associated data field in your form document

5. Insert the other fields (including any punctuation and spaces) and type some boilerplate text, such as in the sample form document shown in Figure 28-14. (The Insert Field dialog box may be left open while typing text.)

6. Close the document, saving it as MERGETEST.FRM.

Tip

Place any formatting for margins, line spacing, and so forth in the Document Initial Style (see Chapter 15, "Formatting Your Document"). This way, the merge won't have to insert individual codes in each merged document.

Right-click any graphic, click Contents, and specify Image on Disk so the actual graphic won't be inserted in each merged document (see Chapter 9, "Working with Graphics").

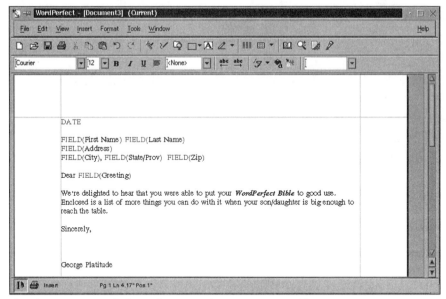

Figure 28-14: Sample form document for your mass mailing

Performing the Merge

Now that you've created your form document, perform the merge to produce three form letters, one for each record in the data file:

1. Click Tools ➪ Merge ➪ Merge.

2. Click the arrow next to the Form File list, click Select File, and then select your MergeTest.frm file (see Figure 28-15). Your merge data file should appear automatically as your data source. If not, select it now.

Figure 28-15: When specifying the form document, its associated data source is selected automatically

3. Click Output File ➪ New Document (if necessary), then click OK.

During the merge, WordPerfect displays a "Merging" message. With a small merge, the result should be nearly instantaneous (depending on the speed of your computer).

The merged document contains the text for all three letters, separated with hard page breaks. Read through the letters to make sure the proper data was inserted into each field. You can save the document or print it now.

Stopping a Merge

To stop a merge in progress, press Esc.

Including Envelopes in Your Merge

You've seen how to create merged form letters, but what about envelopes in which to stuff them? Surprise! You can create envelopes for your form letters at the same time:

1. Click Tools ➪ Merge ➪ Merge.

2. Select the form document and data source (if necessary), then click Envelopes.

3. Select or type your return address.

4. Click the mailing address box, then click Field in the lower-right to select fields for the mailing addresses just as with the form letter. Type any additional punctuation.

5. To include the POSTNET bar code, insert the Zip field in both the mailing address and the POSTNET Bar Code box (see Figure 28-16).(Zip+4 codes are required for bulk mailing discounts in the United States.)

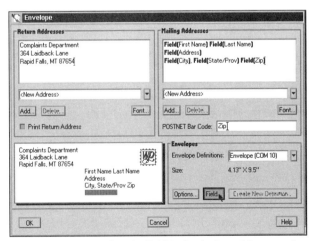

Figure 28-16: Put the Zip field in both the address and the POSTNET Bar Code boxes

Tip   If you don't see the Bar Code box, click Options and choose to include the Bar Code either above or below the address.

 6. If necessary, select an envelope definition or create a new one.

 7. Click OK.

The output document now contains all your form letters, followed by all the envelopes.

To include graphics in your merged envelopes, set up an envelope form document similar to that for the mailing labels discussed in the following section. (For more on printing envelopes, see Chapter 10, "Printing Documents, Booklets, and Envelopes.")

Using Merge for Envelopes Only

Instead of including envelopes with your merge, you may only want to produce the envelopes for your mass mailing, such as when you're sending out wedding invitations or a preprinted brochure:

 1. In a blank window, click Tools ➪ Merge ➪ Form, then select the data file to associate with the envelope.

 2. Click Format ➪ Envelope, then follow Steps 3–6 in the preceding "Including Envelopes in Your Merge" section.

 3. Click the Save button to save your form file.

 4. Click Merge on the toolbar, then click Merge ➪ Output File, select Printer to print your envelopes now (or New Document to print them later), then click OK. (Print to a document when testing the merge.)

Creating Mailing Labels with Merge

The trick to creating mailing labels instead of envelopes is to set up a separate form document for your labels.

Creating the Label Form Document

To create the label form document:

 1. Open a new document window and click Tools ➪ Merge ➪ Form, then click "Use file in active window" and click OK.

 2. Specify the associated data source, then click OK.

 3. Click Format ➪ Labels and select a label definition.

4. Type the return address and any other information that stays the same from label to label.

5. Click Insert Field to insert fields from the associated data file. Because the codes don't print, click Options ➪ Display as Markers to get a better view of where the data will go (see Figure 28-17).

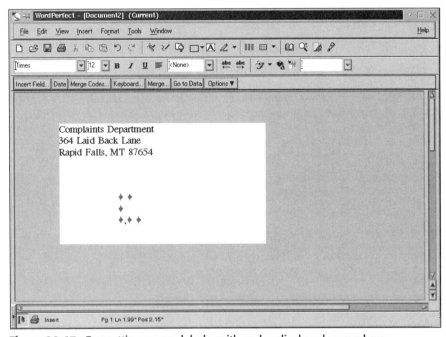

Figure 28-17: Formatting merge labels, with codes displayed as markers

6. To include the POSTNET bar code for U.S. addresses, click Options ➪ Display Codes (if necessary), click Merge Codes, type **po** to highlight the POSTNET merge code, then click Insert. Next, click Insert Field to insert the Zip field into the POSTNET code. The codes should appear as "POSTNET(FIELD(Zip))."

7. Save the file as MERGELABEL.FRM or your own filename.

Printing the Labels

To print the labels from the label form document:

1. Open a new document window and click Tools ➪ Merge ➪ Merge.

2. Select your label form document, then click OK.

3. Click File ➪ Print to print the labels. (Click the Zoom button and zoom to full page for a print preview.)

Merge Techniques

Now that you've mastered the merge basics, including how to create envelopes and labels, you're ready for some intermediate techniques on using data sources, form documents, and other merge features to produce precisely the output you want.

Editing Data and Form Documents

Because data files and form documents are WordPerfect documents, you can open a file and edit it directly. With a table data file, you can edit the structure as well, by using standard table-editing techniques described in Chapter 16, "Formatting with Columns and Tables." For example, you can rename a field by editing the column header or add a field by inserting a column. You can edit the cells (fields), or insert and delete rows to add or delete records. (Insert and delete rows or columns from the Merge bar.)

Tip   Switch between the data file and form document with the "Go to..." button on the Merge bar.

For more controlled editing of a text or table data file, use the Quick Data Entry dialog box:

1. Open the data file, then click Quick Entry on the Merge bar to edit the current record (see Figure 28-18).

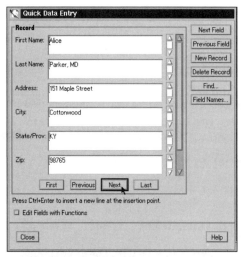

Figure 28-18: Using Quick Data Entry to edit a record

2. Click any of the following options:

- *Next Field* (Tab) or *Previous Field* (Shift+Tab) to scroll the fields
- *First*, *Previous*, *Next*, or *Last* to move among records
- *Find* to locate records containing particular text
- *Field Names* to edit, add, or delete field names for all your records
- *New Record* to add a record
- *Delete Record* to remove the current record

3. To edit fields containing styles, graphics, font changes, and so forth, check "Edit Fields with Functions." (If you don't want to lose these features, edit the text directly.)

4. To edit the record structure, click Field Names, then select or enter a field name (see Figure 28-19) and click any of the following:

- *Add* to insert a new field after the highlighted field in every record
- *Add Before* to insert a new field before the highlighted field
- *Replace* to rename the highlighted field (change associated references in the form documents as well)
- *Delete* to remove the field and its contents from every record

Figure 28-19: Editing the record structure

Directing the Merge Output

When performing a merge, you can click the Output File button to direct the merged text to any of the following locations:

✦ *Current Document* to append it to the text in the screen document.

✦ *New Document* (the default) to send it to a new, blank document.

✦ *Printer* to print the output of the merge immediately.

✦ *File* to send output directly to a disk file.

Specifying Merge Output Options

When performing a merge, you can click the Options button (see Figure 28-20) to specify any of these options:

✦ *Separate Each Merged Document With a Page Break* is the default for producing form letters, mailing labels, and so forth. Remove the check to produce a continuous list (such as an inventory of your CDs or a phone directory).

✦ *Number of Copies for Each Record* enables you to output multiple copies of business cards and so forth from a single copy in your document.

✦ *If Empty Field in Data File* enables you to remove blank lines from your output, such as when you have two address fields but only one is filled.

✦ *Display Options* lets you show or hide codes during the keyboard merge, or show them as markers.

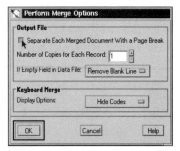

Figure 28-20: Specifying merge output options

Selecting Records

Often, you'll want to merge with only certain records from an address book, customer file, or other data source. Click Select Records when performing the merge, then click one of the following:

✦ *Specify Conditions* to designate record-selection criteria (see Figure 28-21).

✦ *Mark Records* to check the records you want to use manually (see Figure 28-22).

Check to specify a range of records

Select fields to set conditions for

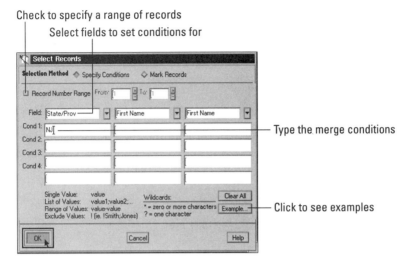

Type the merge conditions

Click to see examples

Figure 28-21: Selecting records by specifying conditions

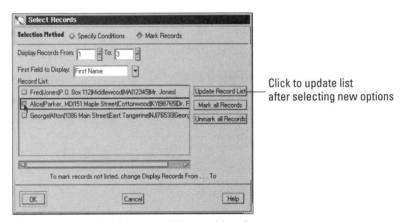

Click to update list after selecting new options

Figure 28-22: Selecting records by marking them

Sorting Data Records

To sort records after you select them (for example, by ZIP code for mailing), click Options ⇨ Sort on the Merge bar or click Tools ⇨ Sort. See Chapter 22, "Sorting Information," for more on sorting records.

Merging from Other Sources

WordPerfect can merge data from many sources, as long as the data format permits the program to identify the fields and records.

Merging from a WordPerfect table

You can merge from any WordPerfect table, as long as you specify the field names in the first row of the table. You can also convert the table (with the field names in the first row) to a merge data file—but work from a copy of the table if you want to preserve the original. Select the entire table, press Delete, then click "Convert to Merge Data File (first row becomes field names)" (see Figure 28-23).

Figure 28-23: Converting a table to a merge data file

Merging from a spreadsheet or database

To use a file in any of the common spreadsheet or database formats as your merge data source:

1. Click Insert ➪ Spreadsheet/Database ➪ Import.

2. Select the data type to import (Spreadsheet, Database, or ASCII).

3. Select Merge Data File from the "Import As" list (see Figure 28-24).

Figure 28-24: Importing a spreadsheet as a merge data file

4. For a spreadsheet, you can specify the range of data to import. For a database, you can check the fields you want to use.

5. Click File ⇨ Save As, then save the file with a new name.

Caution

Be sure to use Save As. Don't perform a regular save: you'll wipe out the original spreadsheet or database.

6. If you're importing a spreadsheet, go to the top of the file, click Merge Codes, insert the FIELDNAMES code, and enter the names of the fields.

Merging from ASCII-delimited text

You can import records from any program that can save records as ASCII-delimited text, enclose fields in quotation marks, separate fields by commas, and end records with carriage returns:

```
"Fred","Jones","P.O. Box 112","Middlewood","MA","12345","Mr. Jones"
"Alice","Parker","MD","151 Maple
Street","Cottontown","KY","98765","Dr. Parker"
"George","Alton","1086 Main Street","East
Tangerine","NJ","76530","George"
```

To turn the ASCII file into a merge text file:

1. Click Insert ⇨ Spreadsheet/Database, set the data file type to ASCII (DOS) Delimited Text (see Figure 28-25), and click OK.

Figure 28-25: Opening an ASCII delimited text file

2. Select Merge Data File from the "Import As" list, specify any delimiters and characters, if necessary, check if the first record has fieldnames, then click OK.

3. Click File ⇨ Save As, then save the file to a new name.

4. If field names aren't included in the file, go to the top of the file, click Merge Codes, insert the FIELDNAMES code, and enter the names of the fields.

Gaining Control with Merge Commands

By adding *merge commands* to your form document or data file, you can control the process of your merge and tell it what to do in special situations.

Many merge commands supply additional information with *parameters* (or arguments) enclosed in parentheses. The IFBLANK command, for example, requires a field. When two or more parameters are used, separate them with semicolons.

Caution   The parentheses for parameters are part of the merge code. Don't type them yourself!

Merge commands are similar to those used in macros and in various programming languages. Indeed, you can assign variables and use hundreds of merge expressions and programming commands to control the input, processing, and output of your merges. Table 28-1 contains some commonly used merge commands. Codes used in the following examples are indicated by an asterisk (*).

Note   The discussion of macro programming concepts in Chapter 29, "Automating with Macros," also applies to merges.

Table 28-1
Commonly Used Merge Commands

Command	What It Does	Basic Syntax
ASSIGN	Assigns a value to a *variable* (such as the name or balance due) to be used somewhere in the merge.	`ASSIGN (var; value)`
BEEP*	Gets the user's attention.	`BEEP`
CALL	Tells the merge to transfer execution of the labeled subroutine, then return to the point immediately after the call when RETURN is encountered.	`CALL (label)`
CHAINFORM	Tells WordPerfect to continue with an additional form file after the current file is done. (Use this command to create envelopes for your form letters.)	`CHAINFORM (formfile)`
CHAINMACRO	Executes a macro when merging is finished. (Use this command to do actions merges cannot, such as open or save files.)	`CHAINMACRO (macro)`

Command	What It Does	Basic Syntax
CHAR	Displays a message box and waits for a single keystroke. A common use of the CHAR command is to display a message asking for a Yes (Y) or No (N) response.	`CHAR (var; prompt; title)`
CODES*	Allows formatting (such as hard returns and tabs) to merge commands without replicating them in the finished merge.	`CODES(merge codes and formatting)`
COMMENT*	Adds non-printing comments to your merges. (Use this command to hide simple formatting, such as a hard return or tab).	`COMMENT (text)`
DATE*	Inserts the current date.	`DATE`
DISPLAYSTOP	Stops the display of text (normally after the KEYBOARD command).	`DISPLAYSTOP`
DOCUMENT*	Inserts the entire contents of a document into the merged output. (Use it to import boilerplate text as part of the merge.)	`DOCUMENT (documentname)`
ENDFIELD*	Indicates the end of a field in a merge data file.	`ENDFIELD`
ENDRECORD*	Indicates the end of a record in a merge data file.	`ENDRECORD`
FIELD*	References a field defined in a merge and inserts the field's contents in the merged output.	`FIELD (field)`
FIELDNAMES*	Specifies the names for fields used in each record in a data file. If the FIELDNAMES command isn't used, the fields must be referenced in the form file by number (FIELD 1, FIELD 2, and so forth).	`FIELDNAMES (name1; name2; ...)`

Continued

Table 28-1 *(continued)*

Command	What It Does	Basic Syntax
GETSTRING*	Displays a message with a text box for the user's response. The GETSTRING variable can then be used elsewhere in the merge.	`GETSTRING (var;message;title)`
GO*	Tells the merge to skip to the commands located after a specified label, without returning. Compare to CALL.	`GO (label)`

IF / ELSE / ENDIF*	Executes a set of commands if the logical expression you define is true. When ELSE is included, the commands between IF and ELSE are executed when the expression is true; the commands between ELSE and ENDIF are executed when it is false.	`IF (expression)`
		`Do this if the expression`
		`              is true`
		`ELSE`
		`Do this if the expression`
		`is false ENDIF`

IFBLANK	Executes a set of commands when the specified field is blank	`IFBLANK(field)`, followed by an optional `ELSE`, and ending with `ENDIF`, as with `IF / ELSE / ENDIF`
IFNOTBLANK	Executes a set of commands when the specified field is not blank.	`IFNOTBLANK(field)`
INSERT*	Writes text within a CODES command. (If you don't use a CODES command, you don't need INSERT, as any text in the form document appears in the merged output.)	`INSERT(text)`
KEYBOARD*	Pauses the merge so the user can type in data.	`KEYBOARD([prompt])`
LABEL*	Identifies an area of the merge form file to which to jump and execute by using the GO and CALL commands.	`LABEL (label)`
NESTFORM*	Turns control over to another form, then continues with the next command after the nested form is done.	`NESTFORM(form)`

Command	What It Does	Basic Syntax
NESTMACRO	Executes the named macro, then continues with the next statement.	`NESTMACRO(macro)`
NEXTRECORD*	Tells the merge to stop processing the current merge data record and go to the next.	`NEXTRECORD`
PAGEON / PAGEOFF	Tells WordPerfect whether to insert a page break between each output record (PAGEON) or to print the records continuously (PAGEOFF).	`PAGEON / PAGEOFF`
PROMPT	Displays a message onscreen to the user.	`Prompt(message)`
QUIT	Terminates all merge execution and outputs any remaining text in the form file. (Compare to STOP.)	`QUIT`
REWRITE*	Rewrites the screen, showing the current state of the merge.	`REWRITE`
STOP	Terminates all merge execution and output.	`STOP`
SUBSTDATA	Switches to the beginning of another data file.	`SUBSTDATA(filename)`
SWITCH / ENDSWITCH / CASEOF	Makes a decision based on specific data in the data file, or data provided by the user.	`SWITCH (expression)` `CASEOF x: Do this if expression equals "x"` `CASEOF y: Do this if expression equals "y"` `CASEOF z: Do this if extExpression equals "z"` `ENDSWITCH`
VARIABLE*	"Returns" the contents of a variable. For example, if the variable contains the name "Fred Smith," that name is inserted into the merged output.	`VARIABLE(Var)`
WHILE / ENDWHILE	Repeats text and commands within this loop until the test expression used with the WHILE command is no longer true.	`WHILE (expression)` `Repeat this part until the test expression is false` `ENDWHILE`

*These commands are used in various examples throughout the chapter.

Checking for a Blank Data Field

Assume that you want every form letter to have an entry in the address field. (Won't get too far without it!) By entering the following IFBLANK command in the form file, the merge stops and ask you to enter the address from the keyboard whenever it encounters a blank address field:

```
CODES(
IFBLANK(Address)
REWRITE KEYBOARD(Address missing: please type it now...)
ELSE
FIELD(Address)
ENDIF
)
```

 Tip The CODES command lets you format multiple merge commands for readability, without inserting the extra hard returns and tabs into the output document. The REWRITE command displays the text that has been merged so far, so you can see whose address is missing.

To insert a merge command while editing a form document or data file, click Merge Codes on the Merge bar. Scroll down the list, or type the first characters of the merge command you want (see Figure 28-26). Double-click the command or click Insert to place it in your document. (When editing a form document, click the Merge bar buttons to enter the date code or keyboard commands.)

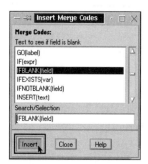

Figure 28-26: Inserting merge codes

WordPerfect prompts automatically for any command parameters. You should supply the parameters when you insert the commands, but you can also insert the command as is and type its arguments later.

Merge commands are inserted into the document like any WordPerfect formatting code. When you open Reveal Codes, the merge commands don't appear like typed text.

The PROMPT command, which displays a message in a box on your screen, is a good example of a one-parameter command. Open your MERGETEST.FRM document (created in the preceding "Creating the Form Document" section), position the insertion point at the top, click Merge Codes, type **prom**, click Insert, then fill in the prompt parameter with your message, such as "Merging address records to produce form letters and envelopes."

When you click OK and then Close, you see PROMPT(message) on the screen.

In Reveal Codes, you see [MRG:PROMPT]message[MRG:PROMPT].

As with formatting codes, deleting one paired merge code deletes the other as well. Merge commands with no parameters display as single codes.

Click Options on the Merge bar to hide your merge codes or display them as markers. To change your default merge code display, switch to the WordPerfect program window and click Preferences ⇨ Display ⇨ Merge.

Supplying Keyboard Merge Input

The KEYBOARD command described in Table 28-1 has many uses. You can, for example, replace the impersonal "your son/daughter" in the boilerplate merge form with a specific term for each letter:

```
BEEP REWRITE KEYBOARD(Type name of kid or creature . . . then
press Alt+Enter.)
```

The BEEP keeps you from falling asleep at the keyboard.

When the merge stops at a prompt, you can either enter the data for which you're prompted or:

✦ *Skip* the record (don't include it in the output)

✦ *Quit* the merge at the end, but ignore any further commands

✦ *Stop* the merge entirely

Making Merges That Think

The ordinary merge extracts the data from each record and creates a separate form letter for each record. You can make your merges "smart" by testing for some value in one of the fields. For example, if one of the fields is a ZIP code, you can test whether the ZIP code is greater or less than some value. That way, you can send out letters to a select group of people who live in a certain area.

The IF command is most often used to provide decision-making capabilities to merges. The IF expression tests the value in one or more fields, and takes appropriate action depending on whether the outcome is TRUE or FALSE.

For the example in this section, create the merge data table as shown in Figure 28-27 and save it as MRGADV.DAT. (Add more records if you like.)

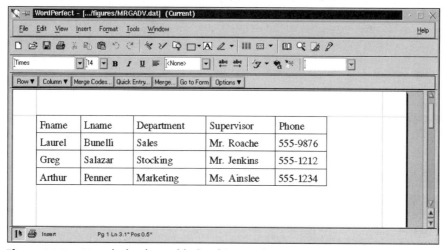

Figure 28-27: Mrgadv.dat data table for this exercise

Now suppose you want to generate a memo to people in the Sales department. Create the form file as follows:

1. Open a new, blank document.

2. Click Tools ➪ Merge.

3. Click Form and enter **mrgadv.dat** as the associated data file.

4. Insert the following codes (in bold) and text into the file as shown in Figure 28-28 (enter a blank IF code, then insert the Department field within the parentheses):

```
LABEL(loop)
IF("FIELD(Department)"="Sales")
MEMO
DATE
```

From: Sam Adams, President

To: **FIELD**(Fname)**FIELD**(Lname)

Subject: Raises

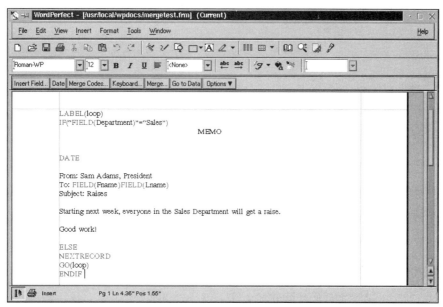

Figure 28-28: Completed form file

Starting next week, everyone in the Sales Department will get a raise.

Good work!

```
ELSE
NEXTRECORD
GO(loop)
ENDIF
```

5. Check your work for typographical errors. (Watch those FIELD names!) Then save the form as MRGSMART.FRM and close it.

6. Click Tools ➪ Merge ➪ Merge, then specify Mrgsmart.frm as the form document, with the associated Mrgadv.dat data file. Output the merge file to New Document (see Figure 28-29).

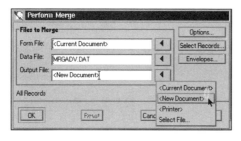

Figure 28-29: Running the merge

7. Click OK to output a single memo for Laura Bunelli in Sales (see Figure 28-30).

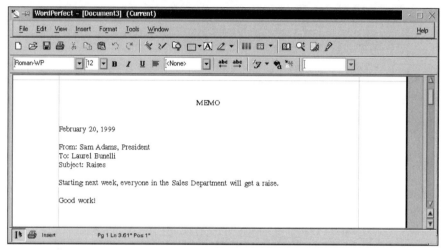

Figure 28-30: Merged memo

The IF expression looks for "Sales" in the Department field and generates a memo if "Sales" is found. If the Department doesn't equal "Sales," the record is skipped by using NEXTRECORD.

Formatting Merge Codes

If you're familiar with programming WordPerfect macros, you know that commands are easier to read when you format them by using hard returns and tabs. The same is true of merge commands, but with a catch: most formatting in the commands ends up in the merged output, even though the commands themselves do not. In the previous exercise, the output memo didn't start at the top of the page for this reason.

To hide the hard returns in your example from the merge output, you can use the COMMENT command as follows:

```
LABEL(loop) COMMENT(
)IF("FIELD(Department)"="Sales")COMMENT(
) MEMO
DATE
```

From: Sam Adams, President

To: **FIELD(**Fname**)FIELD(**Lname**)**

Subject: Raises

Starting next week, everyone in the Sales Department will get a raise.

Good work!

Sam

```
ELSE COMMENT(
)NEXTRECORD COMMENT(
)GO(loop)COMMENT(
)ENDIF
```

Here's a simpler solution: enclose whole groups of codes within a CODES command, in which both the codes and their formatting are ignored:

```
CODES(
LABEL(loop)
IF("FIELD(Department)"="Sales")
) MEMO
DATE
```

From: Sam Adams, President

To: **FIELD**(Fname)**FIELD**(Lname)

Subject: Raises

Starting next week, everyone in the Sales Department will get a raise.

Good work!

```
CODES(
ELSE
NEXTRECORD
GO(loop)
ENDIF
)
```

Tip   Select the codes you want to enclose before selecting the CODES command.

You can also enclose the entire form within a single CODES command, then enclose the text and fields you want to write out within INSERT commands.

Commenting Your Merge Form

You saw how the COMMENT code can be used to hide code formatting, but its main purpose is to document your merge form to make it easier for you and others to maintain. For example, you may want to include the following comment at the beginning of your raise memo form:

```
COMMENT(Be sure to update the Department before running the merge.)
```

Generating Menus and More

Menus help guide an inexperienced user through the merge process. For example, you may build a merge project that asks the user which of three files, if any, to insert as part of the merge. The user doesn't have to know the names of the files, but instead just enters the number displayed in the menu.

Using the MERGADV.DAT file from the previous example, suppose you have three different form letters, depending on whether the person get a raise, gets transferred, or gets fired. The menu example shown in Figure 28-31 uses three text documents (DOC1.WPD, DOC2.WPD, and DOC3.WPD) to customize the letter based on the answer to the menu prompt. There's also another form, OPENDOC.FRM, with standard opening text and codes.

Figure 28-31: Responding to the GETSTRING prompt when running the merge

1. Create three documents using the names "DOC1.WPD, DOC2.WPD, and DOC3.WPD." Have the first document contain the text variable "raise", the second document contain "reassigned," and the third document "outsourced."

2. Open a new, blank document, click Tools ⇨ Merge ⇨ Form, and enter **mrgadv.dat** as the associated data file.

3. Insert the following codes (in bold) and text into the new file:

```
CODES(
LABEL(Top)
GETSTRING(doc;Type the number of the letter to send to
FIELD(Fname)FIELD(Lname):
```

    1 (You got a raise!)

    2 (You've been reassigned!)

    3 (You've been outsourced!)

    0 (Don't send a letter.)   ; Specify the Merge Document

```
IF(VARIABLE(doc=1)
NESTFORM(DocOpen.frm)
```

```
DOCUMENT(Doc1.wpd)
ELSE
IF(VARIABLE(doc)=2)
NESTFORM(DocOpen.frm)
DOCUMENT(Doc2.wpd)
ELSE
IF(VARIABLE(doc=3)
NESTFORM(DocOpen.frm)
DOCUMENT(Doc3.wpd)
ELSE
NEXTRECORD
GO(Top)
ENDIF
ENDIF
ENDIF
)
```

Tip

Use the Copy and Paste commands to repeat code.

4. Check your work for typographical errors, then save the form as MRGDOC.FRM and close it.

5. Create OPENDOC.FRM with the following code (you can add more spacing between lines) and associate it with MRGADV.DAT:

```
INSERT(DATE
```

From: Sam Adams, President

To:**FIELD(**FName**) FIELD(**Lname**)**

Subject: What's Happening to You

Dear **FIELD(**Fname**)**,

Here's the letter you've been waiting for:

6. Click Tools ⇨ Merge ⇨ Merge, then specify MrgDoc.frm as the form document with the associated Mrgadv.dat data file, and output to New Document.

7. Click Merge, then respond to the menu prompt for each record by entering the number of the document to use or any other character to skip the record (refer to Figure 28-31).

Your resulting letters should resemble Figure 28-32.

For explanations of the various codes used in the exercise, refer to Table 28-1.

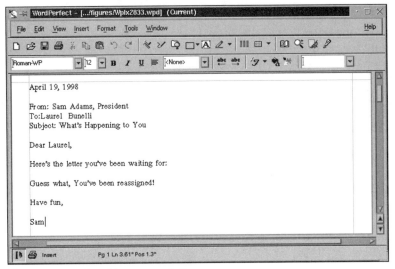

Figure 28-32: Resulting merge letter

Producing Merge Lists

Normally, there's a page break between each merge output record, such as when you produce form letters and so forth. To output a continuous list, as with a telephone directory, you can use the PAGEOFF command:

```
PAGEOFF COMMENT(
)FIELD(Lname), FIELD(Fname)  FIELD(Department)    FIELD(Phone)
```

This command removes the check from the "Separate Each Merged Document with a Page Break" option when performing a merge.

Merging into Tables

The preceding section showed how to use merge to create a list. The final list, formatted into columns, lacks visual impact. To gain this impact, you can merge data directly into a table, then format the resulting table (see Chapter 16, "Formatting with Columns and Tables"):

1. In the form file, create a two-row table with as many columns as you need.

2. In the top-left cell of the table, add the following merge commands:

```
WHILE(1) PAGEOFF
```

3. Insert the FIELD commands for the data as needed. (Place any fields in the upper-left column after the WHILE and PAGEOFF commands.)

4. In the lower-left cell, enter the following merge commands:

```
NEXTRECORD ENDWHILE
```

The merge table form in Figure 28-33 uses the MRGADV.DAT file you created previously to produce the table shown in Figure 28-34.

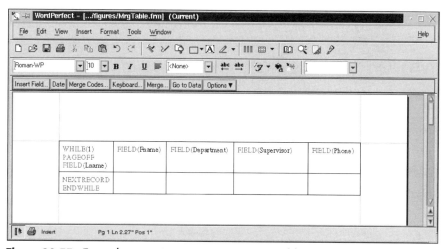

Figure 28-33: Form document set up to merge to a table

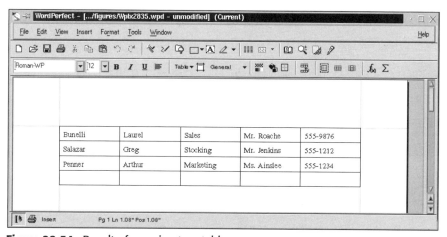

Figure 28-34: Result of merging to a table

Including Document Formatting in Your Output

Document, paragraph, and character formats in the form merge file are normally transferred to the resulting merge documents. You can, for example, set up tabs in the form document before creating the telephone list described in the preceding section. Or, if you want your form letters to have 1½-inch margins, include those formats at the start of the form file.

You can also apply any character format, such as bold or italics, to the boilerplate text of the form merge file. Just write or edit the document in the usual manner and add the appropriate formatting. If you want the variable data from the data file to be formatted in a particular way, apply the formatting to the FIELD code instead.

For More Information . . .

On	See
Creating a custom page definition	Chapter 15
Editing the Document Initial Style	Chapter 15
Printing envelopes	Chapter 10
Using tables	Chapter 16
Using an image on disk	Chapter 9
Sorting records	Chapter 22
Macro programming concepts	Chapter 29

✦   ✦   ✦

Automating with Macros

Tired of performing the same series of actions over and over? Capture these actions as a macro file that you can play back at the click of a button or the press of a key. A macro file can contain:

+ A recording of the results of your actions, including keystrokes, mouse selections, and text you typed

+ Nonrecordable macro *programming commands*, such those as to check your system or present a dialog box with custom selections

You may be surprised to discover how easy it is to automate repetitive tasks with macros. This chapter shows you how to record and play back WordPerfect macros, and gives you an idea of other possibilities with the robust and powerful macro commands.

Why Macros?

Just as a QuickCorrect abbreviation is handy for words or phrases you type regularly, a macro can make quick work of any repetitive task.

Suppose that you create a pointing finger bulleted list frequently, set in from the left margin with a custom indent that puts the bullet and text closer together. Instead of reinventing your custom bullets each time, this chapter shows you how to record them once as a macro, then play them back whenever you need such a list.

For even more power and flexibility, you can work directly in the macro programming language. For example, you can have the macro behave differently depending on the current program settings and conditions.

Tip Check the QwkScreen Web site (http://www.qwkscreen.com) for such great macros as English-Metric conversions, perfectly formatted footnotes and endnotes, and super move, copy, insert, and delete. These macros have been designed to work in WordPerfect for Windows, but most of them work in WordPerfect for Linux as well.

Alternatives to Macros

Although it's easier than ever to record a macro, WordPerfect's improvements may make some macros unnecessary. For example, four clicks were required to display the ruler in WordPerfect 7, but now two clicks do the trick.

With Spell-As-You-Go, Grammar-As-You-Go, QuickCorrect, Format-As-You-Go, SmartQuotes, and other tools, there's less need for custom macros to do everyday tasks. ExpressDoc templates now handle many complicated tasks (such as creating a term paper or resume).

The Power of Macros

So, who needs macros? Well, maybe you don't. But, as the examples in this chapter illustrate, when you're looking for solutions to your particular needs, macros are a powerful and flexible instrument.

Recording a Macro

So much for the theory. To record a macro:

1. Click the New Blank Document button to open a blank document (unless you want to record your steps in the current document).

2. Click Tools ➪ Macro ➪ Record (or press Ctrl+F10).

3. Type a name for the macro, then click Record (see Figure 29-1). WordPerfect gives your macro an extension of .WCM automatically (the macro won't play without this extension). Note that the words "Macro Record" appear on the application bar.

Figure 29-1: Give your macro a name, and then click Record

4. Perform the keystrokes and mouse selections you want to record. (The mouse won't work in the document area—you can't use it to select text.)

5. To end the recording, click Tools ⇨ Macro ⇨ Record (or press Ctrl+F10).

Tip

Right-click the toolbar and check the Macro Tools toolbar for quick access to frequently-used macro features like playing a macro, editing a macro, pausing a macro, and recording a macro. The Macro Tools toolbar is especially convenient when recording a macro.

Playing a Macro

To play a macro:

1. Click Tools ⇨ Macro ⇨ Play (Shift+Ctrl+F10).

2. Specify the macro, then click Play.

To pause a macro that's playing, click Tools ⇨ Macro ⇨ Pause. To cancel a macro that's playing, press Esc.

WordPerfect comes with ready-made macros you can play, as described in Table 29-1.

Table 29-1 Macros That Ship with WordPerfect 8 for Linux	
Macro	**What It Does**
Abbrev	Allows you to create and expand abbreviations
Capital	Capitalizes the first letter of a word
Checkbox	Adds boxes to a document that you can click to check
Closeall	Closes all open documents, prompting you to save changes
Ctrlm	Activates the Macro Command Inserter
Ctrlsftf	Prompts for From and To values in the Equation Editor
Endfoot	Converts endnotes into footnotes
Filestmp	Displays the document's filename and path in the header or footer
Fontdn	Decreases the font size by 2 points
Fontup	Increases the font size by 2 points

Continued

Table 29-1 *(continued)*	
Macro	**What It Does**
Footend	Converts footnotes into endnotes
Graph	Creates graph paper
Lawfax	Fills out a legal fax form
Linenum	Lets you place the insertion point at a particular line number and character when debugging macros
Macrocnv	Starts the macro converter, which enables you to convert macros created in WordPerfect 5.1
Pagexofy	Inserts a "Page *x* of *y*" page number
Parabrk	Inserts graphical breaks between paragraphs
Pgborder	Creates a page border
Pleading	Creates lines and numbers for a legal pleading statement
Reverse	Reverses background and foreground colors in selected text or table cells
Saveall	Prompts you to save all open documents
Softfonts	Displays all Type 1 fonts that come with WordPerfect (see Chapter 8, "Fonts Fantastic")
Transpos	Transposes two characters
Watermrk	Prompts for text or a graphic to insert as a watermark

Creating Some Macro Examples

This section contains three macro examples you can record and play.

Custom Bullet Macro

To create a macro for the custom bulleted list:

1. Open a blank document and click View ➪ Ruler to display the ruler.
2. Make sure QuickBullets is on (Tools ➪ QuickCorrect ➪ Format-As-You-Go ➪ QuickBullets).
3. Click Tools ➪ Macro ➪ Record (Ctrl+F10), give your macro a name (such as "BulletPoint"), then click Record.
4. Drag the tab markers on the ruler to adjust the first two tabs to your liking (for example, move the marker at 2" to 1.75").

5. Press Tab, click Insert ➪ Symbol, and select the pointing finger (WP character [5,43]) or another bullet. Click Insert followed by Close, then press Tab again.

6. Click the Stop button on the Macro Tools toolbar to stop recording and save the macro (see Figure 29-2). (You can also click Tools ➪ Macro ➪ Record or press Ctrl+F10.)

Figure 29-2: Stopping your macro recording from the macro tools toolbar

Tip

If you display the ruler *before* you start recording, it won't display when you play the macro.

QuickBullets must be on for proper playback of the macro. Do you usually leave QuickBullets off? No problem. Turn QuickBullets on when you start recording the macro, then turn them off just before you stop.

But wait . . . QuickBullets will always be turned *off* by the macro, even when you want them on! Later in this chapter (in the "Waving a Flag" section), you see how programming commands can get you out of this dilemma.

Letter-Opening Macro with a Date

Suppose you want to create an informal letter opening, with your address and date at the top, followed by Dear . . . . You could use QuickWords, but a macro has three advantages:

✦ It can open a blank document to begin your letter. (You add the open document command later, instead of recording it.)

✦ It can insert the current date, without using a code that changes the date every time you look at it.

✦ It can pause for you to type the recipient's name, then continue. The pause command is added in a following section.

To record your letter-opening macro:

1. Open a blank document, then click Tools ➪ Macro ➪ Record, and give your macro a name, such as "MyLetter".

2. Put your name, address, and anything else at the top, with your normal formatting.

3. Press Enter a couple of times, then click Insert ➪ Date/Time ➪ Insert.

4. Press Enter a couple of times again, then type **Dear** plus a space and a comma, and press Enter twice.

5. Click the Macro toolbar Stop button on the Macro toolbar to stop recording and save the macro.

Now open a blank document and play your letter macro. The result should resemble Figure 29-3. Of course, this example is far from perfect. In a following section, you customize this macro to make it more useful.

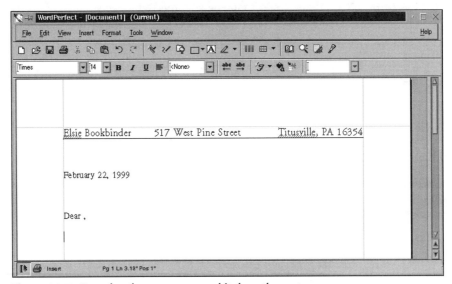

Figure 29-3: You play the macro . . . and it does the rest

Macro to Transpose Two Paragraphs

Now create a macro to transpose two paragraphs when you press Ctrl+Shift+T:

1. Create some text with a few paragraphs and place the insertion point in any paragraph other than the first.

2. Click Tools ➪ Macro ➪ Record, and give the macro the precise name (including case) of "ctrlsftt".

3. Click Edit ➪ Select ➪ Paragraph.

4. Click the Cut button, then press Ctrl+Up Arrow to go up one paragraph and click the Paste button. Click the Macro toolbar Stop button (or Tools ➪ Macro ➪ Record) to stop the recording.

Now, every time you press Ctrl+Shift+T, you transpose the paragraph at the insertion point with the paragraph above it!

Naming Keystroke Macros

The preceding macro is an example of a *keystroke macro* in the form of "Ctrl*x*" (Ctrl and a letter) or "Ctrlsft*x*" (Ctrl+Shift and a letter) that plays without being assigned to a keyboard.

Actual keyboard assignments take precedence (see Chapter 27, "Customizing Toolbars, Menus, and Keyboards"), so you must name the macros for vacant keystrokes. Examine the tables for control-alpha shortcut keys in Chapter 3, "Mastering the WordPerfect Interface," for such vacant keys as Ctrl+H (name your macro "Ctrlh") and Ctrl+Shift+E (name your macro "Ctrlsfte").

Using Shortcuts to Play Macros

When you play macros over and over, you may get tired of typing their names (unless they're Ctrl key macros). Try either of these shortcuts instead:

✦ Assign macros to keyboards or toolbars (see Chapter 27, "Customizing Toolbars, Menus, and Keyboards").

✦ Click Tools ⇨ Macro, then select any of the last nine macros you played from the Macro submenu.

Managing Your Macro Collection

As with other files, macros are stored in directories. When you install WordPerfect, the program sets up a default macro directory where it places ready-made macros.

If you create numerous macros, you should set up a separate directory for them. Be sure to designate the directory as your default or supplemental macro directory (switch to the WordPerfect program window and click Preferences ⇨ Files ⇨ Macros/ Toolbar/Keyboard to specify the macro directories). With this strategy, you can always play your macros by name alone, without designating the path.

Adding Macro Programming Commands

In the preceding section, you learned how to create macro recordings of your actions that you can play back again and again. In this section, you examine how to enhance your macros with nonrecordable macro *programming commands*, using the previous examples.

Macro programming enables possibilities beyond simple macro recording. For example, you can prompt the user for input, evaluate expressions, perform calculations, and make decisions about what happens next in a macro, depending on some input or results.

Understanding Macro Commands

To begin, click Tools ➪ Macro ➪ Edit and open the letter-opening macro you created previously (myletter.wcm), just as you would open a document (see Figure 29-4).

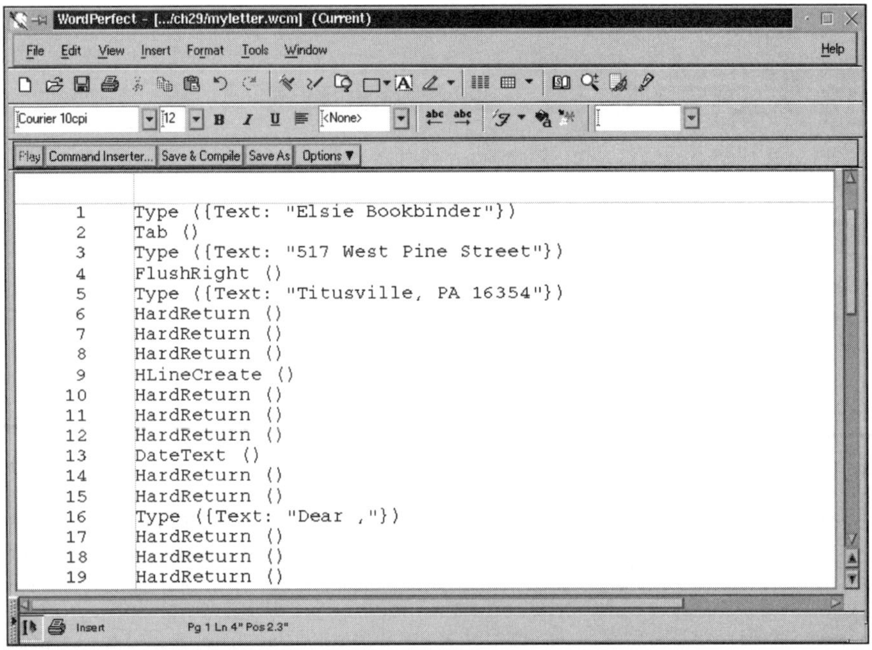
WordPerfect - [.../ch29/myletter.wcm] (Current)
File Edit View Insert Format Tools Window
Help
Courier 10cpi
12
<None>
Play Command Inserter... Save & Compile Save As Options
1 Type ({Text: "Elsie Bookbinder"})
2 Tab ()
3 Type ({Text: "517 West Pine Street"})
4 FlushRight ()
5 Type ({Text: "Titusville, PA 16354"})
6 HardReturn ()
7 HardReturn ()
8 HardReturn ()
9 HLineCreate ()
10 HardReturn ()
11 HardReturn ()
12 HardReturn ()
13 DateText ()
14 HardReturn ()
15 HardReturn ()
16 Type ({Text: "Dear ,"})
17 HardReturn ()
18 HardReturn ()
19 HardReturn ()
Insert
Pg 1 Ln 4" Pos 2.3"

Figure 29-4: Looking at your letter opening macro

Your macro differs, depending on your text and formatting. Examine line 5 in Figure 29-4:

```
Type ({Text: "Titusville, PA 16354"})
```

This line has:

✦ A *Command name* of “Type”

✦ A *Parameter*, in parentheses, of the particular characters to type

Some commands can have multiple parameters, such as:

```
Prompt (Title: string; [Prompt: string]; [Style: enumeration];
[HorizontalPosition: numeric]; [VerticalPosition: numeric])
```

In such cases, semicolon (;) *separators* are placed between parameters. Parameters in square brackets are optional. An *enumeration* parameter lets you specify two or more options, separated with |, such as "StopSign! | Beep!" for the Prompt parameter.

Sometimes, as with the TabSet parameter in your custom bullet macro, you can have a series of repeating parameters enclosed in braces ({}).

What's in a Macro?

A macro can contain various types of statements, including the following:

✦ *Programming Commands* to direct the execution of the macro. For example, you can use the Label command to identify a location in your macro, then use a Go command in another place to jump to the label.

✦ *WordPerfect Commands* that refer to specific WordPerfect functions. For example, you can use the ZoomToMarginWidth command to adjust the zoom settings in a macro.

✦ *System Variables* that you can query to obtain the current state of the environment. For example, ?MarginLeft returns the width of the left margin.

Using the Macro Command Inserter

You can type commands in your macros, just as in an ordinary document. Commands are not case-sensitive, but their wording must be precise. That's one of the reasons why QuickCorrect is suspended (in all your open documents) while you're editing a macro.

You can also use the *Macro Command Inserter* to insert or edit commands in their precise syntax. For practice, let's add some commands to the letter-heading macro you created previously:

1. Place the insertion point at the beginning of line 1 of the letter-heading macro.

2. Click "Command Inserter" on the Macro toolbar and select the WordPerfect commands from the "Command type" list (see Figure 29-5).

3. Type **filen** to select the FileNew command, double-click the command and click Insert (see Figure 29-6), then click Close.

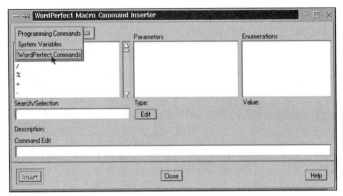

Figure 29-5: Displaying the WordPerfect commands

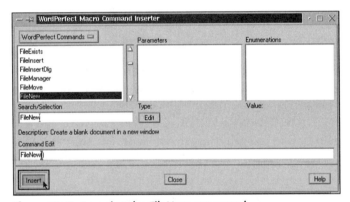

Figure 29-6: Inserting the FileNew command

4. Click "Save & Compile" to record your changes.

The FileNew command has the macro open a blank new document as soon as it starts, so it won't mess up an existing document on the screen. The *compile* part of the "Save & Compile" command puts your text commands into a language the machine can understand. (The text and machine code are in the same macro file — you read one part, your computer reads the other.)

Now make the macro even more useful by adding another command:

1. Click Tools ➪ Macro ➪ Edit and open the letter-heading macro.

2. Edit the macro to insert a pause where you can add the name of the person to which the letter will be sent, before the macro continues:

```
Type ({Text: "Dear "})
PauseKey(Key:Enter!)
Type ({Text:","})
```

Use the Command Inserter to make it easier to add the correct parameters to the PauseKey command (see Figure 29-7).

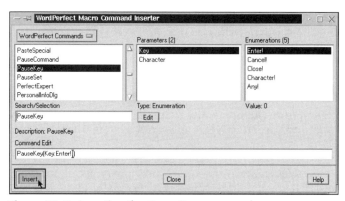

Figure 29-7: Inserting the PauseKey command

3. Click "Save & Compile" to record your changes.

Now when you run the macro, it pauses and waits for you to enter the recipient's name. After you enter the name, the macro creates the rest of the letter heading.

Executing a Command if a Condition Is Met

To get an idea of the cleverness and flexibility available with macros, use the If and EndIf programming commands to execute a command only if the conditional statement's test is true.

You just added the FileNew command to a macro to open a new blank document automatically. But suppose the screen is blank already? To avoid opening another blank screen:

1. Click Tools ➪ Macro ➪ Edit and open the macro containing the FileNew command.

2. Type the following three lines between lines 1 and 2, so that new lines 2–4 read as follows (type the number **0** in line 2):

```
2 If (?DocBlank = 0)
3 FileNew ()
4 EndIf
```

3. Click "Save & Compile" to record your changes.

Tip

You can format your macros with tabs, indents, blank lines, and so forth to make them easier to read. Except in specific instances, the formatting doesn't affect the execution of the macro.

Now your macro asks "Is it not true that the document is blank?" If it is not blank (0), a new blank document is opened. If it is blank (1), the "If" test is not met, so line 3 is skipped.

You can add to the fun with an If-Else-EndIf command sequence, where everything between the If and the Else is run if the test is met, and everything between the Else and the EndIf is run if the test is *not* met.

Waving a Flag

If your head isn't spinning from the preceding example, perhaps you're ready for more. (Again, these scenarios are macro examples, not systematic programming instructions.)

Returning to the custom bullets macro you created previously, recall how you can record the macro one way if you keep QuickBullets on normally, and another if you keep them off normally. However, you can't have it both ways. Well, you *can* have it both ways with programming commands:

1. Click Tools ➪ Macro ➪ Edit and open your custom bullet macro (see Figure 29-8). Don't be shocked ("Did I write all that?") by lines 1–40. Those lines compose one TabSet command—when you change one tab you reset them all.

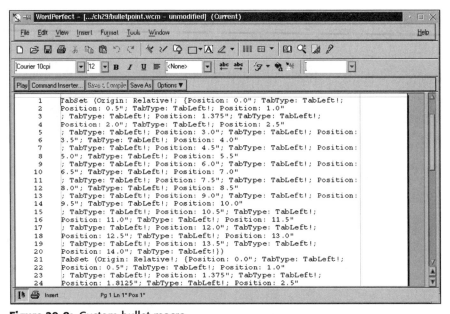

Figure 29-8: Custom bullet macro

2. Edit the macro so lines 1–4 read:

```
1 vFlag := ?QuickCorrectBulletListsQry
2 If (vFlag =0)
3 QuickCorrectBulletListsToggle(State:On!)
4 EndIf
```

3. At the end of macro, add these lines:

```
If (vFlag =0)
QuickCorrectBulletListsToggle(State:Off!)
EndIf
```

Line 1 defines a variable *flag* (an on/off switch to signal a particular condition or status) "vFlag." It then sets the flag to the result of the QuickBullets query command ("0" if off; "1" if on). The If-EndIf instructions in lines 2–4 turn on QuickBullets if they are currently off.

This sequence ensures that QuickBullets will always be on while the macro runs. But when the macro gets to the end, how does it know whether QuickBullets was on or off at the start? That's where your flag enters the picture. The last three lines at the end of your macro are identical to lines 2–4, but this time, if QuickBullets was *off* before you played the macro, the macro returns QuickBullets to off after completion.

Try these changes, both with QuickBullets on and off before you play the macro, and see what happens. (Exit the macro editor first — otherwise QuickBullets is automatically set to off.)

Getting Help on Writing Macros

You can do many more tasks with macro programming. WordPerfect's online help facility contains more information and examples:

1. Click Help ➪ Macros to open the online macros manual (see Figure 29-9).

2. Click the topic on which you want more information. The online macro reference tells you about macro programming and can help you build advanced macros that even display their own dialog boxes.

Figure 29-9: Getting online help in writing macros

For More Information . . .

On	See
Default keyboard assignments	Chapter 3
Assigning macros to keyboards, menus, and toolbars	Chapter 27
Using ExpressDocs	Chapter 20
Using the PerfectExperts	Chapter 5

✦   ✦   ✦

WordPerfect Settings Quick Reference

A *setting* is any element in your working environment that
stays put from session to session. Thus, a change to
the Current Document Style is not a setting, but a change to
the Initial Document Style is a setting because it affects future
documents. A change of keyboards or a customized shortcut
key is also a setting, as it stays put until you change it again.
A custom style or macro is not a setting, as it is only applied
when called. A custom page or envelope size is a borderline
case, as this size could become the new default.

WordPerfect has a large number of settings. While most of
the user settings discussed in this book are found among
WordPerfect's Preferences dialog boxes, many are not. The
user settings in Table A-1 show the chapter where the setting
is discussed, how to access the setting, and, where applicable,
the authors' recommended settings. Most settings can be
adjusted from the WordPerfect program window. For the items
that tell you to click Preferences, you have to switch to the
WordPerfect program window first. Table A-1 also shows the
KDE desktop settings discussed in Chapter 3.

Table A-1
WordPerfect User Settings Quick Reference

Setting	Chapter	How to Access It	Recommended Setting
Administrator settings	26	Preferences ⇨ Administration (requires the -adm startup option)	
Application bar, customizing	26	Right-click application bar, click Settings	
Backup, folder	6, 26	Preferences ⇨ Files ⇨ Documents/Backup	
Bar display	3, 27	View ⇨ Toolbars	
Beeps, program	26	Preferences ⇨ Environment	
Codes, deleting the old DOS way	26	Preferences ⇨ Environment ⇨ "Confirm deletion of codes..."	Leave unchecked
Color settings	26	Preferences ⇨ Colors	
Comment display	13	Preferences ⇨ Display ⇨ Document	Check to see comments
Comment and summary user information	13, 26	Preferences ⇨ Environment	
Convert settings	26	Preferences ⇨ Convert	
Cursor, blinking	27	Preferences ⇨ Display ⇨ Document	
Desktop (KDE)	3	K ⇨ Panel Configure ⇨ Options	Autohide taskbar and panel
Display mode	3, 26	Preferences ⇨ Display ⇨ View/Zoom	
Document backup	6	Preferences ⇨ Files ⇨ Documents/Backup	Timed every ten minutes; no original backup
Document, default extension	26	Preferences ⇨ Files ⇨ Documents/Backup	Leave default .wpd
Document defaults, setting	15	Format ⇨ Styles ⇨ InitialStyle ⇨ Edit ⇨ "Use as default"	

Setting	Chapter	How to Access It	Recommended Setting
Document folder, default	26	Preferences ➪ Files ➪ Documents/Backup	The one you use the most
Document summary configuration	7	File ➪ Properties ➪ Document Summary ➪ Configure ➪ Use as Default	
Directory, default document	26	Preferences ➪ Files ➪ Documents/Backup	
Document summary (automatic) settings	7, 26	Preferences ➪ Summary	Normally leave options unchecked
Endnote options	18	Insert ➪ Endnote ➪ Options	
Envelopes, custom sizes	10	Format ➪ Envelope ➪ Create New Definition	
Envelope options	10	Format ➪ Envelope ➪ Options	
ExpressDoc templates directory	20, 26	Preferences ➪ Files ➪ ExpressDocs	
File-management display	7	File ➪ Open ➪ Display ➪ Change File Manager Setup	
Fast Search indexes (configuring)	7	File ➪ Open ➪ QuickFinder ➪ Indexer ➪ Indexer Options ➪ Preferences	
Fast Search settings	7	File ➪ Open ➪ QuickFinder ➪ Options	
File locking	26	Preferences ➪ File Locking (requires the -adm startup option)	
Find and Replace options	13	Edit ➪ Find and Replace ➪ Options	
Fonts directory	8, 26	Preferences ➪ Files ➪ Graphics Fonts	
Font, document and printer default	15	File ➪ Document ➪ Default Font	

Continued

Table A-1 (*continued*)

Setting	*Chapter*	*How to Access It*	*Recommended Setting*
Font preferences	26	Preferences ⇨ Font	
Footnote options	18	Insert ⇨ Endnote ⇨ Options	
Format-As-You-Go options	4	Tools ⇨ QuickCorrect ⇨ Format-As-You-Go	
Grammatik, customizing checking styles	12	Tools ⇨ Grammatik ⇨ Options ⇨ Writing Style	
Grammatik options	12	Tools ⇨ Grammatik ⇨ Options	
Graphical banner and Startup screen display	26	Preferences ⇨ Environment	
Graphics display	26	Preferences ⇨ Display ⇨ Document	
Graphics folders, default	26	Preferences ⇨ Files ⇨ Graphics	
Guideline display	4	View ⇨ Guidelines	
Hidden text display	13	Preferences ⇨ Display ⇨ Document	Leave unchecked (hidden) and turn on from View menu when you need to see it
Hyperlink activate option	26	Preferences ⇨ Environment	Check
Hyphenation prompt option	14	Preferences ⇨ Environment	When Required
Hyphenation zone, setting	14	Tools ⇨ Language ⇨ Hyphenation	
Keyboard, creating and customizing	27	Preferences ⇨ Keyboard	
Keyboard, selecting	3,27	Preferences ⇨ Keyboard	
KDE desktop	3	K ⇨ Panel ⇨ Configure ⇨ Options	Autohide taskbar and panel

Setting	Chapter	How to Access It	Recommended Setting
KDE menu	3	K ⇨ Panel ⇨ Edit Menus	
Label file and default labels display	28	Preferences Files ⇨ Printers/Labels	Set default labels display to your type of printer
Language tools, selecting	12	Tools ⇨ Language ⇨ Settings	
Macro file settings	26	Preferences ⇨ Files ⇨ Macros/Toolbar/ Keyboard	
Menu display options	26	Preferences ⇨ Environment	Display documents and Quick Tips (view shortcut keys in Quick Tips)
Menu (KDE)	3	K ⇨ Panel ⇨ Edit Menus	
Merge codes display options	26	Preferences ⇨ Display ⇨ Merge	Display codes (setting can be changed during merge)
Mouse, select words with	2, 26	Preferences ⇨ Environment	Check "Select whole words instead of characters"
Page, custom definition	15	File ⇨ Page Setup ⇨ Page Size ⇨ Create	
Page size and orientation	10	File ⇨ Page Setup ⇨ Page Size	
Print, custom settings	10,26	Preferences ⇨ Print	
Print resolution and color	10	Preferences ⇨ Print	
Printing restrictions	26	Preferences ⇨ Print Restrictions (requires the -adm startup option)	
Prompt-As-You-Go	2	Tools ⇨ Proofread	Check unless it slows your computer
Printer, adding	10	File ⇨ Print ⇨ Select ⇨ Printer Create/Edit	
Printer, selecting and configuring	11	File ⇨ Print ⇨ Select	
Property bars, customizing	27	Right-click property bar, click Settings	
Property bar display	3, 27	Right-click property bar, click Settings ⇨ Options	

Continued

Table A-1 (*continued*)			
Setting	**Chapter**	**How to Access It**	**Recommended Setting**
Proofreading-As-You-Go	2, 12	Tools ⇨ Proofread	Grammar-As-You-Go
QuickCorrect options	2	Tools ⇨ QuickCorrect	
QuickCorrect	2	Tools ⇨ QuickCorrect, "Replace words as you type" replacement (on/off)	
QuickLinks	11	Tools ⇨ QuickCorrect ⇨ QuickLinks	
Quicklist, adding to	7	File ⇨ Open ⇨ Quicklist	
Quicklist, update with changes option	26	Preferences ⇨ Files ⇨ Documents/Backup	Leave unchecked
QuickMark, set on save/go to on open	4	Tools ⇨ Bookmark	
QuickTips display	26	Preferences ⇨ Environment	
Redline method, changing	13, 26	File ⇨ Document ⇨ Redline Method, Preferences ⇨ Fonts	
Reformat document for default printer option	26	Preferences ⇨ Environment	Leave checked
Relative font sizes	26	Preferences ⇨ Font	
Reveal Codes display options	26	Preferences ⇨ Display ⇨ Reveal Codes	Wrap lines, show spaces as bullets, show codes in detail
Ruler options	26	Preferences ⇨ Display ⇨ Ruler Bar	Check both options
Save workspace options	26	Preferences ⇨ Environment	
Scroll bar display	3, 26	Tools ⇨ Settings ⇨ Display ⇨ Document	Vertical
Sentence correction options	4	Tools ⇨ QuickCorrect ⇨ Format-As-You-Go	

Setting	Chapter	How to Access It	Recommended Setting
Shadow cursor display	3, 26	Preferences ⇨ Display	Active in Both
SmartQuotes (on/off)	4	Tools ⇨ QuickCorrect ⇨ SmartQuotes	
Spell Check options	12	Tools ⇨ Spell Check ⇨ Options	
Spreadsheet files	26	Preferences ⇨ Files ⇨ Spreadsheets	
Style libraries	20	Preferences ⇨ Files ⇨ Styles	
Symbol display options	26	Preferences ⇨ Display ⇨ Show @symbols	
Table formulas, confirm deletion of	26	Preferences ⇨ Environment	Leave checked
Table gridline display	26	Preferences ⇨ Display ⇨ Document	Leave unchecked, turn on and off from View menu
Table position, default	16	Table ⇨ Format ⇨ Table	
Table, auto calculation	21	Table ⇨ Calculate	Calculate Table
Template (Express Doc) directory	20, 26	Preferences ⇨ Files ⇨ ExpressDocs	
Toolbars, creating and customizing	27	Right-click toolbar, click Settings	
Toolbar display	27	Right-click toolbar, click Settings ⇨ Options	
Toolbar, selecting	27	Right-click toolbar	
Typos, correcting automatically	12	Tools ⇨ QuickCorrect	Check "Correct other mistyped words when possible" (except for scientific writing)
Undo/Redo options	6	Edit ⇨ Undo/Redo History ⇨ Options	
Units of measure	26	Preferences ⇨ Display ⇨ Documents	
View/Zoom, default	3, 26	Preferences ⇨ Display ⇨ View/Zoom	Experiment to find the view and zoom with which you're comfortable

Continued

Table A-1 *(continued)*			
Setting	*Chapter*	*How to Access It*	*Recommended Setting*
Warning beep options		Preferences ➪ Environment	
Word lists, creating	12	Tools ➪ Spell Check ➪ Dictionaries	
Writing tools, disabling	12	Tools ➪ Language ➪ Settings	

✦   ✦   ✦

WordPerfect and Linux Links

As discussed in Chapter 5, "Getting Help," the Internet is an invaluable source of comprehensive, up-to-date information and support. If you want to know more about using WordPerfect, available product updates, your Linux distribution, the KDE desktop environment, or anything else, the Internet is the place to look.

Above all, subscribe to the free support newsgroups at `cnews.corel.com` and join in the lively discussions. No matter what your question — from the most basic to the most obscure — you'll get friendly advice from WordPerfect experts, and, more often than not, two or three alternate solutions!

Note   The authors of this book appreciate e-mail from readers, but they are unable to handle individual queries. Even if they could, the newsgroups are still a better bet, as you'll find experts there in every specialized issue.

WordPerfect 8 for Linux

Check out these links for specific help in using and maintaining WordPerfect for Linux. Above all, subscribe to the newsgroup!

Fonts and printers information	`http://www.channel1.com/users/rodsmith/wpfonts.html`
Macros, manual WordPerfect 8 (Windows)	`http://www.corel.com/support/suite8manuals/macros2`
Macros, WordPerfect Universe	`http://www.wpwin.com`
Printer drivers	`http://www.corel.com/support/printerdrivers/index.htm`
QwkScreen's WordPerfect Information and Tips	`http://www.qwkscreen.com`
WordPerfect 8 for Linux home page	`http://linux.corel.com/linux8/index.htm`
WordPerfect 8 for Linux news	`http://linux.corel.com/linux8/news.htm`
WordPerfect for Linux Newsgroup	`news://cnews.corel.com/corelsupport.wordperfect-linux`

Corel Help and Information

For general support, updates, and the latest information, check out these Corel links. In particular, check out the Knowledge Base used by Corel's support technicians, with its wealth of detailed information on WordPerfect features and solutions to customer problems. (Most of the WordPerfect for Windows information applies to WordPerfect for Linux as well.)

Contact Corel	`http://www.corel.com/contact/index.htm`
Corel Linux Desktop	`http://www.corel.com/news/1999/march/march_2a_1999.htm`
Customer service	`http://www.corel.com/support/customer/index.htm`
FTP site, main	`ftp://ftp.corel.com`
Home page	`http://www.corel.com`

Knowledge Base, all applications	`http://kb.corel.com/search`
Linux home page	`http://linux.corel.com`
Newsgroups server	`news://cnews.corel.com`
Newsgroups, guidelines for use	`http://www.corel.com/` `support/newsgroup.htm`

Product feedback	`https://livewire.corel.com/`
	`cfscripts/Feedback_forms/`
	`feedback.htm`

Purchasing products online	`http://www.corel.com/` `galleria/reference`
Support home page	`http://www.corel.com/` `support/index.htm`

Linux Distributions

While the latest Linux kernel and many supporting programs can always be downloaded for free, most users opt for a convenient package distribution, complete with an installation program, tools, applications, documentation, and limited support. Here are links to the main third-party distributors.

Linux, distributions and FTP sites	`http://www.linux.org/` `dist/index.html`
Caldera OpenLinux	`http://www.calderasystems.com`
Debian Linux	`http://www.debian.org`
Red Hat	`http://www.redhat.com`
Slackware Linux	`http://www.cdrom.com`
S.u.S.E. Linux	`http://www.suse.com`

KDE Software and Support

This book's CD includes the popular KDE software desktop environment in which you can run WordPerfect for Linux. Head to these KDE links for the latest news, updates, and instructions.

KDE	`http://www.kde.org`
KDE downloads	`ftp://ftp.kde.org/pub/kde`

| KDE FAQ | `http://www.kde.org/faq/kdefaq.html` |
| KDE news | `http://www.kde.org/news_dyn.html` |

Linux Distribution Centers

WordPerfect is just one of the growing number of applications (many of them free) available for the Linux environment. These links take you to some of the major distribution centers.

FreshMeat	`http://ny.us.mirrors.freshmeat.net/`
Gnome Software Map	`http://www.gnome.org/applist/list.phtml`
Linux Applications	`http://www.linuxapps.com`
Linuxberg	`http://www.linuxberg.net`
Linux Center	`http://www.linux-center.org/en/applications/index.html`
Red Hat applications, Red Hat list	`http://www.redhat.com/appindex/index.html`

Linux Documentation

In the spirit of open source, there's a growing amount of Linux documentation available for free. Use these links to find excellent help and instructions.

Linux Documentation Project	`http://metalab.unc.edu/mdw`
Linux Help Center	`http://www.linux.org/help/index.html`
Linux Help Menu	`http://home.earthlink.net/~pandsl/unix/Linux/linuxhelp.html`
Linux manuals, PPP, SLIP, Serial, Modems, etc.	`http://help-site.com/c.m/linux/pppslip`
Linux, mini how to	`http://www.linux.org/help/minihowto.html`

Linux, newbies, basic training bookmarks	http://basiclinux. hypermart.net/ basic/bookmarks.html
Linux Org, how to	http://www.linux.org/ help/howto.html
Linux, resources	http://www.linux-center.org/en
RedHat Portal	http://www.redhat.com/ linuxindex/index.html

Linux News

The Linux world is an exciting place. Here are some places to check out what's happening.

Linux.com	http://www.linux.com
Linux Gazette	http://www.linuxgazette.com
Linux Online	http://www.linux.org
Linux Today	http://linuxtoday.com
Linux Weekly News	http://lwn.net
Linux World	http://www.linuxworldexpo.com
Slashdot.org	http://www.slashdot.org
ZDNet Linux Lounge	http://www.zdnet.co.uk/ news/specials/1998/10/ linux_lounge

Other Interesting Links

As you get into Linux, you may want to examine some of these resources and cutting-edge projects.

Double-booting Linux and Windows	http://www.zdnet.com/zdhelp/ stories/main/0,5594, 2218754-1,00.html
FIPS, nondestructive disk splitter	http://www.igd.fhg.de/ ~aschaefe/fips
Gimp, powerful graphics manipulation software	http://www.gimp.org

Gnome, open source graphical desktop environment	`http://www.gnome.org`
GNU project, delivers many of the open source tools and applications included in a Linux distribution	`http://www.gnu.org`
Linux newsgroups	`http://www.iinet.com.au/ ~pdcruze/Resources/linux. news.html`
Linux user groups	`http://www.linuxlinks.com/ UserGroups/index.shtml`
Ranish Partition Manager, free partition manager	`http://www.ml.brooklyn. cuny.edu/~mranish/part`
RedHat list of supported hardware	`http://www.redhat.com/ LinuxIndex/Hardware`
Unix/Linux graphics handling	`http://www.graphics- muse.org/cgi-bin/muse.pl`
Wine open source interface project to port the Windows applications of Corel and others over to Linux	`http://www.winehq.com`
XFree86, free X-Window Server included in many distributions	`http://www.xfree86.org`

Links to Linux Links

You want more links? Hop over to these sites to continue!

Corel's Linux links	`http://linux.corel.com/ links.htm`
Linux Center	`http://www.linux-center.org/en`
Linux Links	`http://www.linuxlinks.com`
Open Directory Project	`http://dmoz.org/Computers/ Operating_Systems/Linux`
Paul E. Merrell's alphabetic listing	`http://n9vst.com/pem/ wplinux.html`
Linux Web Ring	`http://nll.interl.net/lwr`

✦   ✦   ✦

What's on the CD?

You really won't find a bigger bargain than this combination of *WordPerfect for Linux Bible* and the Personal Edition of WordPerfect 8 for Linux software. Mix in the latest KDE desktop environment and a printable listing of the fonts on your CD, and you're ready to do some serious work in Linux!

Installing WordPerfect for Linux Personal Edition

The full Personal Edition of WordPerfect 8 for Linux on this book's CD offers a powerful office solution with an amazing array of features.

Minimum system requirements to install and use WordPerfect 8 for Linux:

- ✦ X86 processor; 486 DX 33 or higher (Pentium processor or higher recommended)
- ✦ Linux release 2.0 or higher
- ✦ libc5 properly installed
- ✦ X-Windows installed and configured properly
- ✦ 9MB memory for first user
- ✦ 43MB to 87MB hard-disk space
- ✦ 32MB swap space

Complete installation instructions can be found in Chapter 1, "Getting Up and Running." (The registration number for the software on this book's CD is located in a text file ("Registration Key") on the CD itself.) If you've already installed a Linux distribution, you'll be using WordPerfect before you know it.

If you're already using the free download version of WordPerfect 8 for Linux, install the Personal Edition software to enjoy additional features, including drawing and charting tools, the equation editor, ExpressDoc templates, the font installer, and a large number of fonts and graphics. (To remove the download version of WP 8 for Linux before installing the Personal Edition, just delete the WP directories and the .wprc directory.)

Installing KDE Desktop Environment

As discussed in Chapter 1, "Getting Up and Running," KDE (the K Desktop Environment) provides an ideal desktop platform for running WordPerfect for Linux. It comes with a powerful X-Window manager and tons of applications, including a file manager, an extended help system, a text editor, viewers, an organizer, a CD player, an e-mail client, a news reader, and lots of games. You name it, it's there!

KDE runs on all the major Linux distributions. The X86 version of KDE 1.1 for Red Hat 5.1/5.2 is located on this book's CD in the KDE Red Hat directory. The Red Hat KDE installation involves the execution of three scripts, as described in the accompanying README file.

If you're running another Linux distribution, such as S.u.S.E, Caldera, Debian, or Slackware, go to the KDE Web site at http://www.kde.org for information on the free version of KDE 1.1 that runs on your system. The latest KDE distribution files can be downloaded from ftp://ftp.kde.org/pub/kde/stable/latest/distribution/.

Please note that KDE is *not* required to run WordPerfect 8 for Linux. Any X-Window manager or X desktop environment can be used.

If you have more questions about KDE, check out the latest KDE FAQ at http://www.kde.org/faq/kdefaq.html.

Installing and Using the WordPerfect 8 for Linux Fonts

Once you have WordPerfect 8 for Linux installed, turn to Chapter 8, "Fonts Fantastic," for instructions on installing the almost 150 high-quality Type 1 fonts located on your *WordPerfect for Linux Bible* CD.

After your fonts are installed, switch to WordPerfect and open the document Linux Fonts.wpd on the CD to display and print examples of the almost 150 fonts.

✦   ✦   ✦

Index

continued

Not equal to operator, 450
NOT operator, 450, 451
NPV function, 448
number formats, 522, 523
Number of Copies for Each Record option, 598
Number of Spaces between List Columns option, 117
numbered lists, 75, 205
    changing the numbering of, 343
    creating, 341-343
Numbering command, 289, 315
Numbering method option, 290, 360
Numbers layout, 345
Numeric Format command, 434
numeric formats, 434-437
numeric keypad, 63

O

objects
    applying effects to, 180
    arranging the order of, 178
    copying, 177
    creating, 179-180
    in the Drawing window, 179-180
    editing, 177
    flipping, 179
    grouping, 178-179
    moving, 177
    overlapping, 178
    reshaping, 177-178
    rotating, 167, 179
    sizing, 177, 180
    skewing, 179, 180
    text, 179-180
    types of, 173
Off codes, 424
one-and-a-half spacing, 287
ON/OFF separator comment, 424
Open button, 111
Open command, 104, 108, 111, 112, 115, 129, 414
Open dialog box, 109, 117, 118, 119, 183
Open File dialog box, 104
open source operating system, 3
Open Window option, 112
OPENDOC.FRM, 612, 613
operators
    arithmetic, 442, 449-450
    creating extraction statements with, 479
    logical, 442, 449-450
    order of precedence for, 451
    text search, 126-127
Options button, 598
Options dialog box, 129
Options menu, 224, 248-256, 350, 517-518, 525, 526, 528, 534
Options tab, 59
OR operator, 450, 477, 479
order of precedence, 451
ordinal numbers, 76
Original Document Backup option, 556
orphans, 265
OS/2 Bitmap file format, 152
Other Codes command, 283
Other palette, 502

Outline Display Icons button, 348
Outline Down Arrow button, 347
Outline Hide Body Text button, 347
Outline Hide Family button, 347
Outline layout, 345, 350
Outline Left Arrow button, 347
Outline Right Arrow button, 347
Outline Set Paragraph Number button, 348
Outline Show Family button, 347
Outline Show Levels button, 347
Outline Tools toolbar, 349
Outline Up Arrow button, 347
outlines
    changing levels in, 346-347
    heading and, 349
    hiding
    layouts for, 349-352
    levels of, 347
    styles for, 349-352
    terminology for, 344-346
    working with, 346-352
Output File box, 478
Output File button, 597
Output File command, 594
Output File list, 582
Output Options command, 188
Output Options dialog box, 185, 188
Overlap style, 531
overlapping objects, 178
overwriting files, 566

P

Page anchor, 163
page breaks
    columns and, 311
    endnotes and, 357
    hard, 263
    inserting, 263, 311
    lists and, 364
page down button, 48
Page Layout command, 381
Page Numbering button, 300
Page Numbering command, 265, 266, 268, 269, 408
Page Numbering option, 377
Page Size command, 187, 191, 296
Page Source command, 207
Page up button, 48
Page view, 57, 61, 253, 263, 296, 300, 302, 317, 355, 356, 496
Page width option, 62
PAGEOFF, 605, 614
PAGEON, 605
pages
    borders for, 496
    creating definitions for, 297-298
    customizing, 293-298
    fills for, 496
    forcing new, 263, 270
    numbering, 187, 265-272, 408
    orientation settings for, 296-297
    printing multiple, 181-186
    size settings for, 296-297
    specified number of, sizing documents to fit, 77-83

IDG BOOKS WORLDWIDE, INC.
END-USER LICENSE AGREEMENT

<u>**READ THIS.**</u> You should carefully read these terms and conditions before opening the software packet(s) included with this book ("Book"). This is a license agreement ("Agreement") between you and IDG Books Worldwide, Inc. ("IDGB"). By opening the accompanying software packet(s), you acknowledge that you have read and accept the following terms and conditions. If you do not agree and do not want to be bound by such terms and conditions, promptly return the Book and the unopened software packet(s) to the place you obtained them for a full refund.

1. <u>**License Grant.**</u> IDGB grants to you (either an individual or entity) a nonexclusive license to use one copy of the enclosed software program(s) (collectively, the "Software") solely for your own personal or business purposes on a single computer (whether a standard computer or a workstation component of a multiuser network). The Software is in use on a computer when it is loaded into temporary memory (RAM) or installed into permanent memory (hard disk, CD-ROM, or other storage device). IDGB reserves all rights not expressly granted herein.

2. <u>**Ownership.**</u> IDGB is the owner of all right, title, and interest, including copyright, in and to the compilation of the Software recorded on the disk(s) or CD-ROM ("Software Media"). Copyright to the individual programs recorded on the Software Media is owned by the author or other authorized copyright owner of each program. Ownership of the Software and all proprietary rights relating thereto remain with IDGB and its licensers.

3. <u>**Restrictions On Use and Transfer.**</u>

   (a) You may only (i) make one copy of the Software for backup or archival purposes, or (ii) transfer the Software to a single hard disk, provided that you keep the original for backup or archival purposes. You may not (i) rent or lease the Software, (ii) copy or reproduce the Software through a LAN or other network system or through any computer subscriber system or bulletin-board system, or (iii) modify, adapt, or create derivative works based on the Software.

   (b) You may not reverse engineer, decompile, or disassemble the Software. You may transfer the Software and user documentation on a permanent basis, provided that the transferee agrees to accept the terms and conditions of this Agreement and you retain no copies. If the Software is an update or has been updated, any transfer must include the most recent update and all prior versions.

4. <u>**Restrictions on Use of Individual Programs.**</u> You must follow the individual requirements and restrictions detailed for each individual program in Appendix C of this Book. These limitations are also contained in the individual license agreements recorded on the Software Media. These limitations may include a requirement that after using the program for a specified period of time, the user must pay a registration fee or discontinue use. By opening the Software packet(s), you will be agreeing to abide by the licenses and restrictions for these individual programs that are detailed in Appendix C and on the Software Media. None of the material on this Software Media or listed in this Book may ever be redistributed, in original or modified form, for commercial purposes.

5. Limited Warranty.

(a) IDGB warrants that the Software and Software Media are free from defects in materials and workmanship under normal use for a period of sixty (60) days from the date of purchase of this Book. If IDGB receives notification within the warranty period of defects in materials or workmanship, IDGB will replace the defective Software Media.

(b) IDGB AND THE AUTHORS OF THE BOOK DISCLAIM ALL OTHER WARRANTIES, EXPRESS OR IMPLIED, INCLUDING WITHOUT LIMITATION IMPLIED WARRANTIES OF MERCHANTABILITY AND FITNESS FOR A PARTICULAR PURPOSE, WITH RESPECT TO THE SOFTWARE, THE PROGRAMS, THE SOURCE CODE CONTAINED THEREIN, AND/OR THE TECHNIQUES DESCRIBED IN THIS BOOK. IDGB DOES NOT WARRANT THAT THE FUNCTIONS CONTAINED IN THE SOFTWARE WILL MEET YOUR REQUIREMENTS OR THAT THE OPERATION OF THE SOFTWARE WILL BE ERROR-FREE.

(c) This limited warranty gives you specific legal rights, and you may have other rights that vary from jurisdiction to jurisdiction.

6. Remedies.

(a) IDGB's entire liability and your exclusive remedy for defects in materials and workmanship shall be limited to replacement of the Software Media, which may be returned to IDGB with a copy of your receipt at the following address: Software Media Fulfillment Department, Attn.: *WordPerfect for Linux Bible*, IDG Books Worldwide, Inc., 7260 Shadeland Station, Ste. 100, Indianapolis, IN 46256, or call 1-800-762-2974. Please allow three to four weeks for delivery. This Limited Warranty is void if failure of the Software Media has resulted from accident, abuse, or misapplication. Any replacement Software Media will be warranted for the remainder of the original warranty period or thirty (30) days, whichever is longer.

(b) In no event shall IDGB or the authors be liable for any damages whatsoever (including without limitation damages for loss of business profits, business interruption, loss of business information, or any other pecuniary loss) arising from the use of or inability to use the Book or the Software, even if IDGB has been advised of the possibility of such damages.

(c) Because some jurisdictions do not allow the exclusion or limitation of liability for consequential or incidental damages, the above limitation or exclusion may not apply to you.

7. U.S. Government Restricted Rights.
Use, duplication, or disclosure of the Software by the U.S. Government is subject to restrictions stated in paragraph (c)(1)(ii) of the Rights in Technical Data and Computer Software clause of DFARS 252.227-7013, and in subparagraphs (a) through (d) of the Commercial Computer — Restricted Rights clause at FAR 52.227-19, and in similar clauses in the NASA FAR supplement, when applicable.

8. General.
This Agreement constitutes the entire understanding of the parties and revokes and supersedes all prior agreements, oral or written, between them and may not be modified or amended except in a writing signed by both parties hereto that specifically refers to this Agreement. This Agreement shall take precedence over any other documents that may be in conflict herewith. If any one or more provisions contained in this Agreement are held by any court or tribunal to be invalid, illegal, or otherwise unenforceable, each and every other provision shall remain in full force and effect.

GNU GENERAL PUBLIC LICENSE

Version 2, June 1991

Preamble

The licenses for most software are designed to take away your freedom to share and change it. By contrast, the GNU General Public License is intended to guarantee your freedom to share and change free software—to make sure the software is free for all its users. This General Public License applies to most of the Free Software Foundation's software and to any other program whose authors commit to using it. (Some other Free Software Foundation software is covered by the GNU Library General Public License instead.) You can apply it to your programs, too.

When we speak of free software, we are referring to freedom, not price. Our General Public Licenses are designed to make sure that you have the freedom to distribute copies of free software (and charge for this service if you wish), that you receive source code or can get it if you want it, that you can change the software or use pieces of it in new free programs; and that you know you can do these things.

To protect your rights, we need to make restrictions that forbid anyone to deny you these rights or to ask you to surrender the rights. These restrictions translate to certain responsibilities for you if you distribute copies of the software, or if you modify it.

For example, if you distribute copies of such a program, whether gratis or for a fee, you must give the recipients all the rights that you have. You must make sure that they, too, receive or can get the source code. And you must show them these terms so they know their rights.

We protect your rights with two steps: (1) copyright the software, and (2) offer you this license which gives you legal permission to copy, distribute and/or modify the software.

Also, for each author's protection and ours, we want to make certain that everyone understands that there is no warranty for this free software. If the software is modified by someone else and passed on, we want its recipients to know that what they have is not the original, so that any problems introduced by others will not reflect on the original authors' reputations.

Finally, any free program is threatened constantly by software patents. We wish to avoid the danger that redistributors of a free program will individually obtain patent licenses, in effect making the program proprietary. To prevent this, we have made it clear that any patent must be licensed for everyone's free use or not licensed at all.

The precise terms and conditions for copying, distribution and modification follow.

TERMS AND CONDITIONS FOR COPYING, DISTRIBUTION AND MODIFICATION

0. This License applies to any program or other work which contains a notice placed by the copyright holder saying it may be distributed under the terms of this General Public License. The "Program", below, refers to any such program or work, and a "work based on the Program" means either the Program or any derivative work under copyright law: that is to say, a work containing the Program or a portion of it, either verbatim or with modifications and/or translated into another language. (Hereinafter, translation is included without limitation in the term "modification".) Each licensee is addressed as "you".

Activities other than copying, distribution and modification are not covered by this License; they are outside its scope. The act of running the Program is not restricted, and the output from the Program is covered only if its contents constitute a work based on the Program (independent of having been made by running the Program). Whether that is true depends on what the Program does.

1. You may copy and distribute verbatim copies of the Program's source code as you receive it, in any medium, provided that you conspicuously and appropriately publish on each copy an appropriate copyright notice and disclaimer of warranty; keep intact all the notices that refer to this License and to the absence of any warranty; and give any other recipients of the Program a copy of this License along with the Program.

You may charge a fee for the physical act of transferring a copy, and you may at your option offer warranty protection in exchange for a fee.

2. You may modify your copy or copies of the Program or any portion of it, thus forming a work based on the Program, and copy and distribute such modifications or work under the terms of Section 1 above, provided that you also meet all of these conditions:

a) You must cause the modified files to carry prominent notices stating that you changed the files and the date of any change.

b) You must cause any work that you distribute or publish, that in whole or in part contains or is derived from the Program or any part thereof, to be licensed as a whole at no charge to all third parties under the terms of this License.

c) If the modified program normally reads commands interactively when run, you must cause it, when started running for such interactive use in the most ordinary way, to print or display an announcement including an appropriate copyright notice and a notice that there is no warranty (or else, saying that you provide a warranty) and that users may redistribute the program under these conditions, and telling the user how to view a copy of this License. (Exception: if the Program itself is interactive but does not normally print such an announcement, your work based on the Program is not required to print an announcement.)

These requirements apply to the modified work as a whole. If identifiable sections of that work are not derived from the Program, and can be reasonably considered independent and separate works in themselves, then this License, and its terms, do not apply to those sections when you distribute them as separate works. But when you distribute the same sections as part of a whole which is a work based on the Program, the distribution of the whole must be on the terms of this License, whose permissions for other licensees extend to the entire whole, and thus to each and every part regardless of who wrote it.

Thus, it is not the intent of this section to claim rights or contest your rights to work written entirely by you; rather, the intent is to exercise the right to control the distribution of derivative or collective works based on the Program.

In addition, mere aggregation of another work not based on the Program with the Program (or with a work based on the Program) on a volume of a storage or distribution medium does not bring the other work under the scope of this License.

3. You may copy and distribute the Program (or a work based on it, under Section 2) in object code or executable form under the terms of Sections 1 and 2 above provided that you also do one of the following:

   a) Accompany it with the complete corresponding machine-readable source code, which must be distributed under the terms of Sections 1 and 2 above on a medium customarily used for software interchange; or,

   b) Accompany it with a written offer, valid for at least three years, to give any third party, for a charge no more than your cost of physically performing source distribution, a complete machine-readable copy of the corresponding source code, to be distributed under the terms of Sections 1 and 2 above on a medium customarily used for software interchange; or,

   c) Accompany it with the information you received as to the offer to distribute corresponding source code. (This alternative is allowed only for noncommercial distribution and only if you received the program in object code or executable form with such an offer, in accord with Subsection b above.)

The source code for a work means the preferred form of the work for making modifications to it. For an executable work, complete source code means all the source code for all modules it contains, plus any associated interface definition files, plus the scripts used to control compilation and installation of the executable.

However, as a special exception, the source code distributed need not include anything that is normally distributed (in either source or binary form) with the major components (compiler, kernel, and so on) of the operating system on which the executable runs, unless that component itself accompanies the executable.

If distribution of executable or object code is made by offering access to copy from a designated place, then offering equivalent access to copy the source code from the same place counts as distribution of the source code, even though third parties are not compelled to copy the source along with the object code.

4. You may not copy, modify, sublicense, or distribute the Program except as expressly provided under this License. Any attempt otherwise to copy, modify, sublicense or distribute the Program is void, and will automatically terminate your rights under this License. However, parties who have received copies, or rights, from you under this License will not have their licenses terminated so long as such parties remain in full compliance.

5. You are not required to accept this License, since you have not signed it. However, nothing else grants you permission to modify or distribute the Program or its derivative works. These actions are prohibited by law if you do not accept this License. Therefore, by modifying or distributing the Program (or any work based on the Program), you indicate your acceptance of this License to do so, and all its terms and conditions for copying, distributing or modifying the Program or works based on it.

6. Each time you redistribute the Program (or any work based on the Program), the recipient automatically receives a license from the original licensor to copy, distribute or modify the Program subject to these terms and conditions. You may not impose any further restrictions on the recipients' exercise of the rights granted herein. You are not responsible for enforcing compliance by third parties to this License.

7. If, as a consequence of a court judgment or allegation of patent infringement or for any other reason (not limited to patent issues), conditions are imposed on you (whether by court order, agreement or otherwise) that contradict the conditions of this License, they do not excuse you from the conditions of this License. If you cannot distribute so as to satisfy simultaneously your obligations under this License and any other pertinent obligations, then as a consequence you may not distribute the Program at all. For example, if a patent license would not permit royalty-free redistribution of the Program by all those who receive copies directly or indirectly through you, then the only way you could satisfy both it and this License would be to refrain entirely from distribution of the Program.

If any portion of this section is held invalid or unenforceable under any particular circumstance, the balance of the section is intended to apply and the section as a whole is intended to apply in other circumstances.

It is not the purpose of this section to induce you to infringe any patents or other property right claims or to contest validity of any such claims; this section has the sole purpose of protecting the integrity of the free software distribution system, which is implemented by public license practices. Many people have made generous contributions to the wide range of software distributed through that system in reliance on consistent application of that system; it is up to the author/donor to decide if he or she is willing to distribute software through any other system and a licensee cannot impose that choice.

This section is intended to make thoroughly clear what is believed to be a consequence of the rest of this License.

8. If the distribution and/or use of the Program is restricted in certain countries either by patents or by copyrighted interfaces, the original copyright holder who places the Program under this License may add an explicit geographical distribution limitation excluding those countries, so that distribution is permitted only in or among countries not thus excluded. In such case, this License incorporates the limitation as if written in the body of this License.

9. The Free Software Foundation may publish revised and/or new versions of the General Public License from time to time. Such new versions will be similar in spirit to the present version, but may differ in detail to address new problems or concerns.

   Each version is given a distinguishing version number. If the Program specifies a version number of this License which applies to it and "any later version", you have the option of following the terms and conditions either of that version or of any later version published by the Free Software Foundation. If the Program does not specify a version number of this License, you may choose any version ever published by the Free Software Foundation.

10. If you wish to incorporate parts of the Program into other free programs whose distribution conditions are different, write to the author to ask for permission. For software which is copyrighted by the Free Software Foundation, write to the Free Software Foundation; we sometimes make exceptions for this. Our decision will be guided by the two goals of preserving the free status of all derivatives of our free software and of promoting the sharing and reuse of software generally.

NO WARRANTY

11. BECAUSE THE PROGRAM IS LICENSED FREE OF CHARGE, THERE IS NO WARRANTY FOR THE PROGRAM, TO THE EXTENT PERMITTED BY APPLICABLE LAW. EXCEPT WHEN OTHERWISE STATED IN WRITING THE COPYRIGHT HOLDERS AND/OR OTHER PARTIES PROVIDE THE PROGRAM "AS IS" WITHOUT WARRANTY OF ANY KIND, EITHER EXPRESSED OR IMPLIED, INCLUDING, BUT NOT LIMITED TO, THE IMPLIED WARRANTIES OF MERCHANTABILITY AND FITNESS FOR A PARTICULAR PURPOSE. THE ENTIRE RISK AS TO THE QUALITY AND PERFORMANCE OF THE PROGRAM IS WITH YOU. SHOULD THE PROGRAM PROVE DEFECTIVE, YOU ASSUME THE COST OF ALL NECESSARY SERVICING, REPAIR OR CORRECTION.

12. IN NO EVENT UNLESS REQUIRED BY APPLICABLE LAW OR AGREED TO IN WRITING WILL ANY COPYRIGHT HOLDER, OR ANY OTHER PARTY WHO MAY MODIFY AND/OR REDISTRIBUTE THE PROGRAM AS PERMITTED ABOVE, BE LIABLE TO YOU FOR DAMAGES, INCLUDING ANY GENERAL, SPECIAL, INCIDENTAL OR CONSEQUENTIAL DAMAGES ARISING OUT OF THE USE OR INABILITY TO USE THE PROGRAM (INCLUDING BUT NOT LIMITED TO LOSS OF DATA OR DATA BEING RENDERED INACCURATE OR LOSSES SUSTAINED BY YOU OR THIRD PARTIES OR A FAILURE OF THE PROGRAM TO OPERATE WITH ANY OTHER PROGRAMS), EVEN IF SUCH HOLDER OR OTHER PARTY HAS BEEN ADVISED OF THE POSSIBILITY OF SUCH DAMAGES.

END OF TERMS AND CONDITIONS

my2cents.idgbooks.com

Register This Book — And Win!

Visit **http://my2cents.idgbooks.com** to register this book and we'll automatically enter you in our fantastic monthly prize giveaway. It's also your opportunity to give us feedback: let us know what you thought of this book and how you would like to see other topics covered.

Discover IDG Books Online!

The IDG Books Online Web site is your online resource for tackling technology — at home and at the office. Frequently updated, the IDG Books Online Web site features exclusive software, insider information, online books, and live events!

10 Productive & Career-Enhancing Things You Can Do at www.idgbooks.com

- Nab source code for your own programming projects.

- Download software.

- Read Web exclusives: special articles and book excerpts by IDG Books Worldwide authors.

- Take advantage of resources to help you advance your career as a Novell or Microsoft professional.

- Buy IDG Books Worldwide titles or find a convenient bookstore that carries them.

- Register your book and win a prize.

- Chat live online with authors.

- Sign up for regular e-mail updates about our latest books.

- Suggest a book you'd like to read or write.

- Give us your 2¢ about our books and about our Web site.

You say you're not on the Web yet? It's easy to get started with IDG Books' *Discover the Internet,* available at local retailers everywhere.